CHARLES COUNTY MARYLAND

A HISTORY

Bicentennial Edition

By

Jack D. Brown
William A. Diggs
Gladys S. Jenkins
J. Karpiak
Elwood M. Leviner
Mary Clare Matthews
Janie MacInnis
Rona R. Schaepman
Frederick Tilp

HERITAGE BOOKS
2008

HERITAGE BOOKS
AN IMPRINT OF HERITAGE BOOKS, INC.

Books, CDs, and more—Worldwide

For our listing of thousands of titles see our website at
www.HeritageBooks.com

A Facsimile Reprint
Published 2008 by
HERITAGE BOOKS, INC.
Publishing Division
100 Railroad Ave. #104
Westminster, Maryland 21157

Copyright © 1976 The Charles County
Bicentennial Committee

Library of Congress Catalogue Card Number: 76-40601
Printed in the United States of America
All rights reserved.
Copyright © Bicentennial Edition

On the cover: The Port Tobacco River Valley, seen from
the bell tower of St. Ignatius Church, Chapel Point.
(*Courtesy of David Warwick Harp*)

All rights reserved. No part of this book may be reproduced or transmitted in any form or by any means, electronic or mechanical, including photocopying, recording or by any information storage and retrieval system without written permission from the author, except for the inclusion of brief quotations in a review.

International Standard Book Numbers
Paperbound: 978-0-7884-1610-1
Clothbound: 978-0-7884-7653-2

Preface

This book is the combined effort of many people, all of them volunteers.

The Charles County Bicentennial Committee, under the dedicated and expert leadership of George Dyson, approached me in early November 1973, and asked that I coordinate the writing of a Charles County history. A plea went out for interested citizens to join in and help with the research and writing of this document. We chose to divide the responsibilities of this book into ten sections, and asked various people to take on the necessary tasks.

Southern Maryland's reliance on and advancement of the oldest occupation, agriculture, was researched by John Karpiak, who brings out some new and interesting points. For Transportation, we are fortunate to have had the services of Frederick Tilp, who has studied the Potomac River for nearly half a century. Janie MacInnis has ferreted fanciful and fundamental facts on the towns and villages of Charles County. The cradle of religious freedom in our country can be found right here, and it has been my privilege to compile this information.

Rona R. Schaepman has completed two chapters of our book, Government and Legends and Folklore, as well as the editing and final production. Black Americans have played a rarely recognized but important part in the development of our County, as William A. Diggs' chapter illustrates.

Professor Milton M. Somers, a well known educator and attorney, began the work on education, but met an untimely death before its completion. It was a pleasure working with him and we shall all miss him. The task was taken over and expertly completed by Elwood M. Leviner. Gladys S. Jenkins adds some fun and frolic to our book with her presentation of the County's social life and entertainment. A unique service is provided by Mary Clare Matthews, who tells readers how they can trace their family histories.

Our approach throughout the book has been to present the basic history of Charles County in ten selected areas. Many facts of significance have been omitted, and quite possibly several points of minimal importance included. This book has been done for you — the citizens of our County and nation — with your concerns and curiosities in mind.

Jack D. Brown
Book Coordinator

Authors

1 Agriculture
M. Johnson
J. Karpiak (c)*

2 Transportation
Robert T. Barbour
Robert Burgess
Calvin Compton Sr.
Dr. Edward J. Edelen
Mary K. Edelen
Harry Jones
Samuel C. Linton Jr.
Lawrence Monroe
Merle Monroe
Frederick Tilp (c)
Elizabeth Wade
Frank Wade Sr.

3 Towns and Villages
Vivian B. Edelen
Janie MacInnis (c)
Moira Mahoney
Gretchen Williams

4 Religion

Episcopal
Rev. William M. Davis
Kathryn C. Newcomb
Maude C. Robinson
Rev. Arnold Taylor
Mary Reeder Tiller

Roman Catholic
Vivian B. Edelen
H. Virginia Mudd
Rev. A. Robert Thoman

Baptist
Rosemary Arbogast
William I. Barkley Jr.
William I. Barkley Sr.
Fannie E. Brown
Jack D. Brown (c)
Christine Bursey
Rev. Donald Chandler
Janette C. Dozier
Lucile Jones
Rev. J. William Lackey
Rev. Clarence P. Moore
Rev. Gleaton R. Rickenbaker
Rev. Ronald Shifflett
Bernice Swann
Anne Lucille Wedding
Kanie B. Wedding
Betty M. Willett

* (c) Chairman of committee

Methodist
Rev. David Argo
Elnora Clark
Rev. Everett W. Culp
Rev. Harvey R. Custis
Virginia Gunter
Joan Hall
Ruth Lantz
Barbara Rowe
Marion Schreiber
Nellie Shelor
Lucille Tolson
John M. Wearmouth
Roberta Wearmouth
Lessie Wheeler
Y. J. Wright

Other County Churches
Rev. Alton H. Flowers
Edward H. Gebauer III
Rev. Jerry S. Jones
LCDR Dewey V. Page, USN
Rev. Eric G. Peterson
Rev. Alvin P. Pisgols
Jerry H. Wilson

5 Government
Pete Castello
John T. Parran Jr.
Rona R. Schaepman (c)
Carroll Stephenson

6 Black History
Veronica Coates
William A. Diggs (c)

7 Education
Margaret Stone Dippold
Elwood M. Leviner (c)
Elizabeth Rowe
Milton M. Somers

8 Sociality
Eleanor (Itzy) Burke
Ruth Fitzgerald
Maisie Gridley
Gladys S. Jenkins (c)
Lois E. Mallory
Courtenay Mitchell Wilson

9 Legend and Folklore
Beverly Argo
Janet Gough
Marti Mumford
Jane Norfolk
Marcia Richard
Rona R. Schaepman (c)
Peggy Valenti

10 Genealogy
Miriam Matthews Cappers
Dolores Laurina DuPont
Mary Keech Edelen
Vivian Bounds Edelen
Mary Clare Matthews (c)
Virginia Turner Mitchell
Marie Shea Nalley

To the People of Charles County

The authors of this *History* would like to thank the people of Charles County, present and past, for living the lives they do and did, and making their stories worthy of relating here.

Specifically, we are grateful to the Board of Directors of the Charles County Bicentennial Committee, under Chairman George Dyson and Vice-chairman Kash McClure, for their formation of the History Writing Committee and their confidence in our success. We thank the Chairman of the Heritage Committee, William A. Bader; Robert B. Case, Celebrations; Richard Gregory, Horizons; Rosemarie Lewis, Publicity; Robert L. Mitchell, Legal Counsel; and Velva Perrygo, Treasurer. And especially Mary K. Edelen, Secretary, who gave generously of her time and knowledge to refresh sections of the text, and Christie Selph, Finance Committee, who helped frequently and in numerous ways.

We appreciate the support of the Board of County Commissioners—President Raymond T. Tilghman, Eleanor Carrico, and James F. Dent—for putting County money where others' hopes were.

For their welcome and often matchless assistance we thank everyone who provided substance for our text, often by sharing precious and private memories. The names of many of these special people are mentioned in our *History*; the identity of others is at times, by chance or by will, obscured.

Finally we thank you, the readers, for taking our *History* in the spirit it was meant. We have written neither a critical discourse nor a panegyric on Charles County, but have presented many points of view. Not all points, for the *History* is certainly not comprehensive.

We have tried to preserve the individual styles of scores of writers and speakers. Citations are made in many ways; they are as accurate as possible, and recorded in the way thought to be most suitable to the context and convenient for the reader. Further information can be obtained in most cases by use of the Bibliography.

Many groups and individuals freely provided their resources and assistance for illustrating this volume. We appreciate the contributions of the Charles County chapter, National Association for the Advancement of Colored People; the Charles County Chamber of Commerce; the Charles County Historical Society; the Department of Tourism, Charles County; the Port Tobacco Restoration Society; and the Tri-County Council. Also Phyllis Seneff, an artist who put pen to paper on a day's notice. We were permitted to use the files and photographs of the three County newspapers—*The Citizen News, The Times Crescent,* and *The Maryland Independent,* which made its most useful 100th anniversary edition available to us. And we are obliged to the helpful staff of the Charles County Public Library for the time and efforts expended on our behalf.

We hope you will read beyond this book. Our greatest disappointment was having to omit or shorten so much of Charles County's rich history. More history is made each day. We encourage you to enjoy it while you make it.

Rona R. Schaepman
Editor

Contents

	Preface	iii
	Authors	v
	To the People of Charles County	vii
1	Agriculture: Still A Tobacco Economy	1
2	Transportation: Mobility on the Potomac	13
3	Towns and Villages: Changes with Transportation	53
4	Religion: Diverse and Free	79
	Episcopal Churches	80
	Roman Catholic Churches	102
	Baptist Churches	131
	Methodist Churches	160
	Other County Churches	180
	Sources	193
5	Government: We The People	197
6	Black History: Here at the Beginning	217
7	Education: How the Public Schools	235
8	Sociality: Jousting, Joining, and Cooking	271
9	Legend and Folklore: Who Are the People?	305
10	Genealogy: Do Your Own History	319
	1) Early Charles County, People and Sources	319
	2) Sources for Genealogical Research	330
	3) Charles County Census of 1850, by district	339
	4) Lists of Married and Professional Persons in Charles County	376
	5) Writing Your Personal History	388
	Bibliography	393
	Photographs	401
	Index	459

CHAPTER 1

AGRICULTURE: STILL A TOBACCO ECONOMY

Although they endured some hardships, early settlers of Charles County generally were blessed with what were perhaps the best possible farming conditions of any of the early English colonies. A favorable climate, abundance of wildlife, friendly Indians, and rich soil, together with a ready market in England for any surplus of farm products, all aided Charles Countians in surviving the hardships of the New World. And in prospering, when settlers of other colonies were barely surviving.

The Environment
The climate was especially praised (Calvert, p. 20):

> The colonists had every reason to be satisfied with their new abode. They had emigrated to one of the most beautiful countries in the world. . . . The climate of Southern Maryland is, perhaps, the most delightful on the American continent. It is a happy medium between the extreme heat of the South and the extreme cold of the North. The winters are mild, but the atmosphere is sufficiently bracing to nerve the system for exhaustion of the warmer part of the year. The spring is calm, sunny genial, and temperate; the summer is magnificent in the luxuriance of its vegetation and frequency and grandeur of its thunderstorms, which, though sometimes terrific, often cools the air, and relieves the monotony of a sky otherwise

remarkably clear and serene. The autumn is peculiarly delightful in temperature, splendor and variety of color, probably unmatched in the world.

While the Jamestown, Va., colonists were having a difficult time with the heat, and the New England colonists were barely surviving the frigid winters, Charles Countians encountered a climate to which they had been accustomed in their native England.

This enabled them to use the entire year to its fullest advantage. Spring planting and summer growing were as pleasant as harvesting in autumn and hunting in winter.

The abundance of wildlife was another important factor in the early development of the County. The animals provided the settlers with food to supplement their grains, and furs were a valuable supplement to their income.

Wrote Cecil Calvert:

> There are buffalo, elks, bears, and deer there in a great store, in places that are not too much frequented; as also beavers, foxes, otters, . . . Of birds, there is the eagle, . . . falcon, lanner, sparrow hawk, and merlin; also, wild turkeys in great abundance, where many weigh 50 pounds and upwards; and of partridge plenty.

Seafood also added to the diet of the early colonists. The river abounded with all the present forms of fish and shellfish. "For many of them we have no English names," Calvert documented. "There are . . . sturgeons, very large and good, and, in great abundance, grampuses, . . . mullets, trouts, . . . mackerel, perch, crabs, oysters."

Nevertheless, it was probably the Indians native to Charles County that were the greatest single factor in the rapid early development of farming. They exhibited a peaceful attitude towards the colonists, who therefore did not have to work to provide defendable, concentrated living areas. Instead, the colonists were able to spread throughout the County and devote all their time to clearing and growing.

The Indians were helpful. From them, "the settlers learned to grow (and then cook) food from their gardens. They learned new ways of trapping fish and hunting game. They immediately benefited from learning how to grow corn and, a little later, tobacco . . . both native American plants." (Foster, p. 44)

The rich soil was another benefit. Said Calvert (p. 20):

In very many places, you shall have two foot of black rich mould, wherein, you shall scarcely find a stone; it is like a sifted garden-mold and is so rich, that if it be not first planted with Indian corn, tobacco, hemp or some such thing that may take off the rankness thereof, it will not be fit for any English grain; and under that, there can be found good loam.

The Work
Settling upon land was the first concern of every freeman in the new colony. If a man had money enough to transport adult males from England to Maryland, he was given land. This was known as the head right system. Lord Baltimore "promised 2,000 acres of land to every adventurer who would transport five adult males to the colony as settlers. Smaller amounts of land were granted to those who transported fewer people." (Radoff, pp. 13-14)

By 1683 new land could be purchased from the Lord Proprietors. At first the rate was fixed at 200 pounds of tobacco for every hundred acres. By 1783 the price of land had increased to about five pounds sterling for this.

All land granted under the head right system was subject to annual "Quit rents." The rents were modest at the outset, it seems: 10 bushels of wheat for every 50 acres. (Radoff, p. 14)

Even though settlers could acquire land outright and in their own right, they could rarely afford to purchase and operate large manors. Most plantations were 250 acres or less. There were some larger manors, but the cost of operating them was prohibitive to most Countians.

The biggest problem of the infant County was labor. Working a farm for profit in the last half of the 17th century required many hands. One man could not grow and harvest much more than it took to support him and his family. To prosper, he needed cheap or free labor to work the fields.

Indentured servants were the first source of cheap labor. New adventurers from England were advised to take with them as many indentured servants as they could. "In the taking of servants, he may do well to furnish himself with as many as he can, of useful and necessary arts," noted Calvert.

The life of an indentured servant was not always bad. Generally, a person sold himself into indenture knowingly, for reason of poverty, religious persecution, or desire for adventure. He was not taken to the colony against his will, nor was he bound to a master for life. A typical indenture for the person with no needed skill was five years; if the servant had mastered a useful trade, indenture might be only for two or three years.

One of the benefits of indenture to the servant in Maryland was that generally he received from the master all living necessities, including food, clothing, drink, and living quarters. Better still, when an indentured servant finished his term, it was suggested (Calvert, p. 53) that he receive a year's supply of corn and 50 acres of land. How well this suggestion was followed is unknown.

Although the institution of slavery was defined by law in Maryland in 1663, there were relatively few slaves in Charles County towards the end of the 17th century. But as the large landholders prospered, so the number of slaves entering the County increased. By 1725 indentured servants were almost exclusively tradesmen and teachers, while field labor and domestic services were provided by slaves.

Because they were needed, it may be that slaves were treated fairly well. Their lot was probably similar to that of the small farmer. They lived for the most part in communal one-room cabins, with adequate food and clothing to assure their ability to work the fields. There were some slave revolts in Maryland, but none was recorded in Charles County. (Radoff, p. 411)

So important was cheap labor to the plantation owners that at the end of the Civil War, with the abolition of slavery, Charles County suffered an agricultural depression from which it did not fully recover until the 1920s.

The Tobacco Industry

Tobacco in Charles County predates the white man's arrival. Long before any farmers arrived in the County, the Indians grew and harvested tobacco, mostly for ceremonial purposes and religious rites.

It was only natural for the settlers to farm tobacco. The land was well suited to it and the Virginia colonies had for some time been growing tobacco and selling it to England at a nice profit. So, with the Indians teaching them how best to grow tobacco, and Virginia providing an improved type of seed, Charles Countians began an agriculture process that was to change little in the next 300 years.

By the time the County was chartered in 1658, tobacco was already the major field crop. It was grown almost to the exclusion of food crops.

This trend did not go unnoticed, and laws were enacted early to increase the acreage of crops other than tobacco. In March 1639 an Act of the Assembly required

> that every person, inhabitant, of this colony shall, yearly, at the beginning of the season plant and tend of cause to be planted and tended two acres of corn for his own food and two acres of corn more for every person in his family planting tobacco.

That the Assembly found it necessary to enact laws to force farmers to grow food is evidence of the commitment to tobacco. Further evidence is found in a report from Benedict Leonard Calvert to Charles Lord Baltimore:

> Tobacco is our staple, is our all and leaves no room for anything else; it requires the attendance of all our hands, and exacts their utmost labor the whole year round; it requires us to abhor communities in townships.

The determination of the County farmers to grow tobacco soon led to overproduction. This has been a constant problem for local farmers, and still persists. Every few years, a new law either limited or banned the production of tobacco in the Southern Maryland counties. But most of the laws were not enforced.

It was not necessarily the farmers' greed that caused overproduction. The market was at the mercy of a number of factors. England, for instance, insisted that all tobacco from Maryland (and other colonies) be shipped first to her, then exported elsewhere. When England was at war with other nations, the tobacco remained unsold.

When the first settlers arrived, the tobacco grown by the Indians was harsh and strong, generally unsuitable for sale in England. This "Rustica" also grew smaller than other tobacco varieties. The Virginia colony imported Orinoco seed from the West Indies. From Orinoco, three other types of tobacco were derived: lizard tail, sweet scented, and broadleaf. It is generally believed that the broadleaf, imported from the West Indies, is the parent of tobacco grown in Maryland until the 20th century. (Middleton, p. 98)

Tobacco farmers learned quickly that tobacco had to be grown on newly cleared land for maximum production per acre. After the third crop on one field, the tobacco would grow slower and smaller than earlier crops. This necessitated constant clearing of new lands for better yields. During the early 18th century, farmers learned to rotate crops to rejuvenate fields for replanting tobacco. Fertilizers did not come into use until after the Civil War.

Once the tobacco was cured, or dried out, it was ready to be packed for shipment. It was placed in large wooden barrels, called hogsheads. Shipping costs were determined by the number of hogsheads, not their weight, so the size of the hogsheads varied. Generally, they measured about three feet across and four feet high. Care had to be taken not to pack the tobacco too tightly, for if the hogsheads were to break, the tobacco would be ruined.

Since few farmers had their own ship landings, the hogsheads were constructed so they could be rolled to the nearest shipping point. An axle was placed in the hogshead, and servants, slaves, or animals pulled the tobacco over roads built for this purpose, the so-called "rolling roads."

After the tobacco left the farmer's hands, he had no control over its handling. It was subject to abuse by mariners, inspectors, and warehousemen. Sailors frequently helped themselves to handfuls for chewing, or to bagfuls for sale. Inspectors and warehousemen would sell tobacco that had been rejected as inferior. But abuse of his tobacco was hardly the worst of the planter's problems.

It was the practice for the planter to consign the tobacco to a merchant in London or some other port in England. Until the tobacco was sold, it remained the property of the planter. The merchant arranged handling and storage, paid duties, and set up the sale. Once the tobacco was sold, the merchant deposited the proceeds, less expenses and two or three per cent commission, in the planter's account. The planter could then draw on his account with a bill of exchange. (Middleton, pp. 104-09)

With his tobacco, the planter usually sent the merchant a list of items he wanted purchased. These ranged from farm implements to household articles and clothing to luxury items. This system proved expensive and even dangerous for the planter. The merchant, his agent, charged a commission on the purchases, inflated the prices, and was negligent in the handling of the articles.

If the planter ordered more goods than he could pay for, he found himself in debt to the merchant. Credit would be extended and the planter would slip further into debt. The debts increased annually, and would be passed from father to son. Once a planter was in debt to a merchant, he was forced to consign all his tobacco to that merchant, accepting any terms the latter dictated, however unsatisfactory they were. It took a careful and prudent man to avoid falling into this trap.

The consignment system, with its problems and abuse, became extremely unpopular. At the beginning of the 18th century it gave way to the outright sale of tobacco in the colonies. Although the planter received lower prices for his crop, he did not have the worries of shipping, the difficulties of dealing with unfamiliar agents, or debts.

By the time of the Revolution, a full three-quarters of the tobacco grown in Charles County was sold before it was shipped. The rest was the produce of large plantation owners, who could afford the risks and expense of gambling for the higher price available in England.

From 1776 to 1860 the farmer enjoyed a quiet period. There were few innovations in agriculture. The County went through cycles of prosperity and recession. With victory over Great Britain in 1814, the planter was free to ship his tobacco to the country willing to pay him the best price.

Probably one of the most significant trends of the period was the migration of farmers out of the County. Most emigres went to Kentucky or South Carolina. Many of the families in those states today are of Southern Maryland descent.

With the end of the Civil War and slavery, the large tobacco plantation ceased to exist. Small farms, with two to ten acres planted in tobacco, were in the majority in Charles County. Tobacco growing became even more expensive; by the end of the century the sale price barely covered the cost of production. This prompted farmers to try to sell an inferior product. The reputation of Maryland tobacco declined; the price dropped to less than five cents a pound.

Low prices caused County farmers to turn to other field crops, but the crops had to be transported over poor roads to markets in Washington and Baltimore. Bruising and spoilage resulted in Charles County farmers getting lower prices than those obtained by farmers in counties close to the cities. It was during this period that canneries sprouted throughout the County. The first opened in La Plata in April 1883, and many others followed.

But the County never completely turned its back on tobacco. Between 1890 and the end of World War I stricter grading and inspection regulations were enacted. With the tightened control, quality improved, Maryland's reputation grew, and the price crept up.

During World War I, Americans started to smoke cigarettes in ever increasing quantities. Tobacco from Maryland is preferred over that from other states for use in cigarettes, because of its free burning qualities. In 1919, as a result of quality control, farmers were paid 25 cents a pound for their tobacco—18 cents more than they had received 10 years earlier. Nevertheless, the unpredictability of the crop quality, which varies with weather and other factors, and the instability of the market, are constant reminders to Maryland farmers that they must diversify.

Tobacco Today

The County's population has risen rapidly in the last 10 years. By 1970 nearly 50,000 people resided here. But the number of farmers is decreasing. Today Charles County has only 700 to 1000 people who make their living from farming.

To accommodate the fast growing population moving in with new industries, much of the land once used to farm tobacco is no longer put to that use. In 1900, 9,002 acres supported tobacco only. In 1960, the figure dropped to 8,735 acres, and in 1964, to 8,198. Even more significant is that in 1900, 1,900 farms produced tobacco; in 1960, only 1,101 farms grew tobacco; in 1964, 1,009.

Nevertheless, although the acreage used for tobacco has dropped, the County's farmers are producing more pounds per acre. Wise use of fertilizer and nutrient additives have brought yields to an average of 1,000 pounds per acre. Before the use of these chemicals, most farms yielded only 500 pounds per acre. (Cooperative Extension Service, Leaflet 30)

To keep their land in good condition, many farmers grow cover crops like wheat, rye, oats, or ryegrass. A good cover crop protects the soil over winter and through early spring; it also adds organic matter and nitrogen. Excellent results have been obtained by adding nitrogen to the cover crop before the land is plowed.

Many different types of tobacco are grown today in Charles County: Maryland 10, Maryland 64, Maryland 609, and Maryland 201, among others. The different types were developed by crossing different varieties of broadleaf and other tobaccoes. Today, as in past years, Charles County is probably best known for its tobacco. For more than 300 years the quality and physical appearance have not changed. Although more corn than tobacco is grown in Charles County, tobacco is still Southern Maryland's major agricultural enterprise, and it accounts for about 75 per cent of the value of farm products sold here.

Growing tobacco is difficult. Many precautions must be observed to produce the best quality and highest value tobacco. Good soil and proper chemicals are important, as are prevention and treatment of disease and insects. The development of Maryland 59 and 609 created tobacco strains resistant to black shank, a disease that affects the lower stem and root of the plant. Maryland 872 is highly resistant to wildfire, a disease prevalent in Southern Maryland and likely to cause heavy damage in the field. The most annoying insects are budworms and aphids, but these can be controlled easily with proper insecticides.

Once the tobacco has been removed from the field, the farmer follows basically the same procedure as did his great-great-great-grandfather. The tobacco is hung in barns for curing. The farmer uses one of two types of curing: air or heat method.

Air curing is most widely used. The tobacco is hung, then vents or boards on the sides of the barn are opened. This usually takes place two to three days after the tobacco is cut. The process of air curing takes two to three months, and greatly affects the color of the tobacco. It also lowers the sugar and starch content. Air curing produces a low nitrogen and nicotine tobacco.

When the curing is completed, the tobacco is loaded and taken to the warehouse. Four warehouses hold the majority of Charles County's tobacco: two at Hughesville, one at Waldorf, and one at La Plata. In the warehouse the tobacco is graded according to 22 strict rules established by the U.S. Department of Agriculture.

Each grade is thoroughly examined—the tobacco must be separated and cleaned, and damaged produce graded a lesser quality. Now the tobacco is ready for sale.

About two-thirds of Charles County's tobacco goes into the production of the American cigarette. Representatives of tobacco companies choose the grades they wish to purchase at the warehouses. Usually they prefer the lower grades.

The other one-third is exported; Switzerland is almost the exclusive buyer of the higher priced, finer quality tobacco produced in Maryland.

The Swiss, together with the tobacco dealers and the State of Maryland, are supporting the Maryland Tobacco Improvement Foundation, Inc. Through research and free seed programs, and extension services, the Foundation will help insure an adequate supply of high quality tobacco. Programs such as these aid the farmers during difficult times.

And Charles County's farmers have seen some difficult times in the last 10 years! A drought in 1966 severely damaged the thirsty tobacco plants. Hurricane Agnes, which hit Southern Maryland in 1972, brought with her a terrible flood. Even more disastrous to the tobacco were the rains that came in early summer of 1975. The total amount of that loss is not yet official, but some farmers lost as much as half their tobacco crops.

Still, most of them feel the great effort put into growing tobacco is worth it. Charles County's tobacco is thin and fluffy, low in tar and nicotine; it has a high filling power, a free burn, and a pleasant aroma.

Now that's something to be proud of!

CHAPTER 2

TRANSPORTATION: MOBILITY ON THE POTOMAC

The waters of the Potomac were naturally the first roadway known to Charles Countians. It was a roadway that needed no building, it never called for repairs, it came to every man's landing. It so established itself in the life of its people that supporters of land roads had great difficulty in ever getting them cut through the forests, much less built, or improved, or repaired.

Early Roads, Taverns, Ferries
For ocean travel, in addition to the larger sailing ships, there were barks, brigs, brigantines, ketches, pinks, and snows. For use exclusively on the river and for occasional adventures into the Chesapeake, there developed the shallop, schooner, sloop, longboat, and the canoe.

For restricted use between neighboring landings, on opposite shores, or up the creeks, the planters maintained rowboats manned usually by four black uniformed oarsmen. If the sun beat uncomfortably, they rigged an awning. Such water vehicles darted between Marshall Hall and Mount Vernon and across the Wicomico to St. Mary's County, back and forth among the great places in the Port Tobacco neighborhood, carrying the family to church, the young folk to parties, and guests on to other hospitalities in the chain of great houses on both shores.

Water travel held a practically exclusive sway along the river shores during the early years. The first roads were not highways but mere private roads leading from the tobacco barns in the fields down the hill across the bottoms to the river landings. They were called "rolling roads," as their reason for existence was to provide a clear way over which the huge tobacco containers were rolled or pulled by oxen directly from the curing and prizing barns (a barn that housed the leverpacking equipment) to the ships that would carry them down the river and across the sea to England.

The next type of road was the "wood road" from the plantation buildings into the forest, as a way over which to haul out the firewood and building timbers that played so important a part in domestic life. Though called "roads," they were in fact only rough clearings.

In the light of modern tidewater roads it is difficult to imagine the "highways" the crowded settlers used to reach the landings, and which the waterside planter used to journey overland to church, court, the gristmill, the Jesuit establishment at Chapel Point, or the State House at Saint Mary's City.

The roads eventually evolved from Indian trails to bridle paths to a winding ribbon of clearing, flanked by forests or fields, and apparently obstructed by gate after gate. A reason for the gates was that a planter economized on fencing which he ran along only one side of the road. The way, in effect, led over one edge of field after field or over one grazing enclosure after another, and the gates were necessary to prevent the loss of stock. Phillip Vickers Fithian, a plantation tudor, riding home to New Jersey in 1774, noted "thirteen gates on the few miles of road from Squire Lee's near Hooe's Ferry at Passaquahanna Creek to Port Tobacco; between that town and Piscataway, fifteen gates."

All who traveled by wheeler vehicles carried axes. The primitive roads were so narrow that two conveyances could not pass except when they met happily in the open fields. If they met in the forest, a roadside clearing was cut away. When ruts ahead were forbiddingly deep, and mire or chuckholes menaced, axes were swung to clear a detour around otherwise impassable places. An old law of 1657 speaks volumes on the state of the first roads there. It required that all roads be "cleared yeerly."

The first road law, passed in 1666, was entitled "an act for making Highwaies Ec making the heads of Rivers, Creeks, Branches and Swamps passable for horse and foote"; and with a few amendments it was in force until 1704.

The establishment in 1695 of a regular post route from the Potomac River to Philadelphia via Annapolis was followed in 1704 by further legislation vesting roadmaking power in the County. This law called for the clearing and grubbing of all public and main roads, 20 feet wide, and a system of highways in Southern Maryland that still survives.

In 1702 a road-making law prescribed "three equidistant notches on the face of a tree to indicate a road to a ferry; two notches with a third high above for a road to a court house; and two notches with a slip down the face for a road to a church."

This main road through Charles County running north and south was termed "Three Notch Road," and laid as high as possible ("following ridges on the dryest lands").

In wet weather and in winter the roads were fairly impassable. The creek heads, as at Allen's Fresh and Nanjemoy, were marshy, and where the tide had forced a channel, a bridge was required. Not that there always was a bridge at such a point. Often the traveler crossed farther up where the creek was shallower, or he swam and led his horse across the watery barrier, for bridges were few, and poorly maintained.

When the way was shortened by an attempt to bridge a creek in its narrower reaches, the "inconveniency" seems not to have been wholly eliminated. In such a place, a "floating bridge" was the earliest device. Logs of wood were placed side by side on the surface of the water and planks were lashed to them. Such a bridge floated high, but only somewhat dry, until weighed with vehicle and horses. Then it sank to a depth proportionate to the weight upon it, and the animals splashed their way across on an invisible floor. The floating bridge was scarcely a dry walk even for a foot passenger.

Attempts to ferry vehicles across the runs and creeks were as ludicrous as they were ingenious and difficult. It was one thing to find the ferry, another to find the ferryman, and still another that he be sober. If the ferry were a dugout or a canoe, the traveler rode in the boat and swam his horse across. Often it was necessary to take wheeled vehicles apart in order to get them aboard the primitive boats, or for the vehicle to straddle the boat with the wheels cutting the water on both sides. When two boats were available, if one of them was not large enough for the job, they were lashed parallel and the wheels of one side of the vehicle rested in one boat and those of the other side rested in the other boat. In such manner even horses were ferried, with their forefeet in one canoe, and their hind legs in another.

The first road travel was on horseback and the earliest cartage was the rolling tobacco cask. Then followed the high-wheeled carts, with the wheels of solid planks drawn by yoked oxen. These powerful, slow moving beasts were not unfamiliar on the roads near the shores and meekly obedient to a word from the carter or a gentle touch from his firmly directed wand.

The first county roads were built and maintained by tax money or physical help in kind. County tax monies were used to employ road superintendents and to furnish road equipment and wagons. Farmers and merchants, and their tenants and hired hands supplied the labor.

On October 12, 1854, the *Port Tobacco Times* printed this notice,

> To Whom It May Concern—All persons who wish to have good roads in the Fourth District (between Newport and Dents Corner) are requested to be punctual in sending their hands when called on. So often they refuse as some gentelmen have done and then will be the first to complain. I pledge myself to devote my whole attention to the roads and early attendance of hands will be required and no man doing a days work at

home before sending him on the roads for the future. I shall send all hands back that do not come at 9 o'clock A.M. which is the regular hour.

Signed J.H.H. (Road Superintendent)

Undoubtedly, the road superintendents were handicapped in building and maintaining the road system with so uncertain a labor supply. Mud and chuck holes were not the only handicap to travelers on early roads, because from the same newspaper in 1869, "Persons having fences encroaching upon the Public Roads in the County are hereby requested to remove them else it becomes the duty of the Superintendent to do so. Signed N.C. Page, Supt."

Stagecoaches, usually covered with mud from top to wheel, rattled along, sometimes overturning, and frequently sinking into bogs at roads crossing the headwaters of such creeks as Mattawoman or Nanjemoy, and the Wicomico River at Zekiah Swamp.

Communications between Charles County and the outside world was not easy. Geographically, Charles and St. Mary's counties occupy a peninsula between the Potomac and Patuxent rivers, with the only land outlet to the north. Originally, the only stagecoach line operated through the County from Annapolis, across the Potomac to Williamsburg; and it did not take on local passengers. Horse paths were the only means of family communication.

Even the United States mail service traveled only a small part of the County and then at infrequent intervals. In 1839 one route from Washington touched Piscataway, Pleasant Hill (near Waldorf), Port Tobacco, Allen's Fresh, and Newport, thence into St. Mary's via Chaptico and Ridge. Mail usually was carried on privately owned mail-stagecoaches along with passengers and small freight items.

The *Port Tobacco Times* in 1845 announced mail stage arriving from Washington Mondays and Thursdays between 3 and 4 p.m. and leaving Wednesdays and Saturdays between 7 and 8 a.m.

Another mail line and passenger public transportation advertised in an 1848 issue:

> Leaving Washington Monday and Thursday 6 A.M., returning the following day. Leaving Newport in time to be at Port Tobacco at 8 A.M. Arriving in Washington before the (railroad) cars leave for Baltimore . . . thus enabling persons from Newport and Port Tobacco going to Baltimore to get there the same day they leave home. Fare to Port Tobacco $2.00, Newport $2.50

The first reference to daily mail service was in 1855. Another daily mail service is noted in 1868, between Glymont and Port Tobacco. This stage left Glymont on the arrival of the "mail steamer" from the District of Columbia at 8 a.m., arrived at Port Tobacco at 11:30 a.m.; picked up the mail at 12:30 p.m. and met the steamer at Glymont on its return trip from Aquia Creek, Va. Stagecoach fare was $1.50. Until World War I, all Charles County mail was taken by horse and wagon to Glymont for shipment to Washington on the steamboat as chartered by the U.S. Post Office. An alternate route from the County seat was by way of Bumpy Oak Road to Marshall Hall, boarding the steamer to Washington.

The Potomac River was the most economical and practical route for transportation of freight, passengers, and mail. The most difficult part was getting the goods or persons from the hinterlands to the river landings. Fortunately, most of Charles County is blessed with excellent deposits of gravel, and with this material passable summer-time roads could be built. However, during winter freezing spells, long stretches became quagmires because of the soft mud under the gravel.

For nearly 200 years tidewater Potomac stretched from northwest to southeast—a bridgeless, watery barrier between the north and south Atlantic coasts sending nearly all land travel across its fresh water at or above Georgetown, with ferry fees paid in shillings or pounds of tobacco. After the Federal capital came to the river, many ferries were established.

It has been said that "nearly all land travel was formerly deflected above Georgetown, as there were no bridges below this point. Eight ferries were established in Charles County alone as essential units in north-south travel, and as travel links between the Maryland and Virginia colonies.

One of the first acts of the Charles County Court was to establish a ferry over the Wicomico River. On June 4, 1658, at the second annual meeting of the Court, it was ordered "by the Governor's Council and the County Commissioners that one Samuel Harris should keep a ferry for more safe and commodious passage of people to and from over the Wicomico River" (Rock Point to Bushwood in St. Mary's County).

Curiously, the colony of Maryland seems not to have passed any laws to establish ferries over the Potomac. Virginia provided for several. The first of these was ordered, in 1705, "In Stafford County from Col. William Fitzhugh's landing in Potomac River (near Metomkin Point, Va.) over to Maryland" (near Riverside). Another ferry was established in 1720, destined to be the main link between lower Tidewater and the north, "from Col. Rice Hooe's (near Persimmon Point, Va.) to Cedar Point in Maryland" (near the present PEPCO plant). From 1732 to 1766, 13 other ferries were ordered across tidewater Potomac by the colonial legislators.

Hooe's Ferry (at the site of the present Gov. Harry W. Nice Bridge) perpetuated the name of Rice Hooe, who came to Virginia in 1621 and whose descendants settled on the river just south of Mathias Point in 1715. There they built Barnsfield, which was a Hooe home until it was burned during the Civil War by Federal order, as it was believed that Charles County blockade runners were guided by signals given by lights in its windows. Although the statutes routed Hooe's Ferry to "Cedar Point," a map accompanying the Maryland volume of the first U.S. census (1790) shows the eastern landings to have been just above Pope's Creek, and another at Passaquahanna Creek. Presumably the passengers were disembarked at several landings (Blossom Point, Port

Tobacco, or Pope's Creek) according to the tide, the wind, and their own preferences.

George Washington found this a convenient route from Mt. Vernon to his brother in Westmoreland, and thence to Williamsburg. When Henry Laurens of South Carolina was on his way home from Congress in 1779, prior to going abroad as our Minister to Holland, Richard Henry Lee of Chantilly, Va., wrote him:

> I shall continue to entertain the very agreeable hopes of being honored with your company in your way Southward. Your route is through Baltimore, across the Potomac at Hooes, and from Mr. Hooey you will get exact direction to my house.

Ferrymen were the keepers of the local news, travel data, and directions for confused strangers, and feeders of horses. Above all, the keeper of the tavern or "small tippling house" usually had female attractions at his ferry dock.

In 1775 Isaac Weld came across the ocean to view the new country as a possible haven from the political storms at home, and returned to Europe to publish an account of his travels and observations. He had an unhappy time before and after crossing the Potomac, and included this experience with Hooe's boats:

> The river at the Ferry is about three miles wide and with particular winds the waves rise very high; in these craft they always tie the horses, for fear of accidents, before they set out; indeed, with the small open boats which they make use of, it is what ought always to be done for in this country gusts of wind rise suddenly, and frequently when they are not at all expected: having omitted to take this precaution, the boat was on the point of being overset two or three different times as I crossed over.

Charles County travelers crossing waterways required two types of ferry: one that crossed a narrow river or creek in well protected waters (Rock Point to Bushwood) and another type that crossed a wide expanse of water like Hooe's Ferry near

Lower Cedar Point, where a sudden squall might raise a rough sea. The boats used were quite different. The former was "a kind of flat bottomed lighter or scow" with "upright sides of about two or three feet and sloped at each end so as to ride over the waves." Drawing very little water, it could come close to shore, and the lowering of a gangplank or apron allowed passengers to go directly from the ferry to dry land.

Sometimes as much as thirty feet long and eight feet wide, these ferries carried from three to six horses besides passengers. The ferryman rowed, poled, or pulled the boat across the estuary by means of a rope. Rope ferries slid along a fixed line, the propulsion being accomplished by means of a notched "heaver" and the ferryboat was thus "walked" across the stream to and from the mainland Cobb Island. Other ferry companies used nothing more than two large canoes tied together; large enough for eight horses and three men in a party—all transported at one time.

Gusts and squalls so characteristic of the Potomac Region made ferrying dangerous even where the creeks were narrow. Newspaper reports cite many drownings when ferryboats were struck by a violent squalls that made horses lose their footing and caused apprehension on the part of the passengers. This happened many times, especially at the Potomac crossing at Chapman's Landing, which is exposed to violent northwest winds.

Because of the frailty, ferryboats of this sort were not used on the lower Potomac. Such waters required more seaworthy vessels, propelled by other means than poling or pulling ropes. Usually sail rigged as sloops or schooners and occasionally decked, the vessels used for this purpose were generally called "passage boats" or "packet sloops." They had to be trim craft of good construction. To encourage men to engage in operating ferries, the Virginia assembly required in 1705 that all persons attending on ferryboats should be free from public and county levies and from such public services as musters, constables, clearing highways, and impressment, and should have their licenses without fee or paying a reward for obtaining them. And if the ferryman desired to maintain an "Ordinary" (public inn with alcoholic beverages and girlie entertainment), he should be permitted to do so without fee for the license, but should be required to give bond for security. No other person was permitted to establish an Ordinary within five miles of the ferry keeper. All public messengers of the Government were to be allowed to cross the ferry free. Ministers of the Church were likewise exempt from paying ferriage.

The ferriage system in Maryland differed from that of Virginia in two ways: Maryland was more successful in establishing free ferries, and unlike Virginia, did not license, grant monopolies to, or fix the rates of privately operated ferries. By about 1720 a system of free public carriers existed side by side with private boats charging fees. Most of the sailing ferries on the Potomac and its estuaries were private, while on many of the smaller creeks free ferries supported by county levies flourished. The wages of the public ferrymen varied considerably. Charles County ferrymen in 1719 received only 500 pounds of tobacco, while in 1723 they received 7,000 pounds of tobacco annually.

On several occasions in the 17th century Lord Baltimore sought to gain control over the Potomac ferries of Maryland with a view to augmenting the proprietary revenues. He derived his claim from the Maryland Charter of 1632, which specified that the Lord Proprietor was to enjoy all the rights and privileges in his American palatinate, among them the licensing of ferries.

Great competition existed among those ferries operated by private persons, free from government regulation. When, as often happened, several ferries crossed the same river only a mile or two apart, there was keen rivalry. One of the most vigorous contests occurred in Charles County between 1745 and 1747, when six ferries over the Potomac carried on a verbal battle in the *Maryland Gazette*. Both Richard Harrison and Robert Dade, who operated rival ferries in Nanjemoy, advertised "a good Boat and Hands" and "constant Attendance." One operated from his house, the other from the Nanjemoy post office. Charles Jones, keeper of the

Lower Cedar Point ferry was "by 18 or 20 Miles the nearest Way to Williamsburg." Henry Thompson, on the other hand, expressed his determination to continue his ferry notwithstanding a malicious rumor spread by "some evil-minded, spiteful, Persons in order to prevent me getting Custom to my Ferry." Thompson also stressed the excellence of his boats, saying that he operated "a very good Boat with able Hands" and "a fine Yawl in order to set those over, who do not incline to go with their Horses." He was then building a commodious ferryboat, large enough to carry six horses. The keeper of the Clifton ferry, Virginia to Marshall Hall, pointed out that although the distance from Annapolis to Williamsburg was "something greater" than by other routes, yet "as the great River Potomac is so narrow at this Place, and passable almost in all Weather, it may justly be accounted the readiest way."

The lengths to which ferrymen would go to obtain "custom" may be seen in the advertisement of George Dent, who kept a ferry in Charles County about two miles above Thompson's ferry. His passengers, he said, "avoided a Creek that lies in the usual Way to Thompson's Ferry, dangerous to Strangers: And Marks are set up at convenient Places on the Road from Port Tobacco, for the Direction of those that incine to pass over the said Ferry."

Most ferrymen also operated taverns. Advertisements frequently offered "good Beds, Liquors and Provider for Horses," as well as "good Boats and skillful Hands." As this was an important source of revenue for ferrymen, some who kept free ferries found it worth their while as tavernkeepers to advertise them in the colonial newspapers.

The absence of regulation of ferries in Maryland was not so disastrous as might be supposed. As long as there was competition, the standard of performance remained high and the rates low. In general, ferriage in Maryland was no more costly than in Virginia. Now and again, however, the lack of regulation led to great injustice.

Complaints about colonial ferries were also common. An accusation was made in Prince William County, Va. that the county ferry to Charles County "hath of Late been kept by Negroes whose Master being for the most part absent" have been "very Negligent in Discharging their Duty," and the food and accommodations were poor. Complaints about delay were even more frequent. The heavy scows that served as river ferries were slow and cumbersome. If only one were in operation and the ferryman happened to be on the other side of the river, the traveler had to build a fire in order to make "a Smoak" to attract the ferryman's attention. Then two complete crossings were necessary before the impatient traveler could continue his journey. Even without the indifference and incompetence of ferrymen—and those shortcomings were common—numerous ferries necessarily slowed down one's journey considerably. Eddis, writing in 1769, said that "though every proper method is adopted for expedition yet such a number of considerable waters unavoidably occasion great delays."

All contemporary comments were not critical of the ferries of the Potomac country. At least one British writer, Lord Adam Gordon, had nothing but praise for them. He wrote in 1765 that "the Ferries, which would retard in another Country, rather accelerate" travel in Virginia and Maryland, and the ferryman "assist . . . all Strangers with their Equipages in so easy and kind a manner, as must deeply touch a person of any feeling."

Ferry boat systems developed after the Civil War: Cliftons Ferry (Marshall Hall to Ferry Point, Va.); Chapmans Ferry (Chapman's Wharf to Hallowing Point, Va.); Cooks Ferry (Sandy Point to Clifton Point, Va.); Budds Ferry (Goose Bay or Poseys Wharf to Shipping Pt., Va.); Boyds Ferry (Trews Marsh near Maryland Pt. to Boyds Hole, Va.); Hooes Ferry (Passaquahanna Creek to Barnsfield, Va.); Rock Point Ferry (Rock Point to Bushwood in St. Mary's County); Adams Ferry (Morgantown to Potomac Beach, Va.).

The development of roads on hilltops flanking the river helped establish stagecoach lines and the Ordinary. However, on the Charles County side, there was apparently no stage line along the river. On the Virginia side an important through road connected Georgetown, Alexandria, Occoquon, Dumfries, Fredericksburg, and Richmond.

The stagecoach road from Philadelphia ran to Upper Marlboro, Nottingham (on the Patuxent), Bryantown, and Port Tobacco. From there the driver had three routes: Budd's Ferry towards Dumfries or Maryland Point ferry to Boyd's hole or Hooe's Ferry near Clifton, Md. All three ferries ended at Williamsburg. Over this road rolled the family coaches drawn by four or six horses. At intervals along its way sprang Ordinaries with food and shelter for man and beast. A stage route carried vagrant passengers over these roads, but the conveyance appears to have been no handsome coach but a vehicle offering merely a succession of cross seats, sheltered indifferently, desperately uncomfortable, and expensive.

Hundreds of "ferries" sprang up with the Eighteenth Amendment to the U.S. Constitution. For about 12 or more years, many highpowered speedboats ran across the river from well concealed whiskey stills (producing corn and rye) in Charles County woods to the land of thirsty Virginians. This was especially true at Federal installations in Virginia, such as Fort Belvoir, Quantico, and Dahlgren.

Sailing Boats

For the family wishing to travel, there were always sailing vessels carrying all sorts of cargo to Washington, Norfolk, and Baltimore. Even though the shippers tried to hurry the captains towards early departures and fast sailing, the Potomac atmosphere resulted in a schedule dependent on wind and weather. Except in extreme doldrums or violent storms, a trip to the Capital City was made in 24 hours, one way. This generally carried two fair tidal currents which was (and still is) an advantage.

Numerous types of sailing and rowing craft were employed by Charles Countians on the river. Each type was developed for special uses and cargoes in certain waters and weather conditions. These were the work boats of the river, designed by trial and error over a long period of time to meet requirements of their use, within limitations of low cost and available materials; the vessel must make its owner a living. The account that follows is an attempt to briefly explain types employed in the County from the early Colonial period to World War II.

1. BARGE. Probably the first type built in the County, a flat-bottom, roomy open rowing craft with auxiliary sail, not more than 30 feet in length. Designed originally for carrying a particular kind of cargo such as tobacco hogsheads, cord wood, fish, and passengers. Barges of a later date became a bit longer and more ornate than the usual working barge. Equipped with a colorful canopy and propelled by uniformed slave oarsmen and a white coxswain; a water-taxi for the gentry of Port Tobacco in their visits to the gentry in King George County, Va.

2. PINNACE. The first, the largest, and most famous of pinnaces on the river was the DOVE, which brought the first colonists to Maryland and Father Andrew White to Chapel Point. She was a little boat of 50 tons for ocean crossing. We can easily believe William Fitter, who was passenger on the ship ARK, when he said that the pinnace carried only a few passengers and was towed many times during its 107-day voyage. Pinnaces as used on the river were designed for ocean use, always along with another but larger vessel; round bottom and equipped with oars and sail. Popular in Colonial times for trading alone in nearby waters such as Delaware Bay and the North Carolina inlets.

3. SHALLOP. The first type of sailing boat on the river, a light open boat equipped with oars and a sail. Captain Henry Fleet, who traded much with Indians in Charles County before the arrival of colonists at St. Mary's, used a shallop which, he said, he had "built among the Indians. . .". The little boat was manned by 10 men and all manner of ammunition.

Maryland's Governor in 1639 directed that "five persons from the Wicomico in Charles County be pressed to go (to Virginia) to secure a supply of arms, victualls and liquor." A friend of the Governor in London advised that he was coming to Maryland to spend 30 pounds sterling "for a pretty shallop with oarres, sailes, and netts, to trade, discover and catch fish."

The two sails were generally lug-rigged and might be called the "shallop rig" with origin from the Dutch and French fisherman. There is no evidence of a ketch variation of this rig, with the main sail shorter than the fore, used on the river, despite its popularity up to the early 1900s. Designed as an open boat, a few had a cuddy or small cabin, even with a fireplace. They ranged from 18 to 28 feet on the keel, had round bottoms, and were fitted with leeboards.

Some of the Elizabethan character was painted into these colorful craft as noted in an advertisement: "A lap strake two masted shallop, painted black and yellow, the lower streak Chocolate color, the masts yellow, the top of the foremast black, the top of the Main-mast not black, a graplin on board instead of an anchor."

The shallop became the most popular boat in the colonies: a "workhorse" suitable for exploring creeks, collecting corn from the Indians, military expeditions, taking the family to church, and transporting tobacco to waiting ships bound for England.

It is the most long lived of all the sailing craft, the first used prior to the settlement at St. Mary's in 1634. Archives show commercial shallops used through the early 1900s. A replica of a 30 foot shallop, named AVIZA, was harbored in Neapsco Creek, Va., and was sailed in waters off Mattawoman Creek.

4. CANOE. It was from the aborigines that the Potomac colonists learned the usefulness of the canoe. The canoe was an Indian's sole means of travel. Captain John Smith, on his voyages up the river, encountered many "savages in canoes." Smith tells how the Indians made their two types, one of "the barkes of trees sewed with barke, and well luted with gumme." the other type was much larger, made of

one tree by burning and scratching away the coales with stones and shell, till they have made it in forme of a Trough. Some of them are fortie or fiftie foote in length. Some will bear forty men, but most ordinary are smaller, and will bear . . . according to their bignesse.

Instead of having oars to propel their canoes, the Indians had "paddles and stickes, with which they will row faster than our barges." Colonists found Indian canoes useful for quiet river or creek travel, but dangerous in open waters.

5. SKIFF. Little may be said about the colonial rowing skiff—the name appears to have been used to mean a "dinghy." It invariably had straight flaring sides, was carvel planked, with a cross-planked bottom. Originally designed with leeboards, the more refined had dagger or centerboards. Shallow draft made skiffs particularly well suited for all types of employment and economic limitations—except as a cargo carrier. A low-cost row boat, it was hard to row or scull, and slow under sail.

Another river skiff was the Gunning Skiff; a sophisticated, highly specialized, deceptive little craft originally made by the best boat builders of the day: the men who built pungies and bugeyes. They made this little boat to launch their duck-cannons for slaughtering water fowl. There was room for one man and one cannon.

The kerosene lamps on these skiffs were the finest of "gunning lights" developed. Guns varied from the big gun of two-inch diameter, weighing 200 pounds down to the older flintlock. A typical evening's work resulted in 100 ducks per gunman. Potomac River was reputed to have more than 150 gunning skiffs in the late 1800s, with the majority located in Swan Point and Rock Point areas.

6. DORY-BOAT. The Potomac River Dory-boat and her predecessor, the "Black Nancy," are the only two small sailing crafts with origins on the river. Their two-masted rigs were both a throwback from the Mediterranean lateen, and the Shallop rigs; otherwise they are the river's only true born children. Both types had two leg-of-mutton sails, the foresail being the larger.

During the Civil War all sailing craft were watched closely by the Federal Navy, which seemed to delight in destroying the watermen's small sailing craft. Immediately after the war, there was a boat building boom especially in the lower Potomac on the Maryland shore. Here the "Black Nancy" was born; as "a poor man's boat." Flat bottom, straight with sides of one plank in lengths 18 to 27 feet. Beam usually one-third the length, painted black (this being the cheapest color). The smaller boats were cross planked; the larger ones planked fore and aft with ribs. A completely open boat, no deck or cabin, a fair sailer with centerboard, generally used for oyster tonging and crab dredging.

For many years hundreds of Black Nancies tonged oysters off Maryland's protected shores during the winter's northwest winds between Maryland Point and Port Tobacco, Lower Cedar Point to Cobb Island, and in the Wicomico.

About 1880 oystermen began to demand a more sophisticated design than the popular Black Nancy. A new type was developed on both sides of the river at about the same time—the Potomac River Dory-Boat. The early models ranged from 24 to 30 feet in length; in later years 42 feet was considered a practical and profitable length.

Width, centerboard and rig similar to the Black Nancy, but a much better sailer, fast and easily handled for oyster tonging and dredging. In contrast to the "pirate color" of black on the Nancy, the Dory-boat had white sides, with gay stripes of green, red, and yellow below the gunwales from bow to stern; used for oyster tonging and dredging until 1931 when most Dory's had 7 HP Palmer engines installed for trot-line crabbing.

7. SHARPIE. The sharpie first appeared on the Wicomico River in the early 1870s. The open flat bottom of the sharpie immediately took hold for the ease in handling oysters; long, rather narrow, straight, stem, round sterned, and economical to build.

The Potomac sharpie ranged in length from 18 to 28 feet. Those in the 24 to 28 foot range were halfdecked, the smaller ones entirely open. Used mainly over large "flats," as off Port Tobacco, Swan Point, and Cobb Island bar, where shallow drafted vessels were practical for scraping or oysters or crabs. Due to the flat bottom construction, the sharpie was unable to stand extremely rough or stormy weather. When weakened and ready for "beaching ashore," many sharpies were transformed into fish lighters, for carrying fish in tow to Washington.

8. STURGEON SKIFF. These boats were employed on the Potomac solely between Smith Point and Glymont in Charles County, with an occasional run as far south as Nanjemoy. Designed to carry nearly two tons of fish. Built by Philadelphia boat builders, shipped by railroad, unloaded at Widewater, Va. and sailed to Charles County sturgeon fisheries.

These were powerful craft, as they had to face rough seas and handle a large fish load. Some boats carried two leg-of-muttons with spirit booms, sharpie fashion, with the mainmast as tall as or taller than the fore. The boats had large centerboards, were exceptionally weatherly.

Most Potomac River sturgeon skiffs were 30 feet in length, had a beam of 8 feet 6 inches with a depth of 2 feet 6 inches. In heavy weather they worked under foresail alone; the mainmast and sail were struck and stowed. Sand bags were frequently carried as ballast along with 12 foot oars for rowing in calm weather. This Delaware Bay sturgeon skiff was the only "foreign vessel" to gain popularity on the river. A more able and powerful small working sailing vessel never sailed the Potomac River.

The last active sturgeon skiffs were deactivated in 1926 near the Morgan Monroe Caviar Factory at Liverpool Point; their names were EDYTHE, W.S. CHILD'S, and the BLACK-BOTTOM. The last sturgeon fisherman on the river, Lawrence Monroe, still resides with his wife, Merle, at Doncaster.

Other Charles County caviar factories were operated at Wade's Bay by the Davis Brothers, Liverpool Point by

William T. Baker, Goose Bay by Cox and Sanders with their skiff FIVE BROTHERS, and Glymont by Swan and Travis.

9. SLOOP. During the Colonial period, large sloops were the most popular due to their suitability for river, bay and ocean work. The sloop rig, supposed to have originated in the Netherlands and well known in England, was particularly well-adapted to the Potomac and the Bay. Appearing shortly after 1640, it subsequently became the most common colonial rig. The Maryland archives of 1690 note a sloop, AMY, as being in the tobacco trade between Port Tobacco and London.

10. SCHOONERS. The historical and economic implications of our first specialized trade, slaves, was largely carried on by schooners. Zebecs were the original slavers. The employment of schooners as naval vessels, and illicit traders, assured this type a remarkable popularity in early Colonial days, sailing out of Port Tobacco.

Schooners developed rapidly on the Potomac River and were in great demand because of their practicability and speed. The type was referred to as "Virginia-built," even though Maryland builders contributed to its development. The Revolution and the 1812 War period employed the fast schooners as blockade runners on the lower river.

By the Civil War the round stern had given way to the more handsome square stern and clipper bow, and the schooner became the most popular vessel on the river, carrying every type of cargo; lumber, bricks, cordwood, fertilizer, farm products, seafood. If anything had to be moved, the schooners did it; it was the number one workhorse in the County.

Prior to the use of steam as a means of propulsion, sailing packets were used on the river to carry passenger and freight between the many river landings in Charles County and Washington, Georgetown, Alexandria, New York, Philadelphia, and Charleston, with advertisements in local newspapers promising a passage within a fixed time schedule. (Packet travel firms guaranteed this or refunded the fare.)

Even after power craft had gained a foothold on river commercial and passenger trade, the schooner continued to be regularly employed until 1940.

For many years during the early 1900s, Captain John W. Selby operated a fleet of schooners from Warehouse Landing in Port Tobacco to Baltimore, serving the area with all necessary goods from the "outside world." The last schooners hailing from Charles County were the BERTHA MAY and ARIANNE BATEMAN by Capt'n Parker Gray of Riverside, engaged in the cord wood trade from Nanjemoy to Washington until the early 1930s and CHARLES H. RICHARDSON, Robert Guy Barbour of Port Tobacco was Mate and relief Captain (1885-1958). This schooner maintained regular coal and lumber trade into the Port Tobacco River for many years. Seasonal work was delivery of grain, tobacco, and oysters. During summer months she was employed in "moonlight pleasure excursions" out of Chapel Point. Also the MATTIE F. DEAN, captained by John Shorter of Rock Point, and later by Captain Matthew Bailey of River Springs (just across the Wicomico River). The DEAN was the last sailing vessel actively engaged in a busy trade between Charles and St. Mary's Counties to Baltimore and Washington, mainly in tobacco, grain, and fertilizer.

11. PUNGY-BOAT. "The Pongees, or oyster boats...are the most elegant and yacht-like merchants vessels in the world... It is remarkable that these vessels are intended for the lowest and most degraded offices (carrying manure, oysters, and cord wood): are of elegant and symmetrical proportions." This observation was made in 1852 by an English naval officer, a Captain Mackinnon, R.N., visiting Baltimore.

It is believed this craft was first designed in the 1840s and is a definite and distinct type. The pungy was a deep draft keel vessel, schooner rigged with two tall raking masts and a main topmast.

At the conclusion of the Civil War, the Maryland Legislature, importuned by pungy-boat men, repealed the law of 1820 and passed a bill allowing use of an oyster dredge in the Bay and the River in waters more than 15 feet deep. The pungy-boats were the best of local craft for many years and powerful enough to haul enormous dredges across kettle bottom shoals, but were gradually replaced by the handier, cheaper, shallow-draft bugeys and skipjack. When dredging season had passed, pungies turned to general freighting. Here they were restricted to a certain extent, for their deep draft would not permit them to sail up shallow rivers where bugeyes and centerboard schooners could sail with ease and rest upright on the bottom at low tide.

U.S. Merchant vessel register shows 10 pungy-boats sailing out of Charles County in 1902. AMANDA F. LEWIS, the last pungy-boat on the Potomac, freighted cleaned cargoes such as canned goods from local canneries, wheat, corn, swan lumber, and general produce. Being the aristocrats of the river craft, their skippers refused to carry cord wood, paving materials, fertilizer, or other "dirty freight."

12. BUGEYE. During early years of the Potomac colonies, oysters, though known to be wholesome, were seldom used as a food except when other supplies failed. Later, following the Indians' example, the colonists made oysters a regular part of their diet. All they needed to do for a plentiful supply was to wade or pole a boat of some sort into the shoal waters over an oyster reef and rake up as many as were wanted.

For many years it was "every man for himself" oyster-wise. Then about 1760, instead of each man providing his own food, he began to turn to specialists for various necessary items, thus inaugurating a new business—that of professional oystermen. Within 20 years oysters became such a favorite that many inns and taverns began to specialize in serving them. The boats to supply the markets were at first the log canoe, followed by the brogan, and finally the bugeye.

In its earliest form the brogan was nothing more than an enlarged canoe, 35 to 40 feet in length with a tiny cabin forward. A number of alterations took place until a new variation of the brogan was evolved. The brogan was now a large canoe, from 40 to 54 feet long, still undecked with washboards around the sides. Up forward was a small hunting cabin. Two tall, raking removable masts carried the jib and leg-of-mutton foresail and mainsail.

At first bugeyes ranged from about 50 to 60 feet on deck, built of logs, the later ones up to 85 feet in length, framed and planked. A bugeye has a round bottom, double ended hull with raking stem and sternpost, a straight keel, a centerboard, and a clipper bow, long head, and bowsprit. It has two tall raking masts with foremast placed far forward, setting a jib, and triangular foresail and mainsail, the foresail being the largest.

The last bugeyes hailing from Charles County were the MAUDE S, LOLA TAYLOR, and BESSIE LAFAYETTE owned by Andrew and Joe Kendrick of Crossroads (Nanjemoy P.O.) sailing out of Mallows Bay; Chiccamuxen Creek was home port for ELEANOR RUSSELL, owned by Shannon Brothers, and ISAAC SOLOMON, by William T. Posey of Mallow's Bay; KATHLEEN, owned by Frank Maddox of Mallow's Bay, and the 50 footer, ELLA R LARMORE, owned by Raymond C. Cooksey and Robert T. Barbour sailed out of Charleston Creek until the owners were called to war.

13. SKIPJACK. The last type of sailing craft developed on the Potomac River was the skipjack. According to local authorities, this craft was better known as a "two-sail bateau." It was a design caused not by hydrographic but by economic conditions: the depressed period in business in the early 1800s and the decline in oyster production at the same time. Just as the bugeye had the canoe as its parent, the skipjack was sired by the V-bottom skiff commonly used in sailing along crab trot-lines in shoal waters. Almost any waterman could and did build skipjacks. They were simple in design, required no special tools or much hardware, and had little rigging and equipment; hence they were cheap to construct compared to other vessels. Furthermore, they were low cost in operation—one man could handle a skipjack with ease in a pinch, even take care of the dredge as well in mild weather. The first boats, those of the 1890s, were small and

stayed near home, selling their catch to buy boats from the cities or local oyster houses. By 1901 skipjacks had grown large enough to carry their own catch to Washington and Alexandria.

When loaded with oysters, skipjacks have a reputation for speed and weatherliness, although the flat angle of deadrise caused pounding when the boat sailed with a slight heel on the wind. At one time they were the "all-purpose boat," a poor man's cargo carrier. After the ban of oyster dredging in the river (1931), many of the skipjacks were left to die on the Charles County shores. The last skipjack was the CHAMPION GIRL out of Picawaxen Creek; she sailed profitably until 1926.

14. RAM. A three-masted, schooner rigged vessel with a wallsided, flat bottomed, blunt hull with centerboard, fitted with a clipper bow and spike bowsprit. Carrying a baldheaded schooner gaff rig, these vessels were usually 125 to 135 feet long. This was the largest of all typical Bay craft, deliberately designed for a specified purpose. Although rams were designed primarily for the canal trade to Delaware Bay, they were not confined to this route. Many entered into coastwise traffic carrying stone, coal, lumber, fertilizer, or any cargo that was offered. One of the first built was the CHARLES T. STRANN at Sharptown in 1891, burned in Baltimore, renamed CHARLES L. RHODE, sold to Johnson & Wimsatt Lumber Company of Washington, D.C., and renamed KINKORA. For many years she was the only well known ram on the Potomac kept busy making trips to Mallow's Bay and Wade's Bay with rough sawn lumber. Her last trip was a load of fertilizer to Sandy Point from Alexandria in 1941.

15. LONGBOAT. Referred to as the "Potomac Long-boat." In the days before central heat and cooking by manufactured gas and electricity became commonplace, wood burning fireplaces and ranges reigned supreme in Washington, Georgetown, and Alexandria. The quantities of cord wood consumed by residential, commercial, and industrial plants were astonishing, and astronomical facilities were needed to transport it from riverside forests to the city's Wharves.

Frequently large fleets of vessels were employed by firewood companies. As time was of no concern, only sail power was used, and careful watch was made by the skipper for every favorable tidal current to help his slow moving, always overloaded vessel. The wood was piled so high, the sail was shortened to the "cargo reef point," and he steered mainly by "guess and by God," returning down river loaded with bricks, fertilizer, and flour bags and general produce. An average return load was 25,000 bricks piled to allow for access to the centerboard. During the early 1900s and up until 1940 longboats were crowded along the shores of Mallow's Bay, Wade's Bay, Blue Banks, and up into Nanjemoy, loading cordwood for Washington.

16. FISH LIGHTER. During the later part of the 19th century and early 20th century there was employed in Charles County a special form of lighter, or barge, to transport large quantities of fish to Washington, Georgetown, or Alexandria. Aboard these craft, which were between 45 feet and 60 feet long, the daily catch was placed, and at a fixed time a number of them were picked up by a steam tug and towed to the city. They were loaded for their return trip with salt, building stone, rip-rap rock, or a rough or heavy type of cargo obtained at the city's wharves. The last fishermen to employ these lighters were centered around Riverside: Lou Hayden, Frank Willett, Jim Davis, Morgan Monroe, Emory Bowie, the Burgess Brothers, and Alfred Haislip.

17. SHAD GALLEY. Charles County gained national fame for its excellence of shad and herring. Huge catches were made for food and fertilizer. A plantation that included a favorable shore for fishing was considered to have an asset of real importance, and specialized gear was developed. Where a natural fishery existed, haul seines were usually used, and the catch pulled up onto the beach. A haul seine is a net set with one end on shore and the other carried by a boat in a great circular sweep out into the river and back to the starting point. Haul seines were set from a galley, a large many-oared boat with a large platform in the stern for the net. After being set, the net was hauled ashore with the fish caught in the

bight. A typical Charles County Shad-Seine rowing galley was 75 feet long with a 12-foot beam, carried about 1,200 fathoms of seine made 30 feet deep at the channel, or hauling, end and 12 feet deep at the shore end; stretching from Sandy Point to Quantico. The boats rowed two oars single banked and, depending on their length, 14 to 24 oars double-banked. Nets were carried in the stern and most boats had a net roller on top of the transom. Records of the U.S. Fish Commission in 1892 indicate 53 of these row-galleys stationed between Glymont and Riverside.

Steamboats

Travel by sail was dependent entirely on wind, weather, and tidal current. In the early 19th century the new invention of steamboat service made water transportation faster and more reliable. However, there are a few records of sailing vessels taking stranded passengers from steamboats whose wood-fired engines failed to function properly.

Steamboat service in Charles County waters began in June 1815, with establishment of a ferry from Washington to Potomac Creek, Va., in conjunction with stagecoaches to Fredericksburg, Va., for Richmond and the south. In the fashion of the day, Charles Countians obtained transportation to the nation's capital by use of tall semaphore signals ashore to attract the captain's attention. If nearby wharfage was not available, passengers would be rowed out to meet the steamer, boarding in the main channel.

By 1820 regular scheduled service began between Norfolk and Alexandria, with stops at the river wharves upon signals made by the passengers. Better service was demanded, resulting in the 1827 establishment of the Washington, Alexandria, and Georgetown Steam Packet Company to service the many wharves from Marshall Point southward to Rock Point. Their first steamer was the FREDERICKSBURG; later vessels, the FRANKLIN and COLUMBIA, which made scheduled trips to Washington and Baltimore continuously until 1874. Other vessels to follow were the

BALTIMORE, MD. and the DIAMOND STATE. In 1860 the SAINT NICHOLAS was added, only to be captured by Confederates the following year off Point Lookout; it was converted to a privateer and sunk at Fredericksburg.

Expanded business brought more steamers, with the new Washington & Norfolk Steamboat Company operating OSCELA twice weekly on the circuit between these two cities and Baltimore.

The Civil War virtually stopped all private steamboat activities. Vessels were placed under Government charter by the Army Engineers, continuing to run the many Charles County landings under strict surveillance, as most of Southern Maryland was anti-Union in sympathy. In 1861-62 the Confederates almost completely blockaded the river, causing stoppage of all traffic for six months. Among the few steamers permitted to operate were the PLANTER and KEYPORT owned by different companies in Washington and under Government charter.

Mail was delivered prior to the Civil War by contract with the Washington & Fredericksburg Steamboat Company, running from Washington to Aquia Creek, Va., stopping twice daily at Marbury Landing (the lower of the two Glymont landings) and at Sandy Point, using steamers BALTIMORE and the MT. VERNON.

After the Civil War the Potomac became the most convenient and economical highway to the "outside world" (until the 1930s) due to the geographical isolation caused by the two rivers, Patuxent and Potomac.

A typical advertisement in Washington, Alexandria, and Charles County newspapers read:

> The steamer MAJESTIC is a modern steel hull passenger and freight-carrying steamer and is practically new. During the past three months her state-rooms and saloons have been built new and her main deck entirely remodeled to fit her for the Potomac route on which she is employed. Her 42 state-rooms are all outside ones, and are furnished with brass beds or two metal berths and all the latest equipment. Numerous and skillfully arranged electric (or gas) lamps make the rooms and saloons of the MAJESTIC at night as bright as day. The

dining Room and Saloon are bright and airy apartments and a roomy Smoking Lounge is to be found on the hurricane deck. Competent critics pronounce her the handsomest and most comfortable steamer ever employed on this route. The equipment of the steamer is of the latest type and is complete in every particular.

The time tables shown give the time the steamer should arrive at and depart from the several many landings, but is not guaranteed. Bicycles, when accompanied by owners are carried free, at owner's risk. Baby carriages must be checked at a charge of 25 cents. Staterooms are $1.00, $1.25, $1.50, and $2.00 each according to location and size. Two persons are accommodated in the $1.00 and the $1.25 rooms; the rooms may be occupied by three persons.

Among the steamship companies serving Charles County for many years after the Civil War were the following.

1. The Potomac Transportation Line ran steamers CHARLOTTE VANDERBILT, W. WILDHEN, KENNEBEC, DIAMOND STATE, SUE, and EXPRESS (sunk off Point Lookout in storm).

2. The Peoples Accommodation Line ran the ISAAC P. SMITH.

3. Lewis Brothers (of St. Mary's County) Line ran the JOHN E. TYGERT, SUE, and W.W. COIT.

4. The Potomac Ferry Company opened to Charles County in 1865 with the steamer WAWASET, which ran until 1873 ending with the worst marine disaster in Charles County. On Aug. 8, 1873, at 11:30 a.m., this vessel crowded with passengers and freight left Riverside wharf for Chatterton's Landing across the river, when in mid-channel it burst into flames; within eight minutes, 76 persons had died. There were many collisions caused by the increasing number of steam boats, but none exceeded the WAWASET in casualties. Later, the owners purchased the MYSTIC and T.V. ARROWSMITH for use to Maryland and Virginia ports.

5. The Potomac Steam Navigation Company began in 1873 with the steamer PALISADES, followed with PILOT BOY,

MARY MORGAN, NELLY WHITE, and SARAH K. TAGGART running until about 1880.

6. The Inland & Seaboard Coasting Line entered for river trade in 1875 with the brand new iron steamer, JOHN W. THOMPSON. Although this firm for many years was solely in the "outside route" to New York, they obtained some of the lucrative river traffic.

7. George L. Sheriff purchased the MATTANO, which became one of the most popular vessels serving Charles County landings from 1876 until 1899. Her stops were at Marshall Hall, Pyes (Glymont), Marbury, Grinders in Mattawoman, Posey's in Chickomuxen, Sandy Point at Mallow's Bay, Smith Point, Shamrock Landing, Tolsons in Nanjemoy, Chapel Point, Brents Wharf. She suffered many collisions and even a sinking at Posey's Wharf in 1887.

8. Ephraim S. Randall entered the shipping field on the Potomac in 1870 and became the largest individual owner of steamboats on the Potomac. His first steamboat acquisition, the MARY WASHINGTON, was followed by the PILOT BOY, SAMUEL J. PENTZ, HARRY RANDALL, ESTELLE RANDALL, T.V. ARROWSMITH, WAKEFIELD, KENT, and the GENERAL J.A. DUMONT. This firm served all 25 Charles County landings until 1906. Daily stops were at Marshall Hall, Fenwick, Pyes, Marbury; also, Mattawoman Creek had landings at Grinder's, Winthrop's, Proctor's, Dent's, Mattingly's, and Nelson's; Chickomuxen Creek had Posey's and Linton's wharves, Budd's Ferry, Sandy Point, Liverpool Point, Clifton Beach (Smith Point), Nalley's Landing, Riverside, Tolsons in Nanjemoy, Brent's and Chapel Point in Port Tobacco, Pope's Creek, Lower Cedar Point (Morgantown), and Lancaster's Wharf at Rock Point.

Randall's empire became the Washington & Potomac Steamboat Company; then changed to the Potomac & Chesapeake Steamboat Company. A few more vessels were added: TRENTON, QUEEN ANNE, VOLUNTEER, GRATITUDE, MAJESTIC, DEBARY, and the newly renamed CAPITAL CITY. All left the river by 1922.

9. It was in 1817 that Captain George Weems acquired the steamboat SURPRISE to inaugurate in route from Baltimore to landings on Maryland's Western Shore of the Bay and to the Patuxent River, with an office and terminal in Benedict; he continued this service with little competition until 1905. All Patuxent steamboat work ended by the mid 1920s.

10. Between the years 1920-29 various independent operators ran steamers, OCEAN VIEW, ENDEAVOR, and the popular E. MADISON HALL. The Maryland and Virginia Steamboat Company of Baltimore (a subsidiary of the powerful Pennsylvania Railroad Company) operated the THREE RIVERS, DORCHESTER, and TALBOT from 1923 to 1932 to the many river landings. This firm succeeded the Weems Line.

11. The Weems Line entered the Potomac-landing trade in 1896, adding the steamers POTOMAC, SUE, NORTHUMBERLAND, CALVERT, ANNE ARUNDEL, ESSEX, WESTMORELAND, and LANCASTER. The ANNE ARUNDEL served Benedict three times a week from Baltimore, the last trip in 1923. The last trip to Charles County landings was made by the ANNE ARUNDEL on Feb. 29, 1932. This was the last of the scheduled packet steamboat lines to serve any Charles County landings.

Glymont with the two piers (Pye's and Marbury's) was unquestionably the "hub" of Charles County water transportation for steamers (packets and excursions), ferries, mail boats, and naval ships for more than 80 years. "Glymont" appeared on more newspaper advertisements for scheduled steamer travel than any other landing on the river.

Navy personnel were transported from the Washington Navy Yard to Indian Head, beginning with the launch SANTA BARBARA in 1890, followed by many Navy tugboats, the GRANPUS, MOOSEHEAD, GUARD, and others until World War II.

The demise of steamboat travel was caused by automobiles, trucks and buses, which not only started new towns but killed others, in a long and gradual time period.

Railroads

The need for a railroad to Washington and Baltimore was recognized by fishermen and farmers in the interior of Tidewater Potomac country in Maryland. In 1853 a charter was granted to the Pennsylvania Railroad for construction of a railroad from Baltimore, through Upper Marlboro, Mechanicsville to St. Mary's City and to Point Lookout. Plans were to join this railroad with the national railroad system, especially the coal fields of western Maryland. Southern Marylanders looked favorably on the possibility of coal, as houses were heated by wood burning fireplaces. Spurs from this Southern Maryland Railroad were also planned and were shown on Civil War maps from Brandywine to Port Tobacco, where connections could be made with ferries to lower Virginia river ports, to Trappe (a town near Hilltop at the headwaters of Nanjemoy Creek), thence to Maryland Point, crossing the river by bridge to a spot east of Somerset Beach, Va. Another planned spur was to run from Trappe to Smith Point, Md., with connections by Railcar ferry to the RF & P terminal at Aquia, Va.

The only spur constructed in Charles County ran from Brandywine to Pope's Creek. The main line terminated at Mechanicsville. It was used intensively by farmers, scrap iron dealers, and pulp wood firms. Marine salvage firms operated at Pope's Creek Wharf after World War II, shipping the scrap iron by railroad. Fishermen tended to freight their products to the city by boat, as they were a bit wary of large railroad companies.

This railroad proved a boon to Charles Countians for freight service in tobacco, cord wood, and pulp wood to Baltimore, returning with everything formerly carried by steamboats—even tractors, automobiles, and farm equipment. Passenger excursions were popular among the Charles County gentry, while the city folks crowded the cars for crab feasts and shad bakes at Pope's Creek. Traffic has decreased on this line, until its only use is to carry coal to the power plants on the Potomac River and Patuxent, with return loads of pulp wood.

The Naval Powder Factory operations at Indian Head to the Washington Navy Yard were served by steamboats or tugs and barges. However, Lt. Commander Joseph Strauss in 1900 established a trolley type street car to handle traffic ashore. It was nicknamed the "Toonerville Trolley," with Clarence D. Carpenter of Pisgah as "pilot." At first it was used for passenger traffic around the base. But there were many accidents, and the trolley was converted to carry freight only. Twice a month it was known as the "cash-car," where the employees collected their wages. It has the distinction of being Charles County's only streetcar.

The U.S. Naval Powder Factory railroad, started during World War I, ran from Indian Head along Mattawoman Creek shore, and connected with the Pennsylvania Railroad from Pope's Creek, at White Plains. It was abandoned shortly after the war.

Roads

Before 1910 the only important roads in the county were those connecting the ferry lines across the river, those leading to river landings for steamboat travel to Washington or Baltimore, and those leading to a railroad station. The State Roads Commission planned in 1909 a road from Brandywine in Prince George's County south to Mattawoman Village, to Waldorf, Young's Switch (White Plains), La Plata, Spring Hill, Bel Alton, Faulkner, Newburg, and on to Lancaster's Wharf at Rock Point. Another road ran from Waldorf, to Beantown, Bryantown, Hughesville, and on into St. Mary's County. A third started at La Plata running to Port Tobacco, Welcome, Hilltop, Ironsides, Doncaster, and ending at Riverside wharf. To compete with steamboat service, the State later planned a road system to connect all Potomac River landings from Marshall Hall, along the shoreline to Riverside, with hopes of the new bridge to Virginia; it would by-pass Washington, and direct business to Baltimore. This never materialized.

Samuel J. Vacchino of La Plata relates his father's description of the first State Road building project in 1910. He was superintendent for the H.S. Swann Construction Company, which built the first stretch between Waldorf and La Plata. Grading was done by hand operated metal scoops drawn by a team of horses. Larger portions of earth and hills were removed by coal-fired steam-powered shovels, loading into horse drawn carts and wagons. Originally all roads were paved with oyster sheets, mostly from the vast source deposited by Indians at Pope's Creek. As most of the County has an underlay of gravel, by 1930 the State Roads Commission reported 167 miles of gravel roads here and only 5 miles of concrete highway.

With the increase of agricultural population and the popularity of tobacco, the demand for better roads to Baltimore was answered by Robert Crain, prominent "Squire of Mount Victoria," assisted by State Senators Walter Mitchell of Charles County and Lansdale Sasscer of Prince George's County. Ground was broken Sept. 30, 1922, for a proposed new concrete paved highway to be known as the Southern Maryland Trunk Line; it later was named the Robert Crain Highway. The main route through and to the County is U.S. Highway 301, which has proved to be a quick route to Baltimore, and avoids the nation's capital city. The comparative isolation of Charles County from the "outside world" was ended by this roadway.

Bridges and Bicycles

Within a few years after the State planned roads in 1909, bridges were planned for Burgess Creek and Ward's Run near Hilltop, the creek near Port Tobacco, Mattawoman Creek at Mason's Springs, Nanjemoy Creek near Grayton, Allen's Fresh over the Wicomico, Bryantown over Zekiah Swamp and an 8,000-foot span across the Potomac River to Virginia at Riverside. The Riverside bridge was not built.

The U.S. Navy built the only bascule bridge over a river in Southern Maryland: a 2,000-foot pedestrian span over

Mattawoman Creek from the Powder Factory to Wilford Road in Marbury. The opened bascule draw was 80 feet wide, permitting large coal barges to float upstream to the powder plant of the Naval Powder Factory.

Pres. Franklin Delano Roosevelt promoted the Morgantown (Md.) Bridge, for Rt. 301 extension. It was opened to traffic in 1940, and redesignated as the Gov. Harry W. Nice Bridge in 1967. Length is 11,446 feet from the former Virginia terminal of Hooe's Ferry to the Maryland site of Ludlow House on Passaquahanna Creek.

Bicycles were generally given to youngsters as Christmas presents or as rewards for performing extra chores around the farm. They were used mostly on cow paths and on oyster shell roads between farms and once in a while for an adventure out on the newly graveled road. George Wade of Port Tobacco was the County's first dealer—ordering his "bicycles and tricycles" from Sears & Roebuck or from the Charles King store in Alexandria. Delivery was made by steamboat to Chapel Point.

Automobiles and Tractors

Self-propelled land vehicles using internal combustion engines and known as "automobiles" first appeared in Charles County driven by the affluent gentry of the Nation's Capital, during the early 1900s. Records are scattered and vague as to exactly who owned the first automobile in Charles County. Robert Crain of Mount Victoria operated the first tractor on his farm; it was delivered ashore by steamboat stevedores at Lower Cedar Point Wharf, Morgantown, in 1901. Two years later Adrian Posey became the first dealer of passenger cars in La Plata. The first load of 1903 Buicks arrived by railroad with Posey taking the first delivery and the second (a sports roadster) sold to the dentist of Faulkner, Dr. Aubrey A. Posey.

On Dec. 1, 1908, F. Brooke Matthews and Bernard A. Howard opened their agency in La Plata to sell "vehicles, fertilizer, and farm implements" with branches in Hughesville and Leonardtown (St. Mary's County). Autos sold were Fords and Buicks.

As all roads and traffic led northward it was an honor for Robert Crain Sr. to drive the first auto south of La Plata. The U.S. Vice President James S. Sherman (under President William Taft in 1909) gave Crain the first Stanley Steamer ever to operate in Southern Maryland. The appearance of this "puffing, noisy mechanical monster" frightened horses, oxen and people. When water in the boiler became low and the steam pressure high, the driver would race to the nearest stream. There he sat, for about an hour, allowing the engine to cool; then the boiler was filled with clear stream water, the burner was lit, and off the "monster" would roar to scare more people. Robert Crain's next autos were a Franklin and then a Packard—all with top speed of 25 miles per hour.

In the early years of fast driving around the county there appeared women drivers, attired in dusters (a lightweight coat for protection from dust), bonnets (small brim hats with chin ribbons), and huge goggles for eye protection. Records of who was the first are limited; newspapers name a few: Mrs. Walter J. Mitchell in her 1913 Buick, Mrs. W.W. Keech in her 1917 Ford, Mrs. Carlyle Turner; Miss Katherine Posey, and Miss Louise Matthews.

The early Ford Touring Cars ran on kerosene and had tail lights, rubber tires that went flat every 10 or 15 miles and required frequent stops for inflating the tube, and a radiator cap containing a temperature gauge that was visible while driving. There were no windshield wipers, and the fuel tank sat under the front hood. The hood was hinged in the center, which allowed the sides to fold up for engine inspection. When it rained, the side curtains were brought out from under the seats and secured in place with clips. Air for sounding the horn was produced by squeezing a hard rubber ball located alongside the driver and outside the door next to his seat.

Differential, axles, and running boards were 24 inches above the ground, thus permitting safe passage of the vehicle over deeply rutted or highly crowned roads. A metal tool box was fixed on the running board, filled with tools for the owner's use. If stranded, the driver could obtain service at a local blacksmith forge or shop, although every owner was supposed to be his own mechanic.

A hand crank projected out front, below the radiator. Starting the engine was somewhat dangerous. If the spark were advanced too far, it caused the crank to kick, thus breaking the cranker's arm. Three foot pedals controlled the auto's movement over the roadway: one for gearshifting (you pushed in for low gear, released for high gear); one for reverse pedal; and the brake, which stopped the rear wheels.

The car had wood spoke wheels and a canvas fold-back top. It was affectionately called the "Tin Lizzie," the "Flivver," or the "Model T Jitney."

In 1920 the first "sedan" of the county was driven to St. Mary's Church at Bryantown by Reed Posey. Parishioners were horrified, fearing the family would be cut to pieces. There was some merit to this fear. Frequently a steering tie-rod broke, and the auto overturned, shattering the glass windows.

At first blacksmith shops stored gasoline in 55-gallon drums for sale to motorists; then dealers and service stations opened for business. Among early dealers were:

1915—Leonard Orem in Waldorf.
1918—Hugh Mitchell and Frank Martin in La Plata.
1918—Steve and Ollie Quade in Hughesville.
1921—Harry Moreland in Bryantown.
1922—Harry and Guy Moreland in Waldorf.
1922—Frank Martin in La Plata.
1922—Maxwell Mitchell in La Plata.

Auto trips years ago were real thrillers. Mary Keech Edelen remembers her trips during the early 1920s in the family car:

> In the summer, most roads were deep sand, in the winter, deep mud. Regardless of the make of auto, you got stuck in either

sand or mud. When Aunt Sallie (Mrs. F.W. Wright of Baltimore) came to our farm and took the family to dinner at the Benedict Hotel, it would take two hours and three flat tires; we got stuck in the sand, filled the radiator, and wiped perspiration.

This was typical in the Edelens' seven-passenger Cadillac. Chains were always taken along. When an auto got stuck, it has to be jacked up and the chains put on the wheels. Then, when the car cleared, the chains were removed and returned to the tool box. Drivers traveling to Washington had to borrow or buy D.C. tags and change them as they crossed the boundary line, because every auto in D.C. had to display a D.C. tag.

Mrs. Edelen continues:

Trips to the Capital City were made about twice a year. When Father went to Baltimore to sell his tobacco at the warehouse, he always took me. We'd go first to Hughesville in a buggy or carriage and take the train to Baltimore, where we would visit relatives and friends, crowding in everything possible like buying fabrics, seeing movies, stuffing with candy and ice cream before starting home.

Walking and Horses

Every child walked to school or to the neighbors' homes, up to five miles. For longer trips, a horse or buggy was used. When they walked to school, youngsters would go together, so as to talk or sing; they would pick strawberries and flowers and often eat their lunches on the way to school. Horses were a fine form of transportation—until the steed saw an automobile; then there was a bolting horse or a runaway.

Early public school transportation consisted of walking or being driven in a buggy by adults, as there were no school buses. Male students of Charlotte Hall Academy, or Notre Dame Senior High School at Bryantown or the McDonough Institute at La Plata were required to furnish their own transportation. Stables were provided, and the horses still harnessed were driven under shelter up to the feeding bay or rack. When a hard crusted snowfall occurred, sleds were used in lieu of buggies, and familiar trees served as guides to school. After World War I motorized buses generally provided transportation for most schoolchildren.

Passenger and Freight Motor Lines

The Public Service Commission, which is required to authorized all regularly operated passenger motor bus and freight motor truck routes, appoved a plan to compete with the remaining steamboats running out of Washington and Alexandria. In 1930 plans were made for a passenger bus route through Anacostia, Piscataway, Sharpersville, Accokeek, Mason Springs, Glymont, Marbury, Rison, Chickamuxen, Doncaster, Cross Roads (Nanjemoy), and Grafton, terminating at Riverside. Federal funds were expected to build a bridge across the Potomac to Metompkin Point, Va., thus permitting the motor lines access through Charles County to the South.

Privately owned trucks hauled turkeys, chickens, eggs, and farm animals to the Southeast Washington markets, returning with household goods and fertilizer. Probably the first organized trucking business ran a 1917 advertisement:

> I am making regular trips to Washington markets and if loads can be accumulated, will be glad to HAUL ANY LIVE STOCK or Produce—at reasonable rates. My Two-Ton Packard Insures Rapid Hauling. Edward G. Edelen of Bryantown, Md.

The first passenger line, established in 1917, was the Simms Motor Line, running from Washington out Good Hope Road to Upper Marlboro and through the County to St. Mary's; followed by the Tidewater Line, Southern Maryland Line, and the J.H. Price Company. Many bus and trucking companies were begun after World War II. Among them were the Washington, Marlboro, and Annapolis Line; Bailey's

Express (of St. Mary's County); Atwoods; Kane's Transfer; Maryland Transportation Line; Preston Trucking; and Greyhound Bus Lines.

Emergency Services

Before there were official church graveyards, most families buried their dead on their own property or in their private graveyards. If transportation to the church were required, it was performed by a horse-drawn hearse. Henry A. Penn operated the County's first motorized "Private Ambulance and Limousine Hearse" in 1948, providing "prompt attention, day or night" from his offices in La Plata.

Funeral parlors furnished their hearses for emergency or ambulance work before the Second World War. Later the State Police made a station wagon available, with stretchers. In 1951 the Charles County Ambulance Service was established by the Restaurant and Tavern Owners, who funded the project. In 1952 the Rescue Squad took over this volunteer community work at La Plata and Ironsides.

The first water to extinguish fires was carried by a bucket brigade from the nearby stream, or, if the condition looked impossible, every means was made to remove valuables from the burning building and just let the place burn down. Hand operated pumps were used by the original La Plata Volunteer Fire Department. The first motorized equipment was a Chevrolet Hose Wagon put into service in February 1930, followed by a Seagrave Pumper in June of that year. By 1976 motorized equipment was located at Indian Head, Marbury, Hughesville, Waldorf, Nanjemoy, Benedict, Cobb Island, Potomac Heights, Bel Alton, and Bryan's Road.

Airplanes

Shortly before the turn of the century, air transportation history touched briefly on Charles County. In 1896 when Samuel P. Langley, then Secretary of the Smithsonian Institution, began testing his experimental heavier-than-air flying machine, the unpiloted plane flew over the Potomac River, landing in Charles County. This was the first flight of a heavier-than-air craft to take place in the United States. Langley then started work on a machine that would accommodate a pilot, but required a launching ship to get airborne.

In the summer of 1903, the necessary launching ship was anchored off Liverpool Point, being supplied and serviced by Charles Countians of Mallow's Bay. Unfortunately, the launching apparatus proved faulty and before Langley could make the necessary corrections, the Wright Brothers had made their flight at Kitty Hawk, N.C., thus depriving Charles County of being the birthplace of the air age in America. Charles County pilots who participated in World War I included Brown Keech Turner, Harry White Wilmer, and G. dePriest Larner.

After World War I, privately owned airplanes made emergency landings in open fields, usually because they ran out of fuel or into motor trouble. Great excitement would result from a forced landing, and children would gallop up and down the road on horseback screaming, "Come see the airoplane in our yard!" Phones would ring and, in an hour or so, several hundred people would have gathered. The following day, after making repairs or fueling, the plane would take off midst cheers and good wishes for the pilot and his passenger. The only two private airstrips in the 1920s were owned by Dr. Ernest Spencer of Bel Alton and Robert Crain at Mt. Victoria.

Air-minded enthusiasts who did not have airstrips made friends with Navy pilots stationed at Dahlgren in the 1930s. Roland Burgess of Riverside was probably the first aviator to fly his own plane out of Dahlgren. Shortly after, Samuel C. Linton Jr. of Grayton became his passenger, influencing him to join the Air Force, where he became a member of a flight crew. He now pilots his own plane. Other County air pioneers were Ray Tilghman, Bob Wenk, Bill Gamble, Henry Thomas, Elmer Burns, Charlie Bauserman, Jack Stricker, Jack Crawford, and George Curtis.

Some World War II pilots were George F. Bonifant, Reed McDonagh, C. Maurice Flynn, and James Mudd. The Korean War listed James Wills Jr. Lt. Edward J. Edelen III was recognized in August 1964 as the youngest pilot to make a nonstop crossing of the Atlantic Ocean in a single-seat, single-engine jet fighter plane (F-100), when he was deployed to Hahn, Germany, as part of the D.C. Air National Guard operation, known as "Ready-Go."

In the 1940s Crawford and Bauserman established the County's first public airfield, near Bryan's Road at Pomonkey, trading as Bauserman Service, Inc. The next field to open publicly was Aqualand Sky Park adjacent to the Potomac River Bridge near Morgantown. Today, private airstrips abound in the County, as at Rock Point, Liverpool Point, Budd's Ferry, and Holly Springs Farm. Helicopter pads adorn the Physicians' Memorial Hospital at La Plata, and the State Police Barracks at Waldorf.

We've come a long way from dependence on the river!

CHAPTER 3

TOWNS AND VILLAGES: CHANGES WITH TRANSPORTATION

The towns and villages of Charles County have held a place in the history of the United States for more than 300 years. They were once bustling and important places. In late 17th century England, Port Tobacco was named along with Boston and Philadelphia when people spoke of major New World seaports.

Nature and technology conspired against Port Tobacco, however, and destined her to be little more than a ghost town by the 19th century. Nature and technology also relegated the thriving steamboat river port of Benedict, and the promising mercantile center of Bryantown, to footnotes in history.

Charles County once comprised an area much larger than it does today. The first Charles County was created by Cecil Calvert, Second Lord Baltimore, Oct. 3, 1650. It included all of the present County as well as some of the counties of Calvert, St. Mary's, and Prince George's. On May 10, 1658, the County was rededicated in honor of Charles Calvert, Third Lord Baltimore, and a year later a General Act of the General Assembly defined the present boundaries.

The County covers 502 square miles, 44 of them water. Located on the Southern Maryland Peninsula, it lies between the Patuxent and Potomac rivers. It is bounded on the north and west by Prince George's County and on the east by St. Mary's. How this land mass was and is divided into entities called "towns" is the subject of this chapter.

53

Proprietary Manor Systems

Land in the County was once divided by the Proprietary system. The Lord Proprietor was usually an English nobleman who had been granted the land by the King. He would order surveys, then draw up land divisions known as Proprietary Manors. These were then divided into individual manors that represented the largest of the land grants; smaller grants within a Proprietary Manor were called plantations, or farms. Political divisions of the Proprietary Manors were the "Hundreds."

By 1869, under William and Mary, the system of Hundreds was abolished, and the counties were further divided into parishes. Charles County consisted of seven political parishes.

The Act for Advancement of Trade, passed in 1683, had provided for the establishment of towns and ports to facilitate commerce. Appointed commissioners were empowered to acquire tracts of land from their legal owners so they might establish towns at strategic points of commerce, regardless of whether a settlement already existed at the site. By this method were officially "erected" the port towns of Benedict-Leonardtown (eventually shortened to Benedict, 1683) and Port Tobacco (1684).

In their history of Charles County, P.D. and Margaret Klapthor Brown note that the waterways threading the County "made major seaports unnecessary," since "every planter could have his own landing. . .". In 1669, they say, the Assembly created seaports to serve the thinly settled neighborhoods. As for towns, their erection "was a hobby with the lawmakers and land speculators," and their sites were chosen because of the people's need for market or port. They describe the pattern of town erection:

> Commissioners were appointed to agree with the owner of land for a tract of 50 to 100 or more acres which was then staked off and divided into lots of an acre each, intersected by proper streets, lanes and alleys. The lots being numbered and priced, the owner was allowed to select one lot and the rest were divided among the "taker up" who received the

free-hold in consideration of a yearly quit-rent usually one penny to the Lord Proprietor.

Names of Towns

Once established, towns and villages within the County received their names in a number of ways.

Benedict-Leonardtown was named for Benedict Leonard Calvert, the Fourth Lord Baltimore and Lord Proprietor. A town might be named for the deed holder, who requisitioned it in accordance with the Act for the Advancement of Trade. So named were Dentsville and Marbury.

Marshall Hall took its name from the main house of the estate that once covered the area. Bryantown was named for a prominent citizen, the proprietor of a local inn on the stagecoach route through that part of the County. McConchie was also named for a leading citizen, the Rev. William McConchie. He served both Durham and Port Tobacco parishes, ministering the latter from 1711 till his death in 1742.

A town might be named nostalgically for a place back home, as was Doncaster; or for the geographical features of its site: Cedarville, Cedar Point, Hilltop, Piney, Rock Point. Also, Centreville, Cross Roads, Middletown (now White Plains), Riverside, and Wayside, which suggest locations of other towns or places. Their proximity to thoroughfares led to the names of Berry Road and Bryan's Road.

It was not unusual to assign a romatic name, perhaps in hopes that the new settlement would take on some of the characteristics cited. Sometimes foreign languages were used: Dubois, Bel Alton, La Plata.

Some towns merely wished to stress their newness; therefore they affixed suffixes to the word: Newburg, Newport, and Newton remain today.

The particular Indian tribes that inhabited the area were recalled in some names: Chicamuxen, Mattawoman, Pomfret, Pomonkey, Patuxent, Potomac, and Port Tobacco owe their names to pre-Colonial residents, although the tribal names were sometimes corrupted by newcomers.

Towns are, of course, more than locations and names. How they develop, what they become, is an essential part of a town's history. Four Charles County towns achieved eminence during the Colonial period: Port Tobacco, Benedict, Bryantown, and La Plata. The first two were noteworthy beyond the United States.

Port Tobacco

Just as there were two Charles Counties, so it seems there were two Port Tobaccoes. Reference to this is found in the Land Records of Charles County. The first post-Indian settlement is described as "lying about four miles from the head of Port Tobacco Creek." A drawing of the Courthouse and a copy of the survey plat are also in the Land Records.

The second settlement appeared in 1727 when an Act of the Assembly directed that a new courthouse be erected on the "Eastside of the Head of Port Tobacco Creek, at a place called 'Chandler Town' allowing 3 acres for a courthouse and a jail."

The County seat was first established in the first town of Port Tobacco with the creation of Charles County on April 15, 1658. One month later, on May 10, County Court was held for the first time in Port Tobacco. It appears that private homes and inns were used until 1679, when a courthouse building and jail were completed at Moore's Lodge.

When Port Tobacco was reestablished on its new site in 1727, a courthouse and jail were to be erected. They were completed under one roof two years later. The building is assumed to have been of brick because the records show that it was constructed at a cost of 12,200 pounds of tobacco. Unfortunately no drawings have been found of this courthouse.

At the same time the Assembly provided for a courthouse, it also granted 60 acres to be cut up into lots to form a town. Additionally it sought to change the name of the village to

"Charles Town," but with little success. The area had always been popularly known as Port Tobacco, a corrupted version of the Indian name Potopaco. Through the years the name has been variously pronounced as Portafacco, Potobac, Potobag, and Porttobattoo.

The Potopaco Indians, "peaceful and about 20 men strong," according to a Jesuit missionary account in 1634, were the pioneers of the village that became the town of Port Tobacco. Situated in a fertile valley four miles from the mouth of the Port Tobacco River it had direct access to the navigable waters of the Chesapeake Bay, since the Port Tobacco River flowed into the Potomac River, and that in turn spilled into the Bay. Because of this, Port Tobacco became one of the busiest seaports in the New World.

The mainstays of Port Tobacco were the corn and tobacco harvested on surrounding hillsides. They were carted by oxen or merely rolled in wooded barrels down the sloping hillsides to the wharves. There, on the riverfront, they were bartered for English and French goods—silks, furniture, tea, china.

The houses of Port Tobacco fanned out from the Courthouse. Characterized by massive chimneys and sloping roofs, they sat close to the street and were built of brick, wood, or both.

There was a Public Square in the center of the town. It was bounded by the Courthouse, Christ Episcopal Church (later moved stone by stone to La Plata), and stores and businesses alongside hotels, inns, granaries, and warehouses.

The town's riverfront advantage placed it on the Potomac River ferry route. This in turn made it an important stop on the North-South stagecoach route. Passengers and mail traveled through Southern Maryland from Philadelphia to the South.

For all these reasons, Port Tobacco grew rapidly. Inns and taverns were the St. Charles, the Centennial, and the Indian-King.

Amusement was provided by a racetrack, cock fighting pits, or high stake card games at the inns. Traveling theatrical companies and musicians often played Port Tobacco in

Colonial days, further contributing to the town's central position in the center of the commercial and social life of Southern Maryland.

But her prosperity was shortlived. The wooded hillsides, cleared and planted, gradually washed into the river. The silting of the river was compounded with the deeper draft design introduced into shipping; soon the silting was so complete that the river became unnavigable for even the shallower draft vessels.

Port Tobacco managed to sit out the War of 1812. Her townsmen watched from Chapel Point in August 1814 as the British fleet sailed to and from the sacking of Alexandria, Va., for some reason sparing their town. They heard that the British had landed in another Charles County town, Benedict, and had marched to Washington and burned it to the ground before retreating to their ships at Benedict.

Port Tobacco survived the Civil War as well, although there was much action in and around the town. Southern Maryland's sympathies lay with the Confederacy. Port Tobacco was the center for Confederate blockade runners. It became an important link in the spy underground, transporting both people and mail along the network that linked it to the South, the Northern States, and Canada.

By the early 1890s Port Tobacco was faced with still another setback: The town of La Plata, 3½ miles northeast, asked that the County Seat be moved there. It had good grounds for such a request.

In 1873 the Baltimore and Potomac Railroad had chosen to erect a station, telegraph office, and store on the Chapman farm, "La Plata." La Plata was on their main rail line through Southern Maryland.

The town gradually grew up around the train station. Goods were now transported primarily by rail rather than water. The railroad's bypassing of Port Tobacco in favor of the more direct La Plata line caused Port Tobacco to slide further into decline.

On Aug. 3, 1892, the center of the cross-shaped courthouse at Port Tobacco was burned to the ground. The conflagration came three months after a special election had defeated the move of the County Seat to La Plata. Arson was suspected and somewhat supported when the Courthouse records were found to have been removed intact from the building before it burned. (Because these records were saved, Charles is the only county in Maryland that has an unbroken line of court records.)

As a result of the fire, another special election was held. The vote favored La Plata, where a new Courthouse was erected in 1895.

At the time of the fire Port Tobacco had been the County Seat for 150 years. The night it lost its bid to retain the County government, it still had some 20 shops, two newspapers (*The Maryland Independent* and the *Port Tobacco Times*), three hotels (St. Charles, Centennial, and Smoot House) and 60 to 70 homes.

By 1900 residents had begun to move away. Many tore down their houses and moved their chimney bricks to their new homes. Others sold their homes and joined the general trek westward across the United States. Older homes deteriorated and Port Tobacco took on the appearance of a ghost town.

The Society for the Restoration of Port Tobacco was formed in 1946. Under its 30-year tutelage, the Courthouse (modeled after the one built in 1819 to replace the 1729 building that was leveled by a tornado in 1808) has been restored as a museum. Area homes are being restored by both the Society and private owners. New homes are being constructed as Port Tobacco finds new meaning as a 20th century town.

Benedict

Historic Benedict grew out of the Proprietary System. It was a large political subdivision of a Proprietary Manor, known as "Benedict Hundreds."

The original Benedict Hundreds was an area that extended roughly north of the present Prince George's-Charles County line toward Aquasco, west to what is now Bryantown (then Boarman's Rest), south and east near Charlotte Hall, and all bounded on the east by the Patuxent River.

The early farms and manors within the Benedict Hundreds produced an abundance of tobacco, lumber, and other goods that were shipped within the colonies as well as to England. The goods were carried and carted from the plantations down a road that followed the same track as present Rt. 231. The old road ended on the banks of the Patuxent River. There, docks were built to accommodate the ships that traveled among the plantations of Southern Maryland, stopping at those whose wharves fingered into the major waterways.

The docks at Benedict represented a number of large manor houses and plantations that were part of the Hundreds. Storehouses were built near the wharves, ship building began and a little center of population grew at the river's edge.

By 1683 the Act for the Advancement of Trade was charged with "erecting" towns and ports to facilitate commerce. Ships could no longer stop at privately owned plantation docks, but would instead put in to designated "ports." These ports would be established at strategic points along the commercial water route.

The sole criterion for the establishment of these ports was their location along the existing commercial route. Benedict was one of the first of these.

Shipbuilding began earnestly at Benedict in the late 1600s. Wooden craft of all sizes were turned out by craftsmen who lived in cottages around the wharves and warehouses.

Local manors during this period mainly produced and shipped tobacco. The crop's popularity had spread throughout the colonies as well as Europe, and a high demand existed for it even then.

Benedict grew quietly, content with her role as chief river port on the Patuxent. Then in 1812 British forces landed and marched on the nation's capital, which they burned to the ground. Benedict became famous as the landing place of the only foreign forces to invade the United States mainland.

Benedict's role in the War of 1812 was not part of the British grand strategy. It was, in fact, contrary to the three main objectives of the enemy's expeditionary forces deployed along our coast: The British planned to invade New York at Lake Champlain, cause diversions by attacking coastal cities, and eventually seize New Orleans. But the character of British Rear Admiral Sir George Cockburn changed all that.

When the Americans launched an unauthorized attack on Canadian communities around Lake Erie, Adm. Sir Alexander Cochrane stormed out of Bermuda and into Chesapeake Bay with reprisal on his mind. His initial target was Baltimore, but at the mouth of the Bay he encountered a British fleet at anchor. The fleet commander was Cockburn, who persuaded Cochrane to revenge the attacks by taking the city of Washington. The capture of their capital, argued Cockburn, would deal a demoralizing blow to the government and people of the United States.

After carefully checking out the land, Cockburn reassured his superior that their British forces could land unopposed at Benedict, where they would find good quarters, horses, and food for the troops.

From his flagship anchored off Jerome Point in Chesapeake Bay, Cockburn wrote Vice Adm. Cochrane, July 17, 1814:

"Sir,

.... I feel no hesitation in stating to you that I consider the town of Benedict in the Patuxent to offer us advantages for this purpose (launching an attack on Washington) beyond any other spot within the United States. It is, I am informed, only 44 or 45 miles from Washington and there is a high road between the two places which tho' hilly, is good, it passes through Piscataway near (er) to Fort Washington than four miles, which fortification is sixteen miles below the City of Washington and is the only one the Army would have to pass. I therefore most firmly believe that within 48 hours after the arrival in the Patuxent of such a force as you expect, the City of Washington might be possessed without difficulty or opposition of any kind . . . the ships of the fleet could cover a

landing at Benedict ... The Army on its arrival would be sure of good quarters in the Town of Benedict, and a rich country around it to afford the necessary immediate supplies, and as many horses as might be wanted to transport cannon, etc. ...
The facility and rapidity, after its being first discovered, with which an Army by landing at Benedict might possess itself of the Capitol, always so great a blow to the government of a country ...

Accordingly, four ships of the line, 20 frigates and sloops, and more than 20 transports carrying 4,000 regulars proceeded up the Patuxent River towards the little town of Benedict on August 18, 1814.

Commodore Joshua Barney, U.S.N., and his flotilla of gunboats that protected the Bay and river, fled upstream before the advance of the formidable British fleet. As the line ships kept the Americans running, the British lightly shelled Benedict and the next day disembarked their troops at Town Point, Benedict. A force of soldiers and marines was formed to march parallel with the ships in pursuit of the American gunboats.

On Aug. 22, Comm. Barney, believing the situation to be hopeless, blew up his boats and sent his marines on to defend Washington. The British accomplished their purpose and returned to Benedict unmolested by Aug. 29. The next day they reembarked and sailed downriver. When a red brick house on Steamboat Lane (The Red House) was torn down recently, British cannonballs were found embedded in the walls of the structure.

Benedict again came to the fore during the Civil War. In August 1863 Camp Stanton was established for the purpose of recruiting and training a Black Infantry. Recently liberated Negroes were actively recruited to serve in the Union Army. Army life afforded food, shelter, and pay when little was otherwise available. Recruiting was so successful that the 7th, 9th, 19th and 30th Colored Infantries formed and trained at Camp Stanton.

The winter of 1863 was a hard one for Benedict. Many of the trainees became ill and died during those long months.

The original Peter C. Henderson house was requisitioned for a field hospital. The hospital, along with a military cemetery in the fields behind the house served the camp throughout the remainder of the war. After the war the bodies of the dead soldiers were removed to the newly designated National Cemetery at Arlington, Va.

From 1817 until 1937 steamboats frequented the Benedict docks. They carried freight and ferried passengers from river ports on Virginia's Rappahannock River, the Potomac, the Patuxent, and on up the coast to Baltimore.

George Boyd, 92, the only living steamboat man remaining in the Benedict area, talks about his life on the river:

> The boats would pick up barrels of oysters at Benedict—lumber, big casks of tobacco, wheat, corn, cattle, and sheep were also carried on consignment from Benedict to Baltimore. People would get on the boat in the evening and for two dollars round trip fare, arrive in Baltimore the next morning. Staterooms were 50 cents extra, and meals were 50 cents. There were 50 to 60 staterooms for passengers of the steamboats, depending on the size of the vessel. The rooms were a comfortable size, and only two persons shared each one.

The steamboats stopped running in 1937 because there was not enough freight business. The men from the steamers turned to charters, to fishing and boat rentals, or they left the river. One man, Capt. Peter "Perry" C. Henderson started a ferry service across the river to Holland Point. Today the ferry dock on the Benedict side is recognized by the University of Maryland Estuarian School Laboratory trailer, which occupies it.

The old ferry office no longer stands at the water's edge. It was moved intact to Henderson Lane and is used as a residential cottage.

The old wooden platforms in the river used to be the shipping lane markers. Out of use now, they originally held lanterns, and later battery operated lights. Today they are a haven for the endangered ospreys that build their huge shaggy nests on top of the platforms year after year. The U.S. Coast

Guard plans to remove one or two platforms to their museum in the near future.

At the end of Steamboat Lane, one can see the remnants of an old wharf. The wharf burned to the water some time ago, and part of it has been restored for use by the oyster boats. Scorched pilings are still visible next to the existing pier; they inflate the original size of the old steamboat wharf.

The red oyster house, between the present pier and Toyer's boat rental dock, was once a storehouse for goods shipped and delivered by the "gone-but-not-forgotten" steamboats.

Since Benedict's earliest days inhabitants have harvested from the waters of the Patuxent River and the Chesapeake Bay. Oysters, clams, crabs and a good variety of fish have provided a living for many of the residents up to the present day. The bounty on both fish and shellfish has declined in recent years due to the pollution of the river. Fortunately, this is being brought under control, and harvest prospects have improved.

Tobacco farming still goes on at Benedict. Produce is taken today to the auction warehouses in Hughesville by truck.

The ruins of the old Cannery Mill are near Mill Creek behind the Connick family property; they have preserved the millstones. Produce canning was a local industry. A canning factory stood next to the present site of Adolph Welch's boat rental business.

In what is now "The Grove," where people rent cottages by the season, was a company store, and small company houses for the cannery workers lined the area. Locally, these were called "hickey shacks." The cannery and its buildings burned to the ground in one of Benedict's many sweeping fires; only the vestiges of the shoreline road and the cement slabs on which some of the buildings stood are still visible.

Pleasure fishing and boating are popular in Benedict most months of the year. Hunting season brings sportsmen for duck and goose.

There is still a little commercial trapping done in Benedict. Muskrat pelts are usually taken. Occasionally, however, a mink, beaver, or otter is seen, reminders of the lucrative fur trade that first attracted white men to the area. Trappers from Virginia Colony named the area before Lord Baltimore's colonists arrived.

Charter boats filled the docks on Benedict's shore and boat rentals thrived before the Patuxent River Bridge was built. Business already had declined during World War II, and the easy access to the Chesapeake Bay after the bridge was completed finished it.

The families that catered to those avid fishermen and women kept hotels for the overnighters and vacationers and their restaurants are still remembered with delight. The town bustled when it was a full fledged resort and even Pres. Franklin D. Roosevelt came up the Patuxent to Benedict and spent a day in the village.

Many of the families, adults and children alike, were up before dawn preparing breakfast and picnic lunches for the charter boats, and then worked long hours after the boats came in, getting them ready for the next day's outing.

The people of Benedict still take great pride in their ability to put on "the best oyster roasts and crab feasts" in the County.

La Plata

La Plata has been the County Seat of Charles County since a courthouse was erected there in 1895.

The town is situated on a tract of land donated by the Chapman family. The land was originally part of their extensive, flat acreage that caused them to name their farm "Le Plateau," French for that type of terrain. French names were common in the naming of colonial lands, as was their corruption. Le Plateau was corrupted to La Plata. The name has nothing to do with the Spanish word for silver.

La Plata owes its existence as a town to the Baltimore and Potomac Railroad. In 1873 the railroad announced that it intended to establish a station, telegraph office, and store under one roof, to be known as La Plata Station. A post office was added that November, and the town was incorporated 15 years later, in 1888.

At the time the Chapman family donated land approximately one mile square to accommodate the building of a new town. Streets were laid out and houses built to accommodate the influx of merchants and residents as La Plata took the commercial reins in Southern Maryland.

La Plata actually had supplanted Port Tobacco as a commercial center at the close of the Civil War. The railroad station and transfer of the County government merely made it official. La Plata Station became the most important of the new little villages that grew along the rail line in Southern Maryland.

The town grew slowly at first. However, the extension of U. S. 301 across the newly completed Potomac River Bridge led to an increase in building and population. World War II halted La Plata's growth; but a postwar resumption occurred. Just as the railroad had initiated the town's growth nearly 75 years earlier, now the automobile revived it. U.S. 301 was the principle New York-to-Florida road for commercial and pleasure transport. Motels and restaurants sprang up to accommodate tourists, sportsmen, and others who passed through or stopped in Charles County.

Today La Plata continues to grow rapidly. In 1958 the town built a picturesque new Courthouse, then had to add a wing by the mid-1970s. By then La Plata had spilled over its one square mile plot, expanding in northerly, southerly, and westerly directions. It has a modern hospital, the Southern Maryland regional library, and a growing community college. New residences are being built, their lots woven among the gracious old homes of another era.

Bryantown

The State census of Bryantown Hundred, taken during the period 1775-78 by John Harbin, Constable, lists six persons having the name of "Bryan" in its data on all males 18 or older living in the area. Evidently, the name of the village originated from that of the innkeeper whose hostelry was so vital to travelers.

Looking back in records of land grants, one would think that the village might have received its name from the earliest owner of land in this part of Maryland Colony. Between 1650 and 1699 Lord Baltimore had granted 30 tracts of land totaling 17,000 acres to Major William Boarman, who had come to Maryland in 1645 and served as an officer in the Provincial Militia, as High Sheriff, and as delegate to the Lower House of the Assembly. The land "east of Zachiah Swamp," considting of 3,333 acres called "Boarman's Manor" and "Boarman's Rest," lay in the area now known as Bryantown. Boarman's prominence in the early history of the Colony and his vast holdings in Charles and St. Mary's counties warrant assigning his name to the village.

But the actual history of Bryantown began before even Boarman's acquisition of the land. Bryantown is situated near the head of Zekiah Swamp, which extends from a point about three miles north of the main road to Allen's Fresh, where the main stream becomes the headwaters of the Wicomico River. Prior to the arrival of the English colonists, the swamp was a favorite camping and hunting area for the Algonquin Indians. In fact, the swamp's name is derived from the Algonquin-Fox dialect in which "Sacaya" means "a dense thicket." Through the years there have been many spellings: "Zachiah", "Zachia", "Sakiah", and now "Zekiah". Today it is one of the largest natural frontiers in Southern Maryland. It abounds with wild game of every description, from the white-tailed deer to ducks and several varieties of fish. As important as the swamp has been to the people who have lived in the area, the village might well have borne the name of "Zekiah."

The town's name was not firmly established until January 1920, when the Federal government approved a post office for the community, and appointed Jesse C. Cooke the first postmaster. He was also the first proprietor of a combination hostelry, tavern, and store known as "Cooke's Tavern" and "Bryantown Hotel."

The golden age of Bryantown as a shopping and business center was between 1840 and 1910, but an even earlier "account of Clothing Purchased in Charles County by Daniel Jenifer" shows that on Feb. 2, 1778, "shoes and stockings left at _____ McPherson's and _____ Boarman's store at Bryantown were collected from Edward Boarman, Charles Montgomery, William Montgomery, David Rawlings, and William Roby of Richard." This item in the *Maryland Calendar of State Papers* is perhaps the earliest record of a store in Bryantown.

A topographical map of the swamp area surveyed by John Henry Alexander in 1835 shows Bryantown to have been a village of 17 buildings, including the tavern and a jail, from which a set of "irons" is still in existence. By the time of the 1860 to 1870 census, professional and business people residing in the four-mile area included six medical doctors, constable, hotelkeeper, three blacksmiths and three apprentices, wheelright, coachmaker, two bootmakers and shoemakers, three merchants and four clerks, five mechanics, six schoolteachers, two millers (water mills), magistrate, two lawyers, carpenter, Protestant Episcopal minister, and Roman Catholic priest.

Old letters reveal there was a dancing master as well as a music teacher, so the cultural development of the community was not neglected.

The first educational facility was "St. Mary's Female Seminary," a boarding school opened by the Misses Mary and Winifred Martin in 1859 on the Catholic Church parish grounds. Anna Surratt was a student there. Patronized by local families, it was highly successful until after the Civil War when patrons suffered financial reverses and the school was closed.

During the time of the "Female Seminary," most men in Bryantown received their education at Rock Hill College in Ellicott City or at the Maryland Agricultural College.

Later there were two frame public school buildings in Bryantown. One was on Rt. 232 and the other on Rt. 5. Many children were tutored at home.

Because of its location, Bryantown was a principal stop on the many routes that traversed Southern Maryland. It was the logical stopping-off place for travelers going from Port Tobacco to Benedict or on to St. Mary's City. There were many saloons and at least one or two general stores. Located on the main wagon train route as well as the stage route, it drew traffic from the Virginia Colony as well as from Maryland.

By 1890 Bryantown was the second most important community in Charles County, renowned for its stores and fine homes. Bryantown Hotel and Brick House Lot (1812) are two of the oldest structures still standing. Across from them, overlooking present Bryantown, is the impressive Victorian home, "The Cedars," built about 1870.

Many farm homes in the vicinity were constructed in the 1800s, replacing the 17th and 18th century homes originally built on the plantations that had been in the same families for many generations.

The decline of Bryantown's importance began in 1872, and again it was caused by the railroad. In that year the Pennsylvania Railroad built lines that bypassed Bryantown in favor of Waldorf and La Plata. We have already seen what effect that had on La Plata.

No longer a main stopover for travelers, Bryantown became a residential area. But as late as 1941 two stores stood as remnants of bygone days. John T. Mudd and William T. Bowling had vacated the old store on the corner of the Thomas Edgar Boarman property where they and several previous merchants had conducted business for many years. The other store stood at the base of what is now the Carrico property, last owned by Luke Oswald Downs. Mrs. William M. Boone has the last known picture of this store in existence, showing how the road through Bryantown approached it. The old hotel and these stores once bore the mercantile titles "McPherson's and Boarman's," "Bean's," "Bowling" (Charles Albert), and "Jameson" (Archibald). Sometime after World War II the stores were torn down because of deterioration. A blacksmith shop, a gristmill, a sawmill, and

Harry Moreland's first garage had disappeared from the scene even earlier.

Many "Bryantown Hundred" residents served faithfully for the Colonies during the American Revolution and others signed the Oath of Allegiance to demonstrate their adherence to the cause.

The Civil War created divided sympathies in Bryantown as in other parts of the country, but Southern Maryland was considered enemy territory by Union soldiers. Eleanora Bowling Kane, of Towson, a descendant of Bryantown residents of that period, tells how her Confederate grandfather, Aloysius Bowling, entrusted with secret papers, hid from the Union soldiers in the St. Mary's Church belfry by straddling the beams. From his lofty perch he viewed the Union men fruitlessly searching for him in the Church and on the grounds.

The grave of Dr. Samuel A. Mudd in the Bryantown cemetery is a quiet reminder of the role he was called upon to play in the treatment of John Wilkes Booth's broken leg after the assassination of President Lincoln.

Crossing the village north and south, Rt. 232 retains many of its century-old houses. Residential developments have sprung up, and with them, two large schools. T. C. Martin School is the public educational facility that replaced the old school in Hughesville; St. Mary's School and Convent is in the stead of the original schools and convent the Rev. Patrick E. Conroy established in 1916.

In 1939-40 when a new concrete road was constructed over the old winding one from Waldorf to St. Mary's County, it bypassed the former hotel (then the home of George I. Gardiner Sr.), "Brick House Lot" owned by Louis Steffens, the Eugene Summers home, and the Dr. Louis Carrico home by a few hundred yards. Bowling and Mudd built their new store on the north side of this Rt. 5. It housed the post office and, for a few years after World War II, an Allis-Chalmers tractor business.

The 1970s brought more change to the crossroads village. A dual highway was laid, necessitating another move for

Bowling and Mudd, to a larger building erected on the southbound lane at the point where it meets the old stagecoach road. The new structure houses Bryantown Store and Bryantown Post Office in separate sections. A large parking space for commuters enables easy access to both. Nearby is the Pat Bowling Auto and Marine Sales business.

Bryantown today is a residential village. Some of its farmland is being developed into residential "estates," featuring custom-built homes. Sitting quietly by the roadside, the town appears secure in its contribution to history, and content with its role for the future.

Indian Head

The town of Indian Head was incorporated in 1920. It is one of only two incorporated townships within Charles County. La Plata is the other. (Some old-timers point out that Port Tobacco was incorporated when first established, and that this status was never changed.)

There is some dispute over the origin of the name "Indian Head." One source cites a legend concerning the Algonquin Indian tribe that originally inhabited the area:

An Algonquin chief promised his beautiful daughter to the son of the chief of the nearby Piscataway tribe. Their marriage would unite the two great tribes in Southern Maryland. However, before the wedding could take place, the young maiden met an Indian hunter who had paddled across the Potomac from the Virginia Colony. It was love at first sight, and the young hunter stayed on to woo the Indian princess. The Algonquin chief ordered the stranger to leave. He did so, but not before he promised to come back for the maiden. On the night he was to return, their plan was discovered and the girl was imprisoned in her tent. When the young Indian landed under the cover of darkness, he was seized by Algonquin fighters and beheaded. His head was mounted on a spear and stuck in the sand as a warning to others who trespassed. On the following day the first white settlers came and discovered the head on the spear. Hence the name Indian Head.

A later story claims the town was named Indian Head because it resembles an Indian's head from the air. Since the name was in common use before the airplane was, this story's origin is certainly questionable.

A series of old charts show that Indian Head has had four names since its settlement in Colonial days. On 1776 charts it was called Indian Point; on a chart drawn in 1835, Indian Headlands; Indian Head Point in 1865; and finally Indian Head on area charts dated 1866. A 17th century map of the area catalogued in the National Archives uses the name Indian Point for the peninsula.

In time the English took over the region. In 1636 it was part of a grant the English King made to Gen. Charles Cornwallis. Later records show that it was deeded to George Washington by Cornwallis in 1661.

Because of its location the town grew slowly. Then in 1890 the U.S. Navy decided to move its proving ground from Annapolis to Indian Head. The town was chosen for its strategic location on navigable water between the Naval shipyards at Norfolk, Va., and the Washington Navy Yard on the Anacostia River.

Indian Head at this time was a desolate area. Abandoned fishing shacks from earlier days lined the shore, while farms were scattered throughout the tract. The area was largely marshland divided by a stream. The stream had to be diverted and the marshland drained before the land could support the heavy guns the Navy was planning to use on the proving grounds.

In September 1890 the Navy solicited the help of the area farmers to prepare the site for testing. The farmers were glad to have after-harvest work. They brought their oxen and tools and prepared to clear the land. Some rode 20 miles on horseback for the opportunity to work. They stayed all week in Indian Head, where the Navy provided bed and board in the abandoned fishing shacks; they returned home weekends. Barracks soon were built to handle the influx of workers who came by boat from Washington. But while the work force increased, the town did not.

When it became evident that the United States could no longer avoid involvement in World War I, Indian Head was allotted a healthy appropriation to expand facilities for the manufacture of smokeless powder. Employees flocked to the town. The Naval facility built its own "village" on the base. A school, post office, and 100 houses circled a village green.

Before the coming of the Federal government, boat transportation was an important business. Lumber, food, hardware, and domestic goods were shipped from Alexandria to Glymont wharf. At the wharf they were put on oxen carts or wagons and transported to villages throughout the county.

When the Naval Powder factory, now the Naval Ordnance Station, was established, the Navy provided boat service from Indian Head to the Washington Navy Yard.

That service no longer exists. The mud track that was the main road in Indian Head is a paved highway (Rt. 210) connecting Indian Head to the nation's capital by land.

St. Charles

The town of St. Charles is a unique addition to the County. It is a new town, a "planned town." It is developed around a concept furthered by city and social planners alike, an attempt to recognize people's needs in a community and to plan accordingly to fulfill those needs.

Studies have shown that people like the idea of a neighborhood that has schools within walking distance, open parkland space, community shopping, and recreational facilities. When completed, St. Charles will have 15 such neighborhood clusters, to make up a total of five villages within the town.

St. Charles is a "balanced town," a concept easier to plan than to achieve. To this end, St. Charles has progressed better than many other planned new towns; it is considered successful.

Housing will include low and medium density single-family homes and detached townhouses, as well as attached townhouses, garden apartments, mid- and high-rise apartments and condominiums.

Not only will it function as a residential and commercial community but the complex includes an industrial park. Light industry will be housed in low-slung office buildings set amid the pine and cedar trees that dot St. Charles' 8,000 acres.

Waldorf

The Baltimore and Potomac Railroad established a station at Waldorf in 1872. By 1880 it had a post office. Actually, Waldorf had appeared as a town on a post office map published even earlier. The completion of the Potomac River Bridge contributed to Waldorf's growth, as it had to La Plata's, and to much of the rest of Charles County.

Before slot machine gambling was outlawed in Maryland, night spots lined Rt. 301 north of Rt. 5. The popularity of the slot machines (one-armed bandits) attracted travelers to the restaurants and motels strung out from Waldorf to the Potomac River Bridge.

Nightly entertainment featuring prominent entertainers was offered by the nightclubs that modeled their decor and names after more famous Western gambling houses: the Las Vegas, Desert Inn, and Stardust, to name but a few. Only the Stardust still offers "big name" entertainers in the Rock and Country-and-Western traditions.

With the loss of gambling revenues, some restaurant owners tried to convert their establishments to family dining to keep afloat. Others changed their clubs to bowling alleys, neighborhood bars, stores, and, in one case, an office building.

Waldorf has successfully shifted from a fledgling farming community around a train station, to a tourist attraction of sorts, to a residential area, which supports the County's largest commercial shopping area. A special division of the County's Planning and Zoning Department has been developing a Comprehensive Plan for the Waldorf area in an attempt to modernize the central part of the County.

Other County Towns

ALLEN'S FRESH. This was first called "Allen's Mill." It was one of the original post (mail) towns in the County, so designated as early as 1695. Eight times a year mail would pass through this town, carried by stagecoach. It was one of the Southern Maryland towns in a mail link designed to connect Philadelphia with Williamsburg, Va.

GLYMONT. In 1868 a daily stage carried mail from Glymont to Port Tobacco. A mail steamer would bring mail from Washington, D.C., to Glymont, and it would then be taken by stage to Port Tobacco. It was to the Glymont Hotel that President Ulysses S. Grant is said to have come to fight his battles with alcoholism. The hotel had a mirrored ballroom encircled by a spectator's balcony. In September 1876 a storm washed away a portion of the steamboat wharf.

MARSHALL HALL. William Marshall arrived in the County in 1641, and 10 years later he took up a tract he named "Marshall." This is believed to have been the core of what later became Marshall Hall.

In 1769 George Washington foreclosed a mortgage he had on Capt. John Posey's farm, south of Mt. Vernon. As a result Washington acquired ferryboats and the ferry rights from Posey's landing to the landing at Marshall Hall. Travelers wishing to cross to the Virginia side of the Potomac would depart from the Marshall landing, to which they came by stagecoach out of Port Tobacco over Bumpy Oak Road. Today the only wharves along the whole river frontage that can accommodate boats of any size are those at Marshall Hall, Indian Head, and Rock Point.

HILL TOP. This town first appeared in *A Geographical Description of the States of Maryland and Delaware*, published 1807 at Philadelphia. It was first noted on maps in *Gavy's General Atlas*, 1833.

PLEASANT HILL. In the 1800s this town appeared on Charles County maps. It seems to have been a town of considerable size, possibly located at the edge of the Mattawoman Swamp, where it was crossed by those leaving the County headed north. Pleasant Hill was on the main road between Port Tobacco and Piscataway.

A list of Maryland towns, published in 1871 in the *State Gazette and Merchants' and Farmers' Directory for Maryland and the District of Columbia*, included these 19 from Charles County, with these thumbnail descriptions:

Allen's Fresh——a post village on the Sekiah Swamp Creek, a tributary of the Wicomico River.

Beanstown——a post office in the Northern part of the county.

Bryantown——a small post town, 15 miles from Benedict, containing a Catholic Church, few stores, steam mill, etc.

Bumpy Oak——consisted of Sasser and Warring, General store.

Centreville——consisted of two general stores, two liquor stores and one drug store.

Cross Roads——A post office in the central part of the county.

Doncaster——a post town in the western part of the county.

Duffield (or Middletown, later White Plains)——a post town in the northern part of the county.

Gallant Green——a post village in the western part of the county.

Harris Lot——consisted of two general stores, three physicians, one teacher, dentist and minister.

Hill Top——A small village a few miles from Taylors Landing, on Nanjemoy Creek.

Hughesville——A post town situated in the eastern part of the county near the St. Mary's County line.

Nanjemoy——a post town at the head of Nanjemoy Creek.

Newburg——a small post office in the southern part of the county.

Newport——a post town near Wicomico River, about six miles from its mouth.

Patuxent City——a village situated near Sampson Creek in the eastern part of the county.

Pisgah——a small post office.

Pomonkey——a post town in the northern part of the county.

Port Tobacco——The county seat of Charles County situated at the head of the Port Tobacco River, about four miles from its mouth and 32 miles from Washington, D.C. Considerable trade is carried on between Port Tobacco and Baltimore.

The reason the authors chose to include these particular towns in their directory is explained on the volume's front cover; it is described as

> Giving Places and Style of Business firms and persons engaged in commercial and professional pursuits, together with the names of all the principal Farmers, Agriculturists, and Horticulturists in the State of Maryland . . . . All Cities, Towns and Villages on the various Railroad and Steamboat Lines, geographically located. . .

How little railroad and steamboat lines mean for "commercial and professional pursuits" in Charles County today!

CHAPTER 4

RELIGION: DIVERSE AND FREE

The principle of religious freedom was basic to the thinking of the founders of Maryland. In fact, it was to establish a colony where people of different religions might be free of persecution that George Calvert, First Baron Baltimore, sought a charter from King Charles I of England in 1632.

Other Englishmen already had dared to take up new lives in the untamed New World in their quest for religious freedom, notably at Jamestown and Massachusetts Bay. But it had become clear that to most of those first settlers, religious freedom meant freedom for Protestants, narrowly defined.

Calvert, who drew up the charter but died before it could be granted, was a Roman Catholic; and he had something else in mind. The charter for the territory, which Calvert named in honor of the Queen Consort, Henrietta Maria, was granted to his son. Cecilius Calvert, Second Baron Baltimore, organized the expedition that Leonard Calvert, his brother, landed at St. Mary's in 1634.

Lord Baltimore instructed his brother, whom he designated Governor of Maryland, that in his voyage, he

> be very careful to preserve unity and peace amongst all the passengers on Shipboard, and that (he) suffer no scandal nor offence to be given to any of the Protestants, . . . and that (he) cause all Acts of Roman Catholic Religion to be done as privately as may be, and that (he) instruct all the Roman Catholics to be silent upon all occasions of discourse

concerning matters of Religion; and that the said Governor and Commissioners treat the Protestants with as much mildness and favor as Justice will permit. And this to be observed at Land as well as at Sea.

He also required Leonard to take an oath that he would not,

directly or indirectly trouble, molest or discountenance any person professing to believe in Jesus Christ for or in respect to religion. I will make no difference of persons in conferring offices, favors or rewards for or in respect of religion, but merely as they shall be found faithful and well deserving and endued with moral virtues and abilities; my aim shall be public unity and if any person or officer shall molest any person professing to believe in Jesus Christ, on account of his religion, I will protect the person and punish the offender.

Lord Baltimore's instructions pertained only to Catholics and Protestants because only Christians are known to have accompanied the first voyage. However, when Jews later came to Maryland they too were accorded religious freedom.

While Maryland was never entirely free of the religious persecutions and prohibitions that have marked history, it was usually considered freer than most other colonies and states. The First Amendment provision in the Bill of Rights, that "Congress shall make no laws respecting the establishment of religion or prohibiting the free exercise thereof," was largely the work of native Marylander Charles Carroll of Carrollton.

Episcopal Churches

But even before the Calverts arrived, it seems, religious services had been conducted in Maryland. Services were Episcopal, held on Kent Island at a plantation and trading post set up there in 1629 by Captain William Claiborne under the authority of the Virginia Company.

Captain Claiborne brought the Rev. Richard James, a priest of the Church of England (the established Episcopal church of England, also called Anglican) from Hampton, Va., for the service in 1631, three years before the Calverts were to land at Yacomico with a band of about 200 settlers seeking religious freedom. The majority of those settlers were members of the Church of England, but the leaders of the expedition and the two priests who accompanied them were Roman Catholics.

Protestant clergymen specifically were prevented by the Charter from being aboard because the leaders were sure that their presence would encourage arguments about religion aboard ship, and that would be, in their eyes, unwholesome.

But the Church of England—priests or no priests—brought over the majority of first settlers. They had their Prayer Books and their traditions.

An Indian style shelter was first used by these settlers for religious worship, but by 1638 a brick structure had been erected at St. Mary's City, and it was used alternately by the Roman Catholics and the Protestant Catholics (another name for Church of England members).

That was the beginning of Trinity Church, St. Mary's Parish, in St. Mary's County.

It is important to note that both denominations worshipped in an organized way as soon as they arrived, and have been doing so every since. In large measure Roman Catholic history is intertwined with Episcopalian.

From the beginning Lord Baltimore, Royal Proprietor of the Colony of Maryland, intended that the colonists should enjoy religious freedom. The Charter gave the Church of England inhabitants of the province the same rights as they would have enjoyed had they stayed in England, where the Church was a part of the ruling government. As such, it held a preferential position over other religious traditions.

The Assembly of 1638 declared that the "Holy Church" should "have and enjoy all her rights, liberties, and franchises, wholly and without blemish." Since the Church of England was the only Church established by law in any possession of England, it might be inferred that despite the policy of toleration promoted by the Proprietor, this legislation favored Church of England establishment here.

Differences and frictions developed almost predictably, so that in 1649 an Act of Toleration was passed, to make it clear that in Maryland Colony, at least, persons were free to worship as they wished, and that all denominations were to be equally respected.

Meanwhile, a Puritan Revolution in England was to have an effect on the Colony. Those who were against both the Roman Catholics *and* the Church of England were made bold in their protest against both the civil and religious restrictions here, simply because the Puritan Revolt in England was meeting with success.

In January, 1649, the same year of the Maryland Act of Toleration, the army of Oliver Cromwell in England cut off the head of King Charles I. The Monarchy was ended; Parliament governed. The Book of Common Prayer was outlawed, as were bishops and priests. There followed a period of growth in the diversity of denominations and in the persecution of Roman Catholics, here as well as in England.

But when Oliver Cromwell died in 1658 the power of the Puritan movement died with him. By 1660 the Monarchy was restored under Charles II, and the Church of England began at that time to be re-established both in England and in the Maryland Assembly.

Then in 1689 Maryland had its own mini-revolution. It was a revolt by Church of England people, and others, against the Roman Catholic Proprietor; it found much of its steam in England where the Protestants overthrew the Roman Catholic King James II. But political goals differed. The Anti-Proprietary party in Maryland put down the Proprietor, but they then proceeded to place the Government in the hands of the Crown!

In June 1691 King William III established royal government here and sent a Royal Governor, Sir Lionel Copley, in the following year. His intention was to establish the Church of England as the official Church of Maryland. To do this, he had the Assembly pass the Act of 1692, which divided the 10 counties making up the Maryland Colony into 30 parishes.

At that time Charles County included most of Prince George's County, the District of Columbia, Montgomery County, and beyond.

These parishes were laid out (alphabetically, here):

DURHAM PARISH in western Charles County (also called Nanjemoy Parish in Colonial times); Old Durham Church in Ironsides.

KING GEORGE'S PARISH in the several counties north of Mattawoman Creek (also called Piscataway Parish in Colonial times); St. John's Broad Creek in Oxon Hill.

PORT TOBACCO PARISH in central Charles County; Christ Church, moved from the town square in Port Tobacco near the reconstructed courthouse to La Plata in 1904.

ST. PAUL'S PARISH along the Patuxent River; St. Paul's Church in what is now Baden, Prince George's County.

WILLIAM AND MARY PARISH in southern Charles County (also called Picawaxon Parish in Colonial days); Christ Church, Wayside.

Under the legislation of 1692 the Parish basis for organization of the Church was established. Although it has been modified to accommodate a larger population, it is still the basis for the Episcopal Church.

Each Parish had a Vestry (like a Board of Directors) chosen by the freeholders, or landowners, to hold and dispose of Church property and accept bequests.

The Governor, for the Proprietor of the Colony, appointed the Rector of each Parish from a list on nominees supplied by the Bishop of London. The Vestry was obliged to accept the Governor's candidate, although the wishes of the parishioners occasionally were considered.

The Clergy was supported by an annual tax of 40 pounds on every taxable person—not just churchgoers. This was one practice of a Church established by the Government. Glebe-lands (property for Church use) usually were given by prominent landowners. Consequently many of the oldest

Episcopal Churches are found in sparsely settled areas rather than in towns or villages.

The Bishop of London was the theoretical and legal overseer of the Churches here, but Lord Baltimore selected the clergymen from England, and established them in their livings here. The Bishop licensed them, but the Governor inducted them—and the Governor was the visible head of the Church here, as a representative of the King, who headed the established Church in England.

But the Church also had a duty to the people.

Accurate records of births, marriages, and funerals were to be kept by each Parish, or a fine would be levied. For this reason Church records are accepted even today as proof for birthdates for persons born before the State began keeping vital statistics.

Members of the Vestries also were obliged to be officials of the Government in such roles as inspectors for weights and measures, tobacco inspectors, customs inspectors, and the like. In a sense, they were to be guardians of the morals of people living in the Parish.

Being so much a part of the Government proved a mixed blessing for the Church during the Revolutionary War. On the one hand, the Parishes were used as the basic unit for the collection of subscriptions to raise 800 pounds for the initial military preparations in the State—in the same way that money had been collected for the raising of Churches. On the other hand, in their worship churchgoers read in the Book of Common Prayer words that expressed reverence for the King of England—a traitorous act once the War began!

The outbreak of the War and the Declaration of Independence compelled the Church to reconstitute itself. The Declaration of Rights of the Maryland Convention of 1776 set the direction. No County court could any longer levy a tax on the people for the support of any Vestry or Church. The Church of England in Maryland would have to find its own money from its own people.

The Legislature might impose a general tax to support the Christian religion, but each person could indicate for what denomination his quota would be spent.

The authorities also prescribed a new form of prayer for the Government; and any clergyman who wouldn't use it, or who refused to take an oath of allegiance to Maryland, left his job. Some left the Colony.

In August 1783 the clergy of Maryland convened in Annapolis to agree on new guidelines for organization, to adapt the worship service to the new conditions. They adopted a new name for the Church of England in America: The Protestant Episcopal Church.

By 1787 three Americans had been consecrated Bishop across the seas, and they became overseers of groups of parishes, called dioceses. These were the dioceses of Connecticut, New York, and Pennsylvania. The Diocese of Virginia was gathered in 1790 under a Bishop.

The first Bishop in the Diocese of Maryland was the Right Reverend Thomas John Claggett, elected in 1792, 100 years after Establishment. For several years prior to the War he had been Rector of St. Paul's Parish, in what is now Baden, Prince George's County.

By this time, growth in the newly independent State of Maryland was rapid. By 1775 there were 14 counties in response to population growth, and 46 Parishes—25 in the West and 21 on the Eastern Shore.

There was a slump in the growth of the Church during the War of 1812, but by 1814 the work of the Bishop of Maryland was so taxing that a Suffragan (Assistant) Bishop was elected to oversee the parishes on the Eastern Shore, which later became the Diocese of Easton.

Around the capitol city, however, growth was constant, despite the ravages of the Civil War, and in 1895 Montgomery, Prince George's, St. Mary's, and Charles counties and the District of Columbia all were carved from the Diocese of Maryland and made into the Diocese of Washington. That structure remains today: There are 76 parishes, 9 separate congregations, 6 missions, several chaplaincies, and the National Cathedral in the Diocese of Washington now.

In Charles County where once there were only four parishes, there are now six, and two chapels. On any Sunday as many as 850 persons may be in attendance at the seven Episcopal Churches in Charles County, which held approximately 837 worship services in 1975.

Christ Church, La Plata (Port Tobacco Parish, 1692)
From its vantage point in the center of the town of La Plata, Christ Church Episcopal tranquilly surveys the busy main street of the County Seat. Secure in the knowledge of the important part it has played in the lives of Charles County men and women in their times of peace and war, it lends a bit of Old World aura to the busy 20th century town.

The series of buildings bearing the name of Christ Church began before the Establishment Act of 1692, and have seen their parishioners go to war in the American Revolution, the War of 1812, the Civil War, and the modern World Wars. They have seen them live in peace in their beautiful Colonial homes surrounded by rolling tobacco fields and pleasant river frontages. They were here when the County slowly changed from bucolic countryside to bustling commercialism. Christ Church today offers living witness that she has great "tenacity to follow her people generation after generation through change after change—in times of despair as well as moments of success and stability." The church accepts the challenge to continue this influence on her members' lives and intends to fulfill her destiny to guide each new generation in solving the problems of its time.

Port Tobacco Parish already had a church before the Act of 1692. The Archives of 1683 refer to "the church land on the East side of Portobacco Creek, near the mouth of the creek," and again in 1684 "at the head of the Portobacco Creek near the church there." It seems that the first church was on the west of the creek near the present Rt. 6 bridge; until the 1920s there were vestiges of a graveyard in that vicinity.

The rector of the earliest Christ Church was a Reverend Mr. Moore, who died the same year as the Establishment Act. In 1694 the Reverend George Tubman, a lay reader, conducted services and remained as Pastor of the Church until 1701.

Since tobacco was the money crop of the fledgling colony, taxes were paid in pounds of tobacco, each taxpayer responsible for a levy of 40 pounds to support the church. In 1696 Port Tobacco and William and Mary parishes had 250 Tithables and an income of 10,320 pounds of tobacco. A record of this taxation appears on a Maryland Historical Marker on the grounds of Christ Church in La Plata.

In 1709 a new Episcopal Church apparently was built. Town records, dated Nov. 8 of that year, include a petition from the Vestry of Port Tobacco Parish referring to the amount of money and tobacco already expended on the church building and requesting an additional levy of tobacco to be imposed on the parishioners. The Assembly Act of 1729 concerning "Laying out of Land and Erecting a Town at the Head of Port Tobacco Creek" authorized the Commissioners to "purchase 60 acres of land—to adjoin to and encompass the lands belonging to Port Tobacco Church, and the said Courthouse."

There appears to be no record of another church until 1808, when a wind storm destroyed this 1709 structure. Because, according to assembly proceedings of that year, "the church in Port Tobacco Parish was blown down by a violent gust of wind and is totally incapable of repair," a lottery apparently was authorized to raise $3,000 for building a new church. In 1811 the lottery was raised to $6,000 and in 1816 increased to $20,000. The $20,000 allotment was "for the purpose of paying expenses already incurred in building the church in Port Tobacco Parish, and such further expenses as may be necessary to furnish said Church in a manner suitable for a place of public worship."

Construction was begun about 1815 on a site on the public square of Port Tobacco. A petition locating the site of the church appeared in the Port Tobacco Records of 1810. It was submitted to the Assembly for the authority "to erect a Protestant Episcopal Church on the Public Square in Charlestown." The Levy Court of Charles County was authorized also in 1810 to dispose of any part of the public square in Charlestown upon such terms and conditions as seemed necessary. That this site was close to the other would be established by the Act of the Assembly of 1824, confirming the title to the Vestry of Port Tobacco Parish to a lot containing "two acres, three rods and thirty perches, located between 'Widow's Pleasure' and 'Pleasant Fields' upon which the new church in the upper part of Port Tobacco Parish is erected" and whereas "a church hath stood on said lot of land for nearly a century past."

The Christ Church of this period was of brick and was consecrated as "Christ Church" on its completion. It stood on this site surveying the activities in the Square for the better part of the century. It was there when Capt. William Williams offered Thomas Jones $100,000 for information leading to the capture of John Wilkes Booth.

In 1884, the early 19th century building being in disrepair, it was torn down and a new church of stone built to take its place. When the new Courthouse was built in La Plata, it was decided to move the new Church to the County Seat. It was dismantled stone by stone. The stones were numbered and loaded on oxcarts, and the plodding three-mile journey to La Plata began. The church was reconstructed in the same position relative to the Courthouse that it had occupied in Port Tobacco. Construction was completed in 1904 but a disastrous fire occurred in 1906. The interior was destroyed, then replaced so services could be held in the church to celebrate Easter.

The land upon which the reconstructed church was erected was bought from Mary A. and Adrian Posey for $321.08. The land on which Christ Church now stands was a part of the property of F. Brooke Matthews, known as the "Hermitage."

The present Christ Church building was constructed in the Gothic style reminiscent of the Middle Ages in Europe. With its foundation laid in the traditional shape of the Latin cross, its high vaulted roof and pointed arches windows and doors, it is typical of this period and its ideas of an exalted Christian faith. The medieval builders had developed a method of vaulting the roof to a point in the nave of the church that was one of the great architectural achievements. The eyes are directed upward—most appropriate for an upward-looking faith. A feeling of spaciousness and peace is encountered in Christ Church.

In the 1906 reconstruction, after the fire, the interior of the building was replaced and a Gothic bell tower on the Gospel side of the church was added. Towering to a height of 60 feet, it surveys the town with its castle-like pinnacles decorated with carved stone relief in the form of the Gothic cross enclosing a quatrefoil. Each day its electronically operated carillon sounds the hours of noon and 5 p.m. Externally the church retains its sandstone construction of 1884: the source of the stones is believed to have been the quarry at Port Deposit.

Precautions are now taken to protect and preserve the sandstone from air pollutants, which cause decomposition of the surface. Gothic in its arched windows and door frames on the lower levels and its magnificent rose window over the entrance, the church beckons from its room of another age, its "dog-house dormers" reminiscent of the Victorian period.

Added to the church in 1938 was a Parish House, which blends with the existing stone of the main edifice. In its nearly four decades of existence, it has served as a base for community activities and the Church Sunday School. The coffers of the church have been replenished through use of the Parish House by such public facilities as the Board of Education, the Federal Government, and the County Government, which utilized it as a Court Room during the Courthouse renovation.

The interior of Christ Church is one of quiet beauty; perhaps its most outstanding feature is a collection of stained glass windows, which create an atmosphere of mysticism. The windows reflect both the modern and the medieval approach to the use of stained glass, and embody the belief that one should glorify both God and man with the beauty of this creative art. Names from Colonial times—Stone, Jenifer,

Hamilton, Barnes, Stewart, Robertson, Cox, Hawkins, Wilmer—appear on Church memorials.

A feeling of spaciousness in the nave, the sturdiness of oak vaulting and trim, and the purity of white plaster combine to give a feeling of security. The pews, altar stalls and appointments reflect the Gothic style of design with their pointed arches and quatrefoil reliefs. Backed by intricate oak paneling set in designs of diamonds and crosses is the altar, a mass of gleaming white marble, marked with the Greek letters of Alpha and Omega. It stands in silent memorial to the Reverend Lemuel Wilmer, rector from 1822-69, an ardent Unionist in a parish that thrived on slavery. Due to his belief that slavery was wrong, he prayed for President Lincoln even when the congregation rose to its feet in defiance.

Casting its muted light on this expanse of white is a Renaissance portrayal in stained glass of the Ascension of Christ. In the upper extremities of the sanctuary and the nave are 10 representations in stained glass of the flowers of the Bible and the Holy Land, installed in 1973 to the memory of Philip Smith.

Christ Church has been both the Mother and Parish Church of Port Tobacco Parish since its inception in 1692. Beginning in May 1754, in addition to serving as Rector of Christ Church, the minister and Vestry were empowered to buy and build a Chapel of Ease "at a place called Ivy Spring on a branch called Dressing Branch near Pines." This Chapel of Ease became known as Piney and the responsibility of this Chapel, called St. Paul's, remained with Christ Church's pastor and Vestry until 1967, when it became a self-supporting entity with its own clergyman and congregation.

Other Chapels of Ease were established, but Piney alone continues to the present day. St. Philip's, a plain frame building, housed a black congregation at Salem from 1891 until the early 1900s but difficulty in finding a minister caused the mission to be discontinued. St. James Chapel, also a plain frame building, was established as a parochial mission at Newtown in 1831 and consecrated April 19 of that year by Bishop Stone. It no longer exists, having been discontinued after a little more than 50 years. Provisions always have been made for all blacks who desired to worship at the Parish Church at La Plata and to be members of the Church School. Integration began early at Christ Church.

Christ Church today continues to grow with a progressive Vestry of nine men and women and two junior Vestry members. The Colonial Vestry formerly had only six members. A Senior and Junior Warden aid the Rector. Two lay readers and numerous acolytes of both sexes serve in the liturgy of the church. Its communicants have increased in number to nearly 350, and with this growth has come problems that challenge but do not defeat. To minister to an almost self-contained County Seat, a rural farming and commuter population, members of the fast growing "bedroom" communities of the nation's Capitol, and youth searching for security presents a most difficult and complex challenge. Christ Church accepts this difficult task, as always she has served her people in times of need.

Leading her in this Bicentennial Year is the Reverend Samuel Gouldthorpe Jr., whose ministry serves all, regardless of age, race, or color. His secret seems to be involvement in his church, his community, and the world—involvement with his parishioners of all ages, and accepting their contributions to the growth of his church.

Old Durham Church, Ironsides (Durham Parish, 1692)

In 1692 carriages creaked to rest before a log church at this site, where now stands the warmly mellowed brick of Old Durham Church. Folk came afoot or by horseback over primitive roads to worship here. Early records "resolved that from April to November services be held at eleven on Sundays by the sundial in the churchyard, and on cloudy days a majority of watches that agree shall determine the time." The old sundial beside the walk still marks the hour.

The site for the original log church was purchased from Joseph Harrison in 1692 for 200 pounds of tobacco. Colonial deeds speak of William Dent as "laying off the bounds of the parish," one of the original four into which Charles County was divided in 1692.

The marriage of William Dent and Elizabeth Fowke is the first of record in Durham Parish. It was solemnized in June 1684 by the Rev. John Turling. The Church's Communion silver, still in use, bears the engraving, "William Dent, Esqr., 1707." Two sons of this marriage are buried in the churchyard, the dates 1690 and 1695 still faintly legible on the stones.

Elected to the first Vestry, in 1694, were John Stone, Joseph Manning, Joseph Bullitt, Capt. William Dent, William Stone, and Richard Harrison.

An early pastor of the Church (1711-1742) was the Rev. William Macconchie, who owned an estate near the present town of McConchie, part of the first grant of land in the parish made by Lord Baltimore to Gov. William Stone. In 1732 Parson McConchie guided the building of a one-story brick structure to replace the original log church. The ancient bricks were said to have been brought over from England, and form the lower part of the present building. Parishioners were assessed 32,000 pounds of tobacco to begin the work, and two years later, 16,000 pounds of tobacco to complete it. Ox teams pulled hogsheads of tobacco down "rolling roads" to Nanjemoy Creek, Port Tobacco, and Potomac River shores. The great casks were then hauled onto barges and loaded aboard sailing vessels, to be sold in distant ports.

In 1779, the Rev. Walter Hanson Harrison came to the Parish, at a salary of 20,000 pounds of tobacco and the glebe on the Pisgah road, which rented for two hogsheads of tobacco a year. Parson Harrison rented out the glebe and lived at his own estate, Holly Springs, near Grayton.

Parson Harrison saw the church through anxious years following the separation of Church and State in 1776 and withdrawal of State aid to the churches. It was in 1791-93 that the sidewalls were raised and clerestory windows added, paid for by 192 pounds cash and 33,000 pounds of tobacco. At a meeting in 1788 a new Vestryman, General William Smallwood, was elected. Gen. Smallwood built a special road to Durham Church from his nearby plantation home.

Bishop Thomas John Clagett of Maryland visited the Church Sept. 24, 1809, observing,

> This is a brick Church and in good condition. The Parish has an attentive Vestry, and a faithful and laborious Rector. The congregation was large and remarkable attentive to its several duties. I consecrated the Church, preached the sermon, and confirmed eighty persons.

The Rev. Robert Prout (1824-1840 and 1846-1880) built soundly for the future. By 1843 a distressing need for repairs "pitied all to see it so." A tidy sum was raised, and when the Vestry despaired of reaching its goal, "the ladies of the Parish stepped forward with their characteristic energy and zeal" and raised $200 to complete the work. The interior was reconstructed, galleries being removed from the South and East walls. The Altar was placed at the East, and the present brick Vestry room constructed.

The first organ was installed in the gallery in 1868. Hymnals and prayer books were scarce, so a salaried officer of the Church known as the clerk "raised the tunes" and led the responses.

The Ladies' Mite Society was formally organized and met on June 6, 1876, at the church. Avowed purposes were to sew for the poor and help the needy. Under the same name and bylaws it continues today an energetic force in the life of the parish. Members and friends have embroidered needlepoint tapestries that cover the kneelers. The annual Festival on the second Saturday in August is a day of homecoming for friends of Old Durham, who travel for miles to enjoy the traditional dinner of ham, crab cakes, and fried chicken, and to greet old friends.

Fronting the churchyard is a brick wall erected in 1932 by the Colonial Dames of Maryland. It commemorates the 200th anniversary of George Washington's birth and the Church's rebuilding in brick. Washington wrote in his diary of a visit to Old Durham on March 17, 1771. The 200-year-old handmade bricks were taken from the old Neil Hotel in Port

Tobacco, and laid in what is known as Flemish bond, like the brickwork of the Church.

The bell tower, erected in 1942 largely by token labor, is a memorial to Gen. Smallwood. The bell was a gift, which originated from a ruined church in St. Mary's County. The tower contains 12,000 old handmade bricks taken from a mansion along the river belonging to Gen. Smallwood's sister, who is buried in the churchyard. The wood in the super-structure is redheart cedar from the old William Dent property along Nanjemoy Creek.

The late Rev. Reginald B. Stevenson worked devotedly during his pastorate, from 1925-1953, on the restoration and preservation of Old Durham Church. Since then a large Parish Hall and nine room Rectory have been built, which bear witness to a continuing vigor.

The Rector since 1971 has been the Rev. Arnold G. Taylor, who is much loved by his congregation and admired by others of the community for his involvement in its many activities.

Christ Church, Wayside (William and Mary Parish, 1692)

By the time William and Mary Parish was formed as one of the 30 established by the Act of 1692, a church already existed. It originally served Picawaxon Parish, the boundaries of which are defined in old land records of Charles County. Early reports show that the Reverend Mr. Moore was rector in 1692. The 1696 religious census assigned William and Mary and Port Tobacco parishes a combined total of 250 "Tithables" and an income of 10,320 pounds of tobacco. The incumbent minister for both parishes was the Rev. George Tubman.

We have little information from this period until 1750. In that year, the Maryland Assembly voted funds to enlarge and repair the church under the direction of its rector, the Rev. Samuel Clagett. His son, Thomas John Clagett, became the first bishop of Maryland 40 years later. A wood carving of the consecration of Bishop Clagett adorns the Bishop's Stall in the Washington Cathedral in the District of Columbia.

One of the most prized possessions of the church was acquired at about this time: the silver Queen Anne chalice and paten, from England. The chalice is now used only twice a year, at Easter and Christmas services; the Hall Marks on the silver reveal it was used from 1697 to 1720.

The baptismal font is also of particular interest. It was the mortar used by Dr. Parnham during the 1700s in the preparation of his medicines. The mortar was a gift from Mrs. Eleanor Edelen, a descendant of Dr. Parnham, and a communicant of the church, whose name appears in the 1836 records.

Records are again sketchy for later years. Some records were burned and others lost during the War between the States. However, in the Vestry minutes of 1864 it was voted to suspend services "because of destruction of windows and other acts of violence" until repairs could be made. The church had been used to quarter Union soldiers and also as a stable for their mounts. Not until Aug. 2, 1869, was a contract signed to repair the church. This was done by a Mr. Horn, under the direction of the rector, John Todd. Church services were held during this period at "Mt. Republic," the estate that lies about a mile from the church, on Rt. 3.

The sale of pews was a common practice, and in 1870 it was noted that the best pews of Christ Church would be sold to the highest bidder for a period of one year. Records indicate that a sum under five dollars not be considered in 1872.

Rector Todd must have come close to setting a record for time and devotion to a single flock. His pastorate began in 1843 and ended after 50 years in continuous service to Christ Church. The vases on the altar are a memorial to him.

The church contains many other memorials. Among them is a bronze wall plaque in memory of the family of the Rev. Neale Hammill Shaw, an early 19th century rector, whose family home was "Black Friars," an estate near Mt. Victoria. The stained glass windows, lectern, brasses, cross, and prayer desk were all given as memorials by members of the parish. The wrought iron gates, wall, and brick walks, which conform to the architecture of the period, are a more recently presented memorial. The stones in the church yard follow the pattern of antiquity characteristic of Christ Church parish; they date from the early 1800s. The Record Book containing the Vestry Minutes has been in continuous use since 1864.

Trinity Church, Newport; Oldfields Chapel, Hughesville (Trinity Parish, 1744)

When it was created in 1744 Trinity Parish consisted of those portions of King and Queen Parish (Chaptico) and All Faith Parish (Charlotte Hall) that lay in Charles County. The Vestry was organized in 1750, and on July 16, 1751, the first full-time clergyman, the Rev. Issac Cambell, presented his letter of induction from Governor Ogle. After taking the prescribed oaths, he read publicly the 39 Articles of the Church of England and "thereunto declared his unfeigned assent and convictions." That same year the parish purchased a communion plate and a surplice for 3,600 pounds of tobacco, as well as a large gilt and Turkey leather folio Prayer Book, and a large marble basin (font).

The original Newport Church on Gilbert Swamp was sold to Trinity Parish by the Chaptico Parish after Chaptico built a new church. At a general meeting of the parishioners on Oct. 14, 1751, it was decided to tear it down and sell the bricks so that a new church could be built on two acres of land purchased from Justinian Burch Jr. A year later the contract for the new church was let to John Arias of Westmoreland County, Va., for 54,250 pounds of tobacco and $200 Virginia currency. This church, along with a Vestry House, was completed in 1756. In 1856 the Vestry House was used as a schoolhouse, and William Wirt, the U.S. Attorney General who prosecuted Aaron Burr, attended school here.

On Nov. 25, 1765, the Vestry petitioned the Lower House of the Maryland Assembly to levy 50,000 pounds of tobacco upon the taxable inhabitants of Trinity Parish for the purpose of building a Chapel of Ease in Benedict Hundred. This Chapel was completed and accepted by the Vestry on May 6, 1769. It is still used today as the regular house of worship for those members of the congregation who live in the Hughesville-Bryantown-Benedict area. The bricks that were used to build the Chapel functioned as a ballast in the ships that came from England to buy tobacco for the English gentry. In 1788 an agreement was reached with Zachariah Johnson, to purchase for 45 shillings the land on which the Chapel stands.

On Aug. 14, 1789, the Vestry and parishioners voted for a lottery to raise $1,000 to build a new Parish Church at Newport. The Rev. Hatch Dent by this time was the second Rector of the Parish. On April 27, 1797, at a special meeting of the Vestry of Trinity Parish and the Vestry of All Faith Parish it was decided that the Rev. Henry L. Davis, Rector of All Faith Parish, would officiate on alternate Sundays in each parish. After a Rectorship of more than 13 years, Hatch Dent died on Dec. 30, 1799. His was the second longest rectorship in the history of the parish; the longest was held by his predecessor, the Rev. Isaac Cambell, who served for 33 years.

During the War of 1812 one of the largest enemy forces ever to attack our country came ashore at Benedict. These British forces, which planned to march on Washington and burn the city, camped on the grounds of Oldfields Chapel. Two soldiers died and were buried in the cemetery that surrounds the church.

In September 1817 the committee appointed to purchase a suitable glebe reported that they had obtained the farm of the late Hatch Dent for $2,300. The committee borrowed the money upon their personal security and thus held the property in their names until June 23, 1827, when the congregation paid off the loan. The land was then deeded to the Vestry of Trinity Parish, to hold in "trust for the use, benefit and support of the Rector and for no other use, intent or purpose whatsoever except for the repair and unprovement of the glebe property." This land, the old "Good Will" grant of 1668, and the adjacent land called "Wittam Enlarged," had been the property of William Posten, whose daughter married Rector Hatch Dent. In 1808 a strip of land called the "Tryfle" was added to the property, and it was in this form that Trinity Parish purchased it.

During the 1800s the Parish had substantial growth in its membership. The interior of both churches was changed from Colonial to Gothic. The pulpit was moved from the side wall and placed near the altar and the pews turned to face the altar. The pews previously had faced in the monastic tradition. This was a difficult time to keep a priest. There were no less than 20 clergymen in the parish from 1800 to 1905. One of them, the Rev. Meyer Levin, was a Polish Jew, and the history of the parish states, "His real name was Levininisky and when he became a Christian, the Jews are said to have had a funeral for him."

The Rev. John London became Rector in August 1894 and served until May 1903. During his rectorship Parish Houses were built at both churches and many records that had been lost for 25 years were discovered in the attic of a house near Patuxent City where they had been placed by a former Register, Rufus Robey.

The early years of the 1900s saw a split develop between the parish members and the Rector, the Rev. James W. Smith. The controversy centered around the Parish Hall at Trinity Church, being used as a "dance hall." The Rector closed the hall and asked the leaders of the church to support him. According to the parish history, there was a

> Horrible row. The un-godly raised—rector asks for the excommunication of the un-Godly. A movement began to have the Rector resign. His stipend was held up from March 1, 1913, yet in that year he had the largest confirmation class in the history of the parish—forty. He resigned—to take effect October 1, 1913.

The Rev. E. Lee Birchby began his Rectorship Nov. 1, 1915. During this time the "Old Glebe" was sold and the money from the sale used to purchase the Walter Jameson property in Hughesville as a Rectory. In May 1916 the Vestry paid Jameson $2,500 for a house and five acres of land.

During the 1920s and 1930s extensive remodeling was undertaken at Trinity Church. A Chancel and Sanctuary, Sacristy, and choir room were added to the church. It was consecrated by the Right Rev. Alfred Harding, Bishop of Washington Nov. 30, 1921. By 1935 the extensive restoration at both churches had been completed and adroit plantings added to the picturesque landscape. During this period a native of Charles County, Colonel Frank B. Keech, and his nephews, William C. Turner and R. Alan Turner, were largely responsible for the upkeep of Trinity Church as well as for the perpetual care of the cemetery through endowments left to the parish.

During the years of 1944 to 1961 there was a great interest on the part of the parishioners as well as the clergy in developing a strong Christian fellowship. Much was accomplished during these years. Under the Rev. Walter V. Reed's direction, a women's guild was formed at Trinity Church and worked very closely with the men in the parish to build a new church hall. At Oldfields a new organ was purchased and a Junior Choir formed with 19 members.

The Rev. Joseph Roberts saw the completion of much work begun earlier. The Church Hall at Trinity was completed and the Hall at Oldfields was remodeled with a gift from the Clagett estate. The new Sanctuary and Choir were also added to the Chapel. The new stained glass windows at the Chapel were completed under the rectorship of the Rev. Robert Lawthers. They were designed and installed by Irene and Rowan Le Compte.

The Rev. George H. Price came to the parish Jan. 1, 1966, from the Diocese of New Jersey. He moved into a new, modern Rectory built in 1965 near the Chapel. The present rector is the Rev. William M. Davis. Since he came to the parish a church Thrift Shop has been initiated in Clagett Hall.

Today Trinity Parish seeks in its services and parochial life to express fully the faith and discipline of the Episcopal Church. Mindful that she owes her establishment to the missionary efforts of the Church of England, she takes her place with parishes throughout the worldwide Anglican communion, which are indebted to the Anglican branch of the Church. The worship is centered at the Altar, since the Holy Eucharist is the chief act of Christian worship. Although the parish has great historic significance, it seeks to revere its past and rich heritage without living in the past.

St. Paul's Church, Piney (St. Paul's Parish, 1794)

"Piney," as it was called, dates from a May 29, 1754, meeting of the Council and General Assembly of Maryland, where it was decided "to purchase a quantity of land...and there on to build a Chappel of Ease." The land designated as the site was located "at a place called Ivy Spring, on a Branch called Dressing Branch, near the Pines."

The first chapel was built of logs, like Christ Church and Old Durham, and burned during "a fire that swept through the pine woods." Later Vestry minutes indicate that a contract was let to Ignatius Spalding of Washington, D.C., in 1823 to build St. Paul's Chapel of Ease at a cost of $1,550. The next year the Vestry was ordered to raise funds for pews at this new "Piney." In April 1825 Col. Francis W. Hawkins and Aquila Turner were appointed to serve "as the first wardens to represent Piney."

A Vestry meeting of 1900 determined "that any proposition to divide Port Tobacco Parish at this time is unwise and impracticable," and it was not until Jan. 26, 1968, that Port Tobacco Parish finally was divided, the Chapel of Ease becoming St. Paul's Church of Piney Parish.

The Rev. John Mason was called as Vicar of Piney in 1967, a step preparatory to Piney becoming an independent parish. When this was accomplished the Rev. Marvin A. Gardener Jr. assumed the Piney rectorship on Aug. 10, 1969. He began his service when the area was in transition from a rural community to a sub-urban one, and accommodated a diversified group of people. Many of them had backgrounds quite different from those of the existing congregation. The result was change.

Three services were added, and in September 1971 a new Sacristy was completed. Memorial windows were given in 1974. Throughout the period parishioners organized new committees to increase participation. Soon Piney will move again—to St. Charles.

Over a period of 221 years some 24 Rectors have served "Piney." The Rev. Lemuel Wilmer, who ministered for 47 years, is buried in the church cemetery. His years of service spanned the Civil War, and one parishioner tells how Mr. Wilmer offered up the "bidding prayer" one Sunday to his congregation, which was divided in its sympathies. At first all knelt—Union supporters and Confederate sympathizers alike. But when the Rector said, "Ye shall pray for the President of the United States," the latter rose hurriedly, stood while the name "Abraham Lincoln" was uttered, then calmly returned to their knees for the finish of the prayer. In the cemetery on the right side of the church are nine stones that face the South—grave markers of Southern sympathizers, an unmistakable reminder of the divided loyalties of Charles County during the War years.

St. John's Chapel, Pomonkey; St. James Parish, Indian Head (St. John's Parish, Prince George's County)

St. John's Chapel in Pomonkey, next to the Maryland Airport, was organized in 1834 as a parochial mission of St. John's Parish in Accokeek, the chapel in Charles County, the Parish Church located in Prince George's.

The original structure was a plain small frame building, erected in 1834. It was torn down in 1902 and much of the material removed to Indian Head for the construction of a mission there (St. James), also organized by St. John's.

The present building was erected in 1902 about 300 yards from the original site. It is chapel style, frame, small, with elevated chancel and all wooden furniture. A bell is housed in a small tower over the west entrance.

St. John's Chapel is served by the Rev. Robert Gillespie of St. John's Parish, and its records are included with those of

Christ Church, Accokeek. The congregation is small, but the ministry is important to Charles County in this Bicentennial year.

St. James Episcopal Church in Indian Head was established as a parochial mission of St. John's Parish (Christ Church, Accokeek) in 1902. It is located a short distance from the Naval Ordnance Station and for a time around the 1940s, the vicar of St. James was also acting Chaplain in the Naval Reserve.

The present church building, of red tile in chapel style, and the connecting school building, were completed in 1924. They opened that Palm Sunday, and have been going strongly ever since. St. James grew from the status of a mission to an established Parish and Church in 1966 through the leadership of its present Rector, the Rev. Herbert S. Costain, who has served since 1949.

Roman Catholic Churches

The cradle of the Catholic faith in the 13 colonies was in St. Mary's and Charles counties, Maryland. The first act of the passengers who accompanied Calvert was to come ashore to hear a Mass said by their fellow voyager, Father Andrew White S.J. on St. Clement's Island.

In 1641 Father White took up residence among the Potobac Indians, but there is evidence he visited Charles County earlier. He registered his claim for the St. Thomas Manor lands in 1642, and the deed is dated 1649. It was probably at St. Thomas Manor that Father White composed his grammar, dictionary, and catechism in the native Potobac dialect at least 15 years before John Eliot, English missionary to the Indians of New England, wrote his Indian Bible. Father White was assisted in his missionary work in Maryland by Father John Gravener S.J., Father Thomas Copley S.J., and Brother Thomas Gervase S.J.

St. Ignatius Church, Chapel Point
On the brow of a hill overlooking the verdant hills of Port Tobacco Valley rising one upon the other and the quiet waters

of the confluence of the Port Tobacco and Potomac rivers, stands a church and a residence with a certain majesty that grips the visitor. It is not a majesty of architecture, although the church spire does catch the eye as one approaches over the water, but the impression of a majestic history is strong in the atmosphere, and awe is inspired at being on the spot.

The Church of St. Ignatius at Chapel Point is one of the oldest Catholic churches in continuous service in the United States. The present church was erected in 1778, when Father Charles Sewall S.J. was the pastor. Father Sewall was born at Mattapony-Sewall, near the mouth of the Patuxent River, in St. Mary's County. He was descended from Major Henry Sewall, connected by marriage with the Calverts. Previous to his appointment as pastor of St. Ignatius Church in May 1793 Father Sewall had erected the first Catholic church in Balitmore, and was the first resident pastor in that city and first rector of the Baltimore procathedral. He died at St. Thomas Manor in November 1806.

In 1798 Bishop John Carroll laid the cornerstone of the church, dedicating it in honor of St. Ignatius. On Dec. 27, 1866, St. Ignatius suffered a disastrous fire, which destroyed most of the church records and left only the brick walls standing. In the rebuilding some modifications were made, and in 1963 a Baptistry and Narthex were added and the Sacristy refurbished. Otherwise the structure is as it was originally built.

The present church was preceded by one or more chapels near the river shore and also by the chapel (the present Sacristy), built sometime between 1662 and 1700. In 1662 Father Henry Warren S.J. became pastor, the first of a constant succession of resident pastors. Thus St. Ignatius claims to be the oldest active parish in continuous service in the United States. Father Warren was also Superior of the Maryland Mission, and for 170 years after 1662 St. Thomas Manor was the "Superior's Residence."

The St. Thomas Manor House was built by the Jesuits in 1741, but not completed until Father George Hunter was Superior after 1747. During the suppression of the Society of Jesus from 1773 to 1805, the Jesuits continued their work on the Maryland Mission. It was at St. Thomas Manor that the happy scene of the Restoration of the Society took place in August 1805, when Father Robert Molyneux S.J., Fr. Sewall, and Father Charles Neale S.J. pronounced their vows, and became the first Jesuits in this young nation.

The Jesuits have always been interested in the education of youth, not only in religion but also in the humanities. To this end, Father Bernardin F. Wiget S.J. in 1854 established a school close to the residence, known as the St. Thomas Parish School. It was a college preparatory school for boys and accommodated boarders as well as day pupils. The course of study included catechism, reading, writing, English grammar and composition, geography, history, arithmetic, algebra, geometry, natural philosophy, bookkeeping, Latin, Greek, and French. The school was prosperous while Father Wiget remained at St. Thomas but after he was transferred his successor, Father Robert D. Woodley S.J., closed it because of his difficulty in securing competent teachers.

During the pastorate of Father Francis Neale S.J., 1819 to 1837, a girls' academy had been contemplated; 75 acres of land was donated for this purpose by Thomas Courtney Reeves. However, it was not until 1870 that the first academy for girls was opened in this part of Charles County by Misses Jennie and Nellie Neale at "Mount Air," the home of their father, Captain James H. Neale. After his death the Misses Neale sold their home and opened St. Thomas Academy, a boarding and day school for girls at Chapel Point. The land for the school was donated by St. Thomas Manor. Until 1900 the Misses Neale conducted this academy, which was attended by young ladies from Charles and St. Mary's counties and from Washington. The school building, located near the manor house, stood for many years as a monument to these two ladies who spent much of their lives in the noble work of training the minds and hearts of the children placed under their care.

The sacrifices and examples of the priests attached to St. Thomas fostered religion, influenced people to assist in the establishment of our country, and counseled peaceful forgiveness and calm toleration. Frontier life was not easy, and required men of strength and determination. Many priests served here: Fathers George Hunter, Ignatius Matthews, Charles and Francis Neale, Aloysius Mudd, and James Brent Matthews. Fr. Hunter, Superior from 1747 to 1779, was a friend of George Washington and there is evidence that the President visited St. Thomas Manor on more than one occasion. With the exception of Fr. Hunter, who was from England, all were native Charles Countians.

The Mission Circuit of St. Thomas the Apostle had the Manor House as its center. All of Charles County, part of Prince George's County, and part of Virginia were included in the territory served from this center, but with the increase of population and available priests, the importance of St. Thomas' as a center has declined. Now, under Father A. Robert Thoman S.J., it serves only St. Ignatius, a parish of about 1,000.

St. Mary's Church, Newport

The impression of newness radiated by St. Mary's Church disappears in the parish churchyard. One seeks the old that preceded the new, and the eye finds a venerable building, now the parish hall. It has something of a languid air, and a mellowness that comes with age. Venerable indeed, it marks the spot where the first Franciscan foundation of a church in the colonies was laid by the Franciscan Fathers under the direction of Father Basil Hobart O.S.F. in 1697.

The Franciscan Fathers had come to the Maryland Mission in 1672, led by Father Masseus a Sancta Barbara Massey O.S.F., and his two companions. Two years later Father Basil Hobart, renowned for his great zeal, was sent to the Maryland Mission. After his death, the congregation at Newport was served by the Jesuit Fathers from St. Thomas' Manor until 1881. Since then, the parish has been under the care of the diocese.

A colorful figure in the history of Colonial Maryland was Major William Boarman, whose plantation, "Boarman's Rest," was near the site of the present St. Mary's Church.

Maj. Boarman was one of the few individuals who understood the language and dialects of the various Algonquin Indians then living in Maryland and Virginia. His services as interpreter were in constant demand in all transactions between the colonists and the Indians. His honesty in these dealings and his integrity as a trader are credited with fostering the spirit of friendliness that existed between Indians and settlers from those early times.

A devout Catholic, Boarman is quoted as saying proudly that he "was born and bred" so. When he died, he left his plantation to a son, on condition that he "keep the chapel standing on the plantation in repair."

It is thought that at this chapel the Franciscan Fathers cared for the spiritual needs of the people until 1697, when Fr. Hobart built the first Church of St. Mary at Newport. It is not known how long the chapel at "Boarman's Rest" was in use after the building of the church.

The frame chapel of 1697 was replaced by a brick edifice faced with a wooden tower in 1840. The first residence, a many-windowed structure, was erected by Fr. Wiget around 1855. In 1906 a stucco finished building replaced the old brick church, which was later converted into a hall where the parishioners serve their Southern Maryland dinners, famous in Charles County, Washington, and Baltimore. In 1954 the stucco church was dismantled and the new church and rectory were built.

St. Mary's Church at Newport has been well known for many years because of the Shrine of the Curé d'Ars, St. John Vianney. This shrine was established by the late Father William Baldus.

This church has served the function in the history of the Catholic Church as a Mother Church. From St. Mary's has sprung the church at Issue, and from Issue the church at Rock Point. One can easily trace the line of growth from the early days of the Colonial plantation to the present era. Though the buildings have changed in design and architecture and in location, the Faith of the congregation remains the same.

One local priest, Father Henry Pile, was a descendant of Honorable John Pile, Privy Councillor to the King in 1649, who, during the Puritan ascendancy, came forward and proclaimed himself, in Court, to be a Roman Catholic. Father Pile studied abroad and entered the Society of Jesus in Europe in 1761. He returned to America in 1784 and had charge of the congregations at Newport and Cobb Neck until his death in 1813. He lived at his ancestral home "Salisbury Manor" (Sarum), overlooking the Wicomico River, in the Newport area.

St. Peter's Church, Waldorf

Three miles east of Waldorf is St. Peter's Church, soon to celebrate its centenary year. This church possesses the charm of maturity, but the age of the church is not as great as that of the parish it serves, for it was here that Charles County's third Catholic parish was established in 1700.

St. Peter's Church was preceded by St. Ignatius Church, which was built in the old cemetery, about a mile east of the present church ground. The site of the old cemetery is one that impresses the visitor with a sense of strength and endurance, as he walks among the age worn tombstones, reading names of those who labored to build the old frame chapel that was used for about 150 years.

From earliest times this parish was known as Upper Zachia, as it is located at the headwaters of the present Zekiah Swamp. In 1681 a fort was built on the Zachia Swamp, about four miles southeast of La Plata, to protect the Zachia Indians against the Senecas and Susquehannocks of the north. To this fort were brought the Piscataways when their village was in danger of attack from their common enemy. Gov. Charles Calvert, writing to his brother, Lord Baltimore, spoke of his intent to build a residence "on his Lordship's

Manor of Sachay"; in 1673 he wrote that the house was complete, and he proposed moving from Mattapony to Zachia for greater security. The word "Zachia," spelled Zacchia, Zachaiah, Zakiah, Zekiah, or Sachay, means "where there is a bend."

The Jesuit Fathers from St. Thomas Manor served the congregation of Upper Zachia from 1700 to 1792, when Archbishop Carroll sent Father J. B. David, a Sulpician, and a refugee from the French Revolution, to care for the congregation. Father Robert Angier O.P., a Dominican, was Fr. David's successor from 1805 to 1807; from then until 1816 the parish was cared for by Father John Henry S.J., a Belgian Jesuit, Father Heath S.J., and Father J. B. Cary S.J. from St. Thomas Manor.

In 1816 Fr. Angier returned from Europe where he had gone to solicit financial help for his several parishes, and was again appointed pastor until 1825. In that year Father Enoch Fenwick S.J., a native of St. Mary's County, was pastor for a short time and was succeeded by Father J. V. Wiseman, who remained until 1829, when Father Francis Roloff became pastor until 1838. It was during his pastorate that the congregation at Piscataway became large enough to form a new parish, and Monsignor McColgan was appointed pastor. Upper Zachia was then served from this parish instead of from Bryantown. The village of Piscataway, an Indian word meaning "a high passable bank around a river bend," is about 12 miles west of Waldorf, on the Piscataway Creek.

The record shows that from 1838 to 1851 the congregation was again served at various times from St. Thomas Manor. In 1851 Father John Donelan was sent by the Archbishop to be the first resident pastor of St. Ignatius Church, and from then until 1894 the Diocesan priests served the congregation. Fr. Donelan was considered a talented speaker, as indicated in the *Port Tobacco Times*, Feb. 1, 1855:

An Invitation, numerously signed by persons of different religious denominations in this village and neighborhood, has been sent to the Rev. John P. Donelan, at present Rector

(Catholic) of an adjoining Pairsh, requesting him to deliver in Port Tobacco this winter, a course of Lectures. It is the generally expressed desire here that this popular and eloquent divine will accept the invitation, and favor us with lectures on whatever subjects he may select.

In November 1855 Fr. Donelan sailed for Rome for the restoration of his health, and Father Lanahan succeeded him as pastor of St. Ignatius of Upper Zachia. He immediately realized that the little frame chapel built in 1700 was inadequate to accommodate the congregation.

Thomas Reeves, a faithful parishioner, died in 1825; as he had no children, he willed that his farm, on the death of his wife, be given to the church. Fr. Lanahan decided to build a new church on this property, and for this reason it was often spoken of as "Reeves' Chapel." For many years the old Reeves residence served as the rectory.

The new church was dedicated in honor of St. Peter the Apostle Aug. 15, 1860. The church was a frame building. It was replaced by the present edifice in 1972, by the Rev. Raymond Fanning, present pastor. It stands on a gently rising site, sufficiently elevated to enhance the building.

From 1894 to 1923 Father Narcisse Martin S.S., a Sulpician, was the pastor of St. Peter's. Before coming to Maryland, he was professor of Dogmatic Theology at the Grand Seminary, Montreal, Canada. Fr. Martin was one of the great theologians in the Catholic Church in America, but he led a life of comparative retirement for more than 30 years working for the good of the people in his parish. His "Treatise on the Blessed Sacrament" is an authoritative theological work. Since his death in 1923 the parish has been under the care of the Diocesan priests.

Many priests have served the congregation at Waldorf; some later became eminent in the Church as bishop or monsignor. Among them is Bishop Charles Warren Currier, born of English and Spanish parents at Charlotte Amalie on the Danish Island of St. Thomas. Bishop Currier's first pastorate was at St. Peter's, from 1885 to 1890.

The old cemetery that had served St. Peter's parish since its establishment in 1700 became inadequate and in 1941 a new cemetery was opened near the entrance to the church. At the entrance to the cemetery is a large granite cross with the inscription: "In memory of Thomas C. Reeves who left his property to St. Peter's Church. His burial was in St. Peter's Old Cemetery in 1825. Erected by members of St. Peter's Church in 1941."

In recent years many children of St. Peter's parish have received their education at the parochial school in Bryantown, under the direction of the School Sisters of Notre Dame. As the congregation continued to grow there developed a need for a school in the parish. Father Henry W. Sank helped make this dream a reality: in September 1957 an elementary school was opened under the direction of the Sisters of Charity of Nazareth.

St. Joseph's Church, Pomfret

Set among fields of tobacco and stretches of forest is St. Joseph's Church, homey and comfortable. The cemetery of some eight acres contains graves of venerable heroes of the Revolutionary War, the Civil War, and both World Wars, as well as of civilian parishioners.

The church has an undefinable architecture, what one might call homespun. There is a "family" atmosphere in the surrounding area, with the cemetery on one side and the baseball diamond, the residence, and the parish hall on the other. This church is the center of the spiritual, social, and recreational life of the community.

As is true of other parishes of the County, the parish was founded when "stations" were used in the absence of a parish church. The "stations" in the Pomfret area were located at these homes, and probably at some others: Araby, the home of the Wills family; Green Park, the home of the Green family; Locust Grove, the home of the Thompson family; Pleasant Hill, the home of the Spalding family; Poplar Springs, the home of the Norris family; The Long House, the home of the Mattingly family; and Aguinsick, the home of the Neale family.

Religious services were held in these homes, in the main room of the house, that is, the parlor. The priest usually came on Saturday, heard confessions in the evening, said Mass, preached, and gave Communion on Sunday morning; he instructed the children and catechumens (adults who were being instructed in the Catholic Faith), administered baptisms, and witnessed marriages. Then he would start off on horseback for the next station in that area.

There are no available data on when these stations were begun, but their use was countrywide. In view of the difficulty of travel and the frontier state of the life in those days, one may validly surmise that they were opened whenever a Catholic landowner had sufficient people living or working on his land to constitute a congregation.

The first Catholic chapel in the Pomfret area was built on land purchased by Fr. Hunter in 1763. It was a small frame chapel, which stood on a site about 100 yards northeast of the present church. This small chapel served the purpose of a funeral chapel, while the stations were the centers of religious life in the surrounding area. On Oct. 15, 1790, the Discalced Carmelite Nuns made their home among the parishioners in their new monastery at Mount Carmel, the first convent established in the United States. For the next 60 years the center of Catholic life at Pomfret was at the monastery, where their pastor lived and served as chaplain to the nuns.

Fr. Charles Neale was pastor and chaplain from 1790 to 1823. He lived in a small residence outside the monastery enclosure until his death in 1823. Father Benedict Fenwick S.J. was named his successor as pastor and chaplain, and remained at that post until 1825 when he was consecrated the second Bishop of Boston. He was succeeded by Father Enoch Fenwick S.J. as pastor and chaplain; he died at the monastery in 1827 and Fr. Francis Xavier Neale, succeeded him as pastor. Fr. Neale remained in the post as chaplain for one year, and after that a priest of the diocese became chaplain.

The Discalced Carmelite Nuns moved to Baltimore in 1831, and the chapel at the monastery was used as the parish church. The frame chapel at Pomfret was becoming a hazard, and in 1835 it was demolished. For the next 14 years the congregation at Pomfret continued to use the Mount Carmel Chapel, while funds were being raised to build the present church. Mass was said for the congregation at the monastery, and use of the stations was gradually discontinued. However, in some areas stations remained in use as late as 1914.

A subscription campaign to raise funds for the new church was begun by Father Thomas Lilly S.J. in November 1837. One acre of land was donated by Major Green as the site of the church and the brick was burnt on his farm near the spot. The following year Father Aloysius Mudd S.J., a native Charles Countian, succeeded Fr. Lilly. Until his death in 1844 Fr. Mudd was instrumental in pushing the work forward to raise funds for completing the church. It took 12 years to complete the work, so that Mass could be said for the first time in the new St. Joseph's Church, Jan. 6, 1849. The church was dedicated Sept. 1, 1850, by the Bishop. The dedication exercises were preceded by a three-day spiritual retreat that began each day at 9:30 a.m. and concluded at 5 p.m.

From the beginning of the parish until 1925, the congregation was served by the Jesuit Fathers who came from the residence at St. Thomas Manor. In that year the Jesuit residence at La Plata was opened and until 1966 the pastor of Pomfret made his residence there with his fellow Jesuits.

Among the many eminent men who were pastors of the churches of Charles County was the Most Reverend Benedict Joseph Fenwick. Born near Leonardtown Sept. 3, 1782, he studied for the priesthood at the Sulpician Seminary in Baltimore and entered the Society of Jesus in 1805. He was ordained by Bishop Leonard Neale on June 11, 1808, and began pastoral work in the diocese of Baltimore. He served at New York, as President of Georgetown University, Washington, D.C., the oldest Catholic college in the nation; and as Vicar General at Charleston, S.C.

Between 1823 and 1825 Bishop Fenwick was pastor of St. Joseph's at Pomfret and chaplain of Mt. Carmel. He was then consecrated second Bishop of the Boston Diocese; in 1842 he convened the first Synod for the diocese. When he was consecrated, his diocese had only two priests, one cathedral, and three churches. During his administration, Bishop Fenwick laid the foundation for the large and numerous archdiocese that now exists.

With justifiable pride Charles County can also point to many prominent Catholic laymen who have done outstanding deeds. One of these is Maurice James McDonough, who was a staunch Catholic. Little is known of McDonough's life, except that he was a peddler who walked the length and breadth of the area with his pack on his back, selling his wares to the residents of the western section of Charles County. During his lifetime there were no public schools in the county. He became aware of the needs of education, and in his will dictated that his estate be sold and the income derived from it used to provide for the education of the poor children in the area in which he had worked.

It was nearly 100 years after his death before sufficient funds were accumulated to make possible the opening of McDonough Institute at La Plata. McDonough was the only high school in Charles County until 1924. When the La Plata High School was opened in 1927 it was thought best to sell the McDonough property and use the income to give deserving students in the McDonough district tuition scholarships to college. More than 40 students received such assistance.

In the cemetery at St. Joseph's Church a monument was erected by the Trustees of McDonough Institute on April 4, 1901. The inscription reads: "Sacred to the memory of Maurice James McDonough who died January 9, 1804. He bequeathed the accumulations of a lifetime of toil to be devoted to the education of poor children of the community in which he lived."

St. Mary's Church, Bryantown

This church, located on Rt. 232 near the intersection of Rt. 5, represents one of the oldest parishes in the County. Early records show it began as a log chapel "only 30 feet long on the Boarman Estate near Zekiah Swamp Creek" in 1696. It was this chapel that Maj. Boarman's will directed his son to keep in good repair.

The Jesuit Fathers, from their residence at St. Thomas Manor at Chapel Point, ministered to the faithful in Southern Maryland until 1773, when political upheavals in the Colony brought their service to a close. After the American Revolution "Congregations" began to spring up and, as early as 1793, the one at Bryantown was well organized. Known as the "Congregation of Upper and Lower Zachia and Mattawoman," it included the present sections of Waldorf, Piscataway, and Aquasco (then Woodville) in the "Upper" area and Bryantown and Benedict in the "Lower" one. The name was dropped from Catholic directories after 1841.

The frame church constructed in 1793 had a room or two for the use of the priest and was supported by the parishioners by a tax levy on their property. It has been said that a portion of the land for the church was donated by a Mr. Hayden in 1743 and another part by his son in 1793. The Haydens may have acquired the land from the Boarmans because it was part of the land known as "Boarman's Manor." The pastor of the little church was the Rev. John B. David, a Frenchman of the Sulpician Order, who fled France during its Revolution and studied English on board ship so zealously that he was appointed to this parish immediately upon his arrival in America. The first parish registers of baptisms, marriages, and deaths which he began recording are a treasure trove for the genealogists of today.

The next pastor was Rev. Robert A. Angier, a Dominican from London, who came in 1804 and served until 1808 when the care of the Congregation appears to have reverted to the Jesuits. Rev. John Henry was pastor pro-tem in 1811 and until 1814. The Congregational Roll of 1811 contained 51 names, and at a meeting of the Trustees in 1812 it was resolved to levy on the assessable property of the members a sum of 75 cents on 100 pounds, to be paid each March "for the purpose of repairing the pastor's dwelling-house as well as meeting other necessary expenses."

Father Carey succeeded Fr. Angier from 1814-1816 and then Fr. Angier returned to serve the parish until 1825. Father Enoch Fenwick was in the parish for three months in 1925 and Father J. V. Wiseman from 1825 to 1829. Father James Moynahan helped Fr. Wiseman during this time and when Fr. Moynahan died in 1831 he was buried in the church graveyard. Later his remains were buried under the new church altar.

Church records for the 1830s are scarce, but it is known that Father Francis Roloff ministered to the congregation then, and that the Piscataway parish in upper Mattawoman was formed as separate entity.

In 1842 Father Patrick Courtney was appointed to the parish. He labored for its improvement until 1855, with the help in 1851 of Fr. Donelan. He succeeded in having erected between 1845 and 1849 a new rectangular brick church, 60 by 40 feet (the present middle section), a plain but substantial building without ornamentation.

In 1851 St. Mary's was established as a separate parish from the Waldorf, Aquasco, and Benedict areas. Heretofore, priests had served the entire area but gradually each place had its own church and pastor. A year later, the then Archbishop of Baltimore, Patrick Kenrick, came to St. Mary's to introduce the Forty Hours' Devotion. At this time a part of the old frame church had been moved to a plot near the new church to serve as an Academy for Young Ladies. It was established by Charles Countians, the Misses Mary and Winifred Martin, who were later assisted by Miss Martha Ann Purcell. Patronized by local and distant families, the St. Mary's Institute was the first educational facility in the area, and it was highly successful until after the Civil War when the patrons suffered financial reverses. Mrs. Daniel Majors and her daughters, who had carried on its work after the retirement of Winifred Martin, found it necessary then to close the school. The founders of this school are buried in the part of the cemetery where their building once stood, between the present church and rectory.

Two Jesuit priests, Fr. Wiget and Father Camillus Vicinanza, served the parish in 1855 to 1861. In 1858 funds amounting to $1,503 were raised for enlarging the church but the final cost proved to be $1,756.91. Galleries were put in the church in 1859 and there was a passageway extending from side to side between the sanctuary and Sacristy, used for confessional purposes. The sanctuary was enlarged into this passageway, with small entries on cither side, prior to 1861.

During the difficult Civil War period Father John T. Gaitly held the parish together. After the assassination of President Lincoln, he was suspected of complicity because of his friendship with Mrs. Mary Surratt, whose daughter had been a student at the Misses Martins' school. He escaped imprisonment, and left the parish in 1865. Father Walter Jorden took charge of the parish from 1865 to 1869, opening the rear wall of the church to enlarge the sanctuary section and adding side altars to accommodate statues of the Blessed Mother and St. Joseph.

Father Peter Lenaghan was pastor from 1869 to 1875, when Father Henry Volz arrived to serve a short time. Father Michael Brennan was pastor for six months in 1876 and Father John A. Ahern served from March to June of that year. Father Volz returned for a year and then Father Francis Teves, serving from 1877 to 1882, built a rectory separate from the church in 1879. The highly revered Father Edward M. Southgate came to the parish in 1882 and remained until 1903. He improved the church in 1894 and extended the main section in 1895, removing the old church tower and steeple and replacing them with new ones. The roof was lifted with exposed beams and covered with slate shingles instead of wood ones. The galleries were replaced by a balcony in the rear of the church later. In May 1882 Calvert County was added to his jurisdiction and he established missions at Solomon's Island, Drum Point, Sollers', St. Leonard's, Dr. Jones', and Huntington.

Father Denis C. Keenan was pastor from 1903 to 1912, followed by Father Charles E. Roach who remained only a short time, and was succeeded by Father Patrick C. Conroy in late 1912. An energetic and enterprising priest, Fr. Conroy organized the Holy Name Society in 1913; it undertook the building of two schools in 1915. A convent was constructed to house the School Sisters of Notre Dame and in the same building was a school for white children, with an enrollment of 115. On the other side of the church a school was erected for colored children; it had an enrollment of 122. Two halls were constructed in connection with the schools, to be used for school plays and socials as well as by the adults of the parish. Under the excellent guidance of the School Sisters of Notre Dame, the schools prospered. In 1916 a ninth grade was added to the already existing eight, and commercial courses were started in 1917 and 1918. A senior high was begun in 1921 and an addition was made to the school, from which the first class was graduated in 1924. The State accredited the high school in 1925 and a boarding school that had been started in 1921 functioned until 1931.

Court Bryantown Catholic Daughters Of America received its charter in 1923, and the Knights of Columbus in 1921. In 1925 Father Conroy had the church redecorated with the painting of the "Assumption of the Blessed Virgin Mary" over the main altar, new white statues for the sanctuary and side altars, and a marble communion rail to match the altar.

Father Conroy was succeeded by Father Charles E. Roach, 1927 to 1936; Father Thomas J. McKew, 1936 to 1941; Father James A. Dwyer, 1941 to 1942; and Father Elmer T. Fisher, 1942-1945. As there had been some liturgical changes, Fr. Fisher enlarged the sanctuary of the church by removing excess marble and statues, installing a more simple altar and tabernacle. To reflect his deep devotion to the Blessed Mother, he redecorated the church in lovely pastel yellow and blue, with medium blue brocade and dark blue velvet wall hangings behind the main altar. Father Francis J. Driscoll, during his sojourn here from 1945 to 1950, initiated the scheduling of four Masses in place of the former two, had storm windows installed in the church, and an artesian water system, a gift of His Excellency, Archbishop Patrick A. O'Boyle D.D., installed on the church grounds. In October 1946 Father Driscoll organized the Sodality of the Blessed Virgin Mary and the Knights of St. John in 1947.

With his appointment to the parish, Father Philip J. Brown, a dynamic priest, established the St. Vincent de Paul Society and laid plans for a Five-Point Development Program for the church grounds during his five years as pastor. In 1953 Father Louis A. Albert inherited this project. With his thrift and good management, after paying off the church debt, he subscribed funds that enabled the construction of a new brick rectory on the site of the old frame one, the addition of a kitchen to the old parish hall, the landscaping of a new dual roadway and cemetery in front of the church, and the repainting of the church interior in buff and blue, with red velvet and gold brocade altar draperies. He organized the Knights of the Altar, as well as the Ushers' Society. Father Raymond A. Patch, a priest of great artistic ability, was assigned to the church in 1954 as assistant priest. He was succeeded in 1956 by Father Donald F. M. Kelley, a most capable and dedicated young priest who remained in the parish for 17 years, bearing the burden of parish work longer than any priest who had preceded him. In 1958 Father A. Echle was appointed pastor and he achieved a close rapport with the youth of the parish as well as with the older parishioners.

Early in 1961 Father Edward J. O'Brien assumed the pastorate. He renovated the church in 1962, enhancing its beauty with an interior decor of blue and white. With the untiring help of Fr. Kelley, he was endeavoring to raise funds for a new convent and hall when a fire destroyed the altar section of the church and damaged the entire interior on Dec. 16, 1963. The old parish hall was prepared for immediate use as a chapel, and church affairs were continued there without interruption during the rebuilding of the church from 1963 to 1965. The church was rebuilt around the original stained glass windows with a few new ones replacing those that had deteriorated. The Sanctuary was extended by large wings on each side to create more seating space, one wing designed as a glass-enclosed, soundproof "cry room" for parents with young children. A modern electronic sound system was installed, and a Conn organ with its deep melodic tones. Fine

Italian marble was used in the Sanctuary and side altars where exquisitely hand-carved lindenwood statues of the Blessed Mother and St. Joseph from Switzerland were placed. Similar hand-carved lindenwood Stations of the Cross were hung on the side walls. Russet Oak pews with padded kneeling benches were installed.

On the large marble table in the sanctuary, a tabernacle with doors opening front and back enabled the priests to celebrate Mass facing the congregation in conformance with new liturgical regulations, or in the old traditional way of facing the altar. The entrance to the church was enhanced by the enlargement of the vestibule and a wider portico covered by a gabled roof supported by six white columns. Parishioners contributed generously toward all the needed items. Mass resumed on the Feast of the Immaculate Conception, Dec. 8, 1965, and on May 23, 1966, the church was dedicated by Archbishop O'Boyle of Washington.

The 51-year old school, with a staff of 13 School Sisters of Notre Dame, which had graduated more than 1,000 students, was closed in June 1967. The high school was phased out entirely, but a new elementary school, convent, and hall were completed by November in a complex valued at over one million dollars. The dedication took place that afternoon; in attendance were 52 priests, 56 Sisters, and 48 guests, who enjoyed an open house for the parishioners later.

In 1968 Father Gerald McWilliams replaced Fr. O'Brien as pastor and served until 1970, establishing the Parish Council and instituting many of the liturgical changes recommended by Vatican Council II. He was succeeded in November 1970 by Father Bernard R. Ihrie Jr., the present pastor. An industrious and conscientious priest, he has made great strides in helping pay off the parish debts incurred by the new constructions and has beautified the church grounds with well-kept shrubbery, flowers, and landscaping. Father William B. Purcell has assisted him in his endeavors, and Father Ansgar has helped with the Masses.

At the approaches to the blacktopped roadways leading to the buildings, two metal plaques recall the history of the parish since it was part of Boarman's 3,333-acre manor. St. Mary's Church serves one of the largest congregations in Charles County.

St. Charles Church, Glymont

St. Charles Church at Glymont stands on a small hill just off the main highway to Indian Head. This church and the surrounding area were known from Revolutionary War days until the turn of the century as Cornwallis' Neck, because according to tradition Cornwallis made his headquarters in this area during the war. St. Charles Church has an atmosphere of quiet dignity which invites the passerby to retire from the bustle of a modern world for a visit in the peace of God's house.

The congregation is an example of the historic growth of Catholicism in Southern Maryland. It was first formed at the mission station at "Araby," but barely 37 years after a church was built at Pomfret in 1763, Glymont, only about 10 miles distant, required a church of its own.

The church was built on the site of an old frame chapel erected about 1800, when Charles Pye, an English Catholic, and his wife sold to Father John Montdesir, an English Diocesan priest, a two-acre plot, one acre of which was to be used for the building of a chapel and the other to be set aside as a burial ground. The cost of this transaction amounted to five shillings.

It is not known how long Fr. Montdesir, the first pastor, or the Diocesan clergy retained charge of this mission, nor is there any account of the transfer of this church to the Jesuits. Father Ignatius Combs S.J. was pastor of Glymont in 1826, Father Matthew Sanders S.J. in 1836, and from 1838 to 1844 Father Thomas Lilly S.J. and Father Aloysius Mudd S.J. took care of Pomfret, Newport, and Cornwallis Neck, saying Mass at each place by turns.

When the old Pye Chapel, as it was called, fell into such a state of decay as to be unsafe for occupancy it was replaced by a new structure—in 1913. Father Joseph H. Hann S.J. was pastor at that time and he lived to see the mortgage paid off before his death the following year.

After the Naval Powder Factory was located at Indian Head, when Father William Tynan S.J. was in charge of La Plata, Pomfret, and Glymont, the population became so large that it was necessary to build a church for that congregation; in 1909 the Church of Our Lady, Star of the Sea, was erected. The Mattingly family donated the land for the church, rectory, and hall at Indian Head and for the increase of the parish cemetery at Glymont.

As time went on and growth continued at a rapid pace, the community became so large that it required a resident pastor. The Jesuit Fathers requested Cardinal Gibbons to appoint a priest of the Archdiocese as pastor, and Father Charles R. O'Hara was assigned the post June 7, 1918. The Indian Head area has continued to increase in Catholic population to such an extent that the rectory was built not at the Mother Church at Glymont, but at Indian Head.

St. Ignatius Church, Hill Top; St. Catherine's Church, McConchie

The highway stretches over land covered with farms and verdant forest, leading to St. Ignatius at Hill Top.

A good example of the old "frame chappelle" type of structure is St. Ignatius Church, which celebrated its centennial in 1959. This church is of wood, with little decoration in its architecture, a simple structure with gabled roof and a small belfry surmounted by a short spire.

Early records say there were mission stations at Nanjemoy in 1798 and at Chicamuxen and Cedar Point in 1820. These stations were attended by the Jesuit Fathers from St. Thomas Manor. The date of the establishment of the parish at Hill Top is given as 1851, but there was no church at that time and religious services were held in private homes.

In 1859 Father Samuel Barber S.J. was given charge of the Hill Top congregation and in that year he built St. Ignatius Church for the care of the area's few scattered Catholics.

The deed to the St. Ignatius Church lot is from William J. Owen to His Excellency, Archbishop Spalding, dated Aug. 27, 1869, for one acre of land, a part of which was used for the cemetery. Later a new cemetery was needed, and on Nov. 6, 1904, John D. Bragunier deeded to His Eminence, Cardinal Gibbons, three-fourths of an acre of land lying across the highway in front of the church.

The parish grew after conversion to the Catholic faith. The first pastor, Fr. Barber, was himself a Catholic convert. "Father Sam," as he was affectionately known, came from a prominent New Hampshire family, whose members were converted to the faith in 1816. All four of Father Samuel Barber's sisters entered the convent. He entered the Society of Jesus after his studies at Georgetown University, and was sent to Rome where he finished his studies with honor. For many years he was Master of Novices at the Jesuit Novitiate at Frederick, Md., and later a professor at Georgetown, before he became pastor of the congregation at Hill Top, where he remained until his death in 1864.

By 1911 there was need of another church to take care of the part of the congregation that lived near McConchie. The deed to the St. Catherine's Church lot is from Lemuel B. Owen to His Eminence, Cardinal Gibbons, dated July 25, 1911, for one-and-three-fourths acres of land, along the McConchie road. This church is a small frame building, similar to the church at Hill Top.

St. Ignatius Parish has thus grown into two parishes, but they have always had the same pastor. Until 1925, he made his residence at St. Thomas Manor with the other Jesuit Father, and since then at La Plata.

The record of this area contains the names of many outstanding men. One of the most eminent was Adm. Raphael Semmes of Civil War fame, born at "Efton Hills" in Nanjemoy, in September 1809. His family was descended from one of the original Catholic colonists of Maryland.

Sacred Heart Church, La Plata

Just off Rt. 301 in La Plata, a brick church nestles among the trees, drawing the visitor away from the roaring traffic and into a spiritual atmosphere.

Just such a function did the "Port Tobacco Chappelle" fulfill when it was built by Father Aloysius Mudd in 1839. Sacred Heart Church, young among the churches of Charles County, thus has a venerable predecessor, which served the old County seat at Port Tobacco for nearly 70 years. The Port Tobacco chapel was last used May 12, 1908, and the property was sold in 1914.

By 1890 the Catholic population of La Plata had increased to such an extent that there was definite need of a church. The pastor of St. Ignatius at Chapel Point began to say Mass once a month at the Town Hall in La Plata. On other Sundays, the people traveled to the little chapel at Port Tobacco, or about seven miles to St. Ignatius at Chapel Point, or to St. Joseph's at Pomfret, about 10 miles from La Plata.

The cornerstone of Sacred Heart Church was laid Aug. 12, 1901. Mass was said twice a month at Sacred Heart until 1925, when the residence was built next to the church by the first pastor and Superior, Father James Brent Matthews S.J. Since that date there has been daily Mass and many other exercises of piety. The pastor of Sacred Heart Church was appointed Superior of the Jesuits in Charles County.

Fr. Matthews was a native of Charles County and a lineal descendant of the Brent and Matthews families, which came to Maryland with the first settlers in 1634. Father Matthews was ordained in 1899 and spent three years teaching at St. George College, Kingston, Jamaica, B.W.I. He was then sent back to his beloved Maryland and served 14 years as the Superior at St. Inigoes in St. Mary's County. In 1919 he was sent to St. Thomas Manor, near the place of his birth and the haunts of his boyhood and youth. He moved to La Plata in 1925 and remained as pastor until his death in 1927.

While in St. Mary's County he was influential in opening the first parish schools, and while Superior in Charles County, he bent every effort to secure the same for the children of this County. This work was completed by his successor, Father Charles Hennessy S.J., who formally opened the Sacred Heart School in September, just five months after Fr. Matthews' death.

One of the most outstanding accomplishments of the Catholic Church in Charles County in recent years has been the establishment of Archbishop Neale School at La Plata. This modern consolidated elementary and high school had an enrollment of nearly 800 in 1957-1958. It is the product of the enterprise and daring of the pastors at Chapel Point, Hill Top, Indian Head, Issue, La Plata, Newport, and Pomfret. The school is located within the confines of the boundaries of Sacred Heart Parish, on the site of the old Sacred Heart School. It is directed and taught by the Sisters of the Immaculate Heart of Mary, who cared for the old school during its 27-year existence.

The old church was replaced by a modern large edifice in 1964. The pastorate of this parish was assumed by the diocesan clergy in 1966.

St. Francis de Sales Church, Benedict

This is a fisherman's church, located in an area famous for Benedict oysters and other seafood, and surrounded by wharves, boats, and other equipment of a fishing town.

In the course of the development of the early Jesuit Missions, the congregation at Benedict was attended at various times from St. Thomas Manor. Later the needs of the Catholics of this area were filled for many years by the pastors of St. Mary's Church at Lower Zachia, now Bryantown.

In 1882 Father Edward M. Southgate was appointed pastor at Bryantown and was placed in charge of the missions at Benedict and Solomon's Island in the Patuxent River. Fr. Southgate is named as the founding pastor of the church at Benedict, for it was he who began having Mass regularly here. As there was no church in his time Mass was said in the home of the Johnson family. Benedict remained under the care of Fr. Southgate until the turn of the century when the congregation became large enough to become a parish with a resident pastor.

The congregation at Benedict has the distinction of having as its first resident pastor the First Auxiliary Bishop of the Archdiocese of Washington, Bishop John M. McNamara, who was appointed pastor of Benedict in the fall of 1903. He constructed a church immediately, but this small frame structure burned in 1924 and was replaced by the present church, a stucco building. It stands on the site of the first church, at the entrance to the village of Benedict, overlooking the waters of the beautiful Patuxent River.

As there was no rectory at Benedict at the time of Bishop McNamara's appointment, he resided at the rectory of St. Mary's, Bryantown, for about six months. A frame house formerly belonging to the Roach family was rebuilt and served as the rectory until it burned in 1943. It was then replaced by a modern brick residence.

At the time of his appointment at Benedict, the Bishop also was given charge of the mission at Solomon's Island, which had been served from Bryantown. Later, when the congregation at Solomon's became large enough to have a resident pastor, the mission at Aquasco in Prince George's County was assigned to Benedict; it is still served by the pastor of St. Francis de Sales.

Holy Ghost Church, Issue; St. Francis de Sales Church, Rock Point

In 1642 trader Capt. James Neale was granted 2000 acres on the peninsula between the Potomac and Wicomico rivers, which became known as "Wolleston Manor." Capt. Neale paid for the land with "cub dollars," Spanish silver coins in circulation at that time; for this reason he called it "Cub Neck." Later the name was changed to Cob Neck and then Cobb Neck.

From the beginning Cobb Neck was generally associated with Newport, as the districts were contiguous, and the same priest attended both congregations. Father A. M. Mandalari S.J. was the last Jesuit pastor of these two parishes. Both places were taken over by the Archbishop on Jan. 1, 1881, and since then have been served by Diocesan clergy. From then until 1904 Issue was cared for by the pastor of St. Mary's Church, Newport.

The first church in the Cobb Neck area, St. Mary's, was built, it is thought, soon after 1873. It was a small frame building, located in what is now the old cemetery, about one-half mile west of the present church. Around 1880 St. Mary's Church burned and was replaced by Holy Ghost Church, also a frame building. This church was not erected on the original site as a new road had been built through the area and the new church was located there.

In 1955 Holy Ghost Church was razed and a brick edifice was erected on the same site, and dedicated Sept. 11.

The earliest record of land transferred to the church at Issue was in 1876 when John S. Richmond deeded to the Trustees of the Roman Catholic Church in Cobb Neck approximately 29 acres of land, part of a tract commonly called "Neale's Gift." In the same year, Mrs. Camilla L. Edelen deeded 10 acres of the tract called "Friendly Hall."

In 1904 the Cobb Neck parish was separated from Newport, and Father Joseph Meyer became the first resident pastor of Holy Ghost Church at Issue. The first task to confront Fr. Meyer was the building of a rectory. Before that, when Holy Ghost Church was still a mission of Newport, it had been customary for the priest to come to the church every other Saturday evening for confessions, then stay overnight at a parishioner's home. One room in these homes, known as the "Priest's Room," was reserved entirely for the use of the pastor.

In addition to building the rectory, Fr. Meyer also built a hall and a pavilion where dances and festivals were held. These buildings were erected in Harris Lot, on land given to the church by J. Rufus Perry. At that time Harris Lot was the social as well as commercial center of the area, and it is supposed these buildings were erected here for this reason. Around 1930, the use of this hall and pavilion was discontinued and a new hall was built on the church property at Issue. Fr. Meyer also worked tirelessly to secure telephone service for the area, even to the point of climbing the poles and helping to string the wires. It was through his efforts that the telephone was extended from La Plata to Rock Point.

In 1908 St. Francis de Sales Church was built at Rock Point, about four miles south of Issue. It is a mission church cared for by the pastor of Issue, a small frame building nestled among the cedar trees on the brink of a cliff overlooking the confluence of the Wicomico and Potomac rivers, its wooden cross a welcoming sight to the weary fisherman returning home from his long day's work.

Mt. Carmel, near La Plata

It was to the thriving community at Port Tobacco that Father Charles Neale S.J. came with the four Discalced Carmelite Nuns in 1790 to found the first religious community of women in the United States.

Before that time the establishment of such a community was hindered by anti-Catholic laws. Young Catholic women who wished to enter religious life were compelled to embark on precarious sailing vessels and make a long ocean journey to Europe. The English Carmelite Monastery at Hoogstraeten, Belgium, attracted many young American girls, among them three members of the Matthews family of Charles County.

Ann Matthews went to Hoogstraeten in 1754. She was followed after the Revolution by her two nieces, Susanna and Ann Teresa Matthews. The Prioress of the Hoogstraeten Monastery was the former Mary Brent, in religion, Sister Mary Margaret of the Angels, also a native of Charles County. The confessor of the Monastery was Father Charles Neale, second cousin of the Prioress.

It was only natural that these Marylanders should look to establishing a foundation in their homeland. Mother Margaret wanted to lead a band of sisters to America but died before she could do so, and was succeeded by Mother Bernardina as Prioress. The news of the adoption of the U.S. Constitution in 1789, with its guarantee of religious freedom, gave the nuns new hope. Father Ignatius Matthews S.J., brother of the Prioress, wrote to Mother Bernardina, "Now is your time to found in this country, for peace is declared and religion is free."

Mother Bernardina immediately began preparing for the foundation. The matter was placed before Bishop-elect John Carroll, who was heartily in favor of the foundation, and assured the nuns a cordial welcome. The Bishop of Antwerp approved the undertaking and appointed Mother Bernardina Prioress. She was joined by her two nieces, Sister Eleanor and Sister Aloysia, and Sister Clare Joseph Dickenson, an English woman from the Antwerp Carmelite Monastery. The nuns were accompanied on their journey by Father Charles Neale and Father Robert Plunkett. Since it was not safe for them to travel as Catholics, the sisters changed their religious habits for secular apparel.

They left Belgium April 19, 1790, and were carried down to the Canary Islands, 2,000 miles out of their way on the tiresome and disagreeable journey. The bread was moldy from the first days out to sea, and the other food was equally poor. The water was hardly fit to drink, and Mother Bernardina, for all her holiness, described the captain in her journal as "a poor, little, mean-spirited, stingy Scotchman."

After their arrival in New York on July Fourth, Fr. Plunkett left the group and proceeded overland to Georgetown, Md. He was appointed the first president of Georgetown College by Bishop Carroll. Fr. Neale and the four nuns proceeded to Norfolk. There they hired another vessel for the day's journey up the Chesapeake Bay and into the Potomac River to "Brentfield," home of Robert Brent, brother of Mother Mary Margaret. They were met on landing by Ignatius Matthews, a nephew of Mother Bernardina and brother of Sisters Aloysia and Eleanora. They rested for a few days at the Matthews home, then continued their journey up the Port Tobacco River.

Fr. Neale had inherited from his father "Chandler's Hope," the family homestead situated on a height overlooking Port Tobacco River. The manor was unoccupied at the time of the nuns' arrival, and they took up their abode in it and resumed their Carmelite habits. The nuns must have found the noise and bustle of the busy village disturbing compared to the peace of their Mother Monastery at Antwerp. The buildings at "Chandler's Hope" were not well suited to their needs. Fr. Neale arranged to exchange his property for a much larger tract of 800 acres about three miles north of Port Tobacco, owned by Baker Brooke.

Here the nuns established the first Carmelite Monastery in the United State, Mt. Carmel, on Oct. 15, 1790, day of the feast of St. Teresa of Avila, the foundress of the Discalced Carmelites. This was the first establishment of a contemplative community of Catholic women in the United States.

The Port Tobacco Monastery stood at its original site for more than 40 years. In 1830 Archbishop Whitefield proposed the removal of the convent to Baltimore to the house on Aisquith Street. In 1872 its second change was made, to the present location at Caroline and Biddle streets. The Carmelites are again planning to move to a new and more fitting location.

When they moved from Port Tobacco the Carmelites exhumed the bodies of the nuns who were buried in their little enclosure, with the exception of two. Sister Euphrasia of the Infant Jesus, Ann Mudd, and Sister Magdalen of St. Joseph, Elizabeth Johnson, had died too recently for their bodies to be disinterred. They still repose at the Port Tobacco Carmel, making the place a holy reliquary. As parishioners of Pomfret say, "We still have the Carmelites in Charles County."

The records in the Carmelite Monastery at Baltimore contain the names of many Charles County families, among them the Boarmans, Brents, Edelens, Johnson, Matthews, Mudds, Neales, and Nicholsons.

For nearly 200 years these holy women, wearing the brown habit of Carmel, have moved silently and serenely through their days of prayer and work in the Monastery, assiduously praying for both the material and the spiritual needs of their neighbors. Since 1936 a movement has grown to restore the original Carmel at Port Tobacco and the Sisters who left Port Tobacco many years ago are planning to return to live in Charles County this year. On their return, the Carmelites will find a ready and hearty welcome, for their history and memory have been cherished over the years.

Loyola-on-the-Potomac Retreat House

In today's complicated world it is necessary for the individual to think over the fundamental ideals of Catholic life, and to do so in a place where the distractions of everyday life will not bother him. This is called a spiritual retreat, a refuge prepared by the authorities of the Church to remove a person from the fatigue and cares of the everyday world and give him spiritual rest and quiet.

The Society of Jesus 400 years ago inherited from its founder, St. Ignatius Loyola, the plan and method of retreats in his book, *The Spiritual Exercises*. All the congregations of the County are aware of its contents, for they have enjoyed the spiritual benefits of retreats held in the various churches. At times these exercises have been called "Missions," but in recent years the proper title has come into use. The first recorded lay retreat in the United States was conducted by the Jesuit Fathers in 1638 at St. Mary's City, Maryland.

As a birthday present to Charles County in 1958, its Tercentenary Year, the Catholic hierarchy decided to erect Loyola-on-the-Potomac Retreat House near Bel Alton. This site is not far from the old St. Thomas Manor where so much of the County's Catholic heritage began.

Loyola-on-the-Potomac stands on the 235-acre property known as "Huckleberry," which was originally among the Chandler Land Grants that date back to 1654, when Job Chandler received extensive grants in the Port Tobacco area for development as parts of a growing shipping center. A manor house stands near the entrance of the property, one mile from the Retreat House.

The facilities of the Retreat House include a chapel, private oratory, lecture hall, community room, 75 single rooms for retreatants, kitchen, dining room, and administrative offices and living quarters for the Jesuit staff.

The Retreat House serves the many parishes within the Washington, Southern Maryland, and Virginia areas. It is used by Georgetown University faculty and students, diplomatic personnel of the 78 embassies and legations in Washington, men from the Armed Services, members of the State Department, the F.B.I., and non-affiliated residents.

All are welcomed at Loyola-on-the-Potomac, and from all walks of life men come to enjoy the opportunities for spiritual growth and progress. They partake of traditional Southern Maryland hospitality and learn the "grace-full" way of life.

Baptist Churches

Baptist work in Southern Maryland began in 1790, when four men from Virginia crossed the Potomac and began preaching in Charles County in the Nanjemoy area. In 1791 one acre of ground was purchased for three shillings, for the exclusive use of a Baptist church. In 1793 the Nanjemoy Baptist Church was organized and thus became the mother of Charles County Baptist churches. At that time the church affiliated with the Ketoctin Association in Virginia. In 1836 the Maryland Baptist Union Association, now the Baptist Convention of Maryland, was formed with six churches. Nanjemoy was the first church to join this new association after its formation.

Through the years, member churches have been asked to contribute ever larger percentages of their budgets to the Association to support educational and other programs. Most churches and missions today give at least five per cent; several give larger amounts.

The churches of the Association have performed a number of ministries including a camp for needy boys, a ministry to migrants, jail services, and work in nursing homes.

A spirit of cooperation is found in the churches of the Potomac Baptist Association. With the passing of the years, other missions and churches will be added.

Nanjemoy Baptist Church

Nanjemoy Baptist Church, located in the western section of Charles County, is one of the oldest continuous Baptist churches in Maryland. Its history is unique in that it is the mother of Charles County Baptist churches. As early as 1790 four men from Virginia crossed the Potomac and started to preach the gospel in the Nanjemoy area of Charles County. These men, William Fristoe, Jeremiah Moore, Andrew Leach, and Henry Hagen, were often personally insulted and abused. Hagen was once dragged into the Potomac River and held under until he almost drowned. On raising him, his persecutors asked him if he "believed," for the Scriptures say none but believers should be baptized. Nearly exhausted, Hagen replied, "I believe that you intend to drown me." The opposition called attention to the preaching: the congregations increased, and many who heard the word did "believe" and were baptized.

On Dec. 15, 1791, Thomas Perry sold one acre of land, part of a tract called "Morris Discovery" in Durham Parish, to George Dunnington, Trustee for the Baptist Church in Nanjemoy. The cost of the land was three shillings, and it was to be used only for the Baptist church.

In 1793 the Nanjemoy Baptist Church was organized; it then became a part of the Ketoctin Association in Virginia For many years after its organization the church had no settled pastor. Ministers visited whenever they could. The Ketoctin Association held its yearly meeting at Nanjemoy Meeting house in 1796. At this time Nanjemoy had 57 members, and George Dunnington and William Carpenter were messengers to the Association. William Perry was a messenger in 1797, and John Fitzgerald and John Carpenter in 1799. From 1802 to 1809 there were 50 members. No report was made to the Association in 1810. It seems that due to irregular preaching, deaths, and other causes, the church's membership was greatly reduced; the report in 1811 showed a membership of 28. However, after this low point there was a renewed interest. In 1814, 19 people were baptized, and at the 1817 meeting William Sedwick (probably Sedgwick) and Walter Dunnington, the messengers, reported 82 members. After 1818 Nanjemoy withdrew from the Ketoctin Association and joined the Columbia Association.

Nothing is known of the progress of the Nanjemoy church until 1833 when Rev. Thomas Conduit of Virginia came to Nanjemoy to preach. Through his leadership much progress was made. There was a widespread revival and many were added to the membership. The meeting house was repaired and enlarged, crowds attended the services, and the morality of the entire neighborhood was greatly improved.

Rev. Conduit also served as pastor of the Good Hope Baptist Church at Newburg, which he and the Rev. Samuel L. Straughan had helped organize in 1832. Until 1954 the Nanjemoy pastor preached at Good Hope once each month. Good Hope Church had a large congregation until the Civil War, when most of its male members died. Through the years a faithful few kept the church going. On April 1, 1954, Rev. G.D. Renegar preached the funeral service for one of the members. Only two members remained, and the church was closed. Today only the ruins of the building remain.

The happy days for Nanjemoy were shortlived. Soon after the revival in 1833, Rev. Conduit and several prominent families in the church moved to Alabama, and again the church was without a pastor. However, prayer meetings were kept up, and the first Sunday School was established. Rev. Conduit returned as pastor in about a year, but he soon died, and in 1835 Rev. William Isham Chiles was engaged to preach at Nanjemoy and Good Hope.

In 1836 the Maryland Baptist Union Association (now the Baptist Convention of Maryland) was formed with six churches as founding members Nanjemoy was the first church to join this new association after its 1837 formation.

During the years 1835-59, while Rev. Chiles was pastor, the church was blessed with several revivals and many were added by baptism. There were 35 baptisms in 1837, but only four in 1838. By 1840 these churches had a total of 246 members. Between 30 and 40 persons were baptized in 1856, and in 1858, 20. Rev. Chiles was forced to resign in 1859 because of his failing health.

Rev. I.F. Stidham of Baltimore was invited to become pastor of Nanjemoy in December 1859. He remained during a part of the troubled times of the Civil War. With a depot of military stores on the Virginia side of the Potomac and an encampment of troops on the Maryland side, the minds of the people were in such a state that church services were of little use. Rev. Stidham left in 1863 and was succeeded by Rev. John Bray in August 1864. A few were baptized but because of the war the church had fewer members than it had had for several years. Rev. Bray left in October 1865.

In November 1866 Rev. Chiles, who had been the pastor from 1835-39, was again called to the pastorate.

Business meetings were held about once a year; little was recorded in the minutes. However, the minutes of November 1868 show the appointment of a committee to superintend the rebuilding of the church. It consisted of R. Price, Thomas Wright, and W.P. Flowers.

Rev. Chiles remained pastor until his death in April 1874. For 37 years he had preached in Nanjemoy and had baptized about 400 persons. Many of these were Negroes, who later organized their own church.

Rev. Samuel Saunders was called as pastor in January 1875. He was a faithful and earnest man, deeply loved by the people. In 1876 he resigned to accept a call to an Eastern Shore church, but as the Nanjemoy congregation earnestly and persistently urged him to remain, he did. The large attendance and warm attachment of the people cheered him to do great things for the Lord. During the years 1875 to 1878 the church was greatly revived, and many people were baptized. Despite the fact that some people had to walk three or four miles over bad roads, the Sunday School and prayer meetings were well attended. The people had little money to give. In 1877, $36.86 was received from weekly collections. The pastor was considered a missionary, and part of his salary was paid by the Association.

Rev. Saunders resigned in 1878 and during 1879 and 1880 the church was without a pastor. The pulpit was supplied most of the time, but without a pastor the church did not enjoy a large measure of prosperity. Rev. A. J. Ashburn of Washington, D.C., was pastor from June 1881 until sometime in 1882, when he left to resume his studies at the seminary. There were 30 conversions during his stay, and a total membership of 149 members. A.J. Graves was Sunday School superintendent in 1881 and S.C. Mills in 1882.

From 1883 to 1884, Rev. G.V. Board was pastor. During the winter bad roads and stormy weather interrupted and injured the meetings, but the congregation remained large and the spiritual condition was good. There was a particularly large number of young people.

Rev. E.C. Allard served as pastor for a part of the year 1886, and Rev. T.A. Reid was appointed in June 1886. Dr. John F. Price, the local doctor, was superintendent of the Sunday School.

There were two mission stations under the leadership of Rev. Reid, one in lower Nanjemoy and another in Hilltop. Rev. Reid preached on alternate Sundays at each mission.

Many were added to membership during Rev. Reid's stay. He resigned in October 1890, and again the church was without a pastor for a year. In 1890 J.L. Davis was Sunday School superintendent.

In September 1891 Rev. L.W. Newman took charge, assisted by Brother Owens of King George, Va. The church reported in 1892 that it was without a pastor and badly needed one.

A great increase in interest was reported in 1893 when Rev. J.R. Thomas became pastor. There was a revival meeting when 23 were baptized. At this time Nanjemoy was the only white Baptist church in Charles County.

Rev. Thomas was pastor from 1893 to 1900, and gratifying progress was made at Nanjemoy. There were 222 members. The mission stations were flourishing. A new mission was started at Dentsville with an average congregation of 45, and at Port Tobacco with an average congregation of 65. Rev. Thomas preached at the County jail once a month.

When Rev. Thomas resigned in April 1900, Nanjemoy was without a pastor until Rev. Lewis Jones came in 1901. C.M. Phillips was Sunday School superintendent at that time.

A few were added to the membership from 1901 to 1903 when Rev. Jones was pastor. The missions continued to grow. John M. Scott was Sunday School superintendent. Rev. J.M. Thomas became pastor in 1904. In 1905 the church reported that it had been gloriously revived—30 were converted. The envelope system was introduced that year, and the church building restored. There were 243 members. C.M. Phillips was superintendent of the 113-member Sunday School.

Progress continued under Rev. Thomas' leadership. There was a great interest in missions. He reported in 1908 that the work was too large for one minister. When Rev. Thomas left in June 1911, the church was in good condition financially and spiritually.

The church was pastored by Rev. J.J. Cain from November 1912 to September 1915. Evidently his congregation loved him because according to the church records a horse and buggy were purchased for him in 1912. The records also indicate that 23 people were baptized, and Walter Mills was superintendent of the Sunday School.

During this time some Nanjemoy members who lived in Marbury were thinking of a local church. They started holding services in a private home; later a building was erected with the help of the Maryland Extension Society and lcoal contributions.

Rev. L.B. Kirby was pastor at Nanjemoy from December 1915 to November 1916. He baptized 11 and reported a great increase in gifts for missions. From November 1916 to May 1917, the church was without a pastor. Then Rev. Hugh P. Vinson was named. The report to the Association stated:

"The work has suffered during the pastorless period, but the prospects are bright." Rev. Vinson left in December 1918.

The church was without a pastor until February 1920, when Rev. Lewis Jones became pastor. He stayed a short time, as did his successor, Rev. O.D. Ramey, who came in 1922. In August 1923 when Rev. T.L. Scruggs became pastor, the church moved forward rapidly and continued to grow under his leadership until his resignation in September 1928. Many improvements were made: a lighting system was installed and stained-glass windows put in. The windows were purchased by individuals or families in memory of loved ones at a cost of $20 per window. (According to the men who recently repaired the windows, they are now valued at $350 to $400 each.) A 75-foot steeple was built with a 40-inch, 1500-pound alloy steel bell, which cost $150.

There were 43 people baptized in 1923 and 46 in 1924. The Sunday School grew from 150 in 1923 to 233 in 1924. The pastor was presented with a new Chevrolet car in 1925. In 1927 the church hall was rebuilt and an addition built onto the Parsonage. The five years of Rev. Scrugg's pastorate were an era of prosperity.

In April 1928 the mission at lower Nanjemoy (now Maryland Point) was burned. According to Maryland Baptist Union minutes this mission was influential in that area. After the building burned, services were held occasionally in the yard. In 1941 Rev. Nanney, with the help of some of the men, rebuilt the mission. Service was held each Sunday afternoon and later on Wednesday night until 1958. It was then closed because only those already attending Nanjemoy were attending there.

Rev. Hostetter was pastor of Nanjemoy from October 1928 until July 1929, when, still a young man, he died. Rev. Lewis Jones and Rev. W.R. Vaiden ministered from that time to September 1930.

Rev. Frank E. Clarke became pastor in October 1930. The church reported in 1931 that members enjoyed warm spiritual fellowship, marked growth, and increased interest. They hoped to begin badly needed Sunday School rooms. That year

23 were baptized and Earl Wright was Sunday School superintendent.

The 1932 report was not so bright: "We must face facts squarely and acknowledge the fact that the depression has hit us." Funds were low; however, the church spent a large sum improving the grounds.

The next few years were hard ones. But, according to the minutes, "We have much to be thankful for because we have new members who have put life into the old ones." The spiritual condition was much better than the financial one. In October 1935 funds were low, but the church voted to build the badly needed Sunday School rooms.

On July 4, 1936, Rev. Clarke stated he felt his work with the Nanjemoy church was finished, and he resigned. Attendance had decreased and the church was in debt when Rev. L.P. Barnette became pastor on Dec. 13, 1936. Although he stayed only 19 months, it was a time of prosperity. The church was blessed materially and spiritually. Electricity was installed in the church and parsonage; and, in July 1938 work finally began on the Sunday School rooms.

The years from February 1939 to March 1947 proved greatly successful under the leadership of Rev. C.C. Nanney. The Sunday School rooms were completed and paid for in 1939. In 1941 the first Vacation Bible School was held. The Association report for 1942 states, "We have gone beyond our goal in the Co-operative Program. Our revival, however, was not well attended because of the gasoline shortage and defense work." The church celebrated its 150th anniversary in 1943, and in 1944 the church was remodeled inside and out. Two new Sunday School rooms and an office were added. Theodore G. Davis Sr. was Sunday School superintendent from 1941 to 1946. In 1946 Louis Skinner succeeded him and served until 1960.

The church continued to grow under the leadership of Rev. W.E. Abrams, who became the pastor in April 1947. Many were converted in the revival in July 1948, which was conducted by Dr. Roy Gresham, then pastor of Middle River Baptist Church. New pulpit furniture was purchased before Rev. Abrams moved to another field in February 1950.

Rev. George D. Renegar was pastor from July 1950 to October 1956. The years of prosperity continued and many improvements were made to the church. In 1952 the walls were repainted and the floors refinished before new pews and a carpet were installed. An electric Hammond organ was purchased, and the following year a central heating system was installed.

After Rev. Renegar had left, a committee was appointed to prepare the parsonage for a new pastor's family. Repairs needed were so extensive that plans were made to build a new parsonage.

The history of Nanjemoy church would not be complete without the mention of Dr. F. Paul Langhorne of Colonial Beach, Va., who was the faithful supply pastor from October 1956 to April 1957. On May 1, 1957, Rev. Buford C. Sellers of Mississippi became pastor. The parsonage was completed in 1958. Also the church adopted the first unified budget and started to make plans for an educational building. This building was dedicated March 26, 1961. In 1963 a baptistry was installed. Rev. Sellers, a pastor loved by the community as well as his church members, resigned in June 1963 to resume his studies.

The church was not without a pastor very long. In August 1963 Rev. C.D. Canady, also from Mississippi, became pastor. On Oct. 28, 1963, the seven-month-old Potomac Baptist Association held its first annual meeting at Nanjemoy. The church constitution was rewritten; the system of rotating deacons was adopted in 1964.

Rev. Canady resigned in September 1966. The pulpit was supplied by Rev. Paul E. Hendricks through December.

Rev. Marvin Whisnant became pastor Jan. 1, 1967, and progress continued under his leadership, which lasted until July 1971, when he resigned to become pastor of the David Baptist Church, Kings Mountain, N.C. In August 1971 Rev. Conrad Burch began serving as pastor. He continued until August 1972 when he moved to Baltimore to serve as pastor of the Antioch Baptist Chapel.

The present pastor is Rev. C.S. Hendon, who has served since June 1973.

Pleasant Grove Baptist Church

This church was organized in August 1907 by Mrs. Addie Thomas, who had received early training in Christian principles at Mt. Hope Baptist Church. Her strong faith encouraged the aid of others—including the Rev. R.B. Ward, who often preached services held at Mrs. Thomas' home, Daniel Thomas, Luther Hemsley, and the Rev. Dickson. Eventually services were so well attended that Mrs. Thomas' home would no longer serve, and she convinced Thomas Simmons to donate the land needed to erect a church.

Early parishioners like to tell how the church was named. It seems that Rev. Ward askes Sis. Thomas what name she planned, and she answered, "Greater Grove." The Reverend shook his head, smiling. "You are always smiling so pleasantly," he told her, "why not call it 'Pleasant Grove'?"

The land in the grove was filled with trees and stumps, but these were small obstacles. Each day Sis. Thomas would go down to the grove with her family to dig up the trees and burn brush. A neighbor, Charlie Simpson, stopped every evening on his way home from work to help. In two weeks a quarter of an acre of land had been cleared and the stumpholes filled. Sister Thomas herself built a platform for the preacher and made 25 long benches to seat the congregation. Then she placed three chairs from her house on the platform, brought out the family Bible, and put bushes over the pulpit for shade.

Under the leadership of Rev. Ward, Pleasant Grove became a building by July 1910. Some of the first deacons of Pleasant Grove were: deacons Henry Hemsley, Harrison Mills, John Ball, and John Coleman. Others working with Rev. Ward were Rev. Skipworth and Rev. Jones.

The Sunday School was organized July 22, 1912, by Rev. Ward and Sis. Josephine Henson, Superintendent, Sis. Addie Thomas, Bro. John Coleman, Sis. Nell Henson, and Sis. Minnie Thomas Brooks.

Rev. R.B. Ward served well at Pleasant Grove, and even after he was disabled he continued to attend services and Sunday School until his death. The next pastor of Pleasant

Grove was Rev. G.E. Carter, who served seven years. During his pastorate membership increased, the missionaries and Deaconess Clubs were organized, and the spiritual fire burned.

After Rev. Carter's resignation in 1925, Rev. William Clark was asked to serve as supply pastor until he was ordained the second Sunday in May, 1930. After his ordination, he became full-time pastor of the Pleasant Grove Baptist Church. The church was remodeled and electric lights were installed. Some of the deacons under Rev. Clark were Deacons Eddie King, Samuel Thomas, Arthur Monroe, Robert T. Harris, Robert Hemsley, John Brooks, James Clark, and Frank Thomas. Rev. Clark worked conscientiously until his death in May 1942.

In 1943 Rev. James E. Dews who had served as assistant pastor under Rev. Clark became pastor, and served until his death in April 1953. During Rev. Dews' pastorate the church progressed spiritually. His Christ-like spirit of humility and service will always live in the hearts of the members and friends of Pleasant Grove Baptist Church.

A few months after the death of Rev. Dews, Rev. W. A. Ball was called as supply pastor of Pleasant Grove. He was appointed as pastor of Pleasant Grove in January 1954. He worked conscientiously and was happy to learn that the church had been established on a firm foundation. The pastor who had preceded him had not worked in vain. He sponsored many spiritual programs. He organized a men's club, new members' club, and pastor aid club. He also added improvements to the church. After Rev. William A. Ball's resignation in 1971, Rev. Avra E. Jones was appointed April 1972 as Pastor of Pleasant Grove Baptist Church. Rev. Jones has worked hard during the years he has served in this capacity. He has tried to give every officer and member a chance to make contributions to the church. He urges his members to attend church with their families, and he has sponsored many successful programs for spiritual growth. He has renovated the church, purchased a bus, organized a Jr. Deacon and Trustee Board, organized a male chorus, flower club, pastor aid club, Prayer Band, increased the Trustee Board, and cleared space for the new cemetery. Sept. 8, 1973, saw a ground-breaking service for the new church.

During Rev. Jones' pastorate, membership has increased, church services were broadcasted on radio, and work was begun on the new Pleasant Grove Baptist Church (The Way of Jesus), under a building committee chaired by Deacon Earl King. The church is being built by church members, who hope to finish it by the end of 1976, so they may continue their work and service in the new building.

Marbury Baptist Church

On June 14, 1915, nine members of the Nanjemoy Baptist Church were granted a letter of dismission enabling them to organize a new Baptist Church at Marbury. Two days later they met in their new building and organized themselves into a church. The land and the timber had been donated, and the building already erected.

The first years were difficult, but "a strong Christian fellowship developed." The pastors' salaries were meager and other hardships were common.

But, according to members, the highlights of their church are not the buildings, or even the members, but "those times the church has reached out in love to begin Christian work in other neighborhoods." Among these are the Lexington Park, La Plata, and Welcome Baptist churches, and the White Plains Baptist Chapel.

Interesting sidelights of Marbury include the first baptism service held in the Potomac River, at Glymont Wharf. Marbury has often shared its pastor with other nearby Baptist churches. And many members worked with the Nanjemoy Baptist Church fellowship to carry the word of God to German prisoners of war at Smith Point during World War II. The era of kerosene lamps ended at the church May 15, 1935, when electricity was turned on for the first time.

The goal of the church is to "sensitively minister and be actively involved in the spreading of the Good News through personal relationships and establishing Mission work."

Indian Head Baptist Church

In 1918 and 1919 the few Baptists living at Indian Head attended Methodist services, held in the Masonic Hall. It was due to the efforts of Walter Thomas, son of a Baptist preacher and principal of Lackey High School, that the Indian Head Baptist Church was organized in the fall of 1919 with 15 members.

Thomas traded his two lots for the small Episcopal Church owned by St. James Rectory. He then donated the property and improvements to the Baptist people of Indian Head.

With 15 members, the Indian Head Baptist Church was organized in the fall of 1919, and Walter Allen was called as the first pastor. The first revival service was conducted by Rev. Farley of Philadelphia. Pastor Allen resigned in October 1920 when there were 60 members, and Mrs. Edmund Perry was the clerk of the church.

The church then called as the pastor the Rev. W.W. Westbroom. The church was blessed and continued to grow under his leadership. It was decided to enlarge the church during his ministry. This was done through gifts, donated labor, and contributions from members and friends of the church. A committee was appointed to call on Dr. Baylor, the General Secretary of the Maryland Baptist Union Association, to ask for a donation to assist the program.

In 1921 Rev. Westbroom resigned as pastor and the church called T.O. Jones, a Welshman, to be the pastor in October 1921. Jones was well liked by all the congregation and said to be a splendid worker with the adults and young people. He resigned in 1924 to accept a church in Washington, leaving a small congregation. The church again asked the Baptist board for assistance, and on Dec. 1, 1924, Dr. E. T. Carter, an Englishman, accepted the call as pastor. He resigned in November 1925, with the church owing him more than $200 in salary.

Low attendance and hard times had fallen on the Indian Head church, and it closed in 1925. In December 1927 J. W. Banks, Pastor at Marbury Baptist Church, offered to preach for nothing at Indian Head until a pastor could be called, and for many years the churches shared a pastor.

In December 1941 the church called its first full-time pastor, the Rev. Lee Powell. Mrs. Julia Halla reports, "While Mr. Powell was with us we had several revivals, had additions to the church and everything seemed to awaken again. We bought new electric lights for the church and Mr. Powell installed them himself."

An outstanding thing happened during the second pastorate of the Rev. C.E. LeGates: the decision to erect a new church building by the members of the church. Church records show that:

> The Laying Corner Stone Service was held on November 24, 1946 by Rev. LeGates assisted by Rev. R.I. Berghauser and Mr. Harwood Bagby. Placed in the corner stone was the Holy Bible, membership roll, history of the church, annual report of 1946, and minutes of the Southern District Association.
>
> The Construction of the Church continued on with the fine spirit of the people and their determination to finish the work in spite of the difficulty of getting materials and high costs. Surely our hearts are filled with deep appreciation for the many who gave so much and so often for the building of our church. Finally we were able to have our first service in our new church on the third Sunday in June 1948.

The Rev. Zane Grey Ross was pastor of the church from 1950 to 1957. During this period the church moved out and started two missions, one at Potomac Heights and one at Bryan's Road. It also appointed a committee to draw up plans for an educational building. A new parsonage was purchased, and the entire indebtedness on the church building paid off. The need to provide a way to bring the people to church was met by the purchase of a bus.

The first Homecoming Day of the Indian Head Baptist Church was held Oct. 5, 1952. Five years later a call went out to the Rev. Parker Hooper to become pastor, and he served until August 1964. At the same time the church voted to purchase property for the future Bryan's Road Baptist Church. The Bryan's Road Mission was organized as Grace Baptist Church on Sept. 14, 1958.

At the July 1961 business meeting the church took action regarding the new Potomac Association, and applied for membership. Previously, the church was affiliated with the Southern District Association.

In a specially called business meeting on Feb. 14, 1965, the church extended a unanimous call to the Rev. Clarence P. Moore to become pastor. He accepted, with his ministry to begin March 21. He was pastor of the church at the time of its 50th anniversary observance, Nov. 30, 1969.

On Dec. 4, 1966, the members of the Indian Head Baptist Church came together for the service of dedication of the new educational building and renovation of the building that had been erected in 1946.

The Rev. Donald A. Batson was pastor from May 1971 until February 1975. The present pastor is the Rev. Robert A. Bridgeman, who began his service in September 1975. The church has grown under the leadership of these pastors and is exerting increasing influence in the life of the community.

First Baptist Church of Waldorf

The Waldorf area developed shortly after 1870 as a trading and shipping center for tobacco growers. As early as 1840 efforts were made to begin a church in this area by the Good Hope Baptist Church of Newburg. A local resident, Daniel Monroe, provided the preaching for these first worship services. Monroe was the first schoolteacher in the Waldorf area. It is believed that the first church site was on land once a part of the Monroe farm. The early worship services were held in Monroe's home every second Sunday, and the Good Hope congregation would come every three months to meet with those in the Monroe home.

The Civil War brought an end to these early efforts to establish a church. Many of the male members of the Good Hope congregation had been killed in the War, and the church was depleted of its leadership.

In 1899 a church was organized at Port Tobacco. Attempts were made by the Baptists of Waldorf to join in worship with this congregation, but distance and infrequency of services hindered progress.

Years later, in 1938, Rev. Thomas E. Boorde and a large group from the Anacostia Baptist Church met at the Waldorf home of A.E. Fletcher to pray for guidance as to whether a Baptist church should be formed, but no conclusion was reached. In 1941 Dr. Joseph T. Watts, Executive Secretary of Maryland Baptists, led a group from Baltimore to Waldorf for a meeting. The distance and summer heat prevented good attendance; and, once again, the plan to establish a church in Waldorf had no significant results.

Finally, the concerned Baptists of Waldorf were great enough in number for significant work to begin. A Sunday School was started in 1944. Fletcher was among the adult leaders of the Sunday School.

During this time the need for a church in Waldorf had come to the attention of Rev. C.E. LeGates of Indian Head Baptist Church. The First Baptist Church of Waldorf is the outgrowth of prayer meetings held by a small group of dedicated Christians under his leadership. A report by Miss Amy Fletcher on the first anniversary of the church states, "The prayers of the many Baptists interested in this work were answered, for here was our leader. No obstacle could seem to stop Brother LeGates once he got started."

On Sunday, Feb. 18, 1945, the first service of the Waldorf Baptist Sunday School was held in the old building on Rt. 5 known as Roby's Saloon (now The Friendly Tavern). Miss Fletcher's report speaks of this first meeting.

> Although it was a bitterly cold, wintry day, there were twenty-five people present. Everyone present felt encouraged. . . . Our place of worship, the old Roby's Saloon, was obtained for the sum of $20 per month. This, at first, seemed to be an enormous price for such an old dilapidated building, but later it proved to be a good investment after much cleaning, painting, and scrubbing put it in shape resembling a house of worship.

Another early account states that Roby's Saloon proved inadequate because rats, backless benches that had been used in a World War I prison, and the need to bring firewood from homes to heat the building worked a great hardship on the worshipers.

In spite of the hardships, these months in the first meeting place saw much progress. There was a choir, complete with organist and choir leader. There were regular business meetings, a Vacation Bible School, mission offerings, and a revival at which three souls were saved. A Teacher's Training Class was conducted, and there was a well attended Christmas program. The Sunday School also had an elected treasurer, a librarian, and other teachers and officers.

After several months Roby needed the meeting site for storage, and the worshipers found themselves with no building at all. The Piney Chapel Episcopal Church came to the aid of the Baptists, and the Sunday School found a new home in the Episcopal Church Hall, rent free. This enabled Waldorf Sunday School to put its former rent money into a building fund. The days in Old Roby's Saloon became history, and Miss Fletcher talks about the future of the site: "Our old place of worship was resold for another liquor establishment. We do hope and pray that the Lord will intervene."

In February 1946 construction started on the first building, which was to be known as Grier Hall after Mrs. Bessie J. Grier, a founder of the group. The Sunday School continued to grow until the members realized the need for the establishment of a full church program.

A meeting was called to consider constituting into a church. There were 15 members present. A petition was drawn up and submitted to the Indian Head Baptist Church, the sponsoring church of the Southern Baptist Convention, and on May 2, 1946, the Waldorf Baptist Sunday School became Waldorf Baptist Church, with 16 charter members. Rev. C.E. LeGates was called as the first pastor. On May 12, 1946, the congregation was accepted into the Southern District Association (now the Potomac Baptist Association).

Land was purchased on Rt. 5 down the street from Old Roby's Saloon, opposite the Calvary Methodist Church, and a building program was begun. The first floor, later the basement of the finished building, was constructed, and services were first held on April 14, 1946. Facilities were somewhat spartan at first, without central heating or restrooms. It was also necessary for the members to bring firewood and water. Baptismal services were held either in another Baptist church or in the Patuxent River.

From 1946 to 1951 the church had four pastors: Rev. C.E. LeGates, 1946-1947; Rev. Rip Rockie Hodson, 1948-1949; Rev. Homer Gatewood, 1949-1950; and Rev. Roy H. Martin, 1950-1951. On March 27, 1949, the Training Union was organized with 41 members present, and the Women's Missionary Union was organized May 3, 1949, with six charter members.

In April 1952 Rev. Joseph T. Greene accepted the call as pastor. During this time a parsonage was built and land purchased on Berry Road for a future church site. Under his leadership the membership increased steadily. After Rev. Greene resigned in 1958 the church called Rev. James Carter as pastor, and he ministered until April of 1960.

Rev. John Powell served the church from December 1960 to August 1961. During his ministry construction of the upper level of the building was completed. The added space provided a sanctuary seating approximately 250 worshipers and was completely furnished with pews, pulpit furniture, and a baptistry. These improvements fulfilled a long-sought goal for the church, which had been functioning 15 years in a basement. The lower area was remodeled and divided for Sunday School use.

On Dec. 3, 1961, Rev. Arthur M. Doepp came as pastor. The 1960s were marked by accelerated development of the Waldorf area, with many new residential subdivisions. The church also grew in number and in its witness to the community under Rev. Doepp's ministry.

A kindergarten program was introduced Sept. 9, 1963, with a single class for pre-school age children directed by Mrs. C.C. Masters. The first class had an enrollment of 27. The present director, Mrs. Jean Fowler, became kindergarten director in 1966. Today there are six classes and five teachers, with an enrollment of nearly 100 children.

The rapid growth in membership required additional space, and in the spring of 1967, there was a ground-breaking ceremony for the building of the present church on the corner of U.S. Rt. 301 and Berry Road. The cornerstone was laid in December 1967 and on April 7, 1968, the present church building was apparently dedicated "to God's glory"; it is the first of three units to be built on this site.

The witness of the First Baptist Church of Waldorf is identified by the 70-foot white steel tower with the church bulletin at its base. In December 1969 the tower was given by the Willingham family in honor of Sylvester Willingham. Many fundamentals of the Christian faith are symbolized in the tower's construction. The symbol of the Holy Trinity can be observed in the tripod holding up the tower which converges as one, One God in three persons, upholding the one world of His creation overshadowed by the cross of Calvary. Here the cross stands highest as the one redeeming power of the world. This tower, which can be clearly seen from the highway, has pointed many people to the ministry of the church. When the tower was dedicated, the following prayer was expressed: "May our church ever be the Spiritual Lighthouse at the crossroads of Charles County as represented in these symbols of the tower, built and dedicated to the glory of God."

Two mission churches were begun during Rev. Doepp's eight-year pastorate, one in St. Charles City and one in Prince Frederick. The St. Charles Church was formally constituted May 25, 1969, and the Emmanuel Baptist Church of Prince Frederick was constituted in 1973. In October 1969 Rev. Doepp resigned to accept a call to the North Gate Baptist Church in Silver Spring.

Upon the resignation of Rev. Doepp, Rev. William I. Barkley Sr., retired Superintendent of Missions of the Baptist Association of the Baltimore area, who was living in St. Charles City, was called as the interim pastor. Under his ministry the church continued to thrive and to grow spiritually.

In March 1970 the church celebrated its 25th Anniversary with many guests and former pastors attending.

During the six-month interim the Pulpit Committee was actively seeking a new pastor. Following the suggestion of the committee, Chairman Arnold Ivie interviewed several candidates who were approaching graduation at the Southwestern Baptist Theological Seminary in Fort Worth, Tex. Ivie taped these interviews for the committee to hear. The church voted unanimously to call Ronald Beams as pastor, and he began his ministry on the first Sunday in May.

During the first year of his ministry there were 190 additions to the church, including 112 baptisms, and in the words of one of the members, "We had a twelve-month revival." Many new ministries were added. Among these were a ministry to the correctional camp, a bus ministry, church retreats, a Sunday night radio ministry, a children's worship service, a tape ministry, a church library, and a painting of a river scene, provided for the wall of the baptistry. As attendance continued to climb, the sanctuary was enlarged and pews were added. Two double-wide trailers were obtained to provide Sunday School and office space. The first full-time secretary was employed, and the parsonage was converted into Sunday School rooms for the youth and has come to be known as "His Place."

The growing church felt the need for a full-time Minister of Music and Youth, and Keith Miller was called to this position. The youth ministry increased under Miller's leadership, and the youth enjoyed many activities, including trips to Ridgecrest Baptist Assembly and a mission ministry to Ohio. In the fall of 1973 Miller accepted the call to go to Colesville Baptist Church.

At this time the church made a study of its staff needs. This resulted in Ivie becoming the part-time Minister of Music and in the call of a full-time Minister of Education and Youth, J. William (Bill) Lackey, a recent graduate of Southwestern Baptist Theological Seminary. The church ordained Brother Bill to the ministry of education on Oct. 13, 1974. Also, Don Chandler was licensed to the gospel ministry and became the first part-time Associate Pastor of the church.

In May 1975, Pastor Beams resigned to accept a call to the Denman Avenue Baptist Church of Lufkin, Texas. On Nov. 2, 1975, the Rev. Marvin Simpson became the pastor of the Waldorf Church.

The history of the First Baptist Church of Waldorf would not be complete without a reference to the hundreds of God's people who have faithfully labored over the past 30 years. God has truly blessed and sent some of His choice servants to work alongside His pastors here.

Potomac Heights Baptist Church

The Potomac Heights Baptist Church serves a community of almost 500 homes in the Indian Head area. In has 272 resident members with a full complement of programs consisting of Sunday School (429 members), Church Training, Women's Missionary Union, morning and evening worship services, midweek prayer services, Bus Ministry (five buses), Children's Churches (for four age groups), Music Program (adult, youth, and children's choirs), and an active youth program.

The church began as a mission on April 25, 1954. It started because of a need for a special evangelistic effort for the Potomac Heights community. This need was sensed by the Indian Head Baptist Church, which sponsored the mission. The community is unique from the standpoint of its inception and development. It was built during World War II by the Federal Government to serve as housing for the military personnel stationed at the Naval Ordnance Station. After the war the Government sold the houses to civilians, who established their own internal governing organization, the Potomac Heights Mutual Homeowners Association.

The first "Meeting house" for the mission was the Child Care Building adjacent to the Community Center Building. This meeting place was rented from the community at $5 a month. Rev. Zane Grey Ross, pastor of the Indian Head Church during this period, preached the morning worship service at 9:30 a.m. and Sunday School followed at 11.

Rev. Hoyt Abrams was called to pastor the mission in October 1954. The first parsonage, 1 Fairmont Place, was purchased by the mission from the Homeowners Association for $900 in 1954.

By November 1955 a WMU and Intermediate and Junior Royal Ambassadors groups were organized. In addition, a building fund was started and plans for a church building were beginning to take shape.

Hoyt Abrams resigned as pastor Oct. 1, 1956. Six days later the mission was constituted a church in a special service. The new church had 70 charter members.

The church elected its first deacons in October 1956: T.H. Headley, F.O. Story, and H.D. Carter. They were ordained May 19, 1957.

The church called Rev. Dale Chapman as pastor on Feb. 2, 1957. It was during his ministry, which continued for two years, that the Church purchased land on which to build.

In October 1959 the parsonage at 1 Fairmont was sold and a new parsonage at 10 Glymont Road was purchased. In December the church called Rev. Coy R. Bates as pastor. He resigned in July 1963 after four years of fruitful ministry.

Rev. Donald L. Mentch was called as pastor on September 29, 1963, and during his ministry an active building program was generated. Construction of a church building began in the spring of 1965. The building was completed and dedicated in November 1965. Rev. Mentch resigned on June 1, 1969.

The church called Rev. Richard Markley as pastor the next June. During his ministry the church entered a bond program to provide financing for a new educational building. The church was growing rapidly, and additional space was desperately needed. The youth Sunday school classes had to meet in the Community Building some distance away from the church. The new building was started in January 1973, and Rev. Markley resigned that June.

Before the arrival of a new pastor, the church began a Bus Ministry for the purpose of reaching out into those areas where a need existed. Presently the church operates and maintains five buses. Also in 1973, the church completed and moved into the new building.

Rev. James Morse was called as pastor in September 1973. The church continued to grow during his tenure. A tape ministry, which became part of an overall Media Center, was started for shut-ins and others who wanted to hear taped messages. It was during this time that the Sunday School reached its highest attendance (371). Rev. Morse resigned on March 9, 1975.

Rev. Robert Hudgins was called as pastor in October 1975; he presently serves the Potomac Heights Church.

Grace Baptist Church, Bryan's Road

On April 11, 1957, Rev. Paul Bard, Area Missionary for the Southern District Association, seeking to start new church work in the Bryan's Road area, met with others for this purpose at a home in Bryan's Road. There were 12 people present.

One month later, on May 19, 1957, the first Sunday service of the newly formed mission was held in the Grange Hall at Pomonkey. Rev. Zane Grey Ross, Pastor of the sponsoring Indian Head Baptist Church, preached the sermon.

On July 24, 1957, the Bryan's Road Mission, as it was called, voted to purchase land on which to build a church. On September 14, 1958, the Bryan's Road Mission was constituted as the Grace Baptist Church of Bryan's Road. Soon after, in November, it called as first Pastor the Rev. Eugene Brotherton.

Grace Baptist broke ground for its present church building in January 1960, and in June of that same year held its first Worship Service in the newly constructed building.

In August 1971 preliminary plans for a new Sunday School addition were approved by the church. Dedication of the addition and of the carillon was held Jan. 7, 1973. Shortly thereafter the Church voted to establish a church kindergarten and day care center.

On Sept. 14, 1975, Grace Baptist celebrated its 17th anniversary.

First Baptist Church of La Plata

The First Baptist Church of La Plata was begun Feb. 21, 1960, as a Mission Church of the Marbury Baptist Church. The first services of the church were held on that date with Dr. Paul L. Bard, the Baptist Associational Missionary, serving as Pastor. Dr. Bard served the church as its Pastor until June of that year, and was followed by Rev. Austin C. Matthews, Pastor of the Marbury Church.

In 1961, under the leadership of Rev. Matthews, the mission purchased the building it still occupies on Hawthorne Drive. Evening worship services were led by James McKeown Sr., who served as Pastor from January 1961 to May 1963.

Rev. Arlie A. Watson, the new Pastor of the Marbury church conducted the services until Rev. Everett Hill was called to be La Plata's Pastor in June 1964.

On Feb. 20, 1966, at a Constitution Service, the La Plata Baptist Chapel was constituted as the First Baptist Church of La Plata. Membership had grown to almost 100. Rev. Hill served the church as Pastor until August 1966.

In December 1966 the church called its present Pastor, Rev. Ronald Shifflett. In 1967, under his leadership, the church added a multi-purpose room, to be used for Sunday School and social function.

Also in 1967 the church purchased some adjoining property to allow for the future building of a new sanctuary. A parking lot was added at the rear of the building.

In March 1968 the First Baptist Church of La Plata received a check for $817.63, the balance of a trust fund that was left by the Port Tobacco Church when it disbanded some 20 years earlier.

In November 1968 the church started a mission on Cobb Island. This work began with a Sunday School at the Fire Hall and later at the Community Hall. In April 1969, on Easter Sunday, the mission held its first worship service. The mission, known as Cobb Island Chapel, purchased a building on the island and is now permanently housed there.

The La Plata Baptist Church is currently in the midst of a building program that calls for a sanctuary with a seating capacity of 300.

First Baptist Church of Welcome

The First Baptist Church of Nanjemoy established a Baptist mission in the community of Welcome in 1944. The mission was first under the direction of Rev. C.C. Nanney, then Pastor at Nanjemoy.

Volunteer workers erected a one-room building on Gunston Road; it served as a sanctuary for 26 years. By 1968 a second room was added to the original structure, to be utilized for Sunday School and as a fellowship hall. The land for the building was leased from Carroll Wedding.

By 1947 the Nanjemoy Baptist Church had established a second mission, and because of this transferred the responsibility for leadership of the Welcome Baptist Mission to the First Baptist Church of Marbury. For two years following this shift of leadership, Rev. Charles R. Pierce, Pastor at Marbury, conducted worship services at Welcome each Sunday afternoon.

Regular Sunday morning worship services began when a layman, Franklin H. Harris accepted the mission pastorate in 1949. Pastor Harris served until February 1953; he was the first of several laymen to pastor the work. Others were Stephen J. Puryear, Homer Gatewood, James McKeown Sr., Leon F. York, Paul E. Hendricks. Rev. Frederick Bastian served the mission from October 1955 to September 1966.

Rev. William L. Bort Sr. accepted the Welcome Baptist Mission pastorate on Oct. 6, 1966, and remained with the work until December 1973. During his tenure the mission grew in membership, became self-supporting, and was constituted into a church on Aug. 24, 1969.

The First Baptist Church of Welcome continued to grow and with the assistance of gifts from Wilson Golden and the Marbury Baptist Church, purchased five acres of land for a new church building, located nine miles from La Plata.

The First Baptist Church of Welcome continues to prosper. Six deacons and two pastors have been ordained there. The first was George Leon Bateman, who pastored the church from Oct. 1, 974, until Sept. 1, 1975, when he resigned to continue his education. Upon Rev. Bateman's resignation, Donald R. Chandler accepted the call of the church and is presently serving as its pastor. A special service was held at the church Feb. 29, 1976, to ordain Rev. Chandler into the Gospel Ministry.

The First Baptist Church of Welcome has a resident and non-resident membership of 132 members.

First Baptist Church of St. Charles

The First Baptist Church of St. Charles is the outgrowth of a mission established by the First Baptist Church of Waldorf. The mission began holding services Oct. 5, 1968, in the Samuel A. Mudd Elementary School in St. Charles, with William I. Barkley Jr., Pastor. Because of the size of the community and the number of people involved in the founding of the mission, the mission was almost immediately able to support itself financially and was granted financial independence from the Mother Church in April 1969.

The church was constituted on May 25, 1969; it called Gleaton F. Rickenbaker Jr. as Pastor.

A committee was soon established to plan for a new building. The building was occupied by the congregation on Sept. 5, 1971. It is the first part of a proposed three-stage building program, and contains a Sanctuary and classrooms.

It was evident from the beginning that the building was not large enough to adequately carry out the educational program for the anticipated growth in membership. This limitation and the fact that the rate of development in the community has been slower than expected has affected the growth rate of the church. However, a steady growth has been maintained throughout the short history of the church, the membership having grown from 109 in October 1969 to 289 people five years later.

Hughesville Baptist Church

In November 1969 the Nanjemoy Baptist Church wrote the Potomac Baptist Association Superintendent of Missions expressing a desire to start a mission. The Association suggested that the mission be started at Hughesville.

The first fellowship meeting was held Tuesday, May 26, 1970, at the home of Mr. and Mrs. C. H. Carpenter of Sandy Level Estates, Hughesville. Nine people were present. Plans were discussed and it was agreed to ask Nanjemoy Baptist Church to sponsor the Hughesville work, with assistance from the First Baptist Church of Waldorf.

Rev. Marvin Whisnant, Pastor of Nanjemoy, conducted the fellowship meetings. They continued until the chapel opened for Sunday services, Sept. 13, 1970, in the T. C. Martin Elementary School, Bryantown, with morning worship and Bible study. Leading in the services was Rev. Marvin Whisnant, with greetings from Rev. William I. Barkley Jr., Superintendent of Missions, and Rev. Ronald Beams, pastor of Waldorf Baptist Church. The original members were: the Carpenters, Mr. and Mrs. Bob Smith, Mr. and Mrs. Marshall McLean and Tim McLean, Claud Bates, Mrs. Louise Morse, and Vickie Long.

On Nov. 1, 1970, Rev. William Barkley Jr. began serving as interim Pastor of the new mission, in a new location at the Charlotte Hall Military Academy Chapel. The Rev. William Barkley Sr. assisted by conducting many of the evening worship services.

In April 1971 a survey was made of an eight-acre tract in Hughesville; it was then authorized by the Mother Church for purchase for the future building site.

On Jan. 7, 1973, the chapel welcomed its new Pastor, Rev. Thomas W. Daigle and his wife, Marlene, and children LeAnne and Bryan, from the pastorate of the Bedford Road Baptist Church, Cumberland. Installation services for the new Pastor were held March 25, 1973.

The new church building was constructed within one week beginning July 16, 1973, by a group of Southern Baptists, the "Builders for Christ." They came, 110 of them, from Louisiana, Texas, Pennsylvania, New Jersey, and Oklahoma, to share in the crash program. Each day 20 or more local Baptists joined to help their new friends. The logs were donated by Jim Watkins of Wolfe Creek Industries of Colorado and hauled to the Hughesville site by the Navajo Trucking Company. The group consisted mainly of whole families, many of whom came in campers. The largest group was from Tioga Baptist Church of Louisiana, which supplied 38 people plus $750 cash for the project. This building movement had begun in 1963 when George Carkeet, pastor at Greenwood, La., wanted a church mission project outside his community.

The first services were held in the new building Oct. 27, 1974, with the building almost completed by many loyal friends and members of the Hughesville Chapel. The dedication service was held on Sunday, Nov. 10, 1974, as Dr. Roy Gresham delivered the message.

An evangelistic crusade took place in early February 1975 with Rev. Charles Barnes preaching, and the first ordination of deacons was held April 6, with Brothers Eddie Neill and Joe Wilkerson being ordained. As of May 1975 there were 154 members on the church rolls.

Cobb Island Baptist Chapel

The Cobb Island Baptist Chapel was started because of a mother's desire for a Sunday School for her children. The

First Baptist Church of La Plata conducted a survey on the island in the spring of 1968 and held a Vacation Bible School in the summer. The response to these efforts was so favorable that a Sunday School was established in the Cobb Island Fire Hall on Nov. 10, 1968. For the first Sunday School, there were 26 people present. The Rev. Ronald F. Shifflett, Pastor of the First Baptist Church of La Plata, taught the adult class and volunteers from the church taught other age groups. Pastor Shifflett returned to La Plata each Sunday in time for morning worship at the First Baptist Church.

Soon the Sunday School was moved to the Community Building. On Easter Sunday, April 6, 1969, morning worship was begun, for 32 people. A different minister preached each Sunday. In August 1969, C. W. Britt was called to become the first regular pastor of the chapel.

After Pastor Britt's resignation, Rev. William I. Barkley Sr. came as interim Pastor. During his ministry at the chapel the congregation voted to purchase a dwelling on S. Wicomico Street for use as a chapel building.

Paul Hair began serving as Pastor in April 1971. Other pastors who served following his tenure were Harl Cockrum and Steve Neel. The chapel still is sponsored by the First Baptist Church of La Plata. Mr. Shifflett leads a Bible study on the island each Tuesday morning. The chapel congregation is in the process of securing a regular pastor.

White Plains Baptist Chapel

The White Plains Baptist Chapel was organized Oct. 5, 1975, under the sponsorship of the Marbury Baptist Church. Backyard Bible Clubs and home Bible study fellowships had been conducted for several years in preparation for this work. The chapel meets temporarily in the James Craik Elementary School on Marshall's Corner Road, adjacent to the Charles County Vocational-Technical Center in Pomfret. The chapel is seeking property in the White Plains area.

The Rev. William I. Barkley Jr., Director of Missions of the Potomac Baptist Association, is Pastor of the chapel.

Rev. Barkley's responsibilities with the Association are to coordinate the cooperative efforts of churches in Calvert, Charles, and St. Mary's counties, and to establish new churches in the tri-county area.

Methodist Churches

Records of early Methodism in Southern Maryland are almost nonexistent. But the increasing number of evangelist horseback (or buggy) Methodist parsons made more or less regular trips into Southern Maryland counties from 1785 to well into the 19th century. These early itinerant apostles traveled not from church to church or over an assigned circuit in the earliest years, but rather from house to house or from tent to tent. These were the early days of under-canvas revival meetings with intensive sessions of exhortation—of one-to-two-week long bursts of highly emotional evangelistic effort, whenever and wherever the time and place seemed right. And from these tents and homes the converts, inspired, reborn, by the days of exhortation and spiritual re-creation, returned to their homes and kindled and nurtured the flame for Methodism until there arose in certain communities organized Methodist groups called societies.

Life for a Charles County circuit rider was undoubtedly hard, and often discouraging. The number of Charges and the extremely difficult routes between, general communication problems and straggling infant societies must have taxed the physical and spiritual strength of many an itinerant pastor, and worn threadbare many a pair of trousers. Church records indicate that Methodist ministers in this circuit labored for nearly half a century without a suitable parsonage. The Rev. S.N. Tucker, preacher in charge of this circuit in 1889, complained for the record, "There is no parsonage within the bounds of the work, La Platta being in the St. Mary's Circuit, eleven miles from the nearest Church and eight miles from the nearest member, your Preacher refuses to occupy it." Even the new parsonage at La Plata did not answer all the needs because of the size of the circuit.

Shiloh United Methodist Church

In 1835 a log building, "Halley's Meeting House," was erected for worship. Preacher Richard Halley and his friends decided to replace it with a frame structure in 1881, and Shiloh Church came into being. The building stood on Halley's land, and Halley led services frequently until his health failed.

Originally named Shiloh Methodist Episcopal Church, the name was changed in 1939 to Shiloh Methodist Church, and is now known as Shiloh United Methodist Church. It was at first one of seven churches on the original La Plata Charge, but became independent in 1945 when the Charge was divided by the Conference.

Many direct descendants of the Halley family were active in the work of the Church. Mrs. Estelle Halley Shives, the eldest surviving descendant of the family, and now more than 80 years old, is still an active member of Shiloh Church.

Pastors who served Shiloh include: T.G. Nevitt and his son, Robert, D.M. Brown, H.P. Baker, I. Rider, A.B. Sapp, C.M. Sarver, J.W. Beall, H.I. Burr, J.E. McDonald, C.H. Shaw, C.M. LeFew, H.H. Hoyt, and D.L.C. Wright.

In June 1951 William Balderson, a Westminster Theological Seminary student, was appointed Pastor of Shiloh Church. During the next year a planning committee was formed to discuss the foundations of a Mission Church in Accokeek, and in 1953 the Conference granted permission for its construction, with Rev. Balderson to continue as Pastor of Shiloh and also of the new Mission Church.

The first service was held at the Faith Methodist Church in Accokeek in January 1954, and the formation of the Shiloh-Faith Charge was formally approved and accomplished by the Conference.

Shortly thereafter the Board of Shiloh, still under the pastorate of Rev. Balderson, discussed the construction of a new Sanctuary. With the approval of the Conference, approximately six acres of land on Rt. 210 in Bryan's Road was acquired from Mr. and Mrs. Camillus Murphy. With the property paid for in May 1960, plans were made for the construction of a Sanctuary. Rev. Ramon Reno served as Pastor from 1958 to 1960.

In 1963 with John Pappas, a Wesley Seminary student, as Pastor, the present Shiloh Church was completed. The first service was held in the new church in December 1963.

Others who held pastorates at Shiloh were: Rev. James Allman, 1964-1965, Rev. Everett Waldo, 1965-1966, and Rev. Henry Swain, 1966-1968.

With the growth of the Faith-Shiloh Charge during this period, discussion began as to separation of the two churches. In June 1968 official separation was accomplished, with Rev. C. Earle Cowden as Pastor of Shiloh, now a station church.

During his pastorate, discussion began on the formation of a charge that would include Shiloh Church and Metropolitan Church, the latter a black member church located about a mile from Shiloh, in Pomonkey.

Succeeding Rev. Cowden as pastor was Rev. Domingo Co, appointed in 1969. The formation of the Shiloh-Metropolitan Charge was still being discussed.

In 1970 the Bryan's Road-Pomonkey Charge was officially formed by the Conference, with Shiloh and Metropolitan on this charge. Rev. Edwin Williams, pastor of Metropolitan, was named Pastor of the Charge. The first worship service at Shiloh, under the pastorate of Rev. Williams, was held in October 1970.

Rev. Williams, the first black pastor of Shiloh, served as minister until May 1973. Then at the Methodist Annual Conference in May 1973, the Bryan's Road-Pomonkey Charge was dissolved by Conference action, and Shiloh was once again a station church.

Rev. Edward S. Munney, Ordained Elder, residing in Accokeek, was appointed part time Supply Lay Pastor of Shiloh. He conducted his first worship service on May, 27, 1973. Rev. David Davis, Chaplain at St. Elizabeth's Hospital in Washington, D.C., residing in Accokeek, was appointed to serve Holy Communion at Shiloh.

Chicamuxen United Methodist Church

In 1835 the people of the little community of Chicamuxen felt the need for a church. Land was given and new lumber purchased for the first Northern Methodist Church of Chicamuxen. The church was built near the county road that ran parallel to the Mattawoman Creek. During the Civil War, Union Gen. Joseph Hooker used the church as his headquarters.

In 1904 the congregation wanted to build a larger new church but by this time it had established itself as Southern Methodist, and would not build a new church on the original Northern Methodist land. So a new parcel of land was given joining the old land. By 1905 the Southern Methodist Church of Chicamuxen was completed.

As years passed the dirt county road was replaced by a state road, Rt. 224. This placed the church a couple of hundred feet away from the state road and facing in the wrong direction. In 1933 the church moved to its present site, and became known as the Chicamuxen United Methodist Church.

Pisgah United Methodist Church

Recorded in the Land Records of Charles County is an Indenture made Feb. 16, 1850: a Mrs. Mary Milstead sold to the church "for and in Consideration of the sum of two dollars current money. . ." one and one-half acres on the "main road that leads from Port Tobacco to Counter Mills." The purpose of buying the land, according to the Indenture was a directive for the trustees to "erect and build, or caused to be erected and built thereon, a house or place or worship for the use of the Methodist Episcopal Church in the United States of America."

Pisgah Church's first years were on the Charles Circuit, Potomac District, as a Methodist Episcopal Church of the Baltimore Conference. No record has been found to describe the first building, but some members recall that it was small, had a gallery, and was torn down when the present church building was erected.

In 1872 the church was put on the Charles-St. Mary's Circuit, and during the 1880s a new church building was erected in Pisgah. This building was begun in 1886 under the leadership of a second group of trustees. In 1886 the Board of Church Extension donated $125 toward the Building Fund, and Pisgah became a "mission church."

The new building was dedicated on Sunday, Jan. 19, 1890. The *Episcopal Methodist* said that the idea to build this new church "was conceived as an appropriate monument to a devoted Christian man, who had long communed at the altar of the old church, and whose remains lie in its graveyard, Wm. H. Rowe."

The same periodical also described the building as "tastefully furnished, beautiful for situation, an ornament to the country, and an honor to the congregation. May many sons and daughters be born unto God at its altars."

In 1921 the Charles Circuit became a six-church circuit with Pisgah as one of the points. During the pastorate of the Rev. J. E. McDonald the present church cemetery was laid off in plots and cemetery records were initiated.

In 1940 the church ordered glass from Czechoslovakia to be used for windows. Many of the windows were given as memorials. Blue and rose shades were chosen, but, due to World War II, the shades selected were unobtainable.

The division of the La Plata Circuit occurred in 1946. Bethel, Dentsville, and La Plata became the La Plata Charge. Shiloh was made a station, and Chicamuxen, Indian Head, and Pisgah churches became the Indian Head Charge.

During his appointment to the Indian Head Charge, the Rev. Albert W. Hamilton died and was buried in Pisgah's cemetery. A new parsonage to serve the Indian Head Charge was built in the 1940s. This building was dedicated by District Superintendent Dr. Orris G. Robertson the first Sunday in March 1957.

During the ministry of Rev. Harold L. May a growing congregation built a Fellowship Hall. The building was dedicated in September 1971.

During the pre-Civil War years two, and sometimes three, Circuit Riders were named to a district. The third man was usually a junior preacher in training for the ministry. The records show that Charles and St. Mary's Circuit went with the Southern Methodists during the war. There were no Baltimore Methodist Episcopal appointments of ministers in Maryland from 1862 to 1865. The Southern Methodists had no appointments north of West River during this time.

Shiloh Community United Methodist Church

In 1863, with no church in the community, people held their worship services in various homes. Later a group of Christians donated a building in the area. This structure became a center for marriages as well as spiritual worship. It also served as a public school to which voluntary teachers came to render their services.

There is no record to show when, or for whom, Shiloh Church was named. Its foundation was laid and its program grew under the leadership of the first minister, Rev. Wainwright. Annual camp meetings were held at Wingate's Grove, where a Baptist Church was later erected.

The original church was destroyed by fire. Members again began to assemble in homes for worship services. However, those determined pioneers whom disaster could not defeat united to build a new church. Many God-fearing, loyal men have served Shiloh Church.

When the Elementary School was consolidated in 1951, members, realizing the need for expansion of the church program, purchased the building to be used as a recreation center and dining room. This building was destroyed by fire in February 1964.

In 1960 Rev. Thomas G. Barrington, Pastor of the church from 1959 to 1961, brought to the attention of the officials the inadequate condition of the church. He envisioned a modern building with adequate facilities. A committee was appointed to investigate possibilities and to initiate the plans. Shiloh, again, began to think of a new church home.

In 1961 Rev. James O. Waters continued to work with the members toward building another new church. In 1964, on the completion of the plans, it became necessary for the church to be incorporated. Since there already was one Shiloh Methodist Church in Charles County, members changed the new church's name to Shiloh Community Methodist Church. This name was submitted by a youth of the church, Leland Ray Jones.

On April 10, 1965, a ground-breaking ceremony was held. Rev. Waters presided and the first shovel of earth was lifted by Ollie Thomas, the oldest member of the church at the time. The second shovel was lifted by Carroll Middleton, then Chairman of the Board of Trustees. Construction of the new building began April 15, 1965. The building contained a nave with a seating capacity of 300, a chancel, a choir space, four classrooms, a choir-robing room, Pastor's study, furnace room, and modern rest rooms. To facilitate the activities of the church and the community, an annex consisting of a kitchen and dining room was built. Today this area also houses the local Headstart Program.

The name was changed again during the 1970s to Shiloh Community United Methodist Church.

Although the dreams of yesterday's pioneers have been fulfilled in the construction of a new edifice, members still strive to promote their Christian program under the dynamic leadership of Rev. Walter H. Sewell, who is now beginning his third year of Pastorship at Shiloh.

Metropolitan United Methodist Church

A few years after the signing of the Emancipation Proclamation, some 20 people, led by Brother Henry Datcher, met to hold prayer meetings at Mulberry Grove. For a year they met at several homes on the farms of residents Ivins and Chapman; then they recognized the need of a regular meeting place. Bro. Datcher and Bro. Coates Slater interceded and purchased land from J. C. Brawner, William Boswell, and Josiah Dent. The stated pupose of the purchase was to erect a building to be used as a church and a school for education of colored people of Charles County.

On Jan. 16, 1928, a deed for these premises was made to the Methodist Episcopal Church by Harry Dotson, Henry W. Johnson, Wallace F. Clark, John Bransome, Sydney Thompson, James Clark, and George Thompson, Acting Trustees of the Methodist Episcopal Church.

After the meeting house was built, Rev. Charles Daniel Wheeler was the first pastor appointed by the Washington Conference of the Methodist Episcopal Church. He was placed on the Charles Circuit, which was later changed to the Pisgah Circuit. Preaching services were held once a month. Bro. Datcher was made local preacher and class leader. Rev. Wheeler served four years, with Rev. George R. Williams as his assistant.

Between 1868 and 1883 the Circuit continued to grow; several pastors succeeded Rev. Wheeler. There were 188 members reported on the Circuit.

Under Rev. Charles Price's leadership between 1883 and 1886, the church was remodeled and renamed Price's Chapel. There were 301 members reported on the Circuit at that time.

Between 1886 and 1891 Rev. R. H. Alexander served; under his leadership money was raised to help purchase a parsonage at Pisgah. Three churches were then on the Circuit, and Bro. Datcher was still local preacher.

Between 1891 and 1900 three pastors succeeded Rev. Alexander, and it was during Rev. W. R. Davis' period of service that Price's Chapel was designated as Pomonkey Charge, with 125 members. Rev. J. C. Norris was the first pastor to serve on the Pomonkey Charge. Under his short stay, 1900 to 1901, the first Parsonage was built at a cost of $400. Rev. L. E. S. Nash, who served from 1901 to 1906, built the present church, the Metropolitan Methodist Episcopal Church. The first organ for the church was purchased by J. T. Slater with the assistance of his father-in-law, Rev. John Griffin, and the first choir was organized by Mrs. Rebecca Slater. Rev. A. H. Tilghman served two years, 1906-1908, and was succeeded by Rev. Charles S. Briggs, who held the greatest revival in the history of the church in the fall of 1910 with 150 converts. The youth class for Christian Training was organized by Rev. Briggs and turned over to Bro. William H. Thompson, who led it for many years. During this period the Methodist Brotherhood was organized and the Church Annex was built.

The choir was reorganized under the leadership of Rev. C. S. Harper, who served between 1911 and 1914; the Parsonage was remodeled under Rev. F. F. King, who served from 1917 to 1922. The electric plant was installed in the church with the help of Wallace Clark who did the temporary electric work and Bro. James Clark Sr., who did the permanent electrical work. Both gave their labor and time free.

Rev. C. H. Matthews served one year from 1922 to 1923, and Rev. J. W. Hollins served from 1923 to 1926. He was the most diligent Sunday School worker since the church began a separate charge. The church celebrated its 57th anniversary in July 1925.

During Rev. Preston R. Vaul's administration, 1927 to 1929, the lower floor of the Parsonage was renovated to include a study and some library space. Between 1936 and 1940 the Church Annex was improved—a stage was built and rooms were added to provide space for the choir to change their robes. Bro. J. Wesley Key was made local Preacher in 1938, and Bro. J. T. Slater was made Layleader. Electric lights were installed in the Parsonage, the chancel was remodeled, and a choir loft was built behind the pulpit platform. A pipe organ was also installed, carpeting laid, and a beautiful memorial window placed over the pulpit. This window was presented to the church by Rev. George T. C. Bell; it was painted by his brother, Page, of Baltimore. In 1949, the first church-school bus was purchased, and church attendance increased.

Under Rev. F. D. Bradford's leadership, many more improvements were made. He served from 1949 to 1952.

Rev. L. A. Dyson's administration, 1952 to 1958, saw changes in the church commissions and other departments of the church. The Church School was outstanding under the leadership of Mrs. Lucille Marshall, one of the teachers who had served faithfully under the late Rev. Bro. J. Wesley Key Sr. Also under Rev. Dyson's leadership, a new kitchen, two rest rooms, and two classrooms were added to the Annex—the classrooms on the upper floor. A modern heating system was installed and plans were made to build a new Parsonage. A kick-off dinner was held by the Women's Society of Christian Service, and the first $500 was raised towards this project.

On Feb. 25, 1959, the church incorporated, on the advice of Rev. J. H. Peters, District Superintendent.

Under the leadership of Rev. Howard Hinson, who came in 1959, much was accomplished—committees were appointed and banks consulted to finance construction of the Parsonage, which was completed. During this time Mrs. Rosa Bransome was instrumental in securing an outdoor bulletin board, which was presented to the Church by Mrs. Gladys Mathews in memory of her husband, Theodore, who served as church undertaker for a number of years. Mrs. Bransome also presented the offering table. The Senior Choir, under the leadership of Mrs. H. Datcher, President, and A. Kane, Organist, purchased a piano; and the Junior Choir, led by Miss Eva Williams and Mrs. Lillian Richardson, bought new robes. The church grounds were landscaped under the direction of Bro. Milbourne Hall.

Between 1963 and 1968, Rev. I. A. Sherman and Rev. Joseph Carroll served the church. During this time, the Commissions were reorganized, the mortgage of the Parsonage was ceremonially burned, and plans were made to build a new church. The usher board, under the leadership of French Myers, donated a table to register guests.

In 1968 the name of Metropolitan Methodist Church was changed to Metropolitan United Methodist Church.

A beautiful painting of "Christ In Prayer at Gethsemane" was presented the Church by Leon Connelly in honor of his mother, Mrs. Lucille Marshall.

Under the present Parson, Rev. Edwin Williams, who arrived in 1969, the United Methodist Men organized a Men's Chorus, The United Choraleers, under the leadership of Sister Havannah Morton. The Youth Choir, conducted by Mrs. Joy Hinton, was able to purchase new robes. The various chairmen and presidents attend leadership meetings, district meetings, workshops, and retreats.

In May 1975 the congregation moved into a temporary site, the Masonic Temple, for worship services, pending the construction of the new church.

Alexandria United Methodist Church

Through Christian spirits and experiences the Alexandria United Methodist Church was begun in the home of William Jordan in 1871. A year later the log church was erected on land he donated. He also gave the logs to build the church.

Before the Rev. Alexander became Pastor, the church was known as Jordan's Chapel. In 1888 a frame building was erected, and much was accomplished at that location, until there developed the need for a more modern church. It was built on Rt. 224 in 1951.

The church has been a great inspiration to the community, and many able ministers have served it.

Calvary United Methodist Church

Old records show that an established group of Methodists was working in Charles County as far back as 1846. Written records from 1877 to 1890 tell of the construction of the original church building. It was called the Oakland Methodist Church. Oakland Cemetery is now the landmark of that historic place, located one mile west of Waldorf on Rt. 228. There were approximately 108 members in the Oakland Church. The only surviving member of that Church is Mrs. Ula Huntt Ryon.

During this period the Oakland Methodist Church was one of eight churches on the Prince George's Circuit, and five Sunday Schools were then in progress.

In the early 1900s the old Oakland Church was sold and torn down. A few pieces of wood were preserved and made into two small crosses, kept in the present Calvary United Methodist Church.

When the Oakland congregation decided to build a new church in the town of Waldorf, the land for the church was given to the Methodist Church in 1898 by Philip Sasscer and his wife. The cornerstone for the present church was laid in 1904. Included in the cornerstone were a Bible, a County newspaper, and a paper containing the names of all the people who had contributed a dime to have their names included. There were 62 charter members when the church was moved to Waldorf.

Between 1914 and 1938 Calvary changed from an active church to a small church struggling to stay alive. Although these years were hard, there remained an active Sunday School. When the Prince George's Circuit was reduced in 1938, the District Superintendent thought the church should be closed but due mainly to the efforts of two devoted members, it was revitalized and in 1945 the Rev. Harold Milstead was sent to Calvary. Many said he "woke up" the church; they also referred to him as "the builder." Soon after his arrival the church began to move forward. The year 1948 marked great progress for Calvary Church. The Sanctuary was remodeled and a new chancel was added to the church. In 1948-49 Sunday School rooms and a fellowship hall and kitchens were added to the construction. The Sunday School and Woman's Society of Christian Service were active and the church grew spiritually and in Christian fellowship. Methods of raising funds during this time included strawberry festivals, bake sales, and church suppers.

However, disaster struck. On March 2, 1950, the windiest day of the year, the Parsonage burned. Practically everything was lost—all of the Minister's personal belongings and furniture and many church records. Fortunately, no lives were lost.

At this time the Conference decided to make this a two-point Charge, consisting of Cheltenham and Calvary churches. Through the sacrifice and devotion of the members and help of the people of the community, money was raised to build a modern, brick Parsonage adjacent to the church. Unfortunately, Rev. Milstead never had the opportunity to live in the new Parsonage, as he was transferred.

During 1953, with Rev. Ralph Leonard as a student pastor, the church grew and had excellent revivals; funds were raised to pay off the debt on the church. In 1961 the church mortgage was paid off and a mortgage-burning ceremony held. During the years of Rev. Milstead's pastorate (1945-51) the church was active in fighting the legalizing of slot machines and the granting of more liquor licenses. During Rev. Johnson's tenure (1959-63) the church actively worked to abolish slot machines.

In 1963, under Rev. Dallas Beall, the Sunday School grew so that additional space was needed, and four new rooms were added. In 1966 the church library was organized, there was a great increase in youth activities, and the Ecumenical Thrift Shop was organized with churches of three faiths participating.

In June 1967 the Conference approved the division of the Waldorf-Cheltenham Charge and Calvary became a station church, bought Cheltenham's interest in the Parsonage, and became a part of the Washington East District.

In 1969 the church was one of the leaders in the community, offering facilities for the Government-sponsored Head Start Program. Other groups to use church facilities were Girl Scouts, Boy Scouts, Home Makers, and the School for Retarded Children, which operated from September 1962 to June 1968.

In October 1969 the present Pastor and his wife were assigned to Calvary. Under their leadership the church has experienced spiritual renewal, holding revivals and inviting many missionaries. In June 1969 Zion Wesley was put on the charge with Calvary, one year after the separation of Cheltenham, and it became Waldorf Methodist Charge. In October 1973, because the congregation had grown so large, it was decided to start a Junior Church for children from 4 to 12 years of age: the Junior Church meets at the same time as the regular morning worship service, and has proved successful. Prayer meetings are held on Wednesday nights, and there are Sunday evening services as well as the morning worships. In 1974 Calvary held its first Missionary Conference, which was spectacularly successful, with faith promises exceeding $16,000 received.

Zion-Wesley United Methodist Church

The first church building was a log structure. In the early 1900s Rev. Wesley Dockett undertook the task of erecting a tabernacle of worship on a parcel of land on the northeast side of the road lending from Beantown to Troy, known as "Smallwood's Plains." Rev. Dockett supervised the building, then stayed on for many years as first Pastor.

Following him as Pastor were the Reverends Snowden Hill, Bedford, J.W. Ford, P. C. Butler, C. H. Tolson, N.C. Barnes, William G. Simms, J. O. Waters, R. Owen Johnson, Theodore Swager, and Everett W. Culp.

Rev. Simms served Zion-Wesley, as well as other churches in the area, for about 20 years; his daughter, Rev. Emma P. Burrell, is a member of the Baltimore Conference. The Rev. Waters, who succeeded to the Pastorate, sought financial help from businessmen and other residents of the community to erect the present building.

In 1962 Zion-Wesley was placed under the charge of Rev. Johnson, who was Pastor of the Brandywine Charge. He had the roof of the building finished and made plans to complete construction. Assistance was rendered by his brother-in-law, Tilgham Hawkins, a carpenter. With plenty of volunteer help, the building was completed and consecrated in March 1965. To help avoid running up a church debt, Rev. Johnson served without salary. He recalls that God blessed the church in many ways, through youth rallies, added members, and by establishing vacation Bible School and worship services each Sunday morning.

Calvary United Methodist Church had a Mission Study to consider ways the church could help the community. The outgrowth of this Study was the organization of an Ecumenical Thrift Shop, where people could buy good usable materials at a low price. Zion-Wesley permitted the use of its basement and was joined by Calvary United Methodist, Good Shepherd United Methodist, St. Peter's Roman Catholic, and St. Paul's Episcopal (Piney) churches. St. Paul's withdrew in 1964. The Pastor and three Lay members from each participating church constitute the Board of Directors. Profits are used to care for needy people, and to provide relief in hardship cases.

When the new building was ready to be used, it is said that the old one was in such bad shape that stars could be seen through the roof. Two men put a rope around the old building and pulled it over.

Zion-Wesley for the most part has been on a Charge with several churches served by one pastor, but is reassigned from time to time. Once it was on a Charge with Mitchellville and Newburg. For about seven years it was on with Ashbury and Gibbons. Since 1969 it has been on with Calvary United Methodist Church. Rev. Theodore Swager served as Pastor for about four months after Zion-Wesley was put on the Waldorf Charge with Calvary in 1969. In October 1969 Rev. Everett W. Culp, the present Pastor, was appointed to the Waldorf United Methodist Charge.

In 1973 the congregation made a serious effort to modernize the present structure.

Both Zion-Wesley and Calvary United Methodist churches are currently carrying on full programs in a fine spirit of cooperation, under the leadership of Rev. Everett W. Culp. Pastor, and three assistants, Robert H. Lyles, John C. Benson, and Harold W. Denison.

La Plata United Methodist Church

Existing church records do not give any clue to the precise reasons for the decision to build a Methodist Church at La Plata. The first indication this was to be done is found in the record of the second quarterly conference held at Chicamuxen Church in August 1887. It reads in part: "Joseph V. Padgett, Henry T. Padgett and Joseph N. Penn (of the New Town and Pisgah Churches) were appointed a committee to secure a suitable lot at La Platta on which to build a house of worship." There is no indication that the decision to build at La Plata was directed from outside the circuit. There were some sound reasons why the Reverend Joyce would have wanted a church at La Plata. In the first place, the new Parsonage was built on land in La Plata deeded to the church May 31, 1877, "in and for the consideration of love and affection for the Methodist Episcopal Church, . . .". This now constituted a permanent homebase for the circuit rider's operation. Second, the La Plata area at this time was roughly the geographic center of the preacher's scattered charges. Third, the village of La Plata with its excellent new railroad communication facilities and its rapidly rising political and social eminence in the County gave promise of a vigorous and prosperous future.

All these reasons aside, the New Town church, located only about three miles east of town, may have served the area's church members equally as well as the proposed new structure. There is also an indication that the Pastor's wife exerted more than a little pressure in engineering the new church and its location. All this adds up to an unbeatable combination of reasons for building in La Plata. Finally, at the second quarterly conference held in La Plata Aug. 18, 1890, the following "were elected a committee to build a church at La Plata": Joseph V. Padgett, J. Marion Freeman, J. Samuel Turner, H.G. Robertson, Joseph H. Penn (from New Town and Pisgah Churches) and Charles A. Joyce, Preacher in charge." In other words, it amounted to "Thy will be done"—and it would be done.

The circuit in which the church would be established was titled Charles Circuit and included the following churches or appointments, as the minister described them: Bethel Society with 65 members, Mechanicsville Society with 23 members, New Town Society with 50 members, Pisgah Society with 69 members, and Chicamuxen (Asbury) with 41 members, for a total of 248. Then, the register covering 1881 and 1882 lists church membership for the Charles and St. Mary's Circuit, which included the same churches or societies given for 1873. The roster for 1889 included a Shiloh Society at Pomonkey with 16 members. The Shiloh Church was transferred to Prince George's Circuit in 1893. The quarterly conference records for years 1887-91 refer to Charles Circuit once again, which appeared to include only churches at New Town, Pisgah, and Chicamuxen. The preacher in charge reported a circuit register of 126 members on May 7, 1887. In the year that the building committe started the new church building at La Plata, the circuit consisted of New Town, Pisgah, Chicamuxen, and Shiloh, with a combined enrollment of 250 members.

Few Methodist today, but probably quite a few in the old 1890 Charles Circuit, have heard of John B. McFerrin. However, we may be sure that Rev. Joyce and the lay leaders of the circuit were well aware of the significance of naming the new church McFerrin Memorial. Apparently the name McFerrin was extremely well known in the Methodist Episcopal Church, South, at the end of the last century.

The Tennessee Conference eulogy stated that McFerrin preached the everlasting gospel for 60 years with singular fidelity, courage, and success and it was predicted (at the Conference) that many McFerrin chapels would be built in his honor. Apparently, the founders of the La Plata Church knew this man and his works well; they named their new house of worship the John B. McFerrin Memorial Church.

As the first pastor of McFerrin Memorial Church, Rev. J. C. Sedwick prepared to leave the circuit for another charge early in 1896, he once again voiced his great concern over pastoral instruction of the children, and closed his final Sunday School report with the words "May the Lord help and save the Children."

Quarterly conference records indicate that from the very beginning members of the New Town Church played a major role in the new La Plata Church congregation. Many of them joined the new church in 1897. Late that year the trustees of New Town Church were authorized to sell the New Town Church building and "reserve the funds for the benefit of the burying ground at that place."

With four churches now in the circuit Rev. T.G. Nevitt replaced Rev. John B. Henry in the spring of 1900. The new minister in one of his early quarterly conference reports launched straightaway into a series of lamentations on the condition of the circuit. He

> feared that our paths have not been straight enough to keep the lame in the narrow way . . . Some of our oldest members neglect (worship), some of our youngest ones observe it . . . There is lameness also to some extent in our financial methods, so much as to give doubt of our being able to meet present obligations without pandering to the flesh in a church festival.

In the spring of 1904 the Rev. I. Ryder replaced Rev. T.G. Nevitt. In his first conference report the new and somewhat bewildered Rev. Ryder pleaded that he did not know much about the Sunday Schools as yet. A year later the Rev. D.M. Brown replaced the Rev. I. Ryder as preacher-in-charge of the Charles-St. Mary's circuit. When he left the circuit in the spring of 1909 the best he could say of his four years of labor was that the church could boast only about "the average state of spirituality." He felt the results of his ministry were not all that could be desired. This pastor had added 46 persons to the circuit membership; 80 names had been removed from the registers and 84 infants had been baptized. He summed up his feelings in his final report:

> I trust it may not be presumptuous to claim comfort from the words of the Savior: "One soweth and another reapeth—both he that soweth and he that reapeth may rejoice together." I wish here to record my deep appreciation of the sympathy and support, moral and material, which have been given by our members and friends during the many trying circumstances incident to our living and laboring in their midst.

Before leaving the Charles-St. Mary's charge early in 1913, Rev. Sarver summed up accomplishments of his four-year ministry in Southern Maryland. He stated that during his ministry about 40 members were added to the church rolls, 64 infants were baptized, and 45 names were removed. His parting words were "for four years we have gone forth on this charge sowing the precious seed of the Gospel and we pray that God will give the increase."

Early in 1913 when the Rev. J.W. Beall became preacher-in-charge of the Charles-St. Mary's circuit total church membership stood at 243, nine less than a year earlier.

The Rev. L.B. Atkins moved into the Parsonage early in 1917 and found himself responsible for the spiritual wellbeing of 308 Methodist souls. We do not know whether moving to this circuit constituted a move upward or downward in this Pastor's career, but he was promised a salary of $1150 and an additional $350 was pledged for support of an assistant preacher. His first impressions of the circuit were noted in a typewritten report dated June 23, 1917.

> We feel we have not been on the work long enough to give anything like a competent general report of it.... We regret to report on Epworth League—the one which once existed at Pisgah seems to be entirely extinct... We have seven Sunday Schools... Our Sunday School work seems to be doing fairly well, most of them are preparing for observance of Children's Day in the very near future.

While preparing to leave the circuit early in 1921, Rev. Atkins pronounced the spiritual condition of his charge to be "fairly good, not ideal but hopeful." He praised his parishioners for having shown a "most commendable spirit in responding liberally to the call of the sufferers both in the Near East and China" and for their "liberal support" to the Anti-Saloon League; and he noted that the churches at La Plata and Shiloh "have both had improvements and repairs amounting to approximately $350."

St. Matthews United Methodist Church

St. Matthews African Methodist Episcopal Church, in Newtown, was established in 1898. It was founded because there was not a Methodist church for the Negro worshipers in this part of the County.

Presiding over the newly founded church was Rev. Benjamin W. Brown, 1898-1899, along with many other distinguished members. Since that time, the Church has been blessed with several leaders who have served the Church well.

After standing in a state of incompletion for 10 years, St. Matthews was finally completed under the pastorship of Rev. Benjamin T. Gant, 1917-1926, at a cost of $303.65. "New Life and Activity was Initiated Into the Old Circuit."

In 1926 the late Mrs. Ollie May Lancaster, a former elementary school teacher from Pittsburgh, organized the first choir at St. Matthews, and she continued to direct and maintain it until her death in August 1975.

The present dining hall at St. Matthews was once the elementary school for the Negro children in Newtown.

Rev. Sewall, present Pastor, has contributed like all earlier pastors, toward the achievements, progress, and religious goals of the Church. Helping all of them since 1919 was the late Rev. Alexander Brown, who served as the Sunday School Teacher and Sunday School Superintendent. He was ordained in 1944 by Bishop Shaw as a local preacher, and he would visit many of the churches in the County.

Smith Chapel United Methodist Church

The Smith Chapel Church was organized early in 1901. In May 1902 the building was erected, and since then it has been renovated and expanded.

First ministers were the Rev. John Barnett and the Rev. Smith. Mrs. Carrie Hackerson organized the first choir of the church in 1931.

Good Shepherd United Methodist Church

Good Shepherd Church is the spiritual home of many active families. Its pastor, Rev. Charles Lightner, stresses involvement in the community and the world in his sermons. Worship service is a time to be renewed and to carry that renewal into home and community. Each member is considered an assistant minister.

The church began in 1967, when the Board of Missions of the Evangelical United Brethren Church chose St. Charles as a mission site and Rev. Keith Day was appointed as the first pastor. Since only the Parsonage had been completed, the first services were held in the recently completed Dr. Mudd School on March 18, 1968.

When the Evangelical United Brethren and Methodist Churches merged, Good Shepherd officially became a United Methodist Church.

Good Shepherd opens its doors to many programs for Charles County residents. It sponsors a kindergarten and provides a meeting place for Senior Citizens, Teens, art groups, and other organizations. It donates much time and resources for programs for the needy.

Many activities and classes are offered to members and friends, including trips, bike hikes, sports events, and varied church socials.

In the summer of 1971 the church participated in a Pastor Exchange Program. This involved sending Rev. Lightner to London and receiving Rev. Douglas Wollen of London as pastor of Good Shepherd. This was a wonderful experience for the involved pastors and their congregations, and anticipated our Bicentennial celebration in many ways.

Other County Churches

Lutheranism in Charles County

The first known attempt to establish a Lutheran congregation in Southern Maryland was in 1909, when a young pastor, Rev. Louis J. Roehm, made his first trip to Mechanicsville in St. Mary's County. He met with some Lutherans who were interested in establishing a Lutheran congregation. On Aug. 31, Pastor Roehm and Pastor D.H. Steffens traveled to Mechanicsville to conduct the first Lutheran service there. A total of four services were held there that year.

In 1910 Pastor Roehm heard of a group of Danish Lutherans in the western part of Charles County. On May 17 he took the train to Pomfret, where he conducted his first service in Charles County. Services were later held in La Plata for Lutherans.

In September 1910 Pastor Schumacher of the Iowa Synod bought a farm in the vicinity of Charlotte Hall. When Pastor Roehm came to conduct the service in Mechanicsville on Nov. 15, he was told that Pastor Schumacher had begun conducting services Nov. 6; therefore, Pastor Roehm did not return to conduct services in Mechanicsville.

One would have expected Pastor Schumacher to have taken over the work from that point and to have established a Lutheran congregation in Mechanicsville. But many of the families were not satisfied with this procedure. They decided to organize a congregation at Charlotte Hall. Again they called upon Pastor Roehm, and on Feb. 16, 1911, he conducted the first service at Charlotte Hall at the home of Heinrich Mueller. Seventeen people attended.

Pastor Roehm continued to serve the group, and on Aug. 21, 1911, first steps were taken toward the organization of a congregation. At the organization meeting Dietrich Badenhoop offered three acres of land as a gift to serve as church property. Later the congregation instructed a committee to build a church 18 ft x 28 ft x 12 ft. The church at Charlotte Hall was dedicated Nov. 26, 1911. Pastor Roehm preached in the morning and Pastor Steffens in the afternoon. Each service was attended by 30 people. This building is still in use.

By 1911 Pastor Roehm was serving seven stations: Overlea, Glen Burnie, Bowie, Halls, Charlotte Hall, La Plata, and Pomfret. He reported that he confirmed 32 children that year and traveled 7,975 miles. Since the work at Charlotte Hall was showing signs of progress, it was decided that a resident pastor should be called to serve the area. On Aug. 31, 1913,

Pastor E. Gallmann was installed as the first resident pastor. St. Paul's Lutheran Church, Charlotte Hall, then became the base for all future Lutheran work in Southern Maryland.

In 1916 the congregation formally became a member of the Eastern District (now Southeastern) of the Lutheran Church—Missouri Synod. In the years that followed the growth of the congregation was hampered by several factors. One was the language barrier. The congregation became known in the community as the "German Church" (a name which is still occasionally heard). This, coupled with the sparse population of the area, effectively limited the outreach of the congregation. Another factor disturbing progress was a succession of short pastorates and long vacancies. During its 60 years St. Paul's has been served by at least 19 pastors and vicars, many of them from a distant location or on a part-time basis.

In 1930 Pastor William Moeller offered his resignation as Pastor of St. Paul's and cited the changing character of Lutheranism in America, which necessitated the use of ministers who were proficient in English as well as German. The language barrier was crumbling, and the use of English, together with improved transporation, enabled the congregation to expand its ministry. This expansion seems to have taken the form of serving those Lutherans who lived in a widely scattered area. Nevertheless, the great distances involved made any meaningful participation by these people impossible.

In 1932 Mr. and Mrs. Harold Skone, anxious that Lutherans in Charles County might be served on a more regular basis, opened their home in La Plata as a temporary worship place. Pastor Ziehlsdorff from Charlotte Hall came to conduct services. Soon the group moved to the Grange Hall in McConchie, and finally to St. John's Episcopal Church in Pomonkey, where evening services were held. The group was small in number, but interested and energetic.

The original intent of this group was to establish a congregation in the La Plata area, but the District Mission Board believed Indian Head to be a new and potentially better opportunity for a preaching station. The Naval Propellant Plant seemed to promise a quicker and larger population growth. Wth the aid of District subsidy the Lutheran Church of Our Saviour was eventually established. The La Plata venture was then absorbed into the Indian Head station.

During this period the mission at Indian Head and St. Paul's, Charlotte Hall, were linked from time to time through mutual assistance during vacancies and through dual service by such pastors as Louis Westermann and Theodore Hafner.

Through the years the facilities at St. Paul's underwent some changes. In 1930 a narthex, or vestibule, had been added to the small church. In 1929 a Sunday School had been organized with Louis H. Steffens as Superintendent, and in 1950 a wing was added to the church to provide Sunday School facilities. A new chancel arrangement was effected in 1956 for the church.

With World War II came the development of Patuxent River Naval Air Station at Lexington Park. A new population center began to form in St. Mary's County, and was seen as an opportunity for mission work, with St. Paul's again serving as the base. Pastor Louis Westermann appears to have been the first to do preliminary work in the area. He also gave some service to a small group of Lutherans in Dahlgren, Va. Pastor Westermann was followed by Pastor A.S. Gedwillo, who in the late 1940s was baptizing persons and conducting confirmation classes at Lexington Park. Pastor Paul Single continued to work at Lexington Park until bad health forced him to resign.

Under the leadership of Pastor Melvin Schmidt the work at Lexington Park prospered. During his pastorate the congregation was officially organized in 1954 and modern facilities were constructed. The congregation adopted the name of Trinity Lutheran Church and became part of a dual parish with St. Paul's at Charlotte Hall. Pastor Schmidt served both congregations.

In 1960 Pastor Schmidt accepted a call to New York, and the dual parish became vacant. That September a retiring pastor, Rev. Herbert E. Plehn, came to the Southeastern

District as missionary-at-large to serve in vacancies. He was assigned to the dual parish of Trinity and St. Paul's.

In 1961 Lexington Park became an independent congregation and called its own resident pastor, Rev. Larry Lineberger. Pastor Lineberger had previously served the congregation as a preacher while serving a vicarage in Silver Spring. Pastor Plehn continued to serve the vacant congregation at Charlotte Hall and accepted the assignment to open a renewed attempt at La Plata. The work was begun at the request of a group of members of St. Paul's. The Mission Board was favorably impressed with the potential in the La Plata area and gave assurance of assistance through the missionary-at-large and through financial subsidy.

Facilities were soon found in a vacant frame church building on Kent Avenue in La Plata. This building was originally built at a cost of about $2,000 as the first home of McFerrin Memorial Methodist Church. It was dedicated Aug. 28, 1892. Despite its noble beginning the structure had deteriorated and had been in commercial use as a print shop for many years. It hardly looked like a house of worship. But the small group tackled the task of conversion and transformed the building into an attractive house of worship.

Finally, the church building was ready, and on Oct. 8, 1961, the first worship service was held. The first service was attended by 66 persons, half of whom were residents of the La Plata area. The young congregation prospered as new members joined. In 1962 the congregation was officially organized as Grace Lutheran Church and was received as a member of the Southeastern District.

Jan. 31, 1963, brought the death of the missionary's wife, Mrs. Ruth Plehn. Pastor Plehn, not a regularly called pastor of the congregation, considered it impossible to continue residence alone in La Plata after the death of his wife, and retired. He then established residence with his son at Laurel. In spite of the 50 miles separating the congregation and his residence, Pastor Plehn continued to serve the dual parish until winter weather made the arrangement impractical. In November 1963 Pastor Herbert Plehn, who had so faithfully served the parish and aided in the organization of Grace Church, found it necessary to resign his position.

From November 1963 until July 1964 the Parish was without the services of a resident pastor. On July 12, 1964, Rev. Arthur W. Scherer was installed as the first regularly called resident pastor at La Plata, serving the dual parish of St. Paul's and Grace. With a resident pastor once again at work, the small congregation at La Plata resumed its growth, increased its activity, and began to make plans for the future.

With the aid of a $2,000 grant from the Chesapeake District, the congregation bought a five-acre church site for $8,600; it was able to retire the debt by the end of 1965. In February 1966 an architectural firm was contracted to draw plans for new worship and educational facilities on the site at the intersection of Rt. 6 and Rt. 488. On June 18, 1967, about 57 years after the first Lutheran service was conducted in La Plata, ground was broken for the first permanent home of the Lutheran Church in this area. The first service of worship in the new structure was conducted on Dec. 17, 1967. Formal dedication of the building took place March 24, 1968. Pastor Plehn preached at the morning service, and Dr. Martin C. Poch, President of the Southeastern District, delivered the sermon in the afternoon. Nearly 400 people attended.

With the benefit of new and adequate facilities the La Plata congregation expanded its program and activities and grew in size and strength. On Jan. 1, 1970, Grace Lutheran Church left subsidized mission status and became, like St. Paul's at the same time, a self-supporting parish.

St. Paul's Lutheran Church had once again been the base for the establishment of a new mission. During this period it regained its former strength and carried on a more active program. In 1965 the old Parsonage, which for several years had been used for rental income, was remodeled to serve as a Parish House and educational building. In 1968 the congregation left its subsidized status of many years and in 1970 was recognized as a self-supporting congregation.

On Feb. 21, 1971, Pastor Arthur Scherer delivered his final sermons as Pastor of Grace Lutheran Church and St. Paul's

Lutheran Church. He was installed Feb. 28, 1971, as pastor of Emmanuel Lutheran Church, Hampton, Va.

A call was then extended through the Southeastern District, for a graduate from the Seminary to be the new pastor of Grace and St. Paul's. On June 15, 1971, Rev. Eric G. Peterson, a graduate of Concordia Seminary, St. Louis, was installed as regular pastor. His residence was made in La Plata. The congregations continued to grow and prosper. During the next three years the nature of the Charlotte Hall area began to change. What was once a quiet farm community had become a center of new home construction. In the fifth election district of St. Mary's County, 5,000 homes were approved to be built. In addition, Charles County was growing rapidly, especially in the north. As more people moved into Southern Maryland, need for another pastor to assist with the work became apparent.

In February 1974 St. Paul's congregation voted to call a graduate from the Seminary as its full-time pastor. On July 1, 1974, Rev. James Stoltenberg, a graduate of Concordia Theological Seminary, Springfield, Ill., began serving St. Paul's. On July 7, 1974, he was ordained and officially installed as Pastor. More than 200 people attended the ceremony, and 15 pastors participated. Six days earlier Rev. Eric G. Peterson had begun working full time at Grace Lutheran Church in La Plata.

Meanwhile, the Lutheran Church of Our Savior at Indian Head had grown. Its 1939 organization had been greatly aided by Elmer Biles Sr., a churchgoer who was an ardent listener of the "Lutheran Hour" radio program. He wrote the director of the program requesting aid in starting a Lutheran church at Indian Head; shortly afterward Pastors Pipelow and Wenchel conducted a survey.

Only July 21, 1942, the Lutheran Church of Our Savior was incorporated; it held its first service, at the old Glymont School, Feb. 14, 1943. Three months later Pastor Westermann was ordained and installed. The congregation still worships in the school building, which it purchased at public auction in August 1944. It plans to build eventually on five acres of land it owns at Bryan's Road.

The Church of Jesus Christ of Latter-Day Saints

The Church of Jesus Christ of Latter-Day Saints (better known as the Mormon Church) was organized April 6, 1830, in New York State, under the direction of Joseph Smith, first prophet and president of the Church. He and five other men participated in the formal ceremony.

Smith, born Dec. 23, 1805, in Vermont, in 1823 was directed by the heavenly messenger Moroni to a hill near Palmyra, N.Y. There he was shown a sacred record engraved on metal plates that appeared to be gold. The record contained the religious and secular history of an ancient American civilization. Four years later Smith was allowed to take the plates from the hill. The engravings were translated into English and published as *The Book of Mormon*, named for one of the ancient American prophets and historians who had kept the records.

The Book of Mormon contains a history of several civilizations of ancient America between about 2200 B.C. and 420 A.D. Included in the volume is an account of the ministry of Jesus Christ on the American continent after His crucifixion and subsequent resurrection and ascension in the Holy Land of the Old World.

Persecution forced church members to leave New York. They first established headquarters at Kirkland, O., but were forced to Missouri, then Nauvoo, Ill., and finally Utah.

The church has today between three and four million members throughout the world. In Charles County members worship at the Seventh Day Adventist Church on Berry Road, Waldorf. The Charles Branch was created April 16, 1972, from portions of the Washington, D.C., and Suitland wards, and the Lexington Park Branch. At the time 50 Charles County families were members; by the end of 1975 membership had increased to 78 families.

A new chapel being constructed at White Plains, at the intersection of Rt. 227 and Padgett Road, is scheduled to be completed this summer. The church will have 12 teaching areas, a chapel to seat 280 people, a multi-purpose room, and a baptismal font.

Many practices of the Church of Jesus Christ of Latter-Day Saints appear unique to nonmembers. The church has no professional clergy, and lay members are chosen as regional and local officers; they receive no monetary compensation for their services. The general authorities of the church are headquartered at Salt Lake City.

The major geographical subdivisions are designated "stakes" and "missions." A stake comprises several wards, or fully organized congregations. Missions are broken down into districts and branches.

The women of the Church of Jesus Christ of Latter-Day Saints hold membership in the Relief Society, an organization established in 1842 to minister to the needs of poor and sick members and others in need of compassionate services. These women carry out a program designed to build up and maintain good homes.

Both youngsters and adults attend Sunday School, a program designed to give religious training on levels suited for each age group from three years and older.

The most basic and important unit within the church is the family. Many church activities are designed for family participation. Music is another important aspect of church culture and religious life. The world renowned Mormon Tabernacle Choir is one of the nation's most famous singing ensembles.

Marbury Church of God

The Church of God reformation movement was founded in the 1880s by Daniel Sidney Warner, with national offices at Anderson, Ind. Warner believed that all Christians from all denominations comprised one universal body of Christ, the Church of God. Warner had not intended to start another church, but people who read of his disgust with denominational divisions, expressed in his magazine, *The Gospel Trumpet*, developed into so large a following that a new religious movement emerged. By 1900 it had taken on the form of a separate church.

The Marbury Church of God was organized as a congregation in 1911. It came about when Rev. T.M. Bowie, a resident of Northern Virginia, an itinerate preacher, began distributing literature on the teachings of "The Church of God."

Rev. T. M. Bowie, through literature distribution, stimulated interest so effectively in Marbury that it was decided to hold a series of evangelistic meetings in a "brush arbor" built especially for that purpose. The meeting place was located on property owned by Marbury merchant L.G. Doane. The meeting was led by Rev. William Drew, a minister from Reading, Pa.

As a result of this month-long meeting several young couples accepted the teachings of the Church of God, repented, and were baptized. The brush arbor meetings inspired serious discussions about construction of a church building in the community, and the property located on Rt. 484 at the intersection of the Marbury-Pisgah Road was deeded to the Church Trustees by Mrs. Ora Abell Clark.

The congregation has several times outgrown its facilities and moved to larger accommodations. It marked its 50th anniversary in 1961, with a community celebration; in 1966 plans were laid for another larger building. This was completed in December 1968. It has Christian education facilities and a seating capacity of 200 in the main Sanctuary worship area.

The congregation has been served by many competent and dedicated pastors, some without salary in the early years of the church. Rev. and Mrs. G. H. Pye came to Marbury in 1915 to help with the work. They stayed for about one month, then moved on to help other newly organized congregations. Other ministers came to hold short meetings from time to time and the Rev. Pye returned several times to assist the new and struggling church. Rev. and Mrs. H.D. Freeman were the first regular pastors; they came to the congregation in 1922. Others who served were Rev. Clifton Lord, Rev. Van Hoose, Rev. Reynolds (Pastor from 1931 to 1943), Rev. B. B. Sellers, Rev. J. W. Puller, Rev. Hollis Pistole, Rev. T. M. Mitchell,

Rev. Robert Smith, Rev. Clay Arnold, Rev. Loyal Hire, and currently, Rev. Jerry Jones.

The Marbury Church of God is proud of its heritage, its growth, and of being a part of Charles County. The spiritual growth of the adjoining communities has been nurtured and strengthened by the presence of the Marbury Church of God.

Ripley Community Church

The Ripley Community Church was started about nine years ago, when a concerned family in the community became burdened for a church in the community. The William Pipes family opened their home and meetings were started. The Pipes continued the meetings until the present pastor, Alton H. Flowers, a Christian businessman from the Clinton area, came and began to minister to the church.

From the beginning it was evident that God's blessing was upon the work. The attendance increased and the congregation knew that a building was necessary.

The men of the church were able to construct the first building with an auditorium that could seat 200 and Sunday School space for about 100 or more. The church moved into the building in November 1971 and by March 1972 there were over 300 in attendance.

The church began a bus ministry as soon as the building was completed and at this time there are nine bus routes that carry more than 300 boys and girls. Many adults also ride.

Ripley Community Church is non-denominational, a Bible-preaching and believing church. It preaches salvation by grace through faith in Jesus Christ. The church takes a firm stand for God and Country and has a sincere burden for the community. It is open to all.

Sunday School classes are provided for all ages, with a free nursery. A variety of activities attract members of all age groups. The missionary outreach of the church is not only local but helps support several foreign missionaries.

Church of Christ, Waldorf

The Church of Christ in Waldorf first met for worship services on the Lord's Day, June 20, 1971, to give glory and honor to God the Father and Jesus Christ His Son, by singing, prayer, Bible study, the financial contribution, and commemoration of the Lord's death by assembling around His table to partake of unleavened bread and the fruit of the vine. The first meeting was the direct result of efforts made in February 1971, when 12 families met at the home of Paul Taylor to establish a congregation and incorporate it under the laws of Maryland. This was an evangelistic endeavor, with interest first expressed by members of the Oxon Hill Church of Christ, who lived in or around Charles County.

The initial meeting place was the J. P. Ryon Elementary School, and its facilities were used until December 1971, when the congregation rented the Middleton Building on Old Washington Road at Holly Lane in Waldorf.

The congregation bought approximately three-fourths of an acre of ground near the new Smallwood Village Shopping Center in St. Charles, a residential development in Waldorf. Much of the building work has been done by members at night and on weekends. The new building program was completed in May 1975. The large "L" shaped complex includes eight classrooms, a fellowship hall with kitchen, preacher's office, nursery, two dressing rooms, several storage rooms, baptistry, and large auditorium with a seating capacity of 260.

Brother Oscar McCoy, who was the first located minister to work with the congregation, was a member of the original group that had met at Waldorf. He left in May 1973 to begin another work at Luray, Va.

Brother Robert Zerphey was then retained as a part-time minister. Brother Zerphey had retired from the Air Force and taught high school social studies near Baltimore. He and his family resided in Annapolis and commuted to Waldorf each week to preach, teach, and worship with the congregation.

Brother Jerry H. Wilson began working with the congregation Jan. 1, 1975, on a full-time basis. He is a young native of Limestone County, Tex., who has been preaching 10 years, primarily in Texas and West Virginia. Brother Wilson holds Bachelor of Science and Master of Business Administration degrees from Sam Houston State University, Texas. Both he and his wife have proved a great asset to the congregation.

The Congregation now numbers about 22 families. One of the encouraging features is that growth has been consistent rather than spectacular. At the first worship service, 65 were present; 75 has been the average since then. The average contribution has grown from $250 a week in 1971 to $461 in 1975. Present plans are to grow to about 200 members and then establish other congregations of the Lord's people in Charles County and throughout the world.

NOS Protestant Chapel

The NOS Protestant Chapel of Naval Ordnance Station, Indian Head, has a brief but interesting history. In 1959-60 the Commanding Officer, Capt. Griswold T. Atkins, USN, convinced of the need within the Command for spiritual guidance beyond that available through the endeavors of local pastors, set out to remedy the situation. He believed the military personnel and their dependents required the leadership and inspiration of a military Chaplain.

Consequently, he introduced into the Command the ministry of Lt. George Swanson, a Navy Chaplain serving God and country at Naval Communications Station, Cheltenham. At first Chaplain Swanson visited the Command approximately one day a week for counseling purposes. His efforts evolved until he was conducting worship services at the Station every Sunday. Meanwhile, Capt. Atkins was officially taking steps to establish a permanent Chaplain's Billet within the Command.

In July, 1960, NOS welcomed aboard its first permanent Chaplain, in the person of Lt. John H. Carnes, CHC, USN. The NOS Auditorium was then altered so that it might accommodate Divine Services on Sundays, and serve as a multipurpose building weekdays. It was a rudimentary beginning, to be sure; still, it was a beginning with promise. It has resulted in magnanimous and incomprehensible spiritual blessings.

In June 1972 the Chaplain's Billet was temporarily lost due to peacetime reduction in military forces. Capt. Stanley P. Gary, Commanding Officer, carefully surveyed the need for continuing a counseling/spiritual ministry within the Command. With the help of the Navy Chief of Chaplains, Rear Admiral Francis L. Garrett, he officially restored the Chaplain's Billet to permanent status Feb. 5, 1974.

By March 1974 the NOS Auditorium was in dire need of certain internal improvements. Under the supervisory counsel of LCDR Dewey V. Page, Station Chaplain, plans were drawn up and certain renovations begun. The improvements were completed by Oct. 27, when the Station held the first worship service in the renewed facility. On Sunday, Jan. 25, 1975, Captain John H. Carnes, first permanent Chaplain of NOS, and Rear Admiral Francis L. Garrett, Navy Chief of Chaplains, assisted the Command, during the regular worship service, in the dedication of the Auditorium/Chapel.

Now on Sunday mornings, when "church call" is sounded, NOS personnel gather in the Auditorium "rigged for church." There they worship God and pray for their country as they bow before a beautiful altar in an atmosphere especially conducive to the Praise of Almighty God.

Sources

Arbogast, Rosemary. "Marbury Baptist Church." Church records, unpublished, 1976.

Argo, Rev. David. "Chicamuxen United Methodist Church." Church records, unpublished, 1976.

Barkley, Rev. William I. Jr. "History for the Potomac Heights Baptist Church." Church records, unpublished, 1976.

——. "History of the Cobb Island Baptist Chapel." Church records, unpublished, 1976.

——. "History of the White Plains Baptist Chapel." Church records, unpublished, 1976.

Berkley, William K. Sr. "Southern Baptists in Southern Maryland." Potomac Baptist Association Paper, 1972.

Brown, Fannie, Bernice Swann, and Lucile Jones. "History of Pleasant Grove Baptist Church." Church records, unpublished, 1975.

Bursey, Christine. "History of the Hughesville Baptist Church." Church records, unpublished, 1975.

Clark, Elnora. "The History of Metropolitan United Methodist Church." Church records, unpublished, 1975.

Culp, Rev. Everett W. "Zion-Wesley United Methodist Church." Church records, unpublished, 1975.

Custis, Rev. Harvey R. "Alexandria United Methodist Church." Church records, unpublished, 1975.

——. "Smith Chapel United Methodist Church." Church records, unpublished, 1976.

Davis, Rev. William. "History of Trinity Parish." Church records, unpublished, 1969.

Dozier, Janette C. "Grace Baptist Church of Bryan's Road, Maryland." Church records, unpublished, 1975.

Edelen, Vivian B. "A History of St. Mary's Roman Catholic Church, Bryantown, Md." Unpublished, 1975.

Flowers, Rev. Alton H. "Ripley Community Church History." Church records, unpublished, 1975.

Gebauer, Edward M. III. "The Church of Jesus Christ of Latter-Day Saints." Church records, unpublished, 1975.

Gunter, Virginia P. "Good Shepherd United Methodist Church." Church records, unpublished, 1975.

Hall, Joan. "Shiloh Community United Methodist Church." Church records, unpublished, 1975.

"Inventory," Church Archives, District of Columbia.

Jones, Rev. Jerry S. "Marbury Church of God." Church records, unpublished, 1975.

Lackey, Rev. William. "First Baptist Church of Waldorf." Church records prepared for the 30th Anniversary, unpublished, 1975.

Lantz, Ruth; Schreiber, Marion; and Shelor, Nellie "History of Calvary United Methodist Church of Waldorf, Md." Chruch records, unpublished, 1975.

Moore, Rev. Clarence P. *History of the Indian Head Baptist Church*. Pamphlet, Indian Head, 1969.

Mudd, H. Virginia. "Charles County's Catholic Heritage." Unpublished, 1958.

Newcomb, Kathryn C. "Christ Church Episcopal." Unpublished, 1975.

Page, LCDR Dewey V. CHC USN. "NOS Protestant Chapel." Church records, unpublished, 1975.

Peterson, Rev. Eric G. "A Brief Historical Sketch of Lutheranism in Charles County." Church records, unpublished, 1975.

Pisgols, Alvin P. "The Lutheran Church of Our Savior." Church records, unpublished, 1975.

Rickenbaker, Rev. Gleaton. "First Baptist Church of St. Charles." Church records, unpublished, 1975.

Robinson, Maude C. "History of St. Paul's Church, Piney Parish." Church records, unpublished, 1975.

Rowe, Barbara. "History of Pisgah United Methodist Church, 1850-1975." Church records, unpublished, 1975.

Shifflett, Rev. Ronald "History of the First Baptist Church of La Plata." Church records, unpublished, 1975.

Taylor, Rev. Arnold. "Old Durham Church." Ironsides, 1958.

_____. "St. James' Episcopal and St. John's Chapel." Church records, unpublished, 1976.

Tiller, Mary Reeder. "History of Christ Church, William and Mary Parish." Church records, unpublished, no date.

Tolson, Lucille. "St. Matthew's United Methodist Church." Church records, unpublished, 1976.

Wearmouth, John M. and Roberta. "History of Methodism in La Plata, 1890-1965." Church records, unpublished, 1975.

Wedding, Anne Lucille and Kanie B. "History of the First Baptist Church of Welcome." Church records, unpublished, 1975.

Willett, Betty M. *Nanjemoy Baptist Church*. 175th Anniversary ed., Nanjemoy, Md., 1968.

Wilson, Jerry H. "History of the Church of Christ Waldorf." Church records, unpublished, 1975.

Wright, Y.J. "History of Shiloh United Methodist Church." Church records, unpublished, 1975.

CHAPTER 5

GOVERNMENT: WE THE PEOPLE

The history of the government of Charles County is as much a narrative of its people as of its laws. The County as we know it today did not come into being until April 13, 1658—and then only after the inhabitants of Nanjemoy and Port Tobacco creeks had complained that the distance to the St. Mary's Courthouse was too great for them to travel conveniently, or to conduct business efficiently.

Therefore, the Governor's Council ordered a new county established to take care of the more distant settlements. Originally the new County included all land west of the Patuxent River; in 1695 Prince George's County was created out of part of this area.

Colonial Charles County

Before Charles County was established, Southern Maryland had been marked by political struggle and warfare, largely traceable to the hostility between the Puritan settlers of the colony and Roman Catholic England.

The Lords Baltimore had been Proprietors of the Maryland colony since 1632, when George Calvert, First Baron, received grants for the territory. (It then included present-day Delaware.) His son, Cecilius Calvert, Second Baron Baltimore, headed the settlement expedition, which founded St. Mary's in 1634. Cecilius Calvert envisioned a colony where followers of both Catholic and Protestant faiths might be free of persecution, where religious tolerance might flourish untrammeled.

The men who had been appointed as first County Commissioners, on May 10, 1658, were required to swear to "do equal right, to the poore as to the rich, to the best of your cunning, witt and power and after the presidents and customes of this province and Acts of Assembly...".

But the third Lord Baltimore, Cecilius' son Charles, proclaimed his loyalty to the English king and Roman Catholicism. This was most unpopular among the many Puritan inhabitants of Charles County, and one result was the Fendall uprising of 1659.

It was quickly put down, and Philip Calvert was named the new Governor. Calvert selected from six to ten Justices, or Commissioners, who were to hold administrative as well as judicial powers.

Many of their duties—including the settling of certain taxes, authorization of public expenditures, setting of pay for County employees, supervision of roads, legal custody of orphans, and jurisdiction over the care of the poor, sick, and mentally disturbed—were not unlike the duties now vested in the Charles County Board of County Commissioners. Some, like paying bounty on wolves and wildcats, were.

In 1727 Port Tobacco, or Charles Town, as the official county seat was known, began. For the next 200 years, Port Tobacco/Charles Town was the center of the community's social and political life. It was the only sizeable town in the county, and its location on the river helped make it the natural center of commerce. The Naval Port of Entry, where ships were loaded or unloaded with trade goods, was a short way down the creek.

Meanwhile, Maryland was emerging as one of the colonies most resistant to the British commercial policies. The 1765 Stamp Act required that colonists use special stamped paper for all their legal documents, such as bills, bonds, leases, and notes. The paper could be obtained only by purchase from British officials, and Charles Countians boldly resisted application of this law.

A protest meeting was called at the Port Tobacco Courthouse in June 1774. The people resolved to import no goods from Great Britain after August, and to send representatives to a Maryland colony protest set for Annapolis; they also agreed to terminate trade with any colony that refused to participate in the boycott.

The thoughts of one Charles County resident chosen to attend the September 1774 First Continental Congress meeting at Philadelphia may have been typical of colonists forced to choose between loyalty to their Mother Country and to their new home. (The following anecdote is reproduced with permission from Stephenson, *A Journey to Philadelphia,* to be published later this year.)

"In September 1774, the journey to Philadelphia to attend the First Continental Congress, was for Thomas Johnson, Jr., filled with foreboding for the future of the American colonies, and in particular, his native colony of Maryland. There had been heated debates in the Maryland Convention as to a position to be taken in response to the Boston Port Bill, which had by now reduced the people of the Bay Colony to begging for help. Some were for all out aid to their fellow countrymen who were blockaded in Boston. Others wanted to break relations with Great Britain in protest. Still others advocated a petition to the King, setting forth the many grievances, and reminding him of their rights as free citizens to unobstructed commerce, to levy and collect taxes, to administer justice, and to live in peace and freedom from unwarranted search and seizure. And to provide for their own defense by bearing arms.

"The First Continental Congress as a whole was in agreement with this plan of action. Consequently, after six or seven weeks of debate, the delegates from all the represented colonies signed a Non-Importation Agareement, whereby they all agreed not to accept any goods from Great Britain until the Blockade of Boston was lifted. They also drafted a Petition to the King. It was resolved before adjournment that another Congress would convene in May of 1775 to pursue the courses they had resolved in the weeks just past.

"Upon Thomas Johnson's return to Annapolis for the Maryland State Convention, he found the atmosphere charged with cool, determined resolve. All the counties had sent their committees to Annapolis, with the express charge of positive action to raise money and supplies for the relief of the Town of Boston. And further, to organize their militia to protect the citizens of Maryland from the possibility of retaliation from British troops that might be sent to put down what seemed now to be open rebellion.

"Amongst the county delegates to the Annapolis Convention, Mr. Johnson saw a friend of long acquaintance, with whom he had studied Law in Annapolis. A man he knew to be modest, retiring and unassuming in manner. A man of clear head and sound judgment. For him to see his friend Thomas Stone, standing in front of the Committee of One Hundred from Charles County, he knew that some portentous danger hung over the Colonies. That things were radically wrong. This was not a man moved easily to mount the public rostrum. There was a look of firm and holy indignation about him. It was the clear mark of a man who had given all the effort he could muster, to right the wrongs through the normal channels of petition and legal debate. But now, he was ready with all the same vigor to move to another course of action. He was ready to respond to the will of his country.

"It was no surprise then, on the 8th of December 1774, when Thomas Stone was elected as a delegate to the next Continental Congress which was scheduled to convene on May 15, 1775, in Philadelphia.

"By the time that Congress did convene, the cry of blood from the heights of Lexington and the fields of Concord was ringing in the ears of the delegates. The clash of arms and mortal combat had already commenced. The fury of the revolutionary storm had broken. The fabric of civil government was falling before a foreign military force.

"To meet such a crisis, it would require, wisdom, patriotism, caution, and learning, combined with eloquence, to bring about a just and lasting conclusion to the noble causes for which so many would suffer and labor so long. That conclusion would begin with the Declaration of Independence. And Thomas Hunt Stone of Charles County, Maryland, would emphatically and firmly pen his name to that immortal document."

From that time on, the War for Independence was uppermost in the minds and actions of the people of Charles County. Many of our men fought for the entire duration of the War in the Maryland Line, under General William Smallwood. General George Washington praised Smallwood's troops on numerous occasions, and is said to have wished in public that he "had more like the men of Maryland."

Behind the lines, men of Charles County were also playing major roles in laying the foundations of government for the new nation to be. John Hanson was one of these men. Born in Charles County, he was elected delegate to the Continental Congress in 1780.

One of his leading demands was that the Articles of Confederation not be ratified until all states ceded their western lands to the federal government, as public domain. This meant that such Atlantic coastal states as Maryland and Virginia would give up their claims to ownership of territories that later became Kentucky and Tennessee. States that had been accustomed to sovereignty did not want to relinquish the fertile lands. But many of the delegates agreed with Hanson—especially those from states that had laid no claims to lands. And without the Articles of Confederation, there would be no nation, not even if Great Britain were defeated.

Eventually this principle was adopted, and the Articles were ratified March 1, 1781. The United States of America was a nation!

Hanson, elected Presiding Officer of the Congress that adopted the Articles, was in truth the first President of the nation. In that post, he was succeeded by George Washington, the victorious general.

Hanson and Stone, although the best known, were but two of many Charles Countians to serve in the Federal Government. Nor were they the only ones to affix their names to our most important national documents. In September 1787 Daniel of St. Thomas Jenifer signed the Constitution, a member of that Convention. James Forbes, born 1732 near Benedict, represented Charles County in the Third Continental Congress; in fact, he died while at Philadelphia, in 1780. Benjamin Contee, who was ordained a pastor at Port Tobacco after moving to Charles County, was the fifth man to attend the Continental Congress from Charles. He also represented Maryland in the First U. S. Congress, which began in 1789.

Since Contee, Charles County has provided eleven Representatives to the U.S. House, and one man (or two, depending on the source used) to the Senate. No doubt other men and women from Charles will hold Federal posts. Even now, some have been elected or appointed to statewide positions.

Members of the U.S. Senate from Charles County, and the years of their service are: Alexander C. Hanson, 1817; William D. Merrick, 1838-1845.

U.S. House of Representative members from Charles County: 1789-91, Benjamin Contee; 1794-95, Michael Jenifer Stone; 1793-1801, George Dent; 1796-1801, William Craik; 1833-35, John Truman Stoddert; 1845-49, John G. Chapman; 1863-65, Benjamin Gwinn Harris; 1867-71, Frederick Stone; 1881-83, Andrew C. Chapman; 1885-89 and 1891-95, Barnes Compton; 1889, 1890, 1897-99, and 1901-09, Sydney E. Mudd Sr; and 1915-24, Sydney E. Mudd Jr.

The New Nation

The war was over! The Treaty of Paris was signed and delegates and soldiers returned home to Charles County. They turned to local matters.

In 1798 the Assembly authorized four election districts for the County, and the next year appointed a commission to mark their boundaries.

But war with Great Britain resumed in 1812. This time, Charles County was one of the theatres of war. A British fleet occupied the Patuxent River, as well as the Potomac and Chesapeake Bay. Many residences along the shores of these waters were plundered. On June 15, 1814, a British force made its way up the Patuxent to Benedict, and came ashore to rout some Maryland militia. The British destroyed the weaponry and supplies left behind by the Americans, then returned to their craft.

Benedict was also the British re-embarkation point after the burning of Washington, D.C., that summer. It is a matter of record that flames leveling the government buildings of the nation's capital could be seen in Charles County; also, that the British encountered no resistance to their march from Washington to Benedict after their arson.

In 1815 the second Treaty of Paris marked the end of the second British-American war. By September 1821 a new Courthouse was ready for use at Port Tobacco, which name had become official by now.

For 30 years the County and its commerce grew. But commerce, insofar as it was a tobacco economy dependent on slave labor, was to suffer irrevocable damage from the next war—the War Between the States. The roots of that ordeal extend deep into Charles County.

It is 1825. News of the day, conveyed by word of mouth since the first newspaper—the *State Register*—will not be published until 1842, concerns the new Courthouse and perhaps the meteorite recently fallen (February 10) at Nanjemoy. New towns are being started all around, schools and churches built, traditions of church bazaars and jousting tournaments germinating. The nation is growing as new states join the Union.

Civil War

By 1850 the issue of slavery is paramount in the question of statehood. Maryland, one of the first 13 states, is not directly involved in this conflict, on the political level. But socially, slavery is central to the Old Line State—and to Charles

County. Just across the Potomac, Virginia's landed aristocracy keep slaves; at home, tobacco growers depend on the slaves' dawn to dusk labor.

And Geography has bestowed on Maryland the dubious epithet of "Border State." Northerners, around Baltimore and other heavily industrial Maryland cities, are sympathetic to the abolitionists. There are few fields or farms to labor in, and the population is largely composed of German, Irish, and other European immigrants, who feel a greater kinship to the working classes of Northern cities than to the aristocracies of the South.

Southern Maryland, however, abuts the Deep South; the way of life is almost entirely agricultural, the attitudes conservative, traditional, and Democratic. The South of Maryland, like that of the nation, supports slavery; indeed, it believes its economy depends on it.

Meanwhile, Maryland's roads and trails figure prominently as routes on the Underground Railroad, the system by which fugitive slaves reached freedom in the North and in Canada. Negroes in Maryland are "infected by the general unrest to such an extent that in 1856 it (is) necessary to begin nightly patrols of the County." (Brown, p. 119).

It is significant that in the Presidential Election of 1856, Maryland is the only state in the nation to give its electoral votes—a total of eight—to the candidate of the biased Know-Nothing Party, former President Millard Fillmore. Usually anti-Negro, in this election the Know-Nothings straddle the issue of slavery. They carry only Maryland.

As the election of 1860 draws closer, the nation, the State, and Charles County are confused, upset, and not a little frightened. Not only is preservation of a way of life at stake in this election, but—again—the horror of war. Even so, it is not likely that many could foresee the true horror the Civil War would wreak on Charles County.

During this period, the state is divided. Governor Thomas H. Hicks declares his Union, or Northern, sympathies; but the Legislature, dominated by powerful Southern and Eastern Shore forces, refuses to abolish slavery or to reapportion the General Assembly.

In April, seven months before the election, shots are fired on Fort Sumter, South Carolina. That state secedes from the Union, and the Civil War is underway. In Charles County, sympathizers of the South hope for a special session of the Maryland Legislature, where they too can secede from the Union.

But there are more moderate attitudes as well, and these prevail. Most people regard secession as rash, hasty, and uncalled or. Maryland does not secede. But many who live in Charles County believe their area is being treated by the Union as an enemy state.

A *Port Tobacco Times* editorial, Dec. 19, 1861, titled "Our Situation," captures the mood:

> The State of Maryland has cast her vote for the Union and Government by the largest majority every known to this State . . . Charles County then stands before the Government and the world this day a loyal county. Charles County has ever been loyal; we challenge a disloyal act to be laid at her door — and yet what is her condition? As a loyal county and State, obedient to the recognized law, faithful to the Constitution, the citizens of this State have a right, and undisputed right to protection in their person and property. Twenty thousand Federal troops are stationed upon the soil of Charles County, their camps extending from Mattawoman Creek to Liverpool Point. These troops are here "For our protection," we are told: "to protect us from the Rebels," and yet, in fact, we are exposed to more danger, to more losses and damage or at least as much as if these very Rebels were here. . . .Our negroes,—ah, this is the point,—our negroes—are taken from us time and time again, with no remuneration and the threats of violence if we seek to recover them. . . .

Despite their unwillingness to become secessionists, it must be noted that large majorities of Marylanders, and Countians, do not agree with Unionists. Most especially they do not agree that they should give up their slaves.

Military occupation, as described in the editorial, provokes many young men to cross the Potomac and join the Confederate Army. In 1862 only one Charles County man responds to President Lincoln's call for Union Army recruits. (Brown, p. 127)

Nevertheless, many Countians will fight on the side of the Union, and many more will come to support the cause of abolition—or, at least, favor equality for Negroes.

Among the Union soldiers was the Seventh Regiment Infantry, U.S. Colored Troops, Maryland Volunteers. These black Marylanders had their regimental camp at Benedict. They drilled through the winter of 1863 at Camp Stanton, and were activated in 1864. The regiment fought in all major campaigns of the Army of the Potomac; they suffered many casualties. (Brown, p. 129)

The War ended April 9, 1865, at Appomattox Courthouse, Va. But Maryland had freed her slaves the previous November 1, as required by the State Constitution that had been adopted in 1864.

Reconstruction

In Maryland's emancipation month, the nation re-elected President Lincoln. Thomas Swann became the new Governor. Despite the law, Swann had no intention of cooperating with the Union Party. He joined with the Democrats, who had always supported slavery. To Swann can be attributed much of the influence and power the Democrats retained through the 19th century in Maryland, even under Republican administrations.

Still, Swann was almost an anachronism. For the most part after the War, Charles County seemed a microcosm of the South. Emancipation of the Negro had immediate as well as long range effects on the whole of Southern life—economy, social structure, and, of course, politics.

A "defeatist" attitude was prevalent, and hostility towards abolitionists and Northerners in general, who had destroyed (Southerners thought) the grace and beauty that marked the "old order."

Economically, loss of a cheap and efficient labor force was disastrous. Not only was there no one to work the fields, but the fields themselves were badly ravaged. Charles County lands, in truth, were not as bad off as was much of the Deeper South; but even here, money was hard to come by, collateral for bank credit almost non-existent.

When the 15th Amendment gave the Negro the right to vote, political allegiances switched. The 1868 Legislature redistricted Charles County into nine election districts: Port Tobacco, Hill Top, Nanjemoy, Allen's Fresh, Harris Lot, Middletown, Pomonkey, Bryantown, and Patuxent City. And in 1870, for the first time, voter registration lists showed a Negro majority in the County.

At this time, the Republicans came to the fore, under the guidance of Dr. W.R. Wilmer. Wilmer began recruiting among Democrats, whose party was badly splintered. A "Fusion" ticket, comprised of Republicans and Independent Democrats—who had broken from the conservative Democratic tenets—swept the 1873 election. Thereafter, Independents were linked with, and became known as, Republicans. But since the old Democrats continued to exercise some influence, a two-party system actually was in operation.

The County saw major innovations, in the railroad, the steamship, and, later, the first electrical transmission. Each change had enormous effects on the government. The railroad's was most obvious: It resulted in the County seat being moved from Port Tobacco, whose influence was waning with the decline in water traffic, to La Plata, which was fortunate to host the first major railroad "station" in the County.

The location of the County seat became a political "hot potato," hot indeed when the Port Tobacco Courthouse burned to the ground in 1892. Arson was suspected, but not proved. (All County records had been safely removed from the building before the fire.) Both parties, Republicans and Democrats, had split into similar factions: One in support of continuing Port Tobacco as the County seat, the other opting to move it to La Plata. Elections were decided not on party lines, but on the candidates' choice of County seat site.

Finally, La Plata won out. The new Courthouse there was dedicated in 1896.

The 20th Century

With the turn of the century, Democratic leadership turned to younger men, who aligned Charles County with the "Progressives." But 19th century politics were sealed more by the First World War than by the arrival of the modern century. The personalities that had given the old era its stability and unity passed from the scene. There remained traces of Southern sympathy, and the issue of "white supremacy," but by now the matter was viewed as a definition of States' Rights, no longer purely racial.

Politically, the coming of the 20th century has meant the ascendance of State control over local rule. In the early period, the six Court Justices or Commissioners exercised almost total control over County matters. Today, the three County Commissioners are greatly dependent on the State Legislature for the enactment of local bills. How did this come about?

The State Constitution of 1867 reaffirmed the principle of separation of power among the executive, legislative, and judicial branches of the State government. It did not alter the bicameral form of the Legislature, that is, the two houses. The Senate, or Upper House, consisted of one Senator from each of the 23 counties, and one from each of the six Legislative districts of Baltimore; the House of Delegates was designed to represent the population proportionately.

Apportionment of representation has always been a point of irritation between urban and rural voters. In the past, the inequity of representation heavily favored rural counties. At one time, nine Eastern Shore counties, with a population of just over 200,000 were represented by 26 delegates, while Prince George's County, with a population of over 250,000, had only six delegates. However, the political power base has since shifted, so the most populous urban areas—such as Prince George's, Montgomery, Ann Arundel, and Baltimore counties—have almost total control of the General Assembly. The most recent reapportionment has resulted in Charles County having "to share" one State Senator and three delegates with its neighboring county, St. Mary's. Previously, Charles County had its own State Senator and delegates.

Responsibility for administration and control of local affairs has shifted largely to the State Legislature, where local matters are regularly considered and local bills frequently enacted by all members of that body so that the county governments may properly function.

The policy of placing local bills before the State Legislature created a logjam almost from its inception. Already in 1884 the Governor felt it necessary to speak out against the practice in his message to the Assembly. He cited

> a mass of local bills for separate counties, having relations to hawks, foxes, owls, crows, etc., birds, fish, to change the names of crossroads, to change election district lines, to make new districts, for insurance on public buildings and for addition to others, to build school houses; for drainage, for stock running at large, to open streets, make causeways, . . .".

The number of local bills clogging Legislature sessions has mounted. In the early 1900s, 56 per cent of the bills passed by the Legislature were local in nature; in 1951, 66.9 per cent; and in 1953, 76.9 per cent!

Adoption of Article XI-A permitted the City of Baltimore and all counties to frame their own charters. In 1954 the General Assembly passed a bill that permitted home rule in municipalities when certain conditions were met. But the counties did not take advantage of the home rule provisions at first. Only recently have the counties enacted home rule, and Charles is one of only three that still cling to the archaic commissioner-type county government.

In view of the real and potential growth of our County's economic and residential base, this has become a most serious consideration for the proper, timely, and competent administration and control of County matters.

The enormous growth of the County's budget in the last 30 years is but one reason for adopting home rule.

Fiscal Year	County Tax Rate (per $100 assessed value)	County Budget
48/49	1.35	$365,670
49/50	1.10	$349,503
50/51	1.00	$518,572
51/52	1.30	$546,541
52/53	1.55	$650.392
53/54	1.55	$746,819
54/55	1.55	$850,737
55/56	1.55	$932,479
56/57	1.55	$1,043,641
57/58	1.50	$1,180,667
58/59	1.35	$1,290,319
59/60	1.35	$1,551,277
60/61	1.65	$1,681,364
61/62	1.65	$1,739,917
62/63	1.65	$2,205,861
63/64	1.65	$2,406,723
64/65	1.65	$2,603,404
65/66	1.85 +.10	$3,265,257
66/67	2.15 +.10	$4,161,236
67/68	2.15 +.10	$5,551,983
68/69	2.40 +.10	$6,851,980
69/70	2.80 +.10	$7,909,728
70/71	3.05 +.10	$9,022,620
71/72	3.05 +.10	$12,253,480
72/73	3.00 +.10	$14,413,586
73/74	2.95 +.10	$16,331,993
74/75	2.42 +.10	$19,005,734
75/76	2.42 +.10	$23,562,701

Construction of the Potomac River Bridge over Rt. 301 in 1939 opened the County to the surrounding area. No longer was Charles County a "dead end," returning north. The bridge brought to the County the commerce of traffic "traveling through" to points south, and Rt. 301 became a major north-south artery for goods and tourists.

The expansion of the Naval Propellant Plant at Indian Head during World War II substantially increased the County's economic base. Public housing at Glymont, for example, was valued at $891,000. This housing was needed to accommodate personnel coming into the County as a result of the Defense Plant's growth.

The legalization of slot machine gambling in Charles County meant the mushrooming of motels, restaurants, and cocktail lounges along Rt. 301, from the Prince George's County line to the Potomac River. At one time, the revenue from slot machines, or "amusement devices," as they were officially designated, represented about one-fourth of the County's income. The same electric power that permitted operation of the slot machines proved another boon to Charles County: The Potomac Electric Power Company (PEPCO) plant located at Morgantown is the largest single taxable base in the County.

It is important to understand the impact this phase of the County's economic development had on the nature of local government. Previously, County officials faced no pressing issues other than normal community support functions, facilities, and activities; and, as noted above, many of these authorizations had by law to be submitted for the State Legislature's consideration and action.

The transformation of local government began in the period immediately following World War II, and intensified after the Korean War. New relationships were being formed between local officials and the Federal and State agencies that dealt with the problems of road, highways, housing, public schools, land use, and planning. The responsibilities of the County government were beginning to resemble those of a large corporation—which, in fact, it had become. The functions and interrelationships of the administration were numerous, varied, and technical. In time, many boards, committees, commissions, and agencies were created by the

County Commissioners to deal with, supervise, administer, and account for County programs.

This period also marked great expansion of the public school system through construction of new schools, including the Charles County Community (junior) College. Additional programs generated the construction of new roads, hospital facilities, libraries, parks, and other services. It was now evident that the County's physical plant would have to expand to keep pace with the continuing economic and population growth.

Concomitant with the growth, regulations to provide proper guidelines were needed. The Commissioners and their respective agencies established these rules, as well as attendant fees for: garbage collection, operation of amusement devices, dog kennels, dog licenses, liquor licenses, plumbing, electrical and building codes, operation of eating and drinking establishments, construction and operation of mobile home parks, and many other endeavors.

The pressures of growth and its related problems put many new responsibilities in the hands of the Commissioners. But, despite the fact that many of these obligations had been assigned to particular agencies, there was then, as now, no direct line of authority from the elected Commissioners to their appointed subordinates. In some cases, agencies and employees of the Commissioners retain a quasi-autonomous relationship with the County government; in the most extreme cases, the Commissioners exercise only review and approval authority over agency budgets, seemingly doing no more than rubber stamping agency "requests."

The economic blow suffered by Charles County businessmen from the phase-out of the slot machines in the 1960s did not go unnoticed. The County Commissioners ordered studies to ascertain the extent of revenue loss, which occurred at about the same time a scaledown of employment at the Naval Plant depressed the communities of Indian Head and Bryan's Road.

An Economic Development Committee was established by the Commissioners in 1961, in an effort to induce new business and commerce to locate in the County. A notable accomplishment of recent years has been the construction of a milk distributing plant in the County; other industries have followed. The EDC, with the help of local Chamber of Commerce spokesmen, also put through a plan to reduce interstate freight rates by persuading one trucking company to use a "through-rate" schedule on goods shipped to and from Charles County. Previously freight rates were charged on the basis of two trips, with Baltimore the first terminal, regardless of the point of origin or final destination of the truckload. The new schedule does not require that goods go through Baltimore at all, unless it is on the direct route.

Studies preparatory to drawing up "master plans" for water and sewer facilities in the County were begun in the 1960s. The resulting master plan for Charles County encompasses not only water and sewers, but also transportation systems and new land use recommendations.

By 1968 the population of Charles County had reached 40,000. The construction of large residential subdivisions encouraged more population.

The developments have had paradoxical effects. Although they provide needed additional revenue, largely from property and employment taxes, they have also taxed the County's already strained police, fire, and other protective and supportive facilities.

The 1960s and 1970s were marked by a heavy traffic in re-zoning dockets, reflecting an unusually large number of requests to redesignate rural-agricultural areas as either residential or commercial zones. Charles Countians became concerned about the sudden economic and population spurts. Officials fear the growth may be of such magnitude that it cannot be adequately supported from the existing tax base. That is, the new multifamily residences being built may bring into the County large numbers of people who do not contribute proportionately to the tax revenue. Providing services for so many people would cause a financial drain on County funds; ultimately, the trend would be reflected by an increase in property taxes or suspension of services.

Some residents anticipate a "paved over" Charles County, one that would resemble the untrammeled recent growth of Northern Virginia or Prince George's County, with the attendant problems of congestion and crime.

The Comprehensive Plan for Charles County, the Land Use Bill, was presented for public scrutiny by the Planning Commission in 1974. The plan proposes to properly channel future growth in the County through the year 1994, so as to prevent the haphazard, crazy-quilt type expansion that has been occurring in surrounding urban areas.

As it was originally presented, the plan allowed for a high concentration of growth to occur in the corridor formed by Rts. 301 and 210, from the Prince George's County line south to a point beyond La Plata. To offset this large growth build-up in that corridor, about half of the County's land area was to be zoned rural-agricultural, with a further restriction that only one residence be permitted within each five-acre tract.

Public protest led to the reduction of the R-5 zone requirement to R-3, allowing one residence for each three acres in the rural-agricultural zones. Objections to R-5 were mounted by those who believed the five-acre requirement to be arbitrary and discriminatory against those who owned smaller tracts. Other objectors sought a more equitable distribution of the expected commercial and residential growth, by planning and paying now for the anticipated necessary expansion of water, sewer, road, and protective facilities.

In the nation's Bicentennial year, our County is 318 years old. We face many uncertainties, each becoming more complex as time passes. It is clear that we must approach the future with dedication and unity of purpose. In seeking to chart a course that will assure a good and equitable future for people of the County, some officials and residents are urging two major objectives:

First, re-organization of the County government—to provide for home rule and consolidation of all County functions into four or five departments, which would be directed by professionals in each field, under the direct supervision of elected officials accountable for government administration.

Second, restructuring of the Comprehensive Plan—so the main thrust of the anticipated growth would not be concentrated in one area but would be distributed equitably throughout the County.

These seem fitting goals for the people of Charles County as we celebrate our nation's political independence.

CHAPTER 6

BLACK HISTORY: HERE AT THE BEGINNING

Black people have lived in Charles County since the early days of settlement. Yet Charles Countians know little about their African heritage. They know little about why blacks were brought from their native Africa as slaves to a new land, or about their entry into and support of Charles County's Colonial economy and social life. What part did Charles County play in this transition of a people from one continent to another? What were the characteristics and lifestyles of these Africans who became Americans in Charles County?

Historical omission of blacks in the history of early settlers has served to create the false assumption that blacks have a history and achievement inferior to whites. The tendency has been to ignore African history in our schools, or to relate it only superficially to the facts about slavery in Maryland. Our children are badly served by learning little or nothing of their African heritage.

This chapter attempts to compile the scattered fragments of the African backgrounds, both oral and written, and to give a glimpse of what it has meant to be black in Charles County from Colonial times through the present.

Background

Basic historical accounts of early colonialism would have us surmise that Africa never existed, except as a convenient exporter of slave labor. Early histories for the most part present Egypt as the one part of Africa that was civilized; the rest of the Dark Continent is depicted as barbaric.

However, a more careful review of African history shows that flourishing civilizations occupied that "other" Africa—from which most slaves came to this country. In Central and Western Africa were noteworthy empires: Benin, Yoruba, Melle, Mossi, and others. They had developed their own forms of government, of commerce, and of complex societies. It was from these cultures that Africans of different customs, languages, socialization, and lifestyles were forcibly transferred to Europe, the West Indies, and the Americas.

The Slave Trade

It is common knowledge that slavery has been practiced in various forms throughout history. In war, Romans enslaved captive Germans, and Germans made slaves of captured Romans. Indebted persons were held in bondage for their debts, and Christians enslaved their Christian captives.

Columbus enslaved Indians during his adventures in the New World. Some were sent to Spain, and others were made forced laborers here. Within a few years, however, from overwork, ill treatment, and especially white man's diseases and wars, Indians dwindled away. The Indian slave was then replaced by the African.

The Africans were an experienced labor force. They had farmed their own homelands and had acquired skills. Once in the New World, they learned new crafts, such as carpentry, metal working, shipbuilding, brickmaking, and other construction and artisan trades. Most Charles County slaves, however, were field hands, working on the tobacco crops.

The slave trade, once begun, proved a devastating blight upon Africa's developing civilizations. Whole villages were depopulated as African kings and European merchants turned to an easier way of making a living: trading human beings to satisfy the demand of their European and American brothers for a cheap labor force.

The slave trade coast of West Africa stretched almost 4,000 miles—from the mouth of the Senegal down past the Equator. Merchants transported captive Africans in whatever vessels they could command, many of them too small and ill-equipped to provide for their extensive cargo. The large, sleek ships were to come later after slave importation to North America was declared illegal, and slavetraders found it necessary to outrun British seacaptains who attempted to enforce the law.

These voyages from the African coast were long and painful. Slaves were generally transported in leg irons and handcuffs which, by the end of the voyage, had worn away the flesh. Often unable to move because of overcrowded conditions, blacks were forced to lie in their own filth until they sickened and died. Frequently, a ship lost half its cargo of slaves. Their bodies were thrown overboard, leaving a trail of black corpses all the way across the Atlantic.

Mutiny was not unknown. Africans fought hard to escape enslavement. Whenever the opportunity arose, they would assume control of the ship—only to become lost on the vast ocean because they lacked navigational knowledge. The meeting of "ghost" ships is mentioned frequently in slave trade documents.

These same documents tell of slaves starving themselves to death by refusing to eat, and of others flinging themselves into the Atlantic to drown rather than face the unknown terrors of slavery.

Once they landed, merchants sold their cargoes of slaves either aboard ship or at warehouse auctions. Plantation owners would barter for inexpensive, sturdy labor.

Slavery in Maryland

Records indicate that blacks were among the first settlers to reach the American shores.

Virginia historians have documented that 20 blacks arrived among the Pilgrims in 1620. Paul Rolfe of Virginia reported that 20 blacks were sold. It is further substantiated that 20 blacks were brought to the Virginia colony in 1620 aboard a Dutch ship from the coast of Guinea.

In Maryland, we know that blacks were present not long after the first settlers under the Proprietor arrived, and that importation continued through much of the 18th century.

But the first blacks in the New World did not come as slaves, but as explorers joining with others in the search for new worlds.

History indicates that black men played a part in the early development of Western Civilization. Blacks accompanied Balboa and De Soto in their early 16th century explorations in America. A black man owned land in South America, in Chile, as early as 1555. Black men were a part of the exploring, founding, and developing of colonies in the United States. They accompanied Lewis and Clark at the beginning of the 19th century. Charles County's own Matthew Henson was with Admiral Richard Perry in his quest for the North Pole—and it was Henson who was the first man to stand on top of the world.

A mulatto, Matthew Sousa, is referred to in Father Andrew White's list of passengers who accompanied him. Records also indicate that in 1642 Governor Leonard Calvert referred to the delivery of "fourteen Negro men-slaves and three women-slaves of between 16 and 26 years old. . .".

In the oldest land record book of Maryland a mulatto, Francisco, is mentioned as having been brought to the colony by Father White in 1635. Subsequent entries in the land records indicate that a black woman, Phillis, was transported into Maryland in 1648. It is interesting to note that at this time blacks were considered to be part of the population, not property.

The English had begun the slave trade under a charter from King James I as early as 1618, but indications are that slavery at that time did not prove profitable and so the charter expired. Later, after the English plantation settlements of the West Indies were demanding labor, a second company for African slave trade was established under Charles I (1631).

This indicates that the importation of slaves into the Colony of Maryland may already have been legal at the time of the first settlement in 1634.

Soon American merchant ships loaded with rum were to depart the New England colonies to the West Indies, go on to the African coast to exchange rum for slaves, then back to the West Indies with a cargo of slaves before returning for the Colonies. This "Triangle Trade," as it became known, was to continue to prosper and to supply the colonies with slave labor.

Until 1663 Maryland was not sufficiently prosperous to contract for an entire cargo of slaves from big trading companies. Blacks were obtained in small groups from Virginia and the West Indies.

In 1667 George Thompson of Maryland urged the Royal African Company to take account of Maryland's need for slaves. It may be noted that slavery by law was not established until the Act of 1664; however, the Act clearly recognizes slavery's prior existence.

Slavery in Charles County

The first blacks in Charles County were said to have been imported in the 17th century by Francis Pope, whose land grant on the Potomac River included Pope's Creek.

This settlement brought the African face to face with new conditions of life. He was compelled to make adjustments. His status as a slave exposed him to economic limitations and spiritual domination by whites for more than two centuries.

The slave had no control over his life. He was considered less than human, bargained for and sold like any other property. His status in Charles County was that of one whose task it was to hew wood, draw water, till the soil, and be a servant for the master. He was considered incapable of mental discipline through formal training of any kind. He was denied the rights of citizenship that enabled one to own property and to participate in the affairs of government.

In this strange and hostile environment, it became necessary for the black man to develop techniques of survival.

So he early adopted the tactics of smiling, dancing, laughing, and singing. He developed a keen sense of humor, which enabled him to release suppressed emotions in ways that did not offend, and which at the same time helped him through difficult situations. The poem, "The House Inside," reflects this:

The House Inside

I have a house inside me,
A house people never see;
It has a door through which none pass,
And windows, but they're not glass.

"Where do you live?" ask folks I meet,
And I say, "On such a street";
But still I know what's really me,
Lives in a house folks never see.

Sometimes I like to go inside,
And hide and hide and hide and hide,
And "doctor up" my wounded pride,
When I've been "treated rough" outside.

And sometimes when I've been to blame,
I go indoors and blush for shame,
And get my mind in better frame,
And get my tongue and temper tame.

Then after I've been made strong,
And have things right, that were all wrong,
I come outside where I belong,
To sing a new and happy song.

Author unknown

Life in Colonial Charles County was especially difficult for the slave. Records of the Jesuits indicate that slaves lived on plantations in one-story log cabins, usually with one room on the lower floor for adults and a garret under the roof for the children. The quarters were usually about 14 by 16 by 12 feet, with a hearth located on one wall.

The master provided no bedding except a blanket and old straw sacks, which were placed on planks and wooden horses. Often the men slept on the ground floor around the hearth. Slaves were fed largely on salt pork, herring, and corn meal.

For clothing the men usually received one woolen jacket, one pair of breeches, one pair of stockings, and one pair of shoes every winter. The women received one pair of shoes, one petticoat, and one jacket every year, and one pair of stockings every other year.

In accordance with State laws, white Charles Countians were permitted the privilege of owning slaves as property, which would be willed to their descendants. The following passages are from Wills registered in the County.

> In the name of God Amen, I Walter Beanes of Charles County in the province of Maryland being weak in body but sound in mind and memory do make this my last Will and Testament hereby nulling and revoking all others heretofore made by me.
> ... I give unto the said Elizabeth one Negro called Mingo, one-half dozen silver spoons and all that stock of cattle and other goods.

And,

> I Thomas Stone of Charles County in the Province of Maryland being sick of body and sound of memory do make the said Will. I make and ordaine my loving wife Mary Stone my sole estate. My dear sons William and Thomas Stone that plantation that is near Simor. I give William Stone all my land and plantation as I have. I give my woman Margarett and my black mares.

And,

> I Zachary Wade of Charles County in the province of Maryland ... do make and ordaine this my last will the Fifth day of March 1677. I give and bequeath unto my son Robert 3000 pounds of tobacco and one Negro boy.

Later wills indicate the giving of slaves *and* their potential offspring:

> I, Mary B. Barnes of Charles County State of Maryland . . . do make and ordain this my last will and testament . . . I give and bequeath to my sister Mary A. Barnes, one Negro woman called Alice to be disposed of at her death as she may think proper . . . I give and bequeath to my brother one Negro man called Alexander, also one Negro boy called John . . . I give and bequeath to my niece Elizabeth Briscoe one Negro man named Josias and one Negro girl named Julia Ann, also my guitar, large locket, and one bed and furniture . . . I give and bequeath one Negro man called Bill . . . one Negro girl called Sally . . . to my nephew, Walter H. I. Mitchell, one Negro man called William, son of Milly . . . also the hire of Negro William for the year 1826 . . . to the infant daughter of my niece Elizabeth Briscoe one Negro girl called Dian . . . It is my will and desire that my oldest Negro Milly by free and that she retain the cattle now in her possession for her own use.
>
> I give and bequeath to my grand niece Mary Clagett one Negro girl called Clarissa and in case said Negro have a child previous to or within nine months after my death I give said child to my niece Elizabeth Page. . . .

As is noted by the provisions of these wills filed in Charles County, the families of slaves were continually separated—husband from wife and mother from child.

Slaves often were freed upon their masters' deaths and, on some occasions property and money were willed to them:

> . . . In consideration of the faithful service of my Negro woman Alice, it is my wish and desire that said Negro woman to manumit and free and that my executor pay to her the sum of sixty dollars.
>
> . . . I hereby emancipate, liberate, and set free my Negro woman Mary and direct my heirs to pay her annually on the first of January during her natural life the sum of twenty dollars towards her support and maintenance.

> In the first place I liberate and manumit all my slave property of the following description, namely woman Esther, man Josias, man John . . . woman Hester, and her daughter Jane Julias Love, woman Cecilia and her two children . . . I give and bequeath unto my Negroes all my stock consisting of one man, cattle, hogs, and all the residue of my property . . . to have and hold forever . . . .

The life of the slave was a tenuous affair. From the departure from the African shore, his fate was in the hands of his master. Seldom was he allowed to feel secure.

As the slaves were brought into the ports they were often sold on board the ship that brought them, after there had been widely circulated advertisements:

> Just imported from Africa a parcel of choice slave Negroes which will be to sale this day, on board the ship Kaulikan . . . on Patuxent River, for Bills of Exchange, money or crop tobacco . . . .

Any relationships that had developed among the Negroes were threatened, for sale of a part of a family was common. Slaves were also hired out:

> 1820—with the hire of Negro Smith for this year, $60.00
> 1821—with the hire of Negro Charles for this year, 60.00

Slaves were unquestionably valuable to Charles County society. An inventory published in 1824 testifies to that:

Negroe George	aged 45 (one arm)	$ 80.00
Negroe Lucy	aged 13	200.00
Negroe Molly	aged 10	120.00
Negroe George	aged 7	100.00
Negroe Eliza	aged 4	50.00

For 200 years, between the Act of 1664 that legalized slavery in Maryland and the adoption of the State

Constitution in 1864 that abolished it, black people were the victims of one of the most vicious legal systems in history.

Slaves could not learn or worship, they could not marry free blacks or any whites, and they could not, of course, leave their masters' homes. Slaves were bartered for, hired out, shipped, molested, and branded. Often the harsh treatment drove them to attempt escape. This had its own dangers: A 1723 law gave slaveowners the right to kill runaway slaves without penalty. Sheriffs advertised their capture of runaways, and owners their "losses":

> Run away from the Subscriber, living in Charles County, near Pomonkey warehouse, on Tuesday the 14th Instant, a Negro man named George, just imported in the *Snow Providence*, Capt. Davis from Africa: He is about 5 feet 8 inches high, has a scar on the right side of his head.... Whoever takes up and secures the said Negro, so that I may get him again, shall have a reward of Thirty Shillings Currency, including what the law allows, and reasonable charges brought home paid by Alexander M'Donald. (Maryland Gazette, Sept. 6, 1770)

Again,

> Run-Away from the Subscriber, near Port Tobacco . . . a mulatto slave . . . he is fair as sometimes to be taken for a white man . . . whoever will apprehend . . . said mulatto to his mistress, shall have . . .

The continued increase in the number of runaways, aided by the eventual spread of anti-slavery sentiment, and the growing numbers of free blacks and free-thinking whites, was the beginning of the end of slavery.

Songs of Freedom

After a hard day's work in the tobacco fields the slaves were allowed to visit among themselves. They would go from one plantation to another and exchange stories and laughter. This was a form of entertainment. The slaves in Charles

County had no material possessions to aid in preserving the arts and customs of their homeland. Yet, though empty-handed, they had in their minds and hearts a treasure of complex musical forms, dramatic speech, and imaginative stories to tell.

They told tales of animals, like "The Fox and the Goose," "Ole Sis Goose," "Tar Baby," "Rabbit Teaches Bear a Song," "Brer Rabbit and Sis Cow," and "Why the Fox's Mouth Is Sharp."

The most significant technique of survival slaves developed might be called the "religious" one, represented by spirituals and early efforts to establish and develop the Black Church. The creation of the spiritual was not an accident in slave life, but a necessity so the slave might adjust himself to the strange conditions of life in the New World.

These songs are the expressions of the restrictions and dominations which their creators experienced in the world about them. They represent the soul-life of a people. They embody the joy and sorrow, the hope, despair, and aspirations of a newly transplanted society. Through the spirituals a race was able to endure suffering and to survive. The spirituals were not songs of hate, nor of revenge, but songs of the soul and the soil.

Through their music, slaves in Charles County have left a record of themselves. Spirituals sung in the County tobacco fields revealed the innermost thoughts of the slaves—on religion, for the future, and on slavery itself, with the multitudinous problems faced by a people held in bondage. A constantly recurring theme in all slave songs was the longing for escape.

Among the spirituals that filled the hearts and souls of black Charles Countians were: "Sinner, Please," "Deep River," "Steal Away," "You'd Better Mind," "I'm Bound for the Promised Land," and "When I Die."

Many of the spirituals dwelled on death, for the slave believed that if he could only get to Heaven, God would shelter him from the mighty storm of slavery. A verse from "Thoughts of Death" expresses this:

> Death is gwin'ter lay his cold icy hands on me,
> One morning I was walkin' along
> I heard a voice and saw no man;
> Said go in peace and sin no more,
> Yo' sins fo'given and yo'
> Soul set free. One of dese
> Mornings it won't be long,
> Yo'll look for me an' I'll be gone.

Expressions of faith in the peace and freedom of death were sung over and over, until the singer could think only of God. He forgot the hot tobacco fields, his hewing wood, plowing fields, washing clothes, cooking, and all the other laborious tasks he had to perform. In singing he could imagine he was free, as he longed to be.

Religion

The desire for religious expression played a major role in the establishment of the Black Church in Charles County. Soon after blacks were brought to the New World the question of the enslavement of Christians arose. Since there seemed to be an unwritten law that a Christian could not be held as a slave (not, at least, by other "Christians"), the slaveholders determined that converting slaves to Christianity would lead to a diminished labor supply. They believed that "too much enlightenment" might inspire slaves with the thought of freedom.

However, after laws were passed to assure that slaves' conversion to Christianity would not result in their freedom, plantation owners agreed to limited religious indoctrination for blacks.

There soon developed missionaries who spread the doctrine of Christ. The Quakers were the first to take real interest in the religious lives of slaves. Soon other denominations began to accept blacks into their congregations.

But after the American Revolution the initial movement to allow the slaves some religious training was supplanted by more stringent rules of enslavement.

Blacks, having enjoyed the freedom of religion, were reluctant to revert. This attitude, coupled with the enlarged number of free blacks in the North, asserted itself in the form of independent black missionaries and churches. Since white churches were now strongly opposed to equal acceptance of black worshipers, there arose a tendency toward religious separation. Blacks might still give expression to their religious feelings, but by themselves.

After several insurrection movements by blacks, however, laws were passed to impose new religious restrictions. One incident occurred locally in 1845, when several slaves and a free black were arrested in Charles County for insurrection. The free black was given 40 years imprisonment, and one slave was sentenced to be hung. Most of those who took part in the incident were not brought to trial: they were sold out of Maryland by their masters. A group of citizens requested that the Governor commute the condemned black's sentence from hanging to imprisonment—which required a special act of the State Assembly.

Now laws were passed against slaves' religious practice. Some states made it unlawful for blacks to preach to more than seven slaves at a time; others insisted that slaveowners attend the services. Slaves were again forced to follow their masters' practices; later, white ministers preached to slave gatherings. The few blacks that might attend established churches were segregated in the rear or in galleries, which they entered through a separate door.

During this period of religious oppression in the South, Northern black ministers were crusading for abolition. With the approach of the Civil War black ministers worked hard to free man's body as well as his soul.

The militant attitude of many slaves found expression in the popular verse:

O Freedom; O Freedom; O Freedom over me!
Before I'd be a slave,
I'd be buried in my grave,
And go home to my Lord and be free!

The first black church in Charles County was founded in Chicamuxen in 1866 by the Jordan family. After blacks were set free the family obtained a large tract of land on which they built a log church. People from miles around would attend the Jordan Chapel. Here blacks prayed and sang all night during their big "camp meetings."

A few years later, in 1868, Price's Chapel was started at Pomonkey by a local preacher, Henry Datcher. The Rev. Daniel Wheeler became the first pastor to conduct services monthly, for four years. In 1870 the Smith Chapel was founded for a black congregation.

Initially one preacher was in charge of the three churches. He was known as the "Circuit Rider Preacher" because he would ride from one church to another spreading the good news of Christ to the newly freed people.

BLACK CHURCHES IN CHARLES COUNTY

Name	Denomination	Site
Metropolitan	Methodist	Pomonkey
Smith Chapel	Methodist	Pisgah
Alexander Chapel	Methodist	Chicamuxen
Emery Chapel	Methodist	Grayton
Shiloh	Methodist	Newburg
St. Luke	Methodist	Waldorf
St. Matthews	Methodist	La Plata
Mt. Hope	Baptist	Ironsides
Oak Grove	Baptist	Grayton
Zion	Baptist	Hill Top
Pleasant Grove	Baptist	Marbury
Macedonia	Baptist	Bryan's Road
St. Catherine	Catholic	Port Tobacco

During this time blacks built churches throughout Maryland and in the District of Columbia. The Methodist denomination spread especially fast, and the local congregations felt a need to unite with a large group. They subsequently joined the Washington, D.C., Methodist Conference. Two of the chapels changed their names: Jordan's Chapel became Alexander Chapel, because the first pastor after its union with the Conference was named Alexander; Price's Chapel became Metropolitan M. E. Church. Smith Chapel retained its name. Many Charles County Blacks became Methodists after emancipation.

At this time there came the Rev. A.B. Ward from Virginia, a stirring leader who spread the Baptist faith. He went to many towns and villages, from Mercury to Nanjemoy, spreading the word about John, the Baptist. He believed, like John, that each soul must be baptized to remove his sins. Under his leadership, four churches were built for Baptist services: Oak Grove at Grayton, Pleasant Grove at Marbury, Mt. Hope at Ironsides, and Zion at Hill Top. All these churches are still active.

Education

Blacks' desire for education grew with the abolition of slavery in 1865. The privilege had been denied them for more than 200 years. The most logical way to establish schools was to extend the places for religious worship, which were already doing education of their own. Consequently schools were situated in, beside, or near the church.

The home, the school, and the church were the three main facilities in the black community.

The first schools were established in the western section of the county, where population was greatest. They were located in Chicamuxen, Mt. Hope, Oak Grove, Zion, and Shiloh churches. Attendance ranged from 12 to 30 pupils in each building. As soon as money and land were available, each community built its own school. After the land was purchased and the building erected, the school was deeded to the County. From that moment the school was a County facility, operated as such. Some of the schools were in operation until the middle of the 20th century.

THE COMMUNITY SCHOOL. All schools for blacks in Charles County from 1872 until 1935 were one-room schools. Most of them were built by blacks who lived in the nearby small communities. The buildings were precious to the people, who referred to them as "my school" or "our school." The school was accorded the same respect as the church.

The building served as schoolhouse and also as location for all community functions except religion. Among the activities carried on in the community schools were dances, bake sales, card parties, chicken dinners, movies, public speaking contests, elections, shelter (in time of disaster), and public health clinics.

Young and old alike enjoyed the facilities of the school. It was the center of social life, a place where something was always going on.

Another reason the school was so popular was that during the 1920s and 1930s entertainment in the home was limited for blacks. The school provided amusement. Often a party being given at one community school was attended by people in neighboring communities; the invitations would be reciprocated.

If money were raised from an event at the school, it would go to a worthy cause that was popular in the community. Events were always attended by at least one of the three trustees appointed to that particular school.

Two-Room Schools. When enrollment in the one-room school increased to 45 pupils, a second room was added. The community carried on the same activities in the enlarged building, but more events could be scheduled. Children had a better opportunity to learn in the two-room schools, and the teacher could provide more individual instruction.

The curriculum, too, was larger now; it might include art, music, and physical education.

Many of the schools for blacks were substandard; little thought was given to the health and safety of those attending until after the 1950s. Attempts had been made earlier to correct this, but black schools' requests had little influence with the Board of Education; indeed, most schools, white or black, had to receive most of their help from their own communities.

The Future
Since the abolition of slavery in Maryland, blacks have consistently fought the residue of that destructive system, and they continue to battle the lasting effects of slavery. Their history is as old as the County's—from their arrival at Port Tobacco as slaves in the 17th century, through the plantation labor force of the 18th, emancipation and sharecropping in the 19th, and today's search for equal opportunity and treatment. Black leaders are found in all fields—construction, education, religion, social and cultural endeavors, business, professions, and law. The contribution of blacks to Charles County is not only an historic fact, but a constant, increasing part of modern life.

CHAPTER 7

EDUCATION: HOW THE PUBLIC SCHOOLS

In the Colonial Period wealthy citizens of Charles County considered the education of the young a private matter. They resented the possibility that they might be taxed to educate children from poor white families. And the idea that a Negro, whether slave or free, would benefit from studying the basic elements of reading, writing, and mathematics was foreign to commonly held beliefs.

The offspring of the wealthy usually were taught at home, by clergymen or by tutors brought to the County from another colony or from abroad. Sometimes the older children were sent to Europe to finish their basic education. Others left Charles County for a time to study in other parts of Maryland. For example, about 1745, the Rev. Thomas Craddock of St. Thomas Parish in Baltimore County taught the sons of the Lees and Barneses.

Early County Schools

The Rev. Leo McCormick wrote (*Church-State Relationships in Education in Maryland*, pub. 1942):

> There is good reason to believe that a parish school was opened about 1725 at the Piccawaxen Parish in Charles County, with the Rev. Hugh Jones, then Rector of Christ Church and a former teacher at William and Mary College in Virginia as its able master.

235

No specific reference to schools or to how they should be financed can be found in the original Charter for the Maryland Colony. The first official mention of education is in a Maryland law passed in 1663, "An Act for the Preservation of Orphans' Estates":

> No account be allowed for diet, clothes, physic, or else against any orphan's estate if it will be educated and provided for by the interest of the estate if it will bear it; but if the estate be so mean and inconsiderable that it will not extend to a free education, then such orphans shall be bound apprentices to some handicraft trade or other person, at the discretion of the court, until one and twenty years of age, unless some kinsman or relation will maintain them for the interest of the sale of the estate they have without diminution of the orphans at the years appointed by law.

An Act of 1671 on the same subject directed that children who were orphaned be committed to the care of persons who were of the same religion as the children's deceased parents.

Gov. Francis Nicholson in 1694 persuaded the General Assembly to pass the first act to support the schools. The Act of 1696 was designed to establish a "free school" at Annapolis, and a similar school in each county as soon as the necessary money could be raised. King William's School, now St. John's College, was the only school established under the law.

An Act of 1717 placed a tax of 20 shillings on every Negro imported into the colony. The proceeds

> shall, for the advancement of learning, be applied towards the encouragement of one public school in every county within this province, equal share thereof toward the support of each school, according to the directions of such act or acts of assembly, as shall hereafter direct therein.

In 1720 a tax was placed on the export of tobacco to finance enactment of this legislation.

Under the Law of 1723 provision was made for the establishment of County schools. In each county 100 acres would be bought and used for the support of a school "where all the elements of a liberal education" would be taught. These schools took pupils of all ages and grades and sought to prepare them for college. A duty was placed upon pork, pitch, or tar imported from any other colony. Anyone who failed to pay lost his goods; half the value of the goods went to the schools, half to the person who had informed the authorities.

Twelve "visitors" were appointed by a Law of 1728 to oversee schools in each county. They were charged

> to take all proper methods for the encouragement of good school masters, that shall be members of the Church of England, and of pious and exemplary lives and conversations, and capable of teaching well the grammar, good writing, and the mathematics, if such can conveniently be got.

Charlotte Hall Academy, while not established until 1774, sprang from the provisions of the Law of 1723. Governing officials of St. Mary's, Charles, and Prince George's counties, who did not have enough local money to maintain schools in each county, pooled their resources to build "at the Coal Springs" the Academy, in honor of Queen Charlotte, wife of George III of England.

An Act of Incorporation was passed in 1807 for the McDonough Charity Schools in Charles County. A changed attitude toward the education of the poor is reflected in the language of that charter, for the trustees were to fix the price of tuition, "provided that the children of those who shall be deemed by them unable to pay shall be received and taught without any charge whatever."

By 1811 the necessity for general education had been asserted by the Maryland Legislature, and in 1812 the first effort was made to raise funds for the support of primary schools. The charters of the banks in the State were extended to the year 1835, and they were required to pay $20,000 annually which was "pledged as a fund for the purpose of supporting county schools."

A State Superintendent of Schools, appointed by the Governor and Council, was provided for in an Act of 1825. The same legislation made provisions for the appointment of nine school commissioners of primary schools in each county. Also, "A suitable number of discreet persons, not exceeding eighteen, also appointed by the levy courts, who, together with the commissioners, shall be inspectors of primary schools." They were to hold their jobs for one year. Not trusting to the public spirit of the citizens, the Legislature fined any appointee who failed to take the oath of office the sum of 10 dollars.

Powers of School Officials

The duties of the Charles County school officials can be read in the Maryland Code of Public Local Laws, printed in 1860. It is at this time that the outline of local school governance can be seen clearly. Article Nine begins:

110. There shall be five school commissioners for Charles County, and the Orphans' Court of said county shall fill all vacancies that may occur in the said board.

111. The said commissioners shall elect their own president and make all such by-laws and regulations as they may deem necessary for their government.

112. They shall meet quarterly at the courthouse in Port Tobacco, and the president may call extra meetings whenever, in his judgment, the business of the board requires it.

113. The majority of the board shall constitute a quorum for the transaction of business.

114. They shall annually appoint a treasurer and a register.

115. The duties of the treasurer shall be to receive and disburse all sums of money receivable and applicable to the

primary schools of Charles County, under the direction of the Board of School Commissioners.

116. The duties of the register shall be to register in a book kept for that purpose, all such matters as the board of school commissioners shall direct.

117. The school commissioners shall divide the county into as many school districts as they deem necessary for public convenience; shall number and clearly define each, and from time to time create new ones as necessity may require.

118. They may sell and dispose of any school house that it may become necessary to sell from the formation of new districts, and appropriate the money to the school fund of the county.

119. They shall every two years appoint in each school district five suitable men as trustees for such school district, who shall be notified of their appointment as early as practicable thereafter, and who shall serve for two years from the date of their appointment, and until their successors shall be appointed.

The Legislature of 1865 provided for the appointment by the Governor of a State Superintendent of Schools and a State Board of Education, which would appoint the boards of County School Commissioners. Immediately after the State Constitution of 1867 was adopted, the Legislature passed an act that permitted the voters in the counties to elect their school boards. In 1870 the power of appointing school commissioners was given to the judges of the Circuit Courts. In 1892 the Governor could appoint school commissioners in all of the Counties.

Charles County had three school commissioners in 1913. They were a regularly incorporated body, with the power to hold property as trustees for the public, to choose one of their own number president, and persons not members of the board as secretary, treasurer, and as the superintendent.

Of the District School Trustees, the Law of 1860 stated:

> They shall exercise a supervisory control over the management of the schools in their respective districts, by appointing teachers, determining upon vacations, times for public examinations, persons to conduct the same, and doing such other things as they may deem necessary for the promotion of the best interests of the schools under their respective supervision.

"In effect they were a local district school board," wrote one analyst of the trustees' power before 1916. He went on to enumerate their powers: They could choose and remove the principal teacher in the elementary school of the distruct, levy and collect district taxes, erect the schoolhouse, determine the length of the school term, prescribe the courses to be taught, and select the textbooks. Finally, the principal teacher of every district school was an *ex officio* member of the board of district trustees, and was required to keep a record of all business proceedings.

After 1916 their powers were sharply curtailed: Except in Montgomery County, school trustees throughout Maryland could now appoint the janitors for the schools in their district. Since the children and the teachers did most of the janitorial work, this was no great burden on a trustee.

The local chairman of the board of trustees had charge of the school keys when the term ended. And it was within the trustees' power to let people use the building for "non-partisan, non-sectarian purposes." This included civil, social, and recreational activities.

School Funding

It has long been a principle of public school financing that the State tax the general population, then distribute the funds to the counties. Each county is expected to supplement this minimum support by the State. One can readily see from the records that the principle of minimum support for each school district was practiced. In turn, the patrons, teachers, and pupils were expected to add to the local government's contribution to education.

The amount of public money spent in 1914 for the support of public education in Maryland was about five million dollars. The State's contribution was just under a third of this. Some areas of the State spent as little as $9.17 per child, others as much as $28.81.

The 1916 Report on Public Education in Maryland discussed the financing of education throughout the State, and then compared to it the situation in Charles County. "The wealth of Maryland is unequally distributed," wrote authors Abraham Flexner and Frank P. Bachman. "The increase in school funds has not, therefore, been entirely uniform. Between 1890 and 1900 the increase in expenditures per pupil enrolled was nowhere considerable. . .".

But in Charles County, they reported, there had been a decline in expenditures for this period. Without exception, there had been an increase in per pupil expenditure throughout the State, but the lowest percentage of increase was 50 per cent—in Charles County. For example, the total expenditure per child of school age (5 to 20) in the County in 1914 was $5.34. Of this, the State contributed $3.90, the County $1.44.

For years, little had been provided by Charles County for repairs to the school buildngs. The Commissioners trusted the members of the County School Board to use their ingenuity to keep the schools open and maintain some kind of roof over the heads of the children.

"The very Counties that receive from the State the largest proportion of money spent on local schools, Calvert, Charles, and St. Mary's," said the Report, "are the Counties that have the lowest school tax." It continued, "Indeed, some Counties," and it cited these three, "have had to appeal to the General Assembly to secure funds even for the erection of schoolhouses costing less than six hundred dollars."

The report went on to criticize the procedure by which the County Commissioners granted funds requests from the school boards, charging that it "aid(s) them to shirk their responsibility." Funds are requested, said Flexner and Bachman, by item—definite amounts for new buildings, maintenance, teachers' salaries, and other items; but the Commissioners "as a rule" make a lump allowance, "less than the total sum asked for" and without stating "which items have been granted in full and which cut or refused altogether."

They recommended that the State permit counties to issue bonds to erect new buildings "up to a fixed per cent of the assessable property of the county." They also urged that as a pre-condition to receiving State money, each county be required to make a fixed minimum local school levy. Each county's levy would be no lower than the average local levy. At that time the average was 34 cents per $100 assessed value. The tax rate in Charles County was 17.2 cents in 1914; Garrett County led the State with a tax rate of 45.3 cents.

Flexner concluded that the proposal would materially affect only eight counties. He lumped Charles with the "poor" counties, but judged it to be doing less than it should to finance public schools.

Appearance of Schools

The third annual report of the County School Commissioners for 1867 listed 36 public schools in Charles County. Five of these were built of logs and 31 were of a frame construction. The report to the State Superintendent of Schools for the next year listed six schools for blacks. How did these and other schools, built after the turn-of-the twentieth century, come into being?

"They shall, in any district where there is no school house, select some suitable and central site, secure the same by purchase, gift or condemnation, and make arrangements for the erection and furnishing of a school house thereon." Thus read one paragraph of the 1860 law as it spoke to the power of the trustees for each district. Later this power was transferred to local boards of education.

About the Greenleek School, Theodore Davis wrote, "This school had its beginning about the year 1854. It was a log structure, built parallel to the road with a door to the south side and a chimney on the west side opposite the side facing the road.

"The land, about an acre in size, was donated to the Board of Education for a school by Mr. Thomas M. Maddox, with the understanding that it was to revert back to the donor, in the event (that) the school should be disbanded."

Alex Haislip recalled a log school that once stood at Friendship Landing. His father, Alpheus Haislip, a graduate of the Charlotte Hall Academy, taught at this school in the 1860s.

A sample of what one can find in the land records of the local courthouse follows:

Dec. 10, 1870. Deed made 26th day of November, 1870 by me Carlone C. Jenkins . . . in the consideration of the sum of twenty dollars cash in hand . . . I have bargained and sold to the Board of School Commissioners of Charles County . . . a lot in parcel of land being in the seventh election district of Charles County. Beginning at a stake and stone near the road leading from the "Bumpy Oak" to the Pomonkey Warehouse and running thence with said road south . . . one acre of land. Signed Annie D. Jenners.

The Ripley School, called Pine College by some, was located on Old Annapolis Road, the main thoroughfare from Glymont Wharf to Port Tobacco, was built in approximately 1875, according to Robert V. Norris. The land was granted by Noah H. Lyon, who owned the farm.

Dorothy Artes wrote of the efforts to build a school at Indian Head; until 1904 the children had gone to the Glymont School: "Funds for a school's erection were subscribed to by interested patrons. About $300 was raised. A lot, then surrounded by forest, was donated by Mr. Samuel W. Lloyd on what is now Raymond Avenue. The county authorities had promised the people of Indian Head that if they would raise a certain sum, the County would add as much more."

Another County resident wrote, "Soon the citizens of Marbury realized (that) they needed a school, so Mrs. Joe

Wright, whose oldest daughter was old enough to begin school, said she would donate the land."

A committee drove to La Plata to offer the land to the County Board of Education. The gift was accepted, and the then Superintendent of Schools—Michael Stone—sent someone to survey the land. Continued the writer:

> The classroom was about 40 feet long, and at the front of the building there were two vestibules, one on each side; and a small library in the center. One vestibule was used for the girls and the other one by the boys. There, they deposited their lunch boxes and wraps. And in winter, the boys' vestibule was also used to store wood and kindling to begin a quick fire on a cold snow or rainy morning.

The school that P. P. Williams remembered "had one room" in 1935, and "was 20 by 24 feet."

The Hill Top School for Negroes was very old and dilapidated, according to Mrs. Elsie Harris Davis, who went there to teach on Oct. 3, 1925.

The Wicomico School for Negroes was "in the woods back of the flour mill. I was told it was an old log cabin, crudely put up," wrote Mrs. Minnie Hill, who went there to teach from Pittsburgh, Pa. She went on, "Almost every school that I taught had to be repaired and almost made over."

The Jacksontown School, in use as late as 1939, earlier had been a four-room farm house. Mrs. Madeline Butler remembers, "The upstairs had been closed off, and we used only the downstairs part. The wall between the kitchen and a dining room had been knocked out, so we had one large room, which was heated by a large wood stove."

Alfred Sweeney, who was in the first graduating class of the first County public high school at Tompkinsville, described the high school as "a one-room (with vestibules), new addition to the Tompkinsville grade school."

Indeed, as late as 1952 two-room schools were in use in the County. The springs still bubble that served some of these small primary schools. Some of the large trees that surrounded them, serving as shade for the children, are still standing; but the schools, for the most part, have crumbled, or they have been converted to other uses.

To Build a School
In the May 9, 1933, minutes of the Board of Education of Charles County one reads, "Mr. James R. Gray presented a petition to the board requesting that a new school building be erected in Marbury for colored children." The matter was taken under advisement; the consideration was whether there was money.

On Sept. 12, 1933, "The board decided to build a colored school at Marbury and to accept the proposition made by the colored people of Marbury that they donate $200 and one acre of land, the board to buy an additional acre at $50."

At its meeting on Oct. 10, 1933, "The board agreed that it should have full ownership of the site at Marbury to be used for the new colored school, before the building will be started. It also agreed that if the site ceases to be used for school purposes, it can be sold or disposed of at the discretion of the board. Superintendent Mr. Gwynn was asked to write a letter to Mr. James R. Gray advising him of this decision."

The minutes of the board for Nov. 25, 1933, show that bids for the building of the Marbury School ranged from $1,575 to $2,138.40. "The board did not accept a bid, but left it to Mr. Gwynn to find out all he can about the workmanship of Mr. (H.F.) Lund and Mr. (W.W.) Milstead." It is of interest to read that the lowest bid was George E. Butler's, but apparently Lund got the job.

Of the Turner Gate School, Edna Dyson said, "This ... was a frame building, painted white with red shutters. It was about 50 feet long and 25 feet wide with four windows on each side, one in the rear end, and two doors at the front."

Jane Wheeler said of the Cedar Point Neck School, "Long ago the building disappeared and the land is a cultivated field." Gertrude R. Monroe reported that the old Middletown One-room School near Waldorf, "still stands, though now slightly enlarged and used as a tenant house."

The La Plata two-room school was destroyed by a tornado, just a year after its teachers and patrons had achieved their goal of making it the first "standard two-room schoolhouse in Charles County."

As early as 1914 the State of Maryland had set forth spectific conditions for State aid for public high schools. A school that would be rated as belonging to the "first group" had to have a minimum of 80 students and four teachers of academic courses. The high school must have existed for four years, with a minimum of a 36-week a year program. In addition, the school had to have an approved course in "manual training." This might be home economics, agriculture, or a commercial course.

Such a standard high school had to have a library and a laboratory with a minimum of $250 worth of science apparatus. An alternative might be a two-year high school with lesser qualifications. The Thompkinsville High School had a two-year program. One teacher handled the whole program at first.

In 1915, 40 per cent of Maryland's teachers taught in one-room schools. There were 77 one-room schools and 9 two-room schools in Charles County when Francis B. Gwynn arrived in 1918 as Superintendent. But with the increased use of the automobile, it became possible to contemplate consolidating them.

The first discussion on record concerning school consolidation was at a meeting in 1899 of the State School Commissioners and Examiners. The first permissive legislation on the subject was a general education bill of 1904.

The Equalization Fund Law of 1922, designed to guarantee every child in the State the advantage of a minimum program of education, speeded the consolidation of schools by providing more State money for the County. Established shortly thereafter were: Glasva High School (1924) and La Plata (1926), Hughesville (1926), and Nanjemoy (1930).

The Lackey High School had been built in 1919 by the Federal Government, to provide for the influx of people who came to work at the Naval Powder Factory at Indian Head. In August 1917 the County Board of Education established the Colored Industrial School at Pomonkey. The State gave monetary aid to the County expressly for that purpose. The Bel Alton High School for Negroes was built in 1937.

When Edna Simmons came to the McConchie School in 1922,

> there were two very dilapidated toilets, and there was no hot water supply on the grounds . . . The Board of Education supplied many of our needs. A new floor in the schools was one of those things supplied, and the old falling plaster was replaced with dressed lumber. To ventilate, the trustee cut a three-inch strip from under the top half of the window. When it rained or snowed, this piece of wood was put back under the window to close it.

To Make a Repair

From the minutes of the Board of Education for March 14, 1933, "A delegation of six colored men appeared before the board, asking for repairs for the Mt. Victorial Colored School. The board decided that the repairs for the Mt. Victoria School cannot be made at the present time."

Feb. 14, 1933. "The board decided that the repairs needed at the Wicomico Colored School be made, but that it is to be first investigated... The matter of new window sills is to be looked into for the Holly Springs School."

March 14, 1941. "The board decided not to repair the Wicomico Colored School at the present time,..."

Oct. 14, 1941. "A delegation from the La Plata Colored School was before the board and asked that the ceiling in the old room be repaired, that a new stove be purchased, and that electricity be installed in their school. . . . This request was granted except for the electric lights. The board felt that they did not have the money for lights at this time."

April 14, 1942. "The matter of electric lights for the La Plata Colored School was held over."

Sept. 10, 1946. "The board discussed the matter of securing coal for the schools. It can be purchased from the La Plata Mill and Supply Company, or Hicks and Simpson."

March 11, 1947. "A delegation from the La Plata Colored School came before the board to request aid in having their school wired for electricity. The board agreed to pay one-half of the cost."

April 8, 1947. "The board agreed to accept the bid of B.R. Winkler of $190 for wiring the La Plata Colored School for electricity."

Aug. 12, 1947. "The Parent Teachers Association of the Marbury Colored School requested an additional teacher and walks to the toilets. The additional teacher was granted, subject to Mr. Park's approval. Mr. Gwynn was to look into the matter of the walks."

On Oct. 25, 1949, there was a request before the Board for two additional outdoor toilets at the Bel Alton Elementary School. As late as Dec. 16, 1952, the subject of outdoor toilets for some of the county schools was discussed.

T. C. Martin reported to the School Board on Aug. 18, 1952, that some County children were being transported from Benedict to Pomonkey—a distance of more than 30 miles.

The Board of Education furnished the materials to have a floor put in the Wicomico School, when Minnie Hill came there to teach in 1927. They also saw to the repair of the roof, maintained the stoves, fixed the windows, and kept the wells in good condition. She wrote, "Mr. Gwynn was kind to give me usually what I asked for, especially books, blackboards and desks. It seemed to me I was given the rundown schools to fix up and have repaired for my comfort."

The Board moved at a more leisurely pace in 1932 than it does today, and it took time to consider small matters. One reads in the minutes, for example: "The requests for music books by several schools were not granted"; "The board granted the request of Mr. Donat to pay for the stop watch purchased"; "The board decided that the grates for the Nanjemoy High School furnace be renewed"; and "The request for a desk and chair for Ella Coombs was granted. It was suggested that there might be a desk available in Dent's School."

The Board exhibited a somewhat miserly attitude toward requests from schools. But this was a period of economic depression, from which the County, like the nation, did not really recover before World War II. Therefore, it is not surprising to read, "Mr. Gwynn was given permission to purchase a filing cabinet for the office of the Board of Education (May 8, 1934)."

July 12, 1934. "The board decided to furnish soap and towels for the schools provided the principal takes the responsibility of seeing that they are used properly."

Jan. 8, 1935. "The board agreed to furnish the Marbury White School shades, provided that the patrons pay for one-half."

Around 1940 some schools were exchanging Delco lighting systems for more modern forms of power. "It was agreed to sell Mr. Kragh the old Glasva Delco light plant for $10."

Sept. 10, 1940. "The board decided to replace stoves in the Home Economics Department at La Plata with two electric stoves and one at Glasva."

In October of that year, "A delegation from the Marbury White School was before the board in reference to installing electricity in their school. The board authorized them to get an estimate. Also, it agreed to have the bushes cut back from the school road."

Dec. 10, 1940. "The board decided to pay for the materials for lunch tables in the cafeteria at Nanjemoy High School. It was aso decided to repair their typewriter."

Feb. 11, 1941. "A delegation from the La Plata Colored School was before the board, asking for a circulating heater for each room, and that doors be cut in the back of the building. No action was taken."

In the March meeting of 1941, "The board granted the request of the following for the La Plata High School:

Curtains to darken the assembly hall for movies . . $40.00
Maryland flag and an American Flag $57.00
Electric clock for the assembly hall $27.00
Music books $45.00
Aid to pay for library books $75.00
Material for window boxes $43.20

As a postscript to this largess, "The board also decided to have the ceilings repaired."

Sept. 9, 1941. "A delegation from Pisgah was before the board and requested individual desks for the pupils at Pisgah, and also to have electric lights installed. Both requests were granted. The board also decided to have lights installed in the Marbury School. Both schools are to take care of the monthly bills."

June 8, 1943. "The board agreed to instruct Mr. Parks (a supervisor) to go ahead and get wood for his schools during the summer."

Few persons today can agree on what constitutes a "frill" in public education and what is essential for instruction. A reading of the Board's minutes from 1935 to 1946 leaves the impression that members looked upon shades for the schools as "extras," and expected their cost to be jointly shared by the Board and those who requested them. A change in this attitude is reflected in the minutes of Jan. 8, 1946: "Four shades for La Plata High School were granted. In the future, the board will pay for all shades needed in schools." Later (June 1946), "The board decided to return the money to the various schools which they had sent to the office as their share on shades." However, as late as 1950 members of the Board were requiring petitioners to promise to pay half the cost of gas stoves for any school.

May 14, 1946. "The board decided to lend Mr. Joseph Parks the old adding machine from the office."

On Feb. 5, 1952, a special session of the Board was held in which "Mrs. Bowling made a motion, which was seconded by Mr. Doane, not to grant the request of the La Plata Colored School for a telephone, since the school will soon be consolidated with the new Port Tobacco Elementary School. All members voted in favor of this motion."

April 20, 1954. "A committee from Lackey High School... came before the board to request drapes for the stage and the windows in the multipurpose room. The committee recommended a fiber glass curtain with window drapes to match. They wanted them installed before graduation day. One member of the board pointed out that "rats eat fiber glass." The committee was told that the Board would try to get the drapes for them.

When the Board did not have to concern itself with matters of shades, drapes, or who would pay for gas stoves and telephones, it had to take time to consider "personnel matters."

At first teacher Hill had been taken to stay at a home two miles from the school where she would teach. A trustee of the Wicomico School took her the next day to a home nearer the school, where her lack of transportation would not be an insurmountable obstacle.

On Aug. 14, 1934, "Mr. John E. Massey was allowed $50 additional for transporting himself and the home economics teacher to La Plata and to the Indian Head Schools."

In its meeting in August of the next year, "The board decided not to give Mr. (Starkey D.) Bizzelle lumber and wire to build a chicken shed." (They gave him $25 for that purpose on Jan. 11, 1938.)

The Board found it necessary to increase the salary of the janitor at the La Plata High School from $50 to $60 a month, because he had been offered a job with the Federal government at a higher salary.

At the Board meeting of Aug. 30, 1954, Superintendent of Schools Martin "told the board that since the war emergency regulations were discontinued, it is illegal for bus contractors to employ anyone who is under (age) twenty to drive a public school bus."

We have seen how the patrons of schools in the different communities of Charles County donated land, materials, and labor to build many of the early schools. So it was that when the resources of the local Boards of Education were depleted, or the biases of their memberships got in the way of their supplying the needs of the schools, the citizenry pitched in to make up the difference.

The La Plata Two-room Elementary School for white children had its "Home-School Improvement Association."

"In 1921, we decided to re-name our group and joined forces with the State as a Parent-Teachers Association," wrote Mary Garner. She went on to write of the patrons' attempts "to help out with the playground equipment, . . . beautifying the school ground, digging a well, . . . furnishing ice for the water when the summer days were intolerably hot, (and) serving hot soup on cold days." These acts she described as "little and big things that would mean comfort and growth."

The "big" thing that she wrote about was their achieving a standard for their school that the State Department of Education would approve. Among other things needed were flag poles, lighting, and stoves of standard sizes and fabrication.

What the parents had not done, the teachers and pupils did for themselves. When Minnie Hill saw her first school in the County, she wrote, "My heart sank within me." But this sinking feeling did not prevent her from acting. "I swept the room, and found a rag to dust the desks. Then I looked in the cupboard and found a few books that I was to use.

"There was one toilet for the girls. The boys and I made one for the boys. Since I couldn't drive the nails and cut the boards, the big boys did a good job.

"Whatever entertainment we had at school, we always made very good. The money was used to help to buy paper, pencils, buckets for water and lamps to be used for our entertainments. I would spend my money to help buy a school paper for the grades. This encouraged the parents to buy the newspaper," she wrote.

"A timid, inexperienced, young graduate" is how Edna M. Dyson described herself when she began her career as a teacher in 1908 at the Turner Gate School.

She wrote, "The fire had to be freshly made every morning. Much of the time, I was the janitor. In addition to this, the children and I at the end of each day, cleaned the classroom and left it in readiness for the next day's work." The older children took turns when it came to getting the water they needed from a nearby spring.

In her school at McConchie, Edna Simmons led in organizing a P.T.A. "We used our vestibule for a cloak room and a kitchen. With activities we purchased a two-burner oil stove, bowls and spoons." With this equipment they were able to serve some of the first hot lunches eaten by the children who attended one-room schools.

The Teachers

Written and spoken records of the Charles County schools seem often to be concerned with the quality of education and what constitutes a "competent" teacher. To one person, it is most important that the instructor be moral; to another, kindness is a prime consideration; and to still another, the educator must above all be knowledgeable. Might not a teacher be all these things?

He might—but it wasn't always the case. Let us look at what was expected of teachers who came to Charles County to be mentors of the young.

Hatch Dent kept a "classical" school in the vestry house of Newport Church, shortly before 1773. He is spoken of by a contemporary as "A most excellent man, sincere and pious Christian, and, I presume, a good teacher."

The trustees of district schools in the County had the right under the Law of 1860 "to discharge teachers for . . . immoral deportment."

Major G.M. Thomas and Professor J.F. Coad of the Charlotte Hall Academy lectured in 1899 to County teachers at an "Institute" on "The Moral Functions of the Public Schools." The *Maryland Independent's* Editor thought so much of the speech that he printed it in full the next week.

At a meeting of the School Board on July 20, 1954, a committee appeared on behalf of a teacher whom it thought should be permitted to return as the principal of one of the County schools. "The committee enumerated the good qualities . . . such as her control over the pupils and good moral influence."

It was also "brought out" that she had "broken up the numbers racket so far as children bringing money to school; and that she would not allow men to hang around the school." A teacher can still be fired for "immorality" in Maryland.

There is abundant evidence that the parents and officials of the County expected the teacher to be kind to her charges. This account on the closing of a school, dated June 29, 1883, appeared in the *Maryland Independent:*

The youthful tutor, Miss Margie Howard, has during the short time she has had charge of the school, added by proficiency, and the zealous discharge of her duties, largely to its patronage, and by her gentle manner and kindness of disposition deeply endeared herself to the hearts of her little pupils, who each in turn impressed on her lips a parting kiss while a tear of sorrow stole down many of their cheeks as they bade her adieux for the holiday season.

G. E. Medley wrote to Miss Wade, "Well do I remember the first teacher; a lady of ponderous aspect, stern of mien, but unable to conceal the tenderness that usually goes with the mother instinct." In his fond memories of this lady, other of his teachers suffered by comparison.

Medley also recalled, "The appointment of the teachers was quite an event in the neighborhood. The boss trustee usually prevailed. Educational qualifications being decided by local authorities, the trustees required a certificate be exhibited as a pre-requisite to appointment. Politics, religion and prejudice sometimes counted for or against an applicant." He added, "Let us hope this has passed away." Perhaps; but politics and prejudice may still play a part in some appointments.

Writing in about 1900, Emily Linton said, "Old records refer to men teachers as a necessity to keeping order." Reflecting upon conditions prevailing in the elementary schools today, where very few men are to be found, one reads the Annual Reports to the State Superintendent with mild surprise.

For the year 1874, there were 33 white, male teachers and 29 female teachers. In the schools for blacks, there were 14 male instructors and five females. The ratio of males to females started changing after that.

In the report of 1879, 34 male, white teachers were on the rolls, and 35 females. Of the black teachers, 14 were male and 12 female. By 1889, 25 males were teaching in the public schools for whites in the County, and 43 females. Schools for blacks had six male and 19 female teachers.

Looking back just before the turn of the 20th century a former pupil of one of the old Hughesville schools remembered a Mr. Tycer: "He was quite a character as far as teachers go, but he made you learn." People seemed to be tolerant of mild eccentricities in their teachers, but there were bounds of propriety that one crossed at some risk to himself.

"Both teachers and pupils are prohibited from using tobacco on the school premises during school hours." This was one of the rules governing teachers' behavior around 1913. Also, "Every teacher is required to know the by-laws, rules and regulation of the state board and of the county board. Any voluntary neglect of these is a breach of contract." And, "All messages sent to teachers by parents or guardians, or by teachers to parents or guardians, must be in writing."

In addition to knowing the rules and regulations, a teacher had to know how to teach.

"Many parents were anxious to have their children to excell in reading, writing and arithmetic. This many did!" This is Mrs. Linton's assessment of the situation existing in the Holly Springs Farm School in Nanjemoy. Here are some paragraphs from the regulations governing teachers' certificates in 1913:

> The issuing, grading, and renewing of all certificates is in the discretion of the county superintendent, subject to existing laws. These certificates are registered and arranged as First Grade, first class; First Grade, second class; Second Grade, first class; Second Grade, second class; Second Grade, third class. The grade is determined by the qualifications of the teacher; the class, by professional ability and skill. The subjects required for a first grade certificate are: orthography, reading, writing, arithmetic, geography, United States and general history, English grammar, book-keeping, algebra, natural philosophy, physiology, plane geometry (four books), National and State Constitutions, theory and practice of teaching, and the laws and by-laws of the public school system in Maryland. For the second grade, history of Maryland is substituted for general history; natural philosophy (sciences), book-keeping, and geometry dropped; and algebra limited to quadratics.
>
> The State Board of Education may grant life certificates to those who have fulfilled the following conditions: The

applicant must have been a teacher for seven years, of which five shall have been spent in Maryland; must have the unanimous recommendation of the County School Board; must give satisfactory proof of a liberal education and of professional study; and if required, pass an examination before the State Board.

No person may be employed as a teacher in the public schools of Maryland unless such person shall hold one of the following documents:

1. A certificate issued by the County Superintendent where he or she proposes to teach.
2. A certificate from the principal of a State Normal School or from the principal of the Normal Department of Washington College.

The minimum age for male teachers was 19 years then; for a female, the minimum age was 18.

This news item appeared in the *Maryland Independent* Oct. 12, 1876: "Our village school (Port Tobacco) opened with Miss M. Lizzie Fowler of Prince George's County as teacher."

The writer went on to congratulate the school authorities for having obtained Miss Fowler's services, because she had held a First Grade Certificate in Prince George's County for four years, before coming here.

Two years before Miss Fowler's appearance on the scene, an unsigned Letter to the Editor of the same paper (Sept. 16, 1874) discussed, under the heading "Teaching as a Profession," some of the concerns that those who have studied the subject of licensing teachers have had to the present day.

The writer expressed the view that one who entered a profession entered it for life, after having one time passed an entrance examination. Further, he said that a professional person worked at his profession the full year. Then, using this yardstick, he made some observations about teachers and teaching. He noted that three-fourths of the teachers were in the business temporarily; that the school doors were closed to them for stated periods of the year, thereby denying them the chance to practice their calling; also, that they were put through the examining mill once a year.

He ranged afield to comment on a contrasting situation in Pennsylvania, where teachers could qualify for lifetime certificates. He found merit in that practice, but he had reservations about hurrying to adopt it in Charles County: "The qualifications of the great majority of teachers are too limited and inadequate to permit them to hold the right to teach by a life tenure.... Moreover every system must guard against the negligence and incompetency of those who administer it."

He continued, "Many examiners discharge their dutes in a very indifferent manner, especially toward the colored schools.... I find in the State of Maryland a very few colored schools that have teachers competent enough to hold a certificate to teach orthography, reading, writing and arithmetic, especially in our country schools. And as for English grammer [sic], geography and the history of the United States, they know nothing about either."

The writer closed his letter, "Until the law gives a class of persons the unquestionable right to fill the teacher's office, teaching is not a profession in any true sense of the term."

The Teaching Profession

The elevation of teaching to a professional calling has a long history in the County. Those who are inclined to sneer at early attempts to educate the masses point out that the County often relied upon convicted "criminals" and indentured servants who landed here during the Colonial period. But often many of these criminals had committed no more heinous crime than that of disagreeing with those who held political power.

It is common knowledge that mere "bookish" knowledge was less valued then, if that is possible, than now. The exception was in the attitude towards trained priests and Protestant ministers. And it is from this professional class that the County got many of its teachers. Sometimes, before a young man entered into the ministry, or often as one of his duties to his parish, he found it necessary to teach the young.

Others might teach for a period before going into careers in business, medicine, or the law. Even today, the requirements for entering the teaching profession can be reduced by the State to meet the great need for instructors, especially during labor shortages. Each war has drawn heavily upon people available for teaching.

To obtain a certificate to teach, a candidate had to be certified by two inspectors to be "of good moral character and of sufficient learning and ability and in all other respects well-qualified to teach a primary school." The only difficulty was that the "inspectors" did not themselves have to have any training. In fact, some could not read or write. The Act of 1825, which established the office of State Superintendent of Schools, did not require any specified amount of formal education for the official; the Superintendent is the Governor's appointee, and his political affiliation seems of more interest than his scholarship.

Fortunately for the advancement of learning, the County often got more than the laws required in the way of trained teachers. Alpheus Haislip of the log school at Friendship Landing was a graduate of Charlotte Hall Academy. Thomas M. Carpenter, County Superintendent of Schools from 1912 to 1918, had been graduated from there in 1884.

One citizen remembers having heard her father speak in admiration of John R. McCarthy: "A very strict disciplinarian; and there was no place in his classroom for the loafer and prankster. He demanded the respect and the attention of his class. He made a lasting impression that was forever left in the memories of his pupils."

Robert V. Norris recalled not only that tobacco was bringing only two to five cents a pound in 1896, but that families were moving and the young men leaving for the District of Columbia. "We had many changes of teachers. I had nine from the time I was five until I was thirteen."

Some modern teachers might find much to fault in the emphasis of the Teacher Institute held here in 1899. This is the same institute where Major Thomas held forth on "The Moral Functions of the Public Schools." One of the early charges given County superintendents was to provide opportunities for teachers to improve themselves after they began teaching. That these training sessions were more inspirational than instructive already has been suggested.

In addition to Thomas' address, those attending were treated to an instrumental duet. Mrs. Sidney E. Mudd played the piano and Robert Griffis accompanied her on the Viola "in melodious tones and in a most fascinating manner."

During the last two years of the McDonough Institute course, teacher's training was offered. A number of County residents went directly into teaching after they finished at this local private school.

In 1915 Maryland had two "normal" schools, where white students could train for teaching. One was Towson, established in 1865, and first located in the City of Baltimore; the other was at Frostburg, established in 1897. One normal school for Negro teachers was provided at Bowie.

Prior to 1915 applicants to the two white schools went from the highest elementary grade for four years of work; the first two years were a continuation of what would today be high school work, and the other two were in pedagogy.

To enter the Bowie Normal School, a black had to have completed the equivalent of the sixth grade. A two-year preparatory course was offered and one year in the art and science of teaching. In the school year 1913-14, Bowie had an enrollment of 43.

The 1915 survey looked at the preparation of 3,444 white teachers and about 75 per cent of the 672 Negro teachers in the State. Nearly 13 per cent of the white elementary teachers had only an elementary education. More than 20 per cent had spent only one or two years in high school; fewer than five per cent had received a standard normal school education.

In 1915 there was not a public Negro high school in Maryland outside the City of Baltimore. The Flexner's report, while incomplete by his own admission, estimated that less than eight per cent of the black teachers had a standard normal training. Considering that the elementary school term for blacks in Charles County then ranged from four to ten months, it becomes clear how much less time was spent in formally preparing a black than a white for teaching.

After 1915 the entrance requirement for Towson was two years of high school work. In 1916 the graduates from a four-year high school were admitted to the normal schools for whites.

Salisbury State Normal School was established for whites in 1926. By 1931 teacher training schools were offering three years of work, and by 1934 they had a four-year program. And in 1938 the first class to be graduated by Towson received college degrees. It was in that year Bowie instituted a four-year program.

In the fall of 1957 the Charles County public schools had 264 teachers. Of these, 37 did not have college or university degrees; 174 had baccalaureate (BA) degrees; 53 had master's (MA) degrees.

By 1975 no Charles County teacher, with the exception of those who instructed in the trades and industrial programs, had less than a B.A. degree; and training in the art of teaching has been a specific part of most teachers' preparation.

As late as July 19, 1955, the spokesman for a delegation before the School Board urged that the Superintendency be free of partisan politics. He argued that the Superintendent should be selected on the basis of merit in order to attract and keep the best qualified people. Otherwise, there would be no incentive for good men to come to the county and to remain, "as a man would have no assurance of tenure."

Teachers were expected to do acceptable work, or they were subject to dismissal. In 1932 the State's Attorney General ruled:

> A teacher may be dismissed only by action of the County Board on written recommendation of the County Superintendent, after ten days notice to the teacher, and that teacher shall have the opportunity of being heard before dismissal. In all cases the right of appeal shall be to the State Superintendent of Schools.

A notation in the Charles County Board minutes for the school year 1936-37 indicates that one teacher "did very poor work, due to lack of daily preparation, and should be notified to do better or resign. She needs to be reminded that the attendance (of pupils) was poor, and (the) teacher will be judged according to her ability to get children in school and keep them there."

In April 1957 the Superintendent "reported to the Board that he was receiving an appraisal on all teachers in the County from the principals and the supervisors, and that there would be several teachers whose resignations he would request." Several teachers were indeed dismissed that year.

One former pupil recalled that the pupils always liked to see the School Examiner come to the school, because it meant a half-day holiday for them. A County teacher, writing at the turn of the century, said,

> The School Superintendent would visit usually once a year. Of course, I wanted everything to go smoothly at this time. He always wanted a class taught in his presence. Once he sat down and talked to the one boy in the school who was a problem and whose intelligence was no higher than a first grader. Of course, I was nervous, but the Superintendent seemed to understand the situation.

Joseph Lancaster of England opened a school in his father's house in 1798. There he tried out his educational theories of instruction as the monitorial or "mutual" approach. The older, brighter, or more proficient children were employed to help the teacher instruct other children. In Lancaster's structured and formal classroom, an adult master taught "monitors" of instruction, and each monitor taught his row of 10 pupils the reading, writing, arithmetic, and spelling that society of that day thought children should master in school.

By this method, Lancaster insisted an almost unlimited number of pupils could be instructed by one trained teacher at one time. Steiner wrote, "Though his system is now discarded, it deserves the credit of causing the education of the masses to be looked upon as a thing attainable. The Frank Laubach method of "Each one teach one," as a means of quickly spreading literacy among adults or whole populations, is the spiritual child of Lancaster's teachings.

Lancaster came to the United States in 1818, and went to South America for a little while thereafter. He returned to the U.S. and died in New York in 1958. During his life he traveled widely, talking of his teaching methods.

School Days

Instruction in the small schools of Charles County in the late 19th and early 20th centuries was patterned on Lancaster's methods. Mrs. Louise Haislip Perry wrote, "The average number of pupils on roll was 35-40, grades one to seven. The older pupils, seventh grade, sometimes helped the teacher with 'hearing' the lessons of the smaller grades—reading, number work, spelling, etc."

Of the pupils at an early Port Tobacco School we read, "The older pupils helped teach and care for the younger. Certainly we learned a valuable lesson in co-operation and citizenship."

Elsie Shank, now retired to Union Bridge, Md., wrote, "One thing was frustrating as far as the first grade was concerned. Pupils in the first grade could enter school when they were six, regardless of the time of year." Mrs. Shank was talking about practice, not the Maryland Law on School attendance of six-year-olds. Elsie Harris Davis said, "The pupils ranged in ages from 6 to 20 years. There were grades one through seven."

Pupils assert that reading, writing, and arithmetic were taught to the tune of the hickory stick in the Indian Head One-room School.

Of the instruction at the Pisgah School, Elsie Shank wrote, "I taught one subject to each grade at a time, while the other two grades worked on seatwork, which was usually on the blackboard."

The teachers at the Port Tobacco School, a citizen said, "not only tried to teach reading, writing, and arithmetic; but they tried to guide their pupils in social and moral behavior."

"By charging a small fee—50 cents for the dance, 10 cents for the show—we accumulated a small fund which would be used to buy materials or equipment for the school. At one time, we had sufficient funds to purchase a small victrola. The children enjoyed singing as the records were played."

The Nov. 18, 1898, *Maryland Independent* reported "Mr. John Gibson, Principal of a school on Tilghman's Island was teaching Geography by laying off a large piece of the school yard." His "mountains" were made of oyster shells.

Of instruction during the day at Turner Gate School, Miss Dyson said, "The teacher's desk and chair were in the rear of the room, facing the children; but the chair was rarely ever occupied. In those days, with 30 or more children covering eight grades to teach and supervise, there was little time for sitting."

P.P. Williams spoke of his teacher as "a bright, intelligent man. He not only made his pupils understand the rudiments, but grounded each and every one thoroughly in them. He also taught Algebra, Geometry and Latin...".

Official records convey some idea of changes in school programs. Part of the School Board's minutes for September 13, 1932, was "request for repairs to sewing machine for Industrial School was allowed."

"Requests for desk, a filing case, water and sink in the science room for the Pomonkey School were granted."

Dec. 11, 1934. "The board agreed to pay twelve dollars toward the cost of a Rosenwald Library for any colored school which will raise twelve dollars for this purpose. It was decided to pay one-third of the cost of a set of World Books for any school willing to pay the other two-thirds."

May 10, 1938. "The board decided to put into the budget the salaries of a Home Economics and an Agriculture teacher. The agricultural course is to be put in at La Plata and Nanjemoy. And the Home Economics course is to be at Nanjemoy."

In a letter to the Board that became part of the minutes of Feb. 13, 1939, Milton Somers stated, "Our high school children of Charles County are no less deserving of such facilities (a gymnasium) than the high school children of Prince George's County or of any other county in the State."

As an obvious result of a challenge by an interested person, the State's Attorney General ruled in 1940 that "The Maryland State Board of Education has the right to conduct Vocational training school courses...".

"On April 30 and May 1, the Charles Theater is showing a historical picture, The Land of Liberty, at a cost of 10 cents per school child. The board authorized the county superintendent to invite the children to see the picture. Each school is to stand its own expense," state Board minutes of March 11, 1941.

At that same meeting, "The board decided to purchase a bag of fertilizer and five dollars worth of seed for the Agriculture Department at Pomonkey. In the future, they are to buy their own."

June 10, 1941. "The N.Y.A. Officials requested the use of two home economics rooms for the summer months to can fruits and vegetables for the winter school hot lunches. This request was not granted."

Sept. 9, 1941. "The Board agreed to allow money for library books to the high schools...". La Plata and Lackey received $100 each; Glasva, Hughesville, and Nanjemoy, $75; Bel Alton and Pomonkey, $50.

Oct. 14, 1941. "The board approved the nursing courses in the Home Economics Classes. Dr. Fisher is to be notified to proceed with them."

Nov. 11, 1941. "The board decided to get a full-time shop teacher for La Plata to fill the vacancy of Mr. Martini and a full-time teacher for Lackey, if possible . . . . The board agreed to order two sewing machines for the La Plata High School."

The Board had to delay its response to a request for typewriters for the commercial course at Pomonkey, because of World War II; that request came to the Board's attention on Feb. 9, 1943.

On October 19, 1943, Miss Eva Turner's request to employ Mrs. Louise Ryon at $100 a year to teach music at the

Waldorf School was granted. The next year, the Superintendent asked the Board to permit him to pay transportation costs for some of the hard-of-hearing children in the County to travel to Washington or Baltimore for treatment. The Board granted his request.

March 1944. "The request to use the lumber on hand at the Pomonkey High School to build a cannery was granted by the board." While permission was granted for each high school to play two games with every other, no bus transportation between the schools was provided.

May 1945. "A delegation from Pomonkey was before the board and made the following requests: Commercial course, Spanish, French, and art for the Pomonkey High School. This matter was held over."

July 31, 1945. "The board decided to start a twelve-year school system, with the seventh grade as the first year of a Junior High School."

"The possibility of having driver education classes in the high schools of Charles County was briefly discussed," at a Dec. 19, 1950, meeting.

In his report to the Board, "Superintendent's Report and Recommendations for 1954-55," T.C. Martin wrote, "The board's plan must be progressive enough to keep ahead of the demands of the lay public." Today one might be content if the schools could keep abreast of the public's demands.

Among the programs Martin urged the Board to consider were, "music for all schools" and "art resource teachers."

He wanted the courses in home economics, agriculture, and industrial education expanded. He noted that a reading consultant was needed to help determine the needs of pupils who were not reading at their normal level, yet appeared to have normal intelligence. Finally, he asked the Board for "speech correctionists" and school psychologists. Only in the last two decades has the County seen these persons and programs added to its schools.

Teachers, who are public servants, have always been paid less than employees in private industry with similar formal training. It is evident that many people left teaching during periods of full employment, which we experienced at the beginning of some of our major wars.

In the 1860s teacher Haislip was paid annually in gold—"The equivalent of thirty-three dollars in cash currency." P. P. Williams believed that after the Civil War, the Superintendent received $600 for 10 months' work.

In 1904 Miss Harris came down from Washington to teach at the newly opened Indian Head School. She was paid $30 a month for the nine months of her contract.

Mrs. Edna Simmons wrote that her salary in 1922 was $35 a month, and that she paid $12 each month for room and board.

To pay teachers at all was a struggle for the County in 1933. "A special meeting of the board was called for March 20, to discuss the possibility of getting funds released to pay part of the pay roll for February, 1933."

From the June 1934 minutes: "The board agreed to offer teaching positions to the three graduates from Normal School this year, Dorothy Bean, Dorothy Mudd, and Polly Gwynn, at a salary of $950, less five percent, if half the cut is to be restored for salaries." For some time, teachers' salaries had been cut by 10 per cent. The record reveals that teachers were successful in their appeals to the Board to have that cut restored. In the absence of a uniform method of paying teachers, each employee bargained annually for his wages.

March 10, 1936. "Three teachers representing the County Teachers' Association came before the board and asked that teachers not be 'docked' for time lost on account of sickness. This was not granted."

The issue of equal pay for black and white teachers took more than two years—and a judicial decision—to resolve:

Feb. 8, 1938. "The board had a petition from the colored teachers of the county requesting that they receive equal pay with the white teachers. This was left to be considered at the next meeting, when all members of the board are present."

March 8, 1938. "The matter of equal pay for the white and colored teachers was discussed. Action was deferred until a later date.

April 12, 1938. "Mr. Gwynn was directed to talk with a committee of colored teachers and explain to them why they would not receive equal pay with the white teachers." Again, June 13, 1939. "A delegation came before the board and asked that the colored teachers' salaries be increased. This was not granted."

April 9, 1940. A delegation again appeared before the Board with a request that blacks be paid salaries equal to those of white teachers. At that time the Board passed a resolution to keep things as they were. Finally, the blacks took the matter to the courts and won the right to be paid salaries equal to those of white instructors with similar professional preparation.

Linn Kragh, a teacher in the County schools, appeared before the Baord on July 8, 1941, and asked that the 10 per cent that had been cut from his salary be restored by the Board. In August, "Mr. Kragh's request that his ten percent cut be restored was not granted. The board decided, however, to pay him eighty dollars more for the first two months of school, until the situation is definitely settled. They did not grant his request for a loan of three hundred dollars."

Times were improving by April 1942, when the Board "decided to include a one hundred dollar bonus in the budget for all teachers for the coming term."

May 12, 1942. "The board was in favor of paying the teachers a fifty dollar bonus this year, and ordered that this be done. . . . The board set Mr. Gwynn's salary at $6,000, plus $500 travel expenses for the school year 1947-48."

Finally, in May 1946, "The board decided to establish a salary scale for teachers at one hundred dollars per teacher above the State Minimum Salary Schedule." This is the first available evidence that the Board had accepted a standard salary scale for all teachers in the County.

F.J. Maddox, Examiner for the Charles County Schools in 1890, expressed his views on pupil attendance in the 24th Annual Report for the State Superintendent:

The irregularity with which our pupils attend school does much to discourage both teachers and pupils. This irregularity is not caused from any want of appreciation on the part of our patrons, but it is from the fact of our population being purely agricultural, and forced from sheer necessity to keep their children (many of them), for the most part engaged with the crops from early spring until late fall.

The Maryland Law of 1913 forbade a pupil to enter the public schools until he was six years old, but some patrons winked at the enrollment of a five-year-old, because school enrollment was dropping so low in some areas of the County that the community was in danger of losing its school.

Until well after the turn of the century, children walked or rode horses or wagons to school. Mrs. Hill said that one of the children she taught lived seven miles from the school. She would walk each month to visit that family.

For more than three centuries children in Charles County went to racially segregated schools. But at the turn of this century they were segregated in the school rooms by sex. The boys were seated on one side of the room and the girls on the other. In many cases their teachers had gone to similar schools to train for teaching.

The law forbade profane or unchaste language on the part of a pupil; but Mrs. Eva Turner of the Waldorf Elementary School reported to the Board that her pupils were getting alcoholic beverages from bars near the school. The Board delegated the Superintendent their spokesman to warn the tavern owners to halt this practice.

Some teachers remembered their pupils' accounts of romantic walks to school, with the attendant opportunity to report on the flora and fauna. Others most vividly recall often having arrived at school half frozen in winter. Once there, pupils did more than study their lessons. According to Mrs. Edna Simmons, they "helped do many things to make this a happy place to live. They gathered dry sticks for fires. they scrubbed and oiled the floors, polished the stove, washed the windows and cleaned the yard."

But they also played. At the Port Tobacco School, "The pupils looked forward to the morning and the afternoon recesses, where ice skating and sleigh riding were enjoyed during the winter months. And baseball, dodgeball, and other games were played in spring and summer."

Schools have certainly changed. This may be what Alice C. Wheeler had in mind when she wrote one verse of her poem, "Old Chicamuxen School":

Old time schools are like by-gone days,
And times have changed in many ways;
Children to-day should be glad to say
We're going to school in the new style way.

CHAPTER 8

SOCIALITY: JOUSTING, JOINING, AND COOKING

"I'm from Charles County—God bless you!" So began the chapter in Emily Emerson Lantz's *The Spirit of Maryland*, published 1929. Miss Lantz went on to say that, in the opinion of many, the phrase arose from the customary way the people of Charles County bade farewell to children leaving home, or to parting guests.

The County was then famous for its mint juleps. According to Miss Lantz, "The butlers upon old plantations were wont to say that seventy-five mint julips were the limit of a gentleman's drinking, but 'You'se only had seventy-four, Colonel; jus let me mix you one more!' "

From its 1790 population of 20,613, Charles County has grown to include more than 50,000 people today. There is great diversification of occupation and interests—but it is probably safe to say that nowhere in the County is there a gentleman Colonel sipping at his 75th mint julep!

Already in 1929 Miss Lantz was describing the intrusion of modern life on Charles County. Today, with our many County-operated recreation programs, two fully equipped County parks—and more to follow—a variety of sports events and educational courses, not to mention the active Parks and Recreation Department, it is especially interesting to look back on the Charles County that existed long ago, when "swift riding horses and graceful riders" skimmed the wooded trails.

Or even to look back on Miss Lantz' contemporary Charles County, when, she noted, motorists were constantly halting at the inns and hotels of the towns for meals or to tarry overnight, while every phase of the automobile business, from sale of new cars to repairing and supplying the needs of cars in commission, could be found locally.

The author cited jousting tournaments as one of the oldest customs in the County, a custom she herself experienced, and which is still enjoyed today:

> Knights gayly tilt, blushing girls are crowned queen of love and beauty. Silver-tongued orators still extol the Spirit of Chivalry and give solemn charge to participating horsemen. What with basket lunches and evening ball the whole county comes happily together on these gala occasions, while the financial returns of these picturesque entertainments materially benefit some local church or community enterprise.

Some things have changed greatly, however. Every Charles County plantation used to have its own gristmill, where corn was ground into meal for the making of such pone as is rarely found outside Southern Maryland. Three old recipes follow.

Tar Heel Hush Puppies

1 pound fine corn meal
1 egg
1 tablespoon sugar
1 tablespoon salt
a 'pinch' of soda
1 cup milk

Stir, adding water if necessary, to a thick consistency; drop by large spoon in deep fat. (Does better, at temperature of 375°.)

Corn Bread

½ cup butter
1 cup granulated sugar
2 eggs
1 cup corn meal
½ cup flour
2 tablespoons baking powder
1½ cups milk

Cream butter and sugar; add eggs, beating in well; then dry ingredients; and finally the milk. Bake in greased pan at 375°.

Spider Corn Cake

1¼ cups corn meal	1 teaspoon salt
2 cups sour milk	2 eggs well beaten
1 teaspoon soda	2 tablespoons butter

Mix soda, salt and corn meal; gradually add eggs, well beaten, and then the milk. Heat frying-pan, grease sides and bottom of pan with butter, turn in the batter, place on middle grade in hot over and cook 20 minutes at 425°.

Many of the recipes used throughout this chapter are attached to particular older homes in the County. Some, with stories, appeared in a book by Swepson Earle, *The Chesapeake Bay Country*, published 1923.

One of Earle's stories tells of Mount Republican when it was owned by Franklin Weems. It was said that Weems kept a pack of 100 foxhounds, had a continuous poker game for 40 years, kept his cellar filled with 50 barrels of brandy and best wines, and hosted parties for young people three times a week. He was known as the "King Entertainer of Southern Maryland," and he rightly deserved that title.

Another tale is that Hard Bargain was so named because of a promise made by Gwynn Harris to his brother, Tom: If Tom would drink a glass of wine to the health of Gwynn's wife, Kitty, at the celebration of their golden wedding, he (Gwynn) would purchase the then Digges farm, transport the bricks from England, and build Tom a fine Colonial home. The offer was accepted and the terms complied with, and Tom became the owner of the farm and lovely house.

In Grandma's Day

More stories of life in early Charles County are told in a delightful book written by a lively girl, from whose family many Countians are descended. *Grandma's Stories and Anecdotes of "Ye Olden Times", incidents of the War of Independence, Etc.*, by S. M. X. of the Visitation Academy, Baltimore, Md., was published in Boston in 1899. "Grandma" writes of many social events, two of which we retell here, in her words.

"It was decided to make (it) a legal holiday to perpetuity. The first anniversary, we thought, should be kept with as much pomp as circumstances would permit; meetings were held from time to time to devise means, ways, etc., for the celebration of 1777. The conclusion was to have a barbecued dinner in every district of the country, and a ball at night. Well, such preparations you cannot imagine. Some weeks beforehand, a committee of gentlemen in our district, met for the purpose of selecting a delightful grove for our entertainment.

"They found in my father's wood a very suitable spot and at once had it ploughed, rolled and beaten till the ground, for about a quarter of a mile, was as hard as marble; the dancing grounds, especially, were lovely, and no marble floor of Italy could have been smoother and more fit for dancing. Every family agreed to send supplies for the table, and you know barbecue means that all the animals, poultry, etc., are to be cooked whole, and, my children, it was a curious sight to see the long tables set off with lambs, pigs, chickens, ducks, etc., all looking so lifelike that you might have expected to hear the pigs squeak or the ducks say quack, quack, etc. The desserts were very handsome and delicious; we met about ten am. and danced till half-past twelve, then had dinner which lasted till about two, and after a short recess we danced again till five, when we had supper. . . . The children were sent home about six. We began the ball about eight, danced till twelve, then stopped to take cake and lemonade, resumed the dance and kept it up till broad daylight.

"Now, I must tell you about our dresses. All the ladies agreed to appear in homespun apparel. I made two fine linen dresses for the occasion, and three pairs of sheepskin slippers. One pair I trimmed with blue satin ribbon, another with pink, and the third with white. I danced out the blue trimmed ones before dinner, the pink ones in the afternoon, and the white at night. One of my dresses was stripped with blue and pink the other pure white. The frolicking in our district was continued for several weeks. We had sailing parties on the Potomac, fishing parties, dances at night, etc. . . .

"In those days few ladies had more than two silk gowns, but they were very handsome. It was the custom for every lady to be married in white satin and to have, for what they called 'the second day's dress', a handsome brocade silk; we do not see such silks nowadays.

"I assure you, children, a dress would almost stand alone, so thick and heavy was the material. The young or unmarried ladies seldom wore silk; taffeta and pongee, both a fine texture or fabric of silk thread, or silk and worsted, were their fashionable dress goods, with cambric and muslin of the finest texture, and sometimes very fine linen lawn, though that was considered expensive."

She describes a dance given by General Marquis de Lafayette at Colonel Bradford's Hotel in Bladensburg, Maryland: "I wore a blue taffeta trimmed with white satin, and it was considered a handsome dress. Mrs. Washington wore a brown satin, with pearl necklace and ornaments. She was escorted to the ball by her cousin, Major Fairfax, but would not dance; she said her partner was absent, and there was no enjoyment for her while she knew him to be exposed to the dangers of war. She joined in the promenade and left soon after supper.

"Everything was on the grandest scale; the hall lighted with reflectors and colored lamps inside and outside the house, gave a fairy-like appearance to everything; the scene was enchanting, Lafayette and all the officers wore red velvet coats lined with white satin; the tails of their coats were square and stood out as if stiffened; their waistcoats extended to the hips and showed to perfection the beautiful ruffled shirt bosoms, set off with a diamond or pearl pin. All wore short breeches of a fawn color, either cloth or some other material that we know not the name of; their long white silk stockings were fastened with gold buckles, and their slippers were called pumps. It was the style for both ladies and gentlemen to wear the hair powdered; the gentlemen had long cues tied with ribbon. . . . .

"The ladies wore long trains to their dresses and when they danced the train or trail, as some called it, was thrown over the left arm. The dance of the times was the minuet and at one of the figures the train was dropped for a series of curtsies; it was part of the ceremony for the partner to lift the train at the proper time, and I believe the gentlemen made it one of their practices to do it gracefully."

Newspapers

The appearance of the old *Port Tobacco Times* was much different from that of papers we read today. The first pages were filled with essays, prayers, and verse. One of the main delights of the early colonists was the arrival of papers from "home." These, and the "ladies journals," were much quoted on the inside pages of the *Times*, and local news was limited to a short column buried in the center of the paper. Between 1851 and 1855, the *Port Tobacco Times* printed these notices:

GO IT BOOTS - A Mrs. Boots of Penna., has left her husband, Mr. Boots and strayed to parts unknown. We presume that the pair of boots are right and left. We cannot say, however, that Mrs. Boots is right, but there is no mistake that Mr. Boots is left. [Jan. 1, 1851]

BIRTH NIGHT PARTY - The anniversary of Washington's Birthday will be celebrated by a Party in this village on Monday night, the 24th at Mr. Davis' Hotel. The affair will be got up in handsome style and we presume much of the beauty and intelligence of this and the adjoining counties will be present on the occasion. [Feb. 18, 1851]

The debating club of Port Tobacco at it's last meeting, decided the question "Is Ignorance Bliss?" in the negative. The next question for debate is the following—"Was Mary of Scotland accessory to the death of Lord Darnley?" Messrs. Geo. Brent and R.S. Reeder were appointed to debate in the affirmative and F. Stone and George Digges in the negative. [June 25, 1851]

Celebration of the Fourth - It will be borne in mind that the anniversary of our national independence will be celebrated in the village on Friday next. An oration will be delivered by Thomas Stone, Esq., and the Declaration of Independence read by George Digges, Esq. [July 2, 1851]

The Celebration of the Fourth in Port Tobacco by the Literary Debation Club was conducted in a manner that entitled the young gentlemen of the institution to much credits. A large number of persons of both sexes were present, and everything seemed to contribute to the interest and pleasure of the occasion. The weather was fair, and the atmosphere cool and unusually pleasant for the season; and the speakers, though young, and but little accustomed to addressing so large an audience as was present—acquitted themselves very handsomely indeed, eliciting praise from all who heard them. [July 9, 1851]

After the ceremonies most of the persons retired to their quiet-rural residences, congratulating themselves, and each other, that another Anniversary of our Nation's Birthday found them in the enjoyment of all the blessings of peace and happiness secured by the union of the States, the severance of which was so seriously apprehended 12 months since. Truly we have great cause to be thankful to the Great Disperser of all good for those virtuous sentiments entertained by the people, in which the permanency of the Union is founded.

The Races for this fall, over Farrall's course, near Port Tobacco, will come off on the 28th, 29th and 30th of the present month. There will be enjoyed, we suppose, the usual sports (With the exception, we hope, of the sweatt-cloth, roulette, and the like), by crowds of visitors at this popular course. [Oct. 20, 1851]

The races over Farrall's Course commenced yesterday. There was quite a large number of spectators present. The contest for the purse of $200.00, 3 mile heats, was between Mr. Nubey's "Sam Shelton", Mr. F.H. Edelen's "Christian Knight" and Judge Digges "Beelzebub". The race was won by Mr. Nubey's horse - time 6 minutes. [Oct. 29, 1851]

In the ladies department of the exhibition (fair) our highest admiration was excited for there was blended with beautiful faces lit up with expressions of satisfaction and pleasure, a rich display of the most delicately executed tapestry and fancy needlework, together with fruits preserves and what was no less gratifying to see, an abundance of the more useful descriptions of home manufactures - such as cloths, jerseys, cassinette, flannels, stockings, bread, butter, soap, candles, etc. . . . showing that our industrious farmers and planters wives and daughters are not behind those of any portion of our Country either in refined taste for producing rich ornamental needlework or in skill and industry for manufacturing articles of real utility. [Nov. 19, 1851]

Saturday last was a gala day for the colored population of this neighborhood. A picnic for the benefit of the colored school was held in the wood near Mt. Hill at which large crowds assembled early in the day; continued to increase until night-fall. Addresses were delivered during the afternoon by General Howard, Rev. Mr. Kimball and Dr. W.R. Wilber. All of whom, is said to have given excellent advice in the matter of economy and temperance. [Aug. 13, 1868]

Weddings and Balls
Church fund raisers and evenings of musical tableaux were often mentioned in the local column. It is interesting to note that most large dances and other gatherings were held on Monday nights. Perhaps, since most people came from what in those days was a great distance, they came to town early in the weekend, stayed at one of the flourishing local hotels seeing friends, going to church on Sunday, doing a little shopping, and then attended the party on Monday night, and returned home the next day.

It is also interesting to note that the debating club was always the first organization mentioned in the papers, then the agricultural society, then the temperance society. (Incidentally, the first public lending library in Charles County was started by a petition of the temperance society, for the purpose of "uplifting our young men's minds, to keep them occupied and out of the local bars"!)

Weddings are always of interest. Some newspaper accounts of weddings that took place in the County are reprinted here. (The clippings from which these notices were copied are part of the memorabilia of a native Charles Countian, Miss Louise Matthews, a highly respected and charming lady who resides in La Plata.)

On Jan. 14, 1891, Miss Maria Louise Stone (aunt of Miss Matthews), whose great-great uncle was Thomas Stone, a Charles County signer of the Declaration of Independence, was wed at Port Tobacco. Her great-grandfather was a member of Congress and afterward a Judge of the Southern Maryland Circuit, over which her father, Judge Frederick Stone, later presided "with dignity and ability."

The headlines of *The Baltimore Sun* read: "Picturesque Nuptials of Mr. Crain and Miss Stone—The Well-known young lawyer takes as his bride the charming daughter of Ex-Judge Frederick Stone—Notable Events in a Venerable Town."

"The quaint and venerable town of Port Tobacco, whose history runs back to the earliest period of Colonial Maryland was yesterday the scene of one of the prettiest weddings that Charles County and Southern Maryland have seen for many a year. . . . The Wedding was solemnized in the old though renovated Christ Protestant Episcopal Church that fronts on Port Tobacco Square. . . Christ Church looked quite different from what it did years ago. It was recently rebuilt, softly-tinted stained glass windows filtered the sunlight of a warm and bright Southern Maryland day.

"The atmosphere within was laden with the grateful odor omitted from the fir wreaths that entwined the pillars and gracefully decorated the chancel. (The interior of the Church was decorated for the ceremony by friends of the bride with festoons of evergreens hung along the outside walls and pendants from the pillars and chancel.) Outside were throngs of country people who arrived in conveyances of almost every description, many of them genuine antiques, the sight of which would excite the envy of a curio-hunter. Some of these vehicles probably dated back two or three generations."

From another newspaper: "The groom and his Baltimore friends left Union Station, Baltimore at 10:20 in the morning in a special parlor car. As this was the first car of its kind that had ever run over the Pope's Creek Branch of the Baltimore and Potomac Road, the trip created a great deal of interest. The party reached La Plata at half-past twelve. Here they were met by carriages and driven over to Port Tobacco, a distance of about three miles. Within, the pews were filled with young and old. The young seemed to be in a majority. Bob Crain was raised in Charles. Everybody knew him and his fair bride was a belle of the county. Old city bachelors with critical eyes were forced to admit that they would not see such a large proportion of pretty faces at the most fashionable city wedding.

"It was two o'clock when the bridal party arrived. Reverend James E. Poindexter, the rector, appeared in his gown. Miss Mary F. Boswell struck up the ever popular wedding march from Wagner's 'Lohengrin.' Mr. Crain, accompanied by his Best Man, Dr. Dudley Morgan, of Washington, advanced from the vestry-room, awaiting the bride. The ushers walked up the aisle . . . next came Miss Jennie Stone, the Maid of Honor, who wore a gown of white crepe de chine with fringe trimming; in her dark hair was an aigrette; (Her head dress was a white ostrich feather pompon.) She carried a large bunch of beautiful la France roses. Then came the bride, who looked very sweet and winsome, leaning on the arm of her father, Judge Stone. The bride wore a gown of white faille silk on traine, with ostrich feather and pearl trimmings; her ornaments were diamonds, the gift of the groom, an exquisite diamond star holding her long tulle veil in place; . . . (while in her hands she carried a pearl-covered prayerbook.)

"The ceremony was brief but impressive. The church was darkened for the occasion. In the rear of the chancel, on an improvised altar, one hundred wax lights burned, diffusing a soft radiance throughout the interior. In the midst of it, however, one of the tapers on the altar threatened to set fire to the woodwork. With an agility that was graceful and a deftness that evinced rare skill, Mr. Buck Merryman leaped over the rail and extinguished it with his silk handkerchief. It took him only three seconds to be back in his position, completing the semicircle of ushers that surrounded the bride and groom.

"After the wedding the immediate friends of the family were driven to Idaho, the hospitable home of Judge and Mrs. Stone, where they were most generously entertained. (Luncheon was served.) The bride was the recipient of many lovely presents. (The bridal party and their friends took the Special at La Plata at 5 p.m. for the return trip. Mr. and Mrs. Crain left the car at Bowie for Washington, where they remained last night. They will leave today for an extended tour. On their return to Baltimore they will reside at the Albion Hotel, the present home of the groom.)"

JUNE 17, 1897. MATTHEWS-JONES. "A Pretty June Wedding—The marriage of Mr. F. Brooke Matthews, a prominent young business man of Charles County, and Miss Annie C. Jones, eldest daughter of Dr. George H. and Mrs. Laura A. Jones, which took place Thursday morning at "Willow Glen," the home of the bride near Buena Vista, Calvert County, was one of the prettiest of the season. The handsome parlors of the brick mansion were artistically decorated for the occasion with blooming asparagus, jessamine, ferns, roses and lilies. From the apex of an arch of evergreen, which spanned the double doorway of the two rooms, swung a large floral ball. To the familiar strains of Mendelssohn's wedding march, rendered by Miss Daisy P. Turner, the bridal party entered the parlors.

"The bride appeared on the arm of her father, by whom she was given away preceded by Miss Elsie Jones, maid of honor. The groom, on the arm of Mr. William D. Skinner, entered a door other than that of the bride, preceded by two ushers—Messrs. Walter Mitchell and Julian Blacklock. Rev. Father Southgate met the contracting parties at the archway and, as they stood under the bell whose tones could sound only the cadence of melody, amidst fragrant flowers, as sweet scented as in the Vale of Cashmere 'with its roses the brightest the world ever gave,' performed the ceremony according to the rites of the Catholic Church, that bound these two hearts in an inseparable earthly union. The attractive bride was elegantly attired in white brocade satin, with a tulle vail caught back with orange blossoms and carried a bouquet of choice white roses tied with white ribbon. Miss Elsi Jones, maid of honor and sister of the bride, was gowned in *mousselin de soie* over pink silk, and carried la France roses. The groom wore a black cutaway coat and stripped trousers. . .".

JUNE 15, 1905. MATTHEWS-BLACKLOCK. "One of the sweetest weddings of the season took place Wednesday, June 15, at 1 o'clock, p.m., at "Oakley" the residence of Mr. and Mrs. James F. Matthews, when Miss Elizabeth Sabina Matthews became the bride of Julian Chandler Blacklock. There were no attendants, and only the immediate families of the contracting parties were present. Dr. Ernest Spencer played the wedding march, and the bride and groom entered the parlor together. Magnolias and ferns formed a background for the bridal group. The ceremony was performed by Rev. W. J. Scanlon of St. Thomas' Church. The bride wore a gown of white silk mull, with white lace hat and gloves to match, and carried a bunch of bride roses. The bride is the third daughter of Mr. and Mrs. James F. Matthews of the county, and the groom is the youngest son of the late Sydney Blacklock, of Alexandria, Virginia, and is a thriving and popular merchant of Bel Alton, Maryland.

"Those who witnessed the ceremony were Rev. W. J. Scanlon, Rev. Father Chester, Dr. Ernest Spencer, Mr. and Mrs. J. F. Matthews, Mr. and Mrs. J. Neale Hamilton, Misses Leila and Ellen Matthews, Mary Brent Hamilton, Elizabeth Brooke Matthews, Laura Lancaster Matthews, Messrs. John Ramsey Robertson, Francis P. Hamilton and James F. Matthews, Jr.

"A lunch was served, and Mr. and Mrs. Blacklock left on the afternoon train for Old Point Comfort. The bride's going-away costume was of silver gray voile. On their return they will reside at Bel Alton."

MISS HAMILTON WEDS. BECOMES A BRIDE OF JOHN T. WILLS AT SACRED HEART CHURCH. "The most fashionable and delightful wedding of the season was solemnized at Sacred Heart Catholic Church here at eleven thirty on Wednesday morning when Miss Margaret Jenkins Hamilton, third daughter of Mrs. Cecilia Plowden, and the late John E. Hamilton, of this County, was bound by the bonds of Holy Wedlock to Mr. John Thomas Wills, of Baltimore, son of Mrs. Mary D. and the late F. Hughes Wills.

"The church was beautifully decorated with dogwood and other native flowers and was filled to overflowing by the many friends and relatives of the popular young couple.

"As the appointed hour arrived the strains of Lohengrin's Wedding March softly rendered by Miss Ida Brown, began to float through the crowded edifice and the procession of the bridal party to the Altar began. This was led by the ushers, Messrs. Harry A. Harvey, A. H. Magruder, and S. Henry Hamilton, of Baltimore, and J. Austin Hamilton, of La Plata, in pairs. Each wore Frock coats, and striped trousers with gray gloves and ties, as did also the groom and his best man. These were followed by the four brides maids, Misses Margaret Corbett of North Carolina, Katherine Morgan of Washington, and Jennie Jenkins and Katherine Hamilton of this County. They wore blue crepe meteor with shadow lace, and white lace hats with pink bows, and carried la France roses. Next in line was Miss Sophia Hill Hamilton, sister of the bride who was maid of honor and who wore pink bow and carried la France roses.

"Then entered the bride upon the arm of her brother Mr. George E. Hamilton, who gave her in marriage. She was charmingly gowned in white charmeuse trimmed in rose point lace and orange blossoms, with long tulle veil caught with orange blossoms. Her only ornament was a sunburst of pearls and she carried a large bouquet of brides roses. At the altar she was met by the groom and his best man, Mr. R. Laurie Mitchell, one of his boyhood friends.

"The ceremony was performed by Rev. Father W. J. Tynan, Pastor of the Church. During the marriage 'Beloved it is Morn' was tenderly sung by Mr. W. Griffin Mudd.

"After the wedding, the bridal party and a number of intimate friends and relatives were tendered a most delightful reception at 'Hawthorn,' the home of the bride's mother. Here the rooms were most artistically decorated with cut flowers and palms, the color scheme being pink and white, which was also carried out at the church.

"After being toasted and congratulated the young couple left amid a shower of rice and good wishes enroute on a northern trip. The bride's going-away gown was of blue moire taffeta with hat to match.

"Upon their return they will reside in Baltimore where the groom is successfully engaged in the Photographic Supply Business, and will be at home at 2103 Maryland Avenue after June first.

"Mr. and Mrs. Wills both come of a long line of old Maryland ancestry and are one of the most popular young couples to be named here in a long time. They many beautiful and useful presents attests the extent of their acquaintance and the large number of their friends. Among the gifts was a handsome silver service from the maid of honor. The bride is noted for her charm and her universal popularity, and took a prominent part in the social functions of the County. For several years she was President of the Local Card Club and was closely identified with the local dances and other social events.

"The groom was scarcely less popular. Some years ago he was in charge of the New Wills Hotel here but later moved to Baltimore where he entered the photographic business and where he is now closely identified with the business life of the city."

Newspaper clippings of other social events have been saved:

1880 LEAP YEAR BALL (This is probably from the *Port Tobacco Times*.) "The long looked for and much talked of leap year hop came off at the St. Charles Hotel on Tuesday evening last. The youth, beauty and elite of our neighborhood were present in all their strength and by their agreeable manner and winning smiles rendered the affair a most enjoyable one. The only drawback was in the fact that the gentlemen outnumbered the ladies 3 to 1 and consequently the array of blooming wall flowers was great and sad faces and pleading glances were at a huge discount. . . .

"The ballroom was very tastefully decorated with evergreen festoons which harmonized well with the charming array of beauty and grace that was there assembled and caused the room to present a pleasing picture. The music obtained from Washington was first class and the soul inspiring strains brought on by the hands of the skillful musicians caused the feet of all to move unconsciously to its time, either in the delightful whirling waltz or the most sedate quadrille. . . .

"The two belles, or beau-belles, of our neighborhood, were present and the charming ease and grace with which they flitted from one belle-beau to another asking for dances was universally noticed and admired. One of these, Miss N_____S_____ was very tastefully attired in a toilet of white which was most becoming to her petite figure, her vivacious and charming manner rendered the time of her partners very pleasant. (Note how newspapers of the day preserve "anonymity" by using only initials, instead of the full name!)

"The other, Miss J_____S_____ was attired in a charming toilet of plumb colored silk which fitted her graceful form to perfection and in it she looked most bewitching. Among others we noticed Miss Ellen W_____n who was tastefully dressed in black harmoniously relieved by cardinal bows and sash. . . Miss Eliza J_____s was the possessor of one of the most handsome toilets in the room, a cream colored bunting in which her graceful figure was shown to every advantage; in it she looked most charming."

FROM A WASHINGTON, D. C., PAPER, JULY 19: "WILSON STOPS TO SEE BALL GAME—Leaves auto at La Plata and joins fans. Big pair of goggles did not preclude the President from being recognized—the game stopped while he is given a hearty cheer—watches for half an hour, then continues."

So read the headlines. The story continued, "President Wilson today experienced the excitement of a country baseball game and thoroughly enjoyed it. He happened along in his automobile at La Plata, Md., about 35 miles south of Washington, when he heard a series of wild shouts and cheers from a frantic crowd of fans rooting with all the intensity of a major league struggle for the rival teams. The President wore a big pair of goggles and he thought he could watch the game inconspicuously without being recognized. He stepped out of the automobile at the cross roads general store, a short distance from the diamond. As he cautiously approached the grounds, however, a thousand curious eyes were turned upon him. The feminine rooters of La Plata almost immediately knew his identity.

" 'It's the President,' they chorused as they swooped down on him and greeted him. The players paused and the crowd gave three hearty cheers for their distinguished visitor. The President inquired about the progress of the game and found that the La Plata team was in bitter combat with the Indian Head (Md.) team at a tie score. The President watched the contest for half an hour, enjoyed the antics of the players and the alternating jeers and compliments as they came from the bleachers, but did not wait for the finish.

"Motoring on, the President had to make a wide detour on account of freshly oiled roads, and arrived at the White House just in time for dinner. He had traveled 70 miles. Earlier in the day he played golf. . . ."

Letters

Personal correspondence often gives insight on the life of the times. The following excerpts, of correspondence between Anne Causin Jones and F. Brooke Matthews, were provided by Miss Matthews.

Aug. 17, 1896. "Tomorrow is the day the Republicans have their Congressional Convention at La Plata, where I expect Mr. Mudd will be nominated. I may go up but am not positive. I would only go to hear what the Republicans had to say. I expect there will be a large crowd, this being the first convention held in this county. There will also be a game of ball at Chapel Point, tomorrow, between the Rockville team, and one picked from this county, which I expect will be very interesting, also a Ball at night the girls at home will attend, I may leave out La Plata to accompany them to the point. . .".

March 23, 1896. "The young ladies are getting things in shape for a grand Leap Year dance just after Easter."

Jan. 6, 1897. "I had about as pleasant a time as I could have with you absent, at the New Year Ball. There were more young gentlemen than girls, so I danced every dance, and would have several to ask me for a single set."

Jan. 13, 1897. "We have in view a pleasant day for next Friday, if the weather will permit. We will go fox hunting in the morning and after the hunt is over, we will wind up with a dance at 'Edgehill.'"

More Recipes

Chef George Greenwald created a dish soon popular in Charles County in the 1930s, named after hotelier, Charles E. King III of New York City.

Elegant Chicken a la King

1 cup sliced mushrooms
¼ cup chopped green pepper
6 tablespoons butter
2 tablespoons all purpose flour
2 cups light cream
3 cups cooked chicken
3 egg yolks
½ teaspoon paprika
2 tablespoons dry sherry
1 tablespoon lemon juice
1 teaspoon onion juice
2 tablespoons chopped pimiento

In saucepan cook mushrooms and green pepper in 2 tablespoons of butter till tender but not brown; push vegetables to one side. Blend flour and ¾ teaspoon salt into butter in saucepan. Stir in cream; cook and stir till thickened and bubbly. Add chicken; heat, stirring occasionally. Meanwhile, in small bowl blend remaining butter, egg yolks, and paprika; set aside. To chicken mixture add sherry, lemon juice, and onion juice; bring to boiling. Add yolk mixture, stirring till blended. Remove from heat. Stir in pimiento. Serve over toast points or biscuits. Serves 6 to 8.

During the war years of the 1940s, Charles Countians did as the rest of the nation: ladies met to roll bandages; victory gardens flourished; canning and preserving, always popular in the County, became a necessity. Some of the recipes that were enjoyed then have survived and are still in use; they take time, but the results are worth the effort.

CHILLIE SAUCE

8 qts ripe tomatoes, cut fine
3 cups green peppers
2 cups onions
21 pounds sugar
1 cup salt

1½ quarts vinegar
2 teaspoons ground cloves
3 teaspoons cinnamon
2 teaspoons ginger
2 teaspoons nutmeg

Put all ingredients in large kettle and boil 3 hours. Pour into sterilized jars and seal.

This recipe easily converts to smaller quantities:

1 qt ripe tomatoes, cut fine
3 oz green peppers
2 oz onions
5¼ cups sugar
1/8 cup salt

5 oz vinegar
¼ teaspoon ground cloves
¾ teaspoon cinnamon
¼ teaspoon ginger
¼ teaspoon nutmeg

CHILLI SAUCE

40 large tomatoes
10 large onions
10 large peppers
2 tablespoons of celery seed

2 tablespoons of mustard seed
7 tablespoons of sugar
4 tablespoons of salt
1 teaspoon red pepper
1 teaspoon black pepper

Boil two hours, then add 5 cups of vinegar and then boil 35 minutes; pour into sterilized jars, cool and seal.

Catsup Recipe

Take one bushel tomatoes and boil until soft; squeeze through a sieve.

Add

½ gallon vinegar	1 tablespoon black pepper
1 pint salt	4 tablespoons celery seed
3 tablespoons cloves	5 heads garlic, cut fine
2 tablespoons allspice	2 pounds sugar (brown)
1 tablespoon red pepper	

Boil until reduced to one-half. Put cloves and garlic in separate bags and add to other ingredients in large kettle. After mixture has boiled for ½ hour take bags of cloves and garlic and mash over mixture; drop back in until sauce is done. When catsup is reduced to half take off heat, remove bags of cloves and garlic, and bottle in sterilized containers and cool then seal.

Chow-Chow

½ peck onions	2 dozen green cucumbers
½ peck green tomatoes	1 dozen green peppers

Cut up and sprinkle with one pint salt; let sit over night; in the morning drain through colander and cover with vinegar and 3 pounds brown sugar, cook till tender then add:

1 oz. mustard seed	½ oz. celery seed
1 oz. Pepper	3 tablespoons mustard
1 oz. tumeric	1 small bottle grated
½ oz. cloves	horseradish
	dash red pepper

Taste. If not sweet enough, add more sugar. Remove from heat; cool; pour into sterilized jars and seal.

Grape Jelly

Take as many grapes as you think you will need (not over four pounds for best results); not too ripe. Put into a kettle and mash with a potato masher until the juice runs free. Add 2 cups of water for every four pounds of grapes. Bring to a boil slowly and let simmer 20 minutes. Drain through a cheesecloth pressing a little to get all the juice you can. Now drain through a regular jelly bag or 2 layers of cheesecloth; let drip through without pressing for a clear jelly. Measure juice and put aside an equal amount of sugar. Return the juice to a clean kettle and bring to a boil; boil for five minutes; add sugar bring to a quick boil and let boil without stirring for five minutes or until a drop of the jelly on a cold plate will jell quickly. Take off the heat and let set until it stops boiling; skim and pour into sterilized jelly glasses. Let set till cold and firm before covering with wax and sealing.

Recipe for Soap

Put one can of lye to a quart of water. Put ½ pound of washing soda to a quart of water. Take 3 quarts of grease melted; put one quart of water to that, then, stir lye mixture into the grease; then the soda mixture; continue to stir until it turns to soap; which will be about 15 minutes or longer.

The 1950s brought more leisure—rock and roll, television, and backyard cook-outs.

Deviled Beef Patties

2½ pound ground beef
¾ cup chili sauce
4 teaspoons prepared mustard
4 teaspoons prepared horseradish
4 teaspoons Worcestershire sauce
1 tablespoon chopped onion
2 teaspoons salt
dash pepper

In mixing bowl combine ground beef, chili sauce, prepared mustard, prepared horseradish, Worcestershire sauce, chopped onion, salt and pepper; mix well. Form into 12 patties; broil over hot coals 5 minutes, turn and broil until done. Serve on hamburger buns.

COLE SLAW DRESSING

6 tablespoons thin cream
4 tablespoons vinegar
3 tablespoons sugar
2 tablespoons butter
1 tablespoon dry mustard
salt, pepper
red pepper
3 eggs beaten well

Cook all but eggs in double boiler until well blended. Add eggs and cook for a short time. Cool. Use cold, as dressing for cole slaw; or hot, over beets.

BAKED BEANS

Pick over 1 quart pea beans, cover with cold water, and soak overnight. In morning, drain, cover with fresh water, heat slowly (keep water below boiling point) and cook until skins will burst, which is best determined by taking a few beans on the tip of a spoon and blowing on them, when skins will burst if sufficiently cooked, drain beans; scald rind of 3/4 pound of fat salt pork, scrape, remove 1/4 inch slice and put in the bottom of a bean pot. Cut through rind of remaining pork every 1/2 inch, making cuts 1 inch deep. Put beans in pot and bury pork in beans, leaving rind exposed. Mix 1 tablespoon salt, 1 tablespoon molasses and 3 tablespoons sugar; add one cup boiling water and pour over beans. Cover bean pot, put in oven and bake slowly six or eight hours, uncovering the last hour of cooking, that rind may become brown and crisp. Add water if needed. Many feel that by adding with seasonings 1/2 tablespoon mustard, the beans are more easily digested. If pork mixed with lean is preferred, use less salt.

BAKED BEANS (short version)

1 large can B. & M. Beans
2 tablespoons dark molasses
1/2 cup chopped onions

Combine and bake in a pan or bean pot 30 minutes at 375°.

During the sixties Charles Countians traveled more. They tried new recipes, with a spattering of foreign dishes. Our young men grew hair and the girls' skirts went up and up and up, and fondue pots were in.

CHEESE FONDUE

3 cups shredded natural swiss cheese (12 oz.)
1 cup shredded natural or process Gruyere Cheese (4 oz.)
1 1/2 teaspoons cornstarch
1 clove garlic, halved
1 cup sauterne
1 tablespoon lemon juice
Dash ground nutmeg
French or Italian bread, or hard rolls, cut in bite-size pieces

Combine cheeses and cornstarch. Rub inside of heavy saucepan with garlic; discard garlic. Pour in sauterne and lemon juice. Warm till air bubbles rise and cover surface (don't cover or boil). Stir vigorously adding a handful of cheeses, keeping heat medium (do not boil). When melted, toss in another handful; after cheese is blended and bubbling and while still stirring, add nutmeg and dash of pepper. Quickly transfer to fondue pot keeping warm over fondue burner. If fondue becomes too thick, thin with warmed sauterne. Spear cube of bread and dunk.

As our Country celebrates it's 200th Birthday, we reach backward trying to capture and record that which has gone before. More and more we appreciate the "home made." Somehow, food that is made from scratch tastes better than "mixes" and, when entertaining or taking something to a friend, we go to the trouble of preparing the real thing.

Here are some really old, old, tried and true recipes.

SCALLOPED CRABS

To one pound of well-cleaned crabmeat add a sauce made as follows: blend 4 tablespoons of flour and 4 tablespoons of butter and add one pint of rich milk. Cook over a slow fire, stirring constantly until thick; remove; add one teaspoon of Worcestershire sauce, 1/2 teaspoonful of salt, a few dashes of pepper, and 1/3 cup of dry sherry. Beat in two egg yolks. Mix lightly with crab and place in buttered shells, sprinkle with crumbs, dot with butter and bake.

CRAB IMPERIAL

Take 1 tablespoon of butter, 2 tablespoons of flour, 2 cups of milk, 1/2 green pepper, 1 egg, salt, black pepper to taste; mix with 1 pound of crabmeat. Melt the butter in a saucepan and stir in flour, mixing till smooth; gradually add milk stirring constantly until thick and smooth; season to taste and stir in a well beaten egg. Seed the pepper and chop small; mix with crab and stir into cream mixture; pile into greased shells and cover with buttered bread crumbs and bake till brown.

CRAB SURPRISE

2 cups boiling water
1 cup yellow oatmeal
1 teaspoon salt

Boil until consistency of mush. Pour into greased custard cups or muffin pans until cool. Scoop out enough for a spoonful of crab flakes. Pour over this a teaspoon of sauce and place in oven until hot. When ready to serve, pour white sauce over each.

SAUCE

1 teaspoon butter
1 teaspoon flour
3/4 cup milk

Blend together; pour in milk and cook until thick; season with salt, white pepper and paprika.

MARYLAND OLD HAM

Cover the ham with water and allow it to simmer forty minutes to the pound. When cooked it may be allowed to cook in its own liquor and serve cold, or following the boiling, may be skinned, spiced and basted in the oven. If the meat is very salty it may be improved by soaking thoroughly before cooking. Serve thinly sliced on Maryland biscuits.

Maryland Biscuit

1 pint flour
1/3 cup lard
1 teaspoon salt

milk and water in equal quantities

Mix and sift flour and salt; work in lard with tips of fingers, and moisten to a stiff dough. Toss on slightly floured board, and beat with rolling-pin thirty minutes, continually folding over the dough. When one-third inch in thickness, shape with round cutter 1 inch in diameter, prick with a fork, and place on a buttered tin. Bake 20 min. in hot oven.

Southern Maryland Stuffed Ham

1 regular smoked ham (preferably corn ham)
3 or 4 pounds kale
3 or 4 pounds fresh watercress
3 or 4 bunches spring onions

Boil kale and watercress 5 to 10 minutes to shrink. Cool. Chop onions including green tops and mix well with greens. Sprinkle with black pepper. Remove all skin and most of fat from ham. Cut deep semi-circle gashes in ham and pack greens in same. (Make lots of deep gashes all over ham.) Cover top of ham with left over greens. Wrap stuffed ham in heavy duty foil. Place on rack in roasting pan. Fill pan about half full of water, cover and cook in oven at 325° to 350° for approximately 3 hours. Eat cold. Or, wrap ham in several layers of cheesecloth or an old pillow case and cook at a very low boil in water from blanching of greens, for 4 hours.

Cream Scones

2 cups flour
4 tsps baking powder

1/2 teaspoon salt
4 tablespoons butter

2 teaspoons sugar   2 eggs, one separated
1/3 cup cream

Mix and sift together flour, baking powder, sugar and salt. Rub in butter with tips of fingers; add eggs well beaten (reserving a small amount of unbeaten white) and cream. Toss on a floured board, pat and roll to three fourths inch in thickness. Cut in squares, brush with reserved white, sprinkle with sugar, and bake in hot oven 15 min.

Pie Crust

1 cup lard   1/2 cup boiling water
3 cups flour   1/2 teaspoon salt

Mix up and put in ice-box in the morning. When needed, roll out and put in pie pan. This will make top and bottom of one pie and the bottom of another.

Angel Pie

4 egg whites
1/4 teaspoon cream of tartar
1/4 cup sugar

Beat whites till frothy; add cream of tartar; when stiff enough to hold a point, add sugar gradually. Beat until stiff and glossy. Spread in well greased cake pan with cutter or removeable bottom; bake 20 minutes at 275°; increase heat to 300° and cook for 40 minutes; remove from oven and cool.

Topping

4 egg yolks   2 teaspoons lemon rind
1/2 cup sugar   1/2 pint whipping cream,
3 tablespoons lemon juice   whipped thick and
                             slightly sweetened

Beat yolks until thick; beat in sugar gradually. Blend in lemon juice and rind; cook over hot water till thick stirring constantly; about 6 to 8 minutes; cool. Spread 1/2 whipped cream mixture on baked meringue; cover with cooled lemon filling and top with the rest of whipped cream. Refrigerate in ice-box overnight for 24 hours.

Berry Pudding

1 cup of sugar	1/2 cup of sweet milk
2 tablespoons of butter	1 teaspoon of baking powder
2 eggs	2 cups of flour

Mix smooth and then quickly stir in 4 cups of berries (any kind). Pour into a round deep saucepan with tight cover and steam 2 hours. Serve with hard sauce.

Hard Sauce

1 tablespoon butter	1 tablespoon sweet cream
1 cup of sugar	additional ingredients

Put into a bowl and stir until well creamed, adding a sprinkle of nutmeg or a few drops of any flavoring. When creamed, add, stirring it in lightly, the whipped white of 1 egg. When this is mixed, add 2 more tablespoons of cream. Beat well and pile on a glass dish.

Spanish Cream

1 tablespoon of Knox gelatin	1/4 teaspoon of salt
3 cups of milk	3 eggs (separately beaten)
1/2 cup of sugar	1 teaspoon vanilla

Soak the gelatin in the milk ten minutes. Place over hot water and when gelatin is dissolved, add sugar; pour slowly on the yolks of the eggs (slightly beaten); return to double boiler and cool until thickened somewhat, sitrring constantly. Remove from stove and add salt and vanilla, then add whites of eggs beaten stiff. Turn into molds. Refrigerate until served. Serve with whipped cream.

Cranberry Cupcakes

Cream 1/4 cup shortening and 1/2 cup brown sugar. Add 1 egg. Beat well. Sift, then mix together the following ingredients:

3/4 cup flour
1/2 teaspoon nutmeg
1/2 teaspoon cinnamon

1/4 teaspoon salt
1/4 teaspoon soda

Add
1/4 cup sour cream 1/4 cup cranberry sauce

Cream all together, and add 1/4 cup chopped nuts. Pour into cupcake pans and bake at 350° until done.

Hot Milk Cake

4 eggs beaten together
2 cups sugar
2 cups flour

2 teaspoons baking powder
1 cup milk heated together
with 1/4 pound butter

Beat eggs and add sugar. Put in flour and stir well. Beat in the warm milk and butter. The last thing beat in 2 teaspoons baking powder and 1 teaspoon any flavoring. Bake at 350° until done.

Chocolate Icing

4 squares chocolate
2 cups sugar
1 cup milk or cream

Cook this until you can roll a ball. Have a white of one egg beaten and pour chocolate on egg and beat; last put in one teaspoon vanilla.

Orange Coconut Cake

2 cups cake flour
3 teaspoons baking powder
1/2 teaspoon salt
2/3 cup butter

1/3 cup milk
3 eggs well beaten separately
1 cup sugar

Sift flour 3 times and add baking powder and salt. Cream butter and add sugar and yolks; then flour and milk alternately a small amount at a time, with flour; mix thoroughly then add egg whites stiffly beaten and vanilla. Bake at 350° until done.

Frosting

2 egg whites	1 tablespoon water
1 1/2 cups sugar	1/4 teaspoon cream of tartar

Put eggs, sugar and water and cream of tartar in upper part of a double boiler, beat with beater for several minutes until frosting will stand in peaks, remove quickly from heat and add 1 can coconut and one large orange rind grated. Beat until thick and spread on cool cake.

Almond Cookies

1/2 pound butter	2 egg yolks
1/2 pound granulated sugar	1 whole egg
1/2 pound of almonds	2 teaspoons cinnamon
1/2 pound of flour	1/2 teaspoon cloves
grated rind of 1 lemon	

Chop the almonds fine without blanching; mix sifted flour, sugar, spices and chopped almonds together; add butter which has been thinly sliced; mix well; break whole egg and add to mixture; mix well with wooden spoon; add egg yolks and continue mixing. (Mixture will be thick.) You might find it easier to roll over and over again with a rolling pin. Refrigerate over night. Roll very thin; cut with cookie cutters in any shape and bake at 350° until lightly done.

Brownies

1 cup of sugar	1/2 cup of flour
1/2 cup of butter	pinch of salt
1/4 cake of chocolate	1 teaspoon vanilla
2 eggs (well beaten)	3/4 cup nut meats

Cream butter and sugar and add melted chocolate and beaten eggs add flour and seasonings and mix well. Pour into greased square pan (2 or more) and spread batter fairly thin. Bake at 350° until done. Cut into squares as soon as you remove it from the oven and take out of pan immediately.

Ginger Cookies

1 cup brown sugar
1 cup lard
1 cup molasses
1 teaspoon soda mixed with a little sour milk (makes a buttermilk)
2 tablespoons ginger
1 teaspoon cinnamon
1/4 teaspoon cloves
1 teaspoon salt

Mix together the above and add just enough flour to make a rollable dough. Roll and cut with cookie cutter and bake on ungreased cookie sheet until lightly brown at 350°.

Soft Gingerbread

1/2 cup sugar
1/2 cup shortening
1 teaspoon cinnamon
2 tsps soda dissolved in 1 cup hot water
2 1/2 cups flour
1 cup molasses
1 teaspoon ginger
1 teaspoon cloves
2 eggs beaten

Cream sugar and shortening; add soda water; then flour and spices; add molasses and lastly the beaten eggs. Bake at 350° until done. Serve warm with whipped cream.

Old Fashioned Jumbles

1 quart flour
1 pint sugar
1/4 pound butter
1/4 pound lard
4 eggs
1 nutmeg grated
1 wine glass of brandy
1 teaspoon soda

Mix together eggs, sugar, butter, lard and seasoning, pour on the brandy, then blend in the flour. Form into balls and bake on ungreased cookie sheet at 350° until done; roll in powdered sugar when done. (Nuts may be added if desired.)

Sugar Cookies

3/4 cup shortening
2 cups sugar
Juice of one lemon
3 cups of flour

2 eggs
2 lemon rinds, grated
2 teaspoons baking powder
1/2 cup milk

Cream shortening and sugar; add eggs one at a time beating well; add lemon rind and juice; then flour and baking powder and lastly milk. Refrigerate at least 3 hours and roll and cut with any shape cutters. Bake at 350° until lightly brown.

Clubs, Auxiliaries, et. al.

It is surprising how many different organizations can be found in Charles County. One of the first active organizations in the county was the GRANGE and, as reported in the *Port Tobacco Times*, these agricultural clubs were very active. Today the Charles County Extension Homemaker Council has almost 500 members, who meet in their neighbors' homes. This council began more than 50 years ago, as the County Federation of Rural Women, with home demonstration agents traveling to farms and homes located miles apart. Canning and preserving, sewing, decorating, and homemaking skills have run the gamut all the way to modern methods of canning and preserving, and modern machine sewing, decorating, and homemaking.

Members also learn to make wills and how to cope with teen-age problems, and are informed on landscaping and the latest medical advances. They hold bake sales, white elephant sales, and craft bazaars to raise money; they volunteer time and transportation to those in need of their service.

A diversified group, members range in age from adolescence to the eighties. The County Extension Service is government-sponsored, and State university-affiliated. Its various clubs and services are available to all residents of Charles County.

The Charles County Garden Club, first organized in 1938, had both men and women members at first. An interest in gardening abounded in the County long before its inception—and has led to other gardening clubs being formed since then. The clubs are encouraged by the County Extension Service. This club was forced to disband during the war years because gas rationing made transportation so difficult. It reorganized in 1947, limiting membership to women. Membership is now limited to 75 active members, with a waiting list of approved prospective members.

The **Woman's Auxiliary of Physicians' Memorial Hospital** (La Plata) was formed in 1938, with a membership of 34 volunteers. The Auxiliary has been of great benefit to the residents of Charles County. Its duties are "to assist the Board of Trustees of the hospital in furthering the interest of the hospital and the welfare of the patients by undertaking such work as it elects and which shall be approved" by the Board. Over the years, the Auxiliary has sponsored such fundraising events as dances, card parties, bingo, and suppers; and has mounted drives for donations and membership.

Today the Auxiliary has a membership of some 60 volunteers, and it now accepts men as well as women. Volunteers operate the hospital's snack bar and gift shop, rent colored television sets to patients, and sponsor the taking of photographs of newborn infants in the nursery, with parents' consent. They also man the information desk and serve hot coffee to patients during midmorning hours. One Auxiliary committee is in charge of Candy Stripers.

In March 1954 the **Women's Club of Southern Maryland** was founded, with 23 members. Its aim is to foster civic improvement, scholarships, and general cultural enrichment of the area. Club members are active fund raisers, and have received many awards for their efforts. They staff a souvenir and craft shop in the north wing of the reconstructed Courthouse at Port Tobacco; proceeds are used for scholarships and community projects. There are now 82 members; new prospective members must have the sponsorship of two current members.

The **Business and Professional Women's Club of Charles County** (BPW) was chartered on June 28, 1973, with the largest initial membership of any County organization. BPW's objectives are: to elevate the standards for women and the professions, to promote the interests of business and professional women, to bring about a spirit of cooperation among the business and professional women in the United

States, and to extend opportunities to business and professional women through education along lines of industrial, scientific, and vocational activities.

The Indian Head-La Plata branch of the **American Association of University Women** (AAUW) was formed in 1958 by a group of enthusiastic, community minded women. Through the years AAUW has been an active voice, influencing State legislation and supporting educational and cultural undertakings in the County.

The Charles County League of Women Voters, one of the more recent organizations in the County, began in 1971, for the purpose of encouraging women to take an active interest in their locality. It seems to demonstrate that informed citizens can, and do, influence what happens in Government, and shows that in a democracy, every citizen has this privilege and responsibility.

The League carefully guards its nonpartisan status, although it is active in politics. It supports no political party and no candidate, but members are free to act individually in support of particular candidates. The League prepares voters' guides for the public prior to primary and general elections, in which the candidates state their positions for the public, in response to League questions on timely issues. The League has also worked with the County's Board of Election Supervisors to make citizen registration more convenient, and to help "get out the vote." "Know Charles County," a handbook on County Government, was recently published by the League.

For those interested in partisan politics, both the Republicans and Democrats are well organized in Charles County. The Democrats have four local clubs, in the Southern, Western, Central, and Northern parts of the County. They are not exclusive, and many people belong to two or more clubs, which meet monthly, usually for dinner and business.

Rudolf Ambrose Carrico, who served in the State House of Delegates and as People's Counsel to the Public Service Commission for Maryland, was a member of the Democratic

State Central Committee from 1950 until his death in June 1969. Carrico, born in Bryantown, was active in politics since 1934, and attended the party's National Conventions in 1964 and 1968. While with the Central Committee, he helped organize Charles County Young Democrats, a new chapter of which is scheduled to start this spring.

The Republicans have four chapters of the Charles County Republican Club, as well as a Ladies' Club. The chapters meet in the first, fifth, seventh, and eighth districts, although they are not mutually exclusive.

Both parties have State Central Committees in Charles County; and both are working to involve more young people and to counteract the apathy and disillusionment that seem to have caused loss of interest among Countians in politics.

There are many other organizations, clubs, and affiliations open to residents of Charles County; their exclusion from this essay should in no way suggest that they are of less importance or interest than those mentioned. The Charles County Chamber of Commerce, or the County Public Library, both located at La Plata, would be good sources of additional information.

Charles is an outgoing County, filled with friendly people who like themselves and one another, and enjoy spending time together. It also has fertile soil, abundant water—fairly unpolluted; and it is rural, but close enough to the "big city" (Washington, D.C., or Baltimore) for any who feel its call. In short, it's a wonderful place to call home.

CHAPTER 9

LEGEND AND FOLKLORE: WHO ARE THE PEOPLE?

It seems appropriate to approach the end of this Bicentennial History of Charles County by relating some of its legends and folklore—the ideas, beliefs, traditions, narratives, arts, and customs that make a people what they are, that give them an identity.

Charles County's identity is rich and rewarding. The County is older than the nation: We celebrated our 300th birthday nearly 20 years ago. Our legends and folklore are older still. Many were "old" when the first settlers arrived here, to adapt or just appreciate from afar the myths and memories common to the indigenous population.

But there is danger in trying to compile a non-factual record of a people. Any short treatment must be incomplete; and where there is selection, something—people, places, events—will be left out. Intentionally, we have not repeated many well known stories; other locally popular accounts appear elsewhere in this *History*.

Nevertheless, contemporary readers will remember or be able to produce written recollections of numerous incidents and teachings we do not mention. They will ask, "Why didn't they tell about . . .?" Others will be sure that events or ideas we relate were different. They will read our account and insist, "It wasn't like that!"

All this is good. Here, as in the rest of our History, we have not tried to be comprehensive or incontrovertible; only to give a smattering of the backgrounds and beliefs that have entertained and enriched the people of Charles County. For we believe folklore, past and present, is the stuff dreams are made of.

Another Nation

Before the United States began there was, in Charles County, another nation. Its founders, who molded a confederacy that reached from southern Prince George's County to northern St. Mary's, came to the Potomac several hundred years before Englishmen anchored their ships in the broad tributary to the Chesapeake. This nation was the Piscataway Empire. It disappeared from written Maryland history more than 200 years ago, leaving no flags, no great monuments, no written records—only place names, graves, and people.

The rulers and protectors of the confederacy were the Piscataway. They held dominion over such as the Portobac, Pomonkey, Mattawoman, and Wicomico. They made treaties with representatives of the "great king" across the water, addressed Governor and Council, taught farming and herb lore to a new population, sold land, and were attracted to a new religion brought by Europeans. They sought to use the English people and their cannons as a shield against Iroquoian invaders; they were in turn used by the English to defend the borders of the struggling Maryland Colony.

Decimated and despairing, the Piscataway left Maryland, going first to Virginia then to an island in the upper reaches of the Potomac. They fled northwestward; later they joined the Iroquoi nations under the name Conoy, as a sub-group of the Mohican. Maryland closed her official records on this earlier nation, the Indians of Southern Maryland, in 1705. The tribe would appear in the "white man's record" only once more: In 1793 some 50 Conoy-Piscataway appeared at a treaty council in Detroit, where they used a wild turkey as their signature.

And so the once proud Piscataway nation came to "that misty plateau" where history meets and merges with legend.

Written records have no memory, no heart, no yearnings. Certain Southern Maryland clans and families claim a tie to these vanished people. Studies have described these Marylanders as "mainly of White and Indian blood with an occasional strong infusion of the Negro element" (Brown, p. 7). They call themselves "We-Sorts," a name based on their efforts to define themselves as "we sort of people," tracing their origins to two dominant groups, European and African. Others have called them "Brandywine people." To themselves they are what they are—descendants of Eastern American Indians, a people who have lived in Maryland under at least three nations: Piscataway, British, and American.

For the most part they are remnants of confederacy sub-tribes that chose not to follow the Piscataway group into exile, most authorities agree. There is, further, a legend from the Port Tobacco area that the Piscataway Emperor and a few of his great men and their families did not go with the rest of the tribe when it left the Potomac (Ferguson, pp. 43-44).

The stories say this small band returned to its own lands. The Maryland Archives record a last appearance by the Emperor before the Council in 1700. At that time he came from the Indians' Potomac island retreat near Point of Rocks to renew his treaties. He was urged to return with as many families as would accompany him, and that he could have lands at either Accokeek or Pomonkey. In 1705 the Archives record Council nullification of its Indian treaties "since the Piscataways failed to come."

But, is it not possible that the Emperor and his small band filtered in to live where they chose rather than where they were told they must go? Perhaps they returned anonymously to the waterman's life on their river, the Potomac—for they never by choice dwelt far from its banks. Today the more then 700 Piscataways scattered throughout Southern Maryland are creating their own Indian cultural center.

Early Legends

The Algonquin legend that attributes the name of the town of Indian Head to the mounting of a young brave's skull on a spear has an epilogue, which tells of his beloved Indian princess. When she learned of his murder, it is said, she fled along the bluff of the Potomac until she was exhausted. She then threw herself into the water and was drowned. But a whirlpool formed where her body struck the river—a whirlpool that has existed to this day. Several people can testify to this; sadly, because they have lost friends or relatives in its swirling waters.

On a bluff above the whirlpool once stood the mansion of the De Pye family, naturally landscaped by a long double row of cedars that remain today. But there are wide spaces in Cedar Lane, formed when some of the great trees fell and were removed. This happened in the early days as well. One night one of the De Pye sons, accompanied by a friend, was returning home after a storm. They came upon a fallen cedar, with its foliage on the ground, its roots high in the air. Young De Pye determined to climb the trunk on horseback, thinking it a good challenge for his thoroughbred horse. His friend objected, but De Pye was adamant. The horse stepped surely along the slippery tree trunk and was almost to the top when he slipped. Horse and rider crashed to their deaths. As they fell, the horse gave a piercing shriek. Legend has it that on a winter night when the wind is right, a listener can hear the shriek of the falling white stallion echoing through the tall cedars.

Like the De Pye mansion, every one of Charles County's many historic homes has its own legends, its own mysteries, and its own ghosts. "Laying the ghost" was in fact a common practice at many homes, and still occurs at some. Every so often a family ghost gets active—that is, it makes itself known to those living in the house by various activities. Then the family must call in a priest, often of a particular denomination or parish, to perform certain acts or deliver specific speeches, to set the ghost at ease and discourage its patent behavior.

Many families' legends concern valuable old portraits that hang on their walls. Two paintings of Daniel of St. Thomas Jenifer once graced the historic Hanson home in Charles

County. One has a bullet hole through the head of the subject; the other is said to have fallen off the wall "for no reason" before the subject's death—or his wedding.

The Official State Sport

People associate basketball with Indiana, and surfing with California, but so far as we know Maryland is the only State to have an official sport. Henry J. Fowler, Delegate from St. Mary's County, introduced into the House of Delegates in February 1962 a bill recognizing jousting as the Official State Sport. The overwhelming support in both chambers of the Legislature for this sport of "womanly words and manly deeds," indicates its widespread popularity.

Although the precise origin of jousting in the New World is a matter of disagreement, historians generally concur that it "survived" the 17th century. Some believe it began in Virginia, but many others "stoutly maintain that it originated in what is now Charles County" (Hiss). According to Hiss, it is certain "that the sport has been practiced in the Southern States . . . from the earliest colonial days to the present time."

Tournaments, which were held at Marshall Hall until it faded in the 1960s, featured the "modern form" of jousting, known as the ring tournament, which clearly distinguished the sport from war. (With the invention of gun powder, in fact, waging war by jousting a man from his mount became outmoded.) The ring tournament was first introduced in St. Mary's City, under the rule of the Calverts. It consists of contestants spearing small rings with their lances, a task that requires great skill, fine horsemanship, and good fellowship.

For the spectator, it entails a good deal more, as indicated by a news item in *The Times Crescent*, Aug. 14, 1953:

> In the days of the gas buggy on the banks of the Potomac River under the old Poplar trees, many a rider and follower of the sport would come to Marshall Hall in wagons, ox carts and on horseback several days before the contest. In the evenings, large bon-fires would fill the sky with light while all gathered would spin yarns, sing songs and talk with friends they had not seen since the last tournament.

Jousting is synonymous with Maryland history, and is still practiced throughout the State. It is unique in that it is non-commercial: There are no jousting scholarships and no one has ever made a living by participating in it or wagering on it. Men and women of all ages participate in tournaments, which are held in late summer in the three Southern counties—in Calvert County at Port Republic's Christ Church; in St. Mary's at Sen. Henry Fowler's Horse Range Farm, Mechanicsville; and at the Charles County Fairgrounds, south of La Plata.

But this is just one equestrian sport popular in Charles County. Port Tobacco held horse races on a moderate scale, with small purses, in 1750 and 1767. Early public advertisements show that races took place at Newport in 1764 and 1765, at the dwelling of Anthony Smith in 1753, near Capt. Harwood's home "on the road leading to Jonathan Rawlings," at Walter Maddox's in 1759, and again at Port Tobacco in 1779. At this later date a 375-pound purse was featured "for the first day's running," and 150 pounds for the second day's.

Horse racing was a "gentlemanly" sport, which apparently had the sanction of the Church. Race courses were built close to churches and on Sundays, following the sermon, men would gather at the nearby track for "horse talk." Races also drew spectators and bettors from many miles away.

According to an article in the *Maryland Historical Magazine*, the popularity of horseracing was to blame when "ferry boats sank because racing fans were in haste to reach the race track," and "2000 horses were counted at a race," and "the governors attended and donated prizes for the meetings." The landed aristocracy was largely responsible for the growth of racing; Gov. Ogle, for example, was the first to import thoroughbreds into Maryland Province.

There is also a letter from John Parke Custis to George Washington, Aug. 18, 1771, urging the (then) important Virginia planter to accept accommodations that had been offered him for horse races at Annapolis. For, writes Custis, Washington's would-be host expected "many acquaintances here at the races whom he would be glad to serve should you not come." At race time even George Washington was but one of many fans.

The Fortunes of War

Just a few of the numerous stories about the nation's wars in which Charles Countians were involved substantiate man's fascination with, perhaps his relief at being able to look back on, armed conflict.

Major General William Smallwood's "Old Liners" fought bravely in many Revolutionary War conflicts, including the Battle of Camden (N.J.), Aug. 16, 1780. A captain in the "Line" was John Mitchell of Charles County, who was hit by a musket ball in his chest. A gold watchkey suspended on a chain from Mitchell's neck deflected the ball and saved his life, according to his descendant, MRS. CATHERINE HANSON MITCHELL.

One of the leading Civil War figures was Olivia Floyd of Rose Hill, an agent and messenger for the Confederacy. Miss Olivia, as she was known, let neither her lameness—the result of a back injury that had not been properly set—nor her brother's war death deter her from functioning admirably as the last link in a chain of communications that reached south from Canada into Confederate territory.

On one occasion Miss Olivia held a message requesting the commissions of captured Confederate officers so they could escape being tried by the Union as spies. No sooner had she received it than word came that Union troops were on their way to search her house, as her undercover work was well known. She plunged the life-saving paper into a hollow brass ball crowning a pair of andirons in the Rose Hill parlor. The Union soldiers arrived, searched the house, and even rested their feet on the andirons before departing empty-handed. Miss Olivia then hid the note in her hair and carried it to Pope's Creek. From there it went to Richmond, whence copies of the commissions were sent to Canada in time to spare the lives of the prisoners.

Other stories of Miss Olivia's "rebellion" were told in articles that ran in local papers at her death, long after the war's end.

If Olivia Floyd's connection with Charles County is still remembered here, then John Wilkes Booth's flight through Southern Maryland is recalled throughout the nation. Much of the aftermath of the April 14, 1865, assassination of President Abraham Lincoln is cloudy, but Charles County's geographic role, if not the precise involvement of suspected individuals, is certain.

Booth fled Washington along Rt. 5, hampered by a leg broken in his jump from a box to the stage of Ford's Theater after firing the fatal bullet at the President. He was sequestered for five days by a resident who owned a farm near Bel Alton, until another Charles Countian ferried Booth and his accomplice across the Potomac to Virginia. There the assassin was shot and killed. But before going into hiding in Charles County he sought medical aid of Dr. Samuel Mudd and Mudd was convicted of involvement in the conspiracy. The doctor has since been exonerated of any involvement in the President's assassination, but much that Booth did in Charles County, and whom he met before the killing, has become part of the folklore.

Reminiscences

Interesting stories of life in Charles County are gleaned from talking with residents, many of whom have celebrated their 70th, 80th, 90th, or even 100th birthdays! Some recall horseback mail routes along Rt. 301—some rode them, others merely watched and waited for the post man, as they did for the trains that came into the station at La Plata. Others tell of smugglers who operated in the southeastern portion of the County, and of honest-to-goodness pirates! Some younger residents possess family heirlooms, diaries, or other items of enormous interest and historic revelation.

MRS. GEORGE SMITH, who traces her lineage back to an Irish emigrant who settled in Charles County in the early

1800s, remembers that her family used to sing the verse to "Froggie Went A-Courtin'" differently than is popular today. Her verse went:

> Froggie went a-courtin' and he did ride,
> Rap Trap Bummy Chi Combo,
> Sword and pistol by his side,
> Rap Trap Bummy Chi Combo.

Then,

> Faro, Faro, give to Karo,
> Karo, Karo, give to Faro,
> With a Rap Trap Bummy Chi,
> Yankee Doodle Yellowbug,
> Rap Trap Bummy Chi Combo.

MRS. MARGARET HAMILTON, now living in Texas, has Charles County roots that go back to the English or Scottish emigrant John Hamilton, who came to Charles County in 1674. Among her ancestors was Capt. Henry Hill Jr., of Prince George's County, who raised a troop at his own expense and fought in the Revolutionary War. She has many letters members of her family wrote in the late 18th and early 19th century, which indicate far better than history books or even contemporary newspaper stories the day-to-day concerns of life and the elements of address and respect among people who lived in another era.

DAVID FARR, an older resident of Wayside, relates stories he heard about County life prior to the Civil War. "The ships would come in to load tobacco to take overseas," he says. "So many farms would load the ships in a community effort—everyone would be on one fare and haul crops down to the creek where the water would not be rough and would be deep enough to bring flatboats up close to shore. That man's goods would be loaded, and the people would go to another spot while the boat was unloading and they would have another load ready when the boat came back.

"The river boys used to thrash wheat with steam engines and a thing which was called a thrasher. At least eight or ten farmers would pool labor and team so that it would be possible to operate one of the machines because it took at least 30 men, besides the boys, to operate ox carts behind the machine.

"The thrashing machines would come down the road with 12 ox carts strung out behind and the old engineer with his big greasy cap blowing his whistle now and then and the big confusion of fixing the meals and getting the water boughs ready to hold water and having the wood ready for the engine and bringing it into the field and men would start pitching on the bundles of wheat and would line the engines up with thrashing machine. A big long belt would be attached and then the men would bring in the first line. You could hear the oxen and the fellows cracking their whips—'whoobie, whene'—sounds that are gone forever. There would be the bind cutters, the feeders, the stackers, the measuring man, bag holders, bag tiers, engineer, firemen, and the men in the field called pitchers or loaders. The straw would sprout of the machine and the machine would hum. The work would keep on to lunch and then there would be a big lunch.

"In the evening they would start to work again. Just about an hour before sundown a certain atmosphere would prevail—the preparing of dinner, singing songs about laying their burden down for the day. About the edge of sundown a whistle would blow three times, people would unyoke the oxen, and the old machine would stop. The engineer would have to stay because of fire but the rest of the workers would file into the house and eat. When the evening meal was eaten, instead of walking three or four miles back to their homes, the workers would go to the straw stacks and spread some grain sacks out and lay on them. They would sing spirituals, tell stories, and just talk.

"The change from steam and sail to motor boats and trucks and the decline of seafood has brought a tremendous change to the community in Southern Maryland. During the early part of this century there were no roads and people would walk as far as 10 miles to watch the steamboats come in on Sunday evening. The roustabouts were just one step away from the river boys who poled the big flat boats to take the tobacco out to the big sailing ships. They were trained to move freight fast and had two-wheel trucks that they pushed with their loads. They used to wear two-tone button shoes with leather aprons and would sing coming off the boats. It might be noted that all fertilizer was, at that time, received from Baltimore. Livestock and grain were also shipped to Baltimore.

"Dredging for oysters was also a large business at this time. The first law that was passed not allowing any oysters under two inches to be caught was done for the buyers and not the oysters, because the people thought the oysters would last forever. Well over 100 boats would line the harbor at Rock Point at one time. The store would be crowded with men right off the immigrant boats. One could hear three or four languages at one time—Swedish, Polish, Irish, and German. An old man, born about 1840, by the name of Bill Hanson, played the banjo and held out a cup for people to drop change in. He sang a lot of four-line songs. The most important event of the year was when the boats came in to load. Also, when they used to tread wheat out with the horses was an interesting event because they used to bring in extra horses and extra help from the different farms and make a holiday out of it."

SPEARMAN LANCASTER, another of the older residents of Rock Point, tells of his family before they arrived in Charles County from Lancastershire, England. Someone in the family, he says, "borrowed some sheep from a monastery and the head man put a curse on the family, and they were shipped over here by the government under the Queen's order. Once here, they spread out and raised more sheep. The curse was there would be a sheepherder for every generation of the family until the end of time."

Lancaster goes on to trace his family, and the curse, to modern times, beginning with the legend surrounding Swann Point. This began about 1800, he says, when the Lancaster family sold the property to a man who came up from the Bahamas. The man's name was Capt. Hollis.

"He brought with him Guinea slaves. They were a little different from the ones in Charles County—they were heavier and stronger and had a different language. He also brought a man named Washington Gudrick, who was supposed to be an ex-pirate. He was about 6'2", had a heavy head of curly red hair and a big scar that went down the side of his face. He was the foreman of the plantation. Captain Hollis, moved on the plantation with his two sons, George and Frank.

"After his father's death, George got the big ship that went to China and other foreign countries and Frank got the plantation. One time, after his brother died, George came back from one of his trips and he brought a beautiful tall brown skinned woman by the name of Santasae. She had a beautiful green silk dress and two little boys, about 5 and 7. Capt. Hollis told Gudrick to let her take charge of the big house and tend to the flowers and things, and to give her what help she needed but not to be familiar with her. That worked out for a while but being such a nice looking woman he tried to be fresh and she gave him the cold shoulder.

"To get even, he put the two little boys into a boat that came into Weird Creek and let them drift out into the tide and after that she lost her mind. She would wander around nights singing some kind of pagan chant. Gudrick throught the best thing to do before Capt. Hollis came back was to get her sold down in Georgia. On a ship that came in every spring was the way in which he planned to accomplish this. He put her on a little boat to take her out to the big ship. Just before they got there, she slipped overboard and she went down like a stone and they couldn't find her. When they did find her she was holding on to some chains that she had wrapped around her body under her dress, and which acted as weights. They brought her ashore and buried her.

"That night the slaves all decided they would get rid of Gudrick by worrying him to death. Sounds of drums and chants were heard all over Weird Creek marsh and around the house. The slaves sang songs saying Gudrick was already dead. This would get on Gudrick's nerves. He would shoot his gun at them and curse them. He could not stand the strain and started drinking more. He couldn't get anyone to stay with him. One time in August a big cloud hung over the plantation and there was sharp lightning. After the lightning, people who lived about a mile down the river heard the slaves from Swann Point calling that this man was sick and he had been calling for help—they said he was locked up in his quarters and couldn't get out and they would like for them to come there; the slaves didn't want to break in without their being there. Two white men got in a buggy and drove over to the plantation. When they got there, things were very quiet and the only sounds were those of the frogs in the marsh. They banged on the door in the overseeer's quarters and couldn't get in so they had to get some logs to break the door in. When they broke the door in he (Gudrick) was sitting up in bed with his hands held in front of him and in one hand was a woman's big piece of silk dress like the one the woman was buried in, and he was dead.

"There was no way of anyone getting in there to do it (to kill him) so the coroner's inquest put down died of causes unknown. That night they buried him. They made a grave, built a fire on top of the grave and one old woman, she must have been a witch, had a pot that was smoking—she went around saying chants and would run her hand in the pot and grab out something and would throw it in the fire and the fire would change colors, from blue to green to pink, and she called out a curse and said the curse would affect the place so there would not be any more prosperity there; she also called out a curse on the family.

"From that time on it seemed like everything went wrong with Swann Point. The curse must have had a long arm because the ship that George Hollis was on was never heard from again. What happened to it no one knows. At this point, the County sold the place for taxes. A man bought it and moved on it with his family and three sons."

People familiar with the County today might well agree that "everything" has gone "wrong with Swann Point"!

We could not end this chapter without encouraging further rummaging among the folktales and legends of Charles County. Rewarding discoveries, fascinating histories are encountered in the most unlikely places, as well as in such natural ones as the Charles County Public Library at La Plata, the Historical Society Library, and the Community College Learning Resources Center.

A search for information on Charles County's folklore begins like a search for anything else: go places, ask questions, listen. People who live here—the tobacco farmer, the waterman, the librarian, the churchman, the teacher, the storekeeper, the homesteader—all have wonderful stories to tell, and the listening itself is worth the trip. The Historical Society of Charles County and the Chamber of Commerce (especially in 1958, the section on Old Homes) have published some marvelous pamphlets and articles; Courthouse and Land Records, and Church histories are available on request. You don't have to travel to Baltimore, Annapolis—or even Cobb Island; but if you do, you'll be glad you did. It's all out there, rich and ripe for the plucking—all you have to do is reach. Aren't dreams worth it?

CHAPTER 10

GENEALOGY: DO YOUR OWN HISTORY

From time immemorial, as the Old Testament attests, mankind has been interested in and eager for knowledge of its ancestors.

For that reason members of this committee have compiled lists of Charles County's early residents and of research sources, to make it possible, and relatively easy, for persons who wish to know something of their ancestors here to search them out and, perhaps, to draw their own genealogical charts.

The names of early settlers appearing in these lists are spelled exactly as they are listed in the records; they may no longer appear that way. Also the sources are contained within the chapter rather than in an appended Bibliography, as it is believed they are of more use this way.

It is well to remember two additional factors in doing genealogical research in this area: First, Charles County's boundaries have been redefined several times; and the calendar in common use until 1582 differed from today's.

1. Early Charles County, People and Sources

Charles County has two distinct periods of history. Old Charles County came into formal existence on Nov. 21, 1650.

In the summer of that year, Robert Brooke arrived in Maryland with his second wife, 10 children, 28 servants and a commission dated at London, September 20, 1649, making him Commander of a County to be newly erected and called Charles. He also held a commission as a member of the Council of Maryland. Lands were surveyed and boundaries set, and on November 2, 1650, the first Charles County came into being.

Brooke agreed to bring more colonists to the new County at his own expense, and he commissioned his son, Baker, to undertake that charge. But after a few years the new County failed to achieve the financial expectations of the Governor and Council, and it was abolished. (*Maryland Historical Magazine*, Dec. 1945, p. 262)

The Land Records of Charles County show the following names of people arriving at Maryland from England, at the cost and charge of Robert Brooke, Esq., June 30, 1650:

Robert Brooke	Thomas Brooke	John Brooke
Mary, his wife	Charles Brooke	Wm. Brooke
His children	Roger Brooke	Francis Brooke
Baker Brooke	Robert Brooke	Mary Brooke
		Anna Brooke

MAN SERVANTS

Marke Lovely	Wm. Bradney	Rich. Robinson
Marke King	Phil. Howard	Anthony Kitchin
Wm. Jones	Thos. Joyce	Robt. Hooper
John Clifford	Henry Peere	Wm. Hinson
James Leigh	Thomas Elstone	John Boocock
Benj. Hammond	Edward Cooke	David Brown
Robt. Sheale	Ambrose Briggs	Henry Robinson

MAID SERVANTS

Anne Marshall	Abigael Mountague
Katherine Fisher	Eleanor Williams
Elizabeth Williamson	Agnes Neale
Margarite Watts	Forty other persons

The entire population of Charles County in 1658 is estimated to have been only 800. Population increased to 1,500 by 1665. The settlers must have been concentrated largely in and around Port Tobacco, for Court records of that period give the names of 30 or more householders in the town. Some of those mentioned are Job Chandler, John Jenkins, William Robinson, a carpenter, Henerie Moore, Robert Sly, a merchant, Edward Parks, Henry Adams, George Thompson, Zachery Wade, Thomas Moris, Edmund Lindsey, Robert Troop, John Nevill, Thomas Hussey, Donell Gordion, a constable, Robert Taylor, Simon Oursees, Joseph Harrison, Clemont Theobold, John Scherman, Francis Wine, a cooper, Henry Mees, James and Robert Littlepage, Abraham Rouse, John Pain, Philip Bourne, a merchant, Gils Glour, a merchant, John Rowley, John Roberts, and George English. There must have been other families whose names did not get into the Court records.

Area Sources for Charles County Genealogical Research

HALL OF RECORDS, Annapolis, Md. 21401

An extensive repository of Maryland records, including many Colonial documents from Charles County. Index Holdings, Bulletin #17 may be obtained free on request.

ENOCH PRATT FREE LIBRARY, Maryland Room, 400 Cathedral St., Baltimore 21201

Collection of Marylandia.

MARYLAND HISTORICAL SOCIETY, 201 West Monument St., Baltimore 21201

Volumes of historical information.

THE NATIONAL ARCHIVES AND RECORDS SERVICE, General Services Administration, Washington, D.C., 20408

Records vary; may give complete information about an individual, or little besides name. An excellent guide to using genealogical records at the Archives available at a small fee.

MARYLAND STATE DEPARTMENT OF HEALTH, Division of Vital Records, Central Office, 301 West Preston St., Baltimore 21201

Births and deaths in Maryland, except in Baltimore City; records from Jan. 1, 1898. After Dec. 31, 1972, all vital records, including those of Baltimore City, are recorded by MD. STATE DEPARTMENT OF HEALTH AND HYGIENE. A charge of $2 for each record copy issued.

Guide to Deciphering Old Documents

Research for the alphabet, figures, and calendar was provided by Anna M. Cartlidge, of the Maryland Historical Society, noted Baltimore genealogist, who has deciphered and extracted them from documents used in Colonial times. They may be of help in understanding the lettering, etc., used in those old documents.

Alphabet.

Artwork by Phyllis Seneff

Common Words.

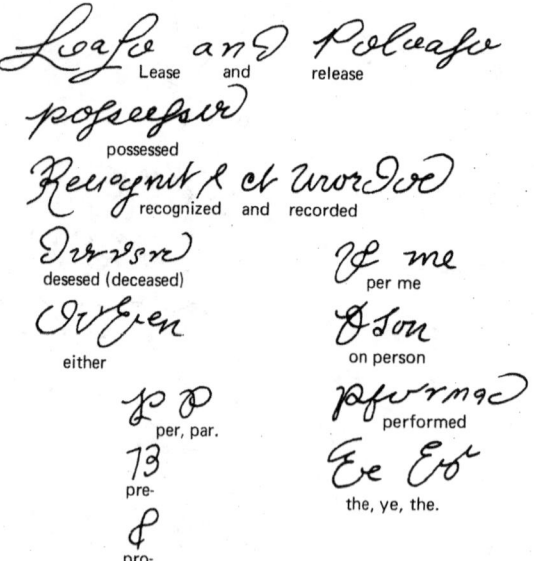

Artwork by Phyllis Seneff

Figures.

1. 1 5 1 8
2. 2 2
3. 3
4. 4 4
5. 5
6. 6 C 6
7. 7 7 7
8. 8 8 0
9. 9 9 9

ƒ pence

ʃ shillings

₽₽ pounds

y = teen
fifty = 15th
j = th
xxviij = 27th
xjx = 6.

Artwork by Phyllis Seneff

Calendar.

OLD STYLE (O. T.)		NEW STYLE (N. T.)
Before 1753, the year began March 25		After Jan. 1, 1753
March (before 1753)	1st Month	January (after 1753)
April	2nd Month	February
May	3rd Month	March
June	4th Month	April
July	5th Month	May
August	6th Month	June
September	7th Month	July
October	8th Month	August
November	9th Month	September
December	10th Month	October
January	11th Month	November
February	12th Month	December

Official Charles County Records.

Circuit Court

LAND AND COURT RECORDS, 1658-1786. Missing: Land Records, 1799-1702; Court Records, 1695, 1716, 1740, 1751, discontinued after 1780. Volumes dated 1658-98,

1710-13 contain both Land and Court Recores; otherwise records are entered in separate volumes, but numbered as a single series. Also includes Probate Recores, 1689-92; Vital Records, 1654-1706; Attachments, Writs, Orders, etc., 1687; Land Commissions, 1716-21; Laws in Force in 1677 and 1688 and Laws Passed in 1692. C.H. 1658-1786 (does not include Court Records, 1696-1710, 1711-80). H.R. (see NOTE) 1658-1786; 1658-1949, microfilm.

INDEX TO COURT AND LAND RECORDS, 1658-1722. Liber index. H.R.

LAND RECORDS, 1786-1810, 1813—. Original volumes for 1810-1813, which are missing, have been replaced by photocopies of the abstracts of the land records contained in these volumes. Most volumes indexed. C.H. 1786—. L.O. 1949—, microfilm. H.R. 1786-90; 1786-1949, microfilm.

ABSTRACTS OF LAND RECORDS, 1810-14. Photocopies of abstracts of land records in Liber I.B. No. 9 and Liber I.B. No. 10. The original volumes are missing from the Land Records. C.H.

INDEX TO LAND RECORDS, 1658-1937. Campbell. C.H. 1658-1937. L.O. 1658-1937, microfilm. H.R. 1658-1832; 1658-1937, microfilm.

INDEX TO LAND RECORDS, 1935—. Cottco Universal. Grantors and grantees in separate volumes. C.H. 1935—. L.O. 1935-48.

MORTGAGE RECORD, 1943—. Earlier mortgages in Land Records. Each volume indexed, 1943-56. C.H.

LAND COMMISSION RECORDS, 1838-85. Each volume indexed. C.H.

COMMISSION DOCKET [COMMISSIONS TO DIVIDE ESTATES], 1844-1903. Indexed. C.H.

PLAT BOOKS, 1933—. Earlier plats in Land Records. Each volume indexed. C.H.

PLAT RECORDS, 1933—. Projection prints of original plats in Plat Books. C.H.

NOTE: Code letters used in listings are H.R., Hall of Records at Annapolis; C.H., Courthouse Records, and L.O., Land Office Records, both at La Plata.

PLAT RECORD [STATE ROADS COMMISSION], 1933—. Indexed. C.H.
TAX SALES RECORD, 1903—. Each volume indexed. C.H.
JUDGMENT RECORD, 1790—. Most volumes indexed. C.H.
JUDGMENT DOCKET, 1846—. Each volume indexed by name of defendant. C.H.
CLERKS DOCKETS, 1864—. Also includes Court Minutes. Each volume indexed by name of defendant. C.H.
STET DOCKET, 1897—. Indexed by name of defendant. C.H.
JUDICIAL RECORDS, 1922—. Each volume indexed. C.H.
BOND RECORDS, 1901—. Each volume indexed. C.H.
EQUITY RECORDS (RECORDS OF EQUITY PROCEEDINGS, COURT PROCEEDINGS), 1796—. Each volume indexed by name of complainant. C.H.
DIVORCE DECREES, 1908—. Earlier divorces in Equity Records. Each volume indexed by name of complainant and respondent. C.H.
EQUITY DOCKETS (CHANCERY DOCKETS), 1811—. Each volume indexed. C.H.
INSOLVENT RECORD, 1879-85. Indexed. C.H.
INSOLVENT DOCKET, 1844-98. Indexed. C.H.
DIVISION OF NATURALIZATION, RECORD OF DECLARATION OF INTENTION, 1908-29. Each volume indexed. C.H.
CERTIFICATES OF NATURALIZATION, 1911-29. C.H.
INCORPORATION RECORDS (INCORPORATIONS, CORPORATION DOCKET), 1877—. Each volume indexed. C.H.
RECORD OF MARRIAGES, 1865-86. Arranged alphabetically by name of male. C.H.
RECORD OF MARRIAGE LICENSES, 1886-1935. Combined Campbell index and record. C.H.
RECORD OF MARRIAGES, 1936—. Applications and Clerk's certificates of ministers' returns. Each volume indexed. C.H.

RECORD OF PUBLICATION OF BANNS [of Marriage], 1905-41. C.H.

APPLICATIONS FOR MARRIAGE LICENSES, 1916—. Each volume indexed. C.H.

RECORD OF BIRTHS, 1865-70. Arranged alphabetically. C.H.

RECORD OF DEATHS, 1865-66. Arranged alphabetically. C.H.

ELECTION RETURNS, 1897—. Each volume indexed. C.H.

REGISTER OF INTENDED VOTERS, 1902-49. Indexed. C.H.

RECORD OF CLAIMS (AFFIDAVITS OF TEMPORARY REMOVAL), 1890-1929. Indexed. C.H.

REGISTRATION BOOKS, 1914—. Each volume indexed by name of voter within each election district. C.H.

TEST BOOKS, 1904—. Each volume indexed. C.H.

TOBACCO INSPECTION RECORDS, 1748-54, 1756-69, 1774-86. Also contains Proceedings of Special Court of Oyer, Terminer and Goal Delivery, June 1755. Each volume indexed, 1748-54, 1774-86. H.R.

ORIGINAL PAPERS, 1844—. Includes Law Papers, 1867—; Equity Papers, 1844—. C.H.

Orphans' Court

TESTAMENTARY PROCEEDINGS, 1716-19, 1760-66. Minutes of the actions taken by the Deputy Commissary for Charles County comparable to the Orphans Court Proceedings. Also contains Wills and Administration Accounts, which have been copied in Wills and in Accounts respectively. Each volume indexed. H.R. has card index.

ORPHANS COURT PROCEEDINGS, 1791—. 1777-91 in Wills. Also includes Accounts, 1908-37. Each volume indexed. H.R. has card index, 1777-91. C.H. 1827—. H.R. 1791-1827; 1791-1951, microfilm.

ORPHANS COURT DOCKETS (TERM DOCKETS), 1897—. C.H.

ADMINISTRATION DOCKET, 1825-1902. See also Estate Docket. Indexed. C.H.

ESTATE DOCKET, 1908—. See also Administration Docket. Each volume indexed. C.H.

WILLS, 1665—. Also includes Testamentary Proceedings, 1716-19, 1760-66; Orphans Court Proceedings, 1777-91; Inventories, 1777-91, 1825; Administration Accounts, 1673-1720, 1760-66, 1777-91, 1825. Most volumes indexed. H.R. has card index, 1665-1825. C.H. 1825—. H.R. 1665-1825; 1665-1955, microfilm.

INDEX TO WILLS, 1665—. Liber index. C.H. 1665—. H.R. 1665-1948, microfilm.

ADMINISTRATION BONDS, 1833—. 1797-1825 in Orphans Court Proceedings. Each volume indexed. C.H.

INVENTORIES, 1673—. 1777-91, 1825 in Wills; 1869-1924, 1933-37 in Orphans Court Proceedings. Also includes Accounts, 1807-24. Inventories of personal and real property recorded in separate volumes beginning in 1946. Each volume indexed. H.R. has card index, 1673-1824. C.H. 1825—. H.R. 1673-1824; 1673-1951, microfilm.

ACCOUNT OF SALES, 1827—. Each volume indexed. C.H.

ADMINISTRATION ACCOUNTS, 1673—. 1673-1720, 1777-91, 1825 in Wills; 1807-24 in Inventories; 1908-37 in Orphans Court Proceedings. H.R. has card index, 1673-1825. Each volume indexed. C.H. 1825—. H.R. 1673-1806; 1673-1955, microfilm.

GUARDIAN BONDS, 1778-1825, 1833—. 1778-91 in Wills; 1791-1825 in Orphans Court Proceedings. Each volume indexed by name of ward. C.H.

GUARDIAN ACCOUNTS, 1788-1823, 1825—. Each volume indexed by name of ward. H.R. has card index, 1788-1823. C.H. 1825—. H.R. 1788-1823, 1788-1823, microfilm.

GUARDIAN DOCKETS, 1792-1890. C.H. 1825-90. H.R. 1792-1824.

RECEIPTS AND RELEASES, 1827—. Earlier record in Court Proceedings. Each volume indexed. C.H.

CLAIM REGISTER, 1854—. Each volume indexed. C.H.

APPRENTICES (INDENTURES), 1915-27. Indexed by name of apprentice. C.H.

MANUMISSIONS, 1826-60. Also includes Rough Minutes of Orphans Court, 1875-87. Indexed. C.H.

PRIVATE ACCOUNT BOOKS. The following records were apparently filed as exhibits in the settlement of estates: Account Book, Orme and Lloyd, Port Tobacco, 1830-34. H.R. Ledger of J.T. Mudd, 1872-75. C.H.
ORIGINAL PAPERS, 1799—. Comprised of: Testamentary Papers, includes wills, inventories, accounts, bonds, and other probate papers. C.H. 1900—. H.R. 1799-1925.
Wills, 1908—. C.H.
Guardian Accounts and Bonds, 1909—. C.H.
Receipts and Releases, 1911-28. C.H.
School Reports, 1833-55. C.H.

County Commissioners

MINUTE BOOKS, 1894—. Earlier records burned. C.H.
ASSESSMENT BOOKS, 1923—. Arranged alphabetically within each district. C.H.
ASSESSORS FIELD CARDS, 1957—. Give more detail about property than Assessment Books. Arranged alphabetically within each district. C.H.
LEVY BOOKS, 1892—. C.H.
SUPPLEMENT TO ASSESSMENT VOLUMES, 1936. Covers small area in 5th election district called "Cobb Island," a summer development. Alphabetical. C.H.
ROAD MAPS, PETITIONS AND REPORTS OF ENGINEER [ROAD RECORDS], 1896—. C.H.

2. Sources for Genealogical Research

The works listed may be of value in researching family names in Charles County. The works marked by asterisk (*) are located in the Charles County Public Library, La Plata. Some works not marked may also be found there. The initials HS following some titles indicates they are in the possession of the Charles County Historical Society, currently housed in the basement of the Public Library.

'GPC' is the code for the Genealogical Publishing Company, 521-3 St. Paul Place, Baltimore, Md. 21202. Other publishers' addresses appear with the entry.

On Genealogy and Historical Research

*Doane, Gilbert H. *Searching for Your Ancestors*. Univ. of Minnesota Press, 1960.
Gibson, Jeremy S. W. *Wills and Where to Find Them* (in Great Britain). GPC, 1974.
Meyer, Mary Keyster. *Genealogical Research in Maryland, A Guide*. HS Pub. Maryland Historical Society, 1972. Contains complete list of sources through publication date.
Pimbley, Arthur F. *Dictionary of Heraldry*. GPC, 1908.
Zieber, Eugene. *Heraldry in America*. GPC, 1909; reprint 1973.
Also see catalogue of Basic Reference Books on Genealogy, Heraldry, and Local History, 1952 to 1973, Genealogical Publishing Co.
Also see Genealogical Records in the National Archives, Washington, D.C. Divisions:

I	Population and mortality census schedules
II	Passenger arrival lists
III	Military records, U. S.
IV	Naval and marine records, U.S.
V	Veterans benefits records
VI	Records concerning the Confederate States of America
VII	Land entry records for the public land states
VIII	Other records of genealogic value

Official Records Pertaining to Charles County, Md.

Archives of Maryland. Vols. 1-71. An invaluable source for records of the State.
Calendar of Maryland State Papers. HS Esp. No. I, *The Black Book*; vols. 1, 2, 3, *The Red Books* (copy, 1950); The Bank Stock Papers, No. 2, No. 4, parts i, ii, iii. Pub. Hall of Records, Annapolis.

Census, 1778, of Maryland. Betty Corothers. Pub. unknown. Primarily a list of names in the counties of Charles, Caroline, and Queen Anne for 1778.

Census of Charles County, Md., taken every 10 years, 1790 through 1890. On microfilm.

Census of Charles County, Md., 1800. 43 pp. Pub. Maryland Genealogical Society, Inc., 201 W. Monument Street, Baltimore 21201, 1967. Cost: $4.

Census, for 1810 and 1830. HS On microfilm.

Chronicles of St. Mary's. Pub. St. Mary's County Historical Society.

Constable's Census of Charles County, 1775-1778 (1,800 persons), for Durham Parish, Benedict Hundred, Port Tobacco, West Hundred; Upper Hundred, East Hundred, Newport; Upper Hundred, Pomonkey; Newport, West Hundred; William and Mary, Lower Hundred; Bryantown Hundred. In *Brumbaugh's Maryland Records*, vol. 1, pp. 297-312. Pub. Williams and Wilkins Co., Baltimore, 1915; vol. II, pub. Lancaster Press, Inc., Lancaster, Pa., 1928.

Heads of Families. First census of the U.S., 1790. Pub. Baltimore Southern Book Co., 1952. For Charles County, see pp. 47-55.

Index to the 1800 Federal Census of Caroline, Cecil, Charles, Frederick, and Kent counties, State of Maryland. By Charlotte and Lowell Volkel and Timothy Wilson, 1968. Available from Heritage House, Rt. 1, Box 211, Thomson, Ill. 61285.

Marriage Licenses, 1777-1886, Prince George's County. By Helen W. Brown. GPC, 1973.

Maryland Account Book #33, 1752. Betty Corothers. Pub. Maryland Publications. This is a reprint of the accounts for the entire State, containing a wealth of genealogical material. Many of those listed did not leave wills; this is the only record of the names of widows, children, marriages, etc. The 56 pages are completely indexed.

Maryland Oaths of Fidelity. Betty Corothers. Vol. 1 includes Charles County.

Maryland Records: Colonial, Revolutionary, County and Church. By Gaius Marcus Brumbaugh. 2 vols.; William and Wilkins Co., Baltimore, 1915.

Maryland Slave Owners and Superintendents, 1798. By Betty Corothers. Pub. Maryland Publications. Vol. 1 contains Charles County information. More than 80 pages, 5,000 names.

Maryland State Papers. Pub. Hall of Records, Annapolis, 1943.

*Maryland, World almanacs for 1920-21.

*Tercentenary History of Maryland, vols. 1-4. Comp. by Henry Fletcher Powell. Pub. S. J. Clarke, Chicago, 1925. Has biographical records of colonists, pioneers, judges, governors, military officers, *et. al.*

Regional Records and Histories that Include Charles County

Banks, Charles Edward, *Planters of the Early Commonwealth.* GPC, 1930.

Almanac, Supplement of the Baltimore Sun, 1876-1916. Baltimore, n.d. List of persons holding public office in Maryland.

Barnes, Robert. *Marriages and Deaths, 1727-1839.* As recorded in the *Maryland Gazette.* GPC, 1973.

Beitzell, Edwin W. *Life on the Potomac River.* HS Published by author, 1968.

*_____, *Point Lookout Prison Camp for Confederates.* Published by author, 1972.

Bell, Landon C. *The Old Free State*, Vol. 2. GPC, reprint 1974.

Bowie, Effie Gwynn. *Across the Years in Prince George's County.* Garrett and Massie, Inc., Richmond, 1944.

Brown, Mary Ross. *An Illustrated Genealogy of the Counties of Maryland and the District of Columbia*; A guide to locating records. HS N.p., n.d.

Burns, Annie W. *Index to Maryland Wills Book.* GPC, n.d.

*Carr, Mrs. Henry J. *Index to Certified Copy of Lists of American Prisoners of War, 1812-15.* GPC, n.d.

Daughters of the American Colonists. Collections of Colonial and Genealogical Records. GPC, 1946.

Davenport, Charles B. *Naval Officers, Their Heritage and Development.* GPC, 1919.

Davis, George Lynn-Lachlan. *The Day Star of American Freedom.* N.p., 1855.

Dielman File: Marriage and death notices from early newspapers, 18th century to date. Maryland Historical Society, n.d.

Hackett, J. Dominick, and C. M. Early. *The Passenger List from Ireland.* GPC, reprint, 1973.

*Hanson, George A. *Old Kent.* Regional Publishing Co., Baltimore, 1967.

Hardy, Stella Pickett. *Colonial Families of the Southern States of America.* GPC, reprint 1974.

Heitman, Francis B. *Historical Register of Officers of the Continental Army During the War of Revolution.* GPC, n.d.

Hinkel, John V. *Arlington, Monument to Heroes.* Prentice-Hall, Inc., Englewood Cliffs, N.J., 1970.

*_____, comp. See *Charles County, Maryland.* Washington, D.C., 1959.

Holten, John C. *Persons of Quality; Original list* (from Great Britain to American Plantations, 1600-1700). GPC, n.d.

Hopkins, G. M. *Atlas of 15 Miles Around Washington, including Prince George's County.* Garamond Pridemark Press, Inc., 714 E. Pratt St., Baltimore 21202, n.d.

Kinnamon, John. "The Public Levy in Colonial Maryland to 1689," *Maryland Historical Magazine*, vol. 53, no. 3 (Sept. 1958). First levy was 1640.

Knowles-Bolton, Charles. *Marriage Notices for the Whole United States, 1785-1794.* GPC, n.d.

*Magruder, James M., Jr. *Index of Maryland Colonial Wills, 1634-1777.* GPC, 1967.

Men of Mark in Maryland. Johnson's Makers of America Series. Bernard C. Steiner, Lynn R. Meekins, David H. Carroll, and Thomas G. Boggs. 4 vols., Johnson-Wynne Co., Washington, D.C., 1907-1912. Biographies of leading men of the State; full index in vol. 4.

Mitchell, John Hanson. "Maryland's Revolutionary Leaders Who Came from Charles County," *The Record*, Charles County Historical Society. HS

*Newman, Harry Wright. *Charles County Gentry.* GPC, reprint 1971. Includes Dent, Edelen, Hanson, Newman, and Warren families.

*_____. *The Flowering of the Maryland Palatinate.* Published by author, 1961.

*_____. *Maryland Revolutionary Records.* Published by author, 1938.

*_____. *Public Officials Reference Book: Seigniory in Early Maryland,* "Manor Lords." N.p., 1949. Descendants of lords of the Maryland manors; see p. 67.

Owings, Donnell M. "His Lordship's Patronage, Officers of Profit in Colonial Maryland." N.p., 1953.

*Parran, Alice Norris. *Register of Maryland's Heraldic Families.* 2 vols., H. G. Roebuck and Son, Baltimore, n.d.

*Pogue, Robert L. T. *Old Maryland Landmarks.* HS Published by author, 1972.

*_____. *Yesterday in Old St. Mary's County.* Carlton Press, Inc., New York, reprint 1972.

*Ridgely, Helen W. *Historic Graves of Maryland and the District of Columbia.* Grafton Press, N.Y., n.d.

Rivoire, J. Richard. *Clifton.* HS N.p., n.d.

*Ross, Nellie Grant. *Tomb-Stones and Bible Records of Charles County, Md.* National Society of the Daughters of the American Revolution. N.d.

Simmons, Julia A. *Men and Women of Note.* GPC, 1935.

*Skirven, Percy G. *First Parishes of the Province of Maryland.* Norman Remington Co., 1923.

*Skordos, Gust. *The Early Settlers of Maryland.* Baltimore GPC, 1968. An index to names of immigrants, compiled from "Records of Land Patents," 1633-1680, in the Hall of Records, Annapolis.

Thomas, James Walter. *Chronicles of Colonial Maryland.* N.p., n.d.

Truitt, Reginald V. *Kent Island.* N.p., 1965. Available from Queen Anne County Historical Society.

Yearbook of the American Gregor Society. HS Vols. 47, 55, 56, 57. American Clan Gregor Society, Inc., 1973.

Genealogical Sources for Charles County Families
Books are listed alphabetically by family name.
ALEXANDER, BROWN, AND CHAPMAN FAMILIES. HS Sigismunda Chapman. Dietz Printing Co., Richmond, 1946.
BAKER AND BUFORD FAMILIES. K.B. Johnson. GPC, 1929.
BAKER FAMILY RECORDS. J.M. Seaver. GPC, 1929.
THE ANCESTRY OF RICHARD BELL AND HIS MOTHER, CLARA GREER BELL. GPC, 1929.
BERRY OF MARYLAND WITH CLAGGETT. Notes and typescript, GPC, n.d.
THE BOONE FAMILY. Hazel A. Spraker. GPC, 1922.
*THE BROOKE FAMILY. In *Maryland Historical Magazine*, vol. 1, March 1906, p. 66. On microfilm.
HISTORY OF THE BURCH FAMILY. HS Frank E. Toon, *et. al.* Unpublished ms., n.d.
THE STORY OF ELIZABETH, Our Country's First Nun. HS Ross L. Martin. Twin Circle Pub. Co., N.Y., 1968.
FOULKE FAMILY. HS Roy A. Foulke. N.p., 1974.
300 YEARS OF MARYLAND GAMBRILLS. Alice M. Bowerman. Maryland Gen. Society, Baltimore, n.d.
HANSON AND CONWELL. John Richardson. Carolingian Press, Stockton, N.J., 1973.
*JOHN HANSON OF MULBERRY GROVE. J. Bruce Kremer. Albert and Charles Boni, Inc., New York, n.d.
JOHN HANSON, OUR FIRST PRESIDENT. HS Seymour Wemys Smith. Heritage Series, n.d.
THE STRANGE STORY OF JOHN HANSON, Our First President. Herbert J. Stoeckel. Hanson House, Hartford, Conn., 1958.
DARK COMPANION. The Story of Matthew Henson. Bradley Robinson. Robert McBride and Co., 1947.
THE THOMAS LAMONTS IN AMERICA. HS Corliss Lamont. A.S. Barnes and Co., n.d.
THE ANCESTORS AND DESCENDANTS OF JAMES W. LEATHERBEE AND HARRIET WILEY. Mrs. A.T. Leatherbee. Md. Book Publishing Co., Baltimore, 1917.

*THE LLOYDS OF SOUTHERN MARYLAND. Daniel B. Lloyd. Published by author, 1971.
*THE LUCKETTS OF PORTOBACCO. Harry Wright Newman. Published by author, 1938.
PETER MANKIN(S), 1770-1881. HS Ouida Hunter Harkreader. Unpublished ms, n.d.
*THE MIDDLETONS AND KINDRED FAMILIES OF SOUTHERN MARYLAND. Daniel B. Lloyd. Published by author, 1975.
*THE MUDD FAMILY IN THE U.S. Dr. Richard Dyer Mudd. Edwards Bros., Inc., Ann Arbor, 1951.
*THE LIFE OF DR. SAMUEL A. MUDD. Nettie Mudd. Neale Publishing Co., New York, 1906.
NEALE FAMILY OF CHARLES COUNTY. Christopher Johnston. *Maryland Historical Magazine*, vol. 7, June 1912, p. 201.
THE NEALES OF MARYLAND AND THEIR DESCENDANTS. HS Published by author, n.d.
NEWTON FAMILY OF VIRGINIA. Mrs. A. Z. Badgley. GPC, n.d. Includes Hyde and Hickey families.
NORMANS OF MARYLAND. HS Zelda Norma Thorne. Published by author, 1944.
SNATCHES OF O'DANIEL, HAMILTON, AND ALLIED GENEALOGY. "A Native of Kentucky." Rosary Press, Somerset, O., 1933.
POSEY FAMILY IN AMERICA. HS Lloyd Franklin Posey and Betty Sue Drake Posey. Hattiesburg, Miss., 1971.
ROHRBACH GENEALOGY. HS Lewis B. Rohrbaugh. Dando-Schaff Printing and Pub. Co., Philadelphia, 1970.
*THE MARYLAND SEMMES AND KINDRED FAMILIES. Harry Wright Newman. J.H. Furst Co., Baltimore, 1956.
*THE SMOOTS OF MARYLAND AND VIRGINIA. Harry Wright Newman. J.P. Bell Co., Lynchburg, Va., 1936.
*THE STONES OF POYNTON MANOR. Harry Wright Newman. Published by author, 1937.
JOHN WHEELER OF CHARLES COUNTY, MARYLAND, AND SOME OF HIS DESCENDANTS, 1630-93. Walter V. Ball. Unpublished ms, n.d.

Baptismal, Marriage, and Death Registers of Catholic Churches

St. Ignatius Church, St. Thomas Manor, Bel Alton. Very early records destroyed by fire; contains records from 1872.

St. Mary's Church, Bryantown. Records from 1793.

St. Peter's Church, Waldorf. Records from 1852.

Holy Ghost, Issue. Records from 1904; cemetery records from 1876.

St. Francis de Sales, Rock Point. Records consolidated with Holy Ghost in 1911.

St. Francis de Sales, Benedict. Records from 1944. Early records destroyed by fire; few left from 1899 to 1900; others at Bryantown.

Sacred Heart, La Plata. Records from 1925; earlier records at St. Thomas Manor, Bel Alton.

St. Mary, Star of the Sea, Indian Head. Records from 1919; earlier records at St. Thomas Manor.

St. Catherine, McConchie. Records from 1952; earlier records at St. Thomas Manor.

St. Ignatius, Hilltop. Records from 1952; earlier records at St. Thomas Manor.

St. Joseph, Pomfret. records from 1925; a few records at Sacred Heart; earlier records at St. Thomas Manor.

Records of Early Anglican Churches

Christ Church, Old Durham Parish; est. 1692. Photostatic copies of Vestry minutes, 1774-1824, 1 vol; some vital records from 1843, in custody of Rector.

Christ Church, Port Tobacco Parish; est. 1692. Vestry records from 1817; vital records from 1869 in custody of Rector.

St. Paul's, Piney; once a chapel of Port Tobacco Parish. Early records a part of Port Tobacco Parish, Christ Church.

Trinity Parish and Oldfields Chapel. Vestry minutes and vital records before 1903 at Hall of Records, Annapolis; records from 1903 in custody of Rector.

Christ Church, William and Mary Parish, Wayside; est. 1692. Vestry Journal, March 2, 1864, through April 5, 1971; vital records Aug. 18, 1874, through Aug. 1, 1963, in custody of Rector.

3. Charles County Census of 1850 (By District)

The Census of 1850 is not complete as printed, because only free heads of families are listed.

The procedure used follows that outlined in the *Guide to Genealogical Records in the National Archives*. For each free person in a household, an entry shows the name and postal address; age, sex, and color (white, black, or mulatto); occupation if over 15 years of age; the value of real estate owned; the State, Territory, or country of birth; and whether he was married within the year.

For each slave, an entry shows the name of the slave owner; the age, sex, color (but not the name) of the slave; and whether he was a fugitive from the State. There is also a column for the number of slaves manumitted by each slave owner. Spellings are copied from the listings.

The date the census was taken and the name of the census taker are also given, as they appear in the records.

Entries in lists show, as available: Name, Age, Sex, Color, Occupation, Place of birth, value of real estate owned.

Allen's Fresh District. July 11, 1850; John M. Hawkins, Asst. Marshal.
1. S. R. Handcock, 42, F, Md.
2. Terresa Padget, 60, F, Md.
3. Mary Dyson, 72, F, Md.
4. Luisa Luckett, 45, F, Md.
5. Uriah Robey, 49, M, Farmer, Md.
6. Edward Gardiner, 40, M, Agent, Md.
7. John G. Chapman, 51, M, Farmer, Md., $50,000
8. John M. Smoot, 66, M, Farmer, Md., $14,000

9. James F. Neal, 36, M, Farmer, Md., $5,000
10. Samuel Cox, 30, M, Farmer, Md., $10,000
11. John O. Maddox, 32, M, Farmer, Md., $12,000
12. John D. Handson, 51, M, Md., $1,140
13. [no entry]
14. Frank Diggs, 65, M, B, Laborer, Md.,
15. William Baker, 36, M, Constable, Md.
16. Charles C. Robey, 42, M, Farmer, Md.
17. Terresa Boswell, 30, F, Md.
18. Hodena Butler, 40, F, B, Md.
19. John B. Maddox, 41, M, Farmer, Md., $1,000
20. Francis B. Wills, 48, M, Farmer, Md., $7,000
21. James F. Stone, 38, M, Farmer, Md.
22. Wm. H. Warthen, 43, M, Farmer, Md., $500
23. James Power, 50, M, R.-C. Priest, Ireland
24. Mary Far, 60, F, Md.
25. E. A. Middletown, 63, F, Md., $7,000
26. Bennett Green, 39, M, Carpenter, Md.
27. Washington A. Posey, 35, M, Farmer, Md., $14,000
28. Robert Diggs, 51, M, Farmer, Md., $10,000
29. John Ware, 32, M, Farmer, Md., $8,000
30. William D. Merrick, 56, M, Farmer, Md., $40,000
31. Milford Jenkins, 30, M, Agent, Md.
32. Robert Oliver, 28, M, Carpenter, Md.
33. Charlotte Herbert, 45, F, Md.
34. E.H. Edelen, 55, F, Md., $10,000
35. William Owen, 39, M, Md., $1,000
36. Harriet Adams, 46, F, M, Md.
37. Alicy Thompson, 53, F, M, Md.
38. Thomas Thompson, 38, M, M, Md.
39. Mary Crane, 57, F, Md., $5,000
40. Ann Brookbank, 46, F, M, Md.
41. Eleanor Roberson, 40, F, $3,000
42. William Boswell, 28, M, Merchant
43. Bennett Neal, 34, M, Doctor, Md., $800
44. Susan Cray, 60, F, B, Md.
45. Maria Bailee, 45, F, Md.
46. L. T. Padget, 26, M, Merchant, Md.

47. Griffin Carter, 45, M, Wheelright, Va.
48. Charles H. Wheeler, 29, M, Tailor, Md., $500
49. Joseph Hutton, 57, M, Undertaker, Md., $1,000
50. Edward Hatcher, 45, M, Shoemaker, Md., $500
51. P. Davis, 40, M, Tavernkeeper, Md., $2,500
52. M. D. Bailee, 52, M, Va., $500
53. Mary S. Smoot, 32, F, Md., $200
54. Lyne Shackelford, 43, M, Tavernkeeper, Va., $3,000
55. Lewis Weeks, 30, M, Merchant, Va., $1,000
56. E. M. Day, 50, M, Merchant, Conn., $2,000
57. David Middleton, 56, M, Tavernkeeper, Md., $800
58. James Swann, 41, M, M, Tavernkeeper, Md., $500
59. E. Wells, 34, M, Printer, Md., $300
60. Francis Wills, 24, M, Doctor, Md., $1,200
61. James O. King, 28, M, Carpenter, Va.
62. Charles W. Barnes, 35, F, Md.
63. Henry A. Neal, 40, M, Farmer, Md., $6,000
64. James H. Norris, 34, M, Capt. of Dept., Md.
65. George W. Lewis, 31, M, Sailor, Md.
66. S. Ferrell, 40, M, Farmer, Md., $5,000
67. Robert Cox, 26, M, Agent, Md.
68. Wm. Nevet, 37, M, Farmer, Va., $4,000
69. Alexander Handcock, 22, M, Farmer, Md., $2,000
70. John Keech, 52, M, Farmer, Va., $500
71. Henry Swann, 30, M, M, Farmer, Md., $500
72. John Thompson, 23, M, M, Laborer, Md.
73. Y. Lloyd, 40, M, Farmer, Md., $5,000
74. Laurence Posey, 28, M, Farmer, Md., $4,600
75. Wm. Homes, 74, M, Farmer, Md., $5,000
76. Wm. Thompson, 30, M, M, Laborer, Md.
77. S. W. Smoot, 54, M, Farmer, Md., $160
78. Matilda Butler, 45, F, B, Md.
79. Ann Homes, 28, F, Md.
80. Ann S. Fowler, 50, F, Md.,
81. Elizabeth S. Pott, 80, F, Md.
82. Mary Tryon, 30, F, Md.
83. Thomas Jackson, 64, M, Farmer, Md.
84. Uz Goldsberry, 58, M, Shoemaker, Md.

85. Rebecca Bateman, 60, F, Md., $5,000
86. S. P. M. Handson, 36, M, Collector, Md.
87. Thomas D. Simpson, 42, M, Agent, Md., $4,000
88. Thomas Posey, 30, M, Agent, Md., $7,000
89. Peter Crain, 48, M, Farmer, Md., $12,000
90. William W. Wood, 32, M, Agent, Md.
91. John Herbert, 41, M, Agent, Md.
92. E. J. Harris, 54, F, Md., $6,000
93. Asa Jenkins, 61, M, Farmer, Md., $1,900
94. James Franklin, 25, M, Agent, Md., $10,000
95. Elizabeth E. Collins, 26, F, Md.
96. Henry Collins, 57, M, M, Farmer, Md., $800
97. Nelly Collins, 59, F, M, Md.
98. Elizabeth Mastain, 35, F, Md.
99. Charles T. S. Briscoe, 51, M, Doctor, Md.
100. Joseph Fowler, 50, M, Farmer, Md.
101. William Shorter, 48, M, Sailor, Md.
102. John N. Xierents, 38, M, Agent, Md., $10,000
103. Eliza Matthews, 47, F, M, Md.
104. Sally Chase, 60, F, M, Md.
105. James E. Goldberry, 26, M, Farmer, Md.
106. Patrick Hamilton, 34, M, Farmer, Md., $8,000
107. Catherine Howard, 47, F, Md.
108. Edward P. Long, 27, M, Md.
109. Wm. P. Flowers, 37, M, Teacher, Md.
110. Benjamin Gunn, 30, M, Farmer, Md., $3,500
111. Notley Dutton, 36, M, Farmer, Md.
112. Thomas Penn, 37, M, Farmer, Md., $2,000
113. Henry R. Harris, 34, M, Farmer, Md., $15,000
114. James S. Willet, 40, M, Agent, Md.
115. Benjamin P. P. Fendal, 27, M, Agent, Md., $3,000
116. Jane Collens, 48, F, M, Md.
117. Francis W. Weems, 23, M, Farmer, Md., $10,000
118. John N. Lomax, 49, M, Agent, Md.
119. Benjamin T. Bateman, 28, M, Farmer, Md., $3,000
120. Charles Bateman, 26, M, Farmer, Md.
121. Andrew E. Lloyd, 25, M, Farmer, Md., $1,000
122. Elizabeth Lloyd, 49, F, Md., $4,000

123. Thomas Lloyd, 30, M. Capt. Lightboat, Md.
124. Thomas S. Smoot, 36, M, Farmer, Md.
125. Letetia Bond, 43, F, Md., $1,000
126. George Bailee, 34, M, Farmer, Md., $500
127. Wm. Rodgers, 32, M, Merchant, Va.
128. Thomas D. Haden, 51, M, Farmer, Md., $3,000
129. Wm. A. Maddox, 45, M, Farmer, Md., $2,800
130. Mary Norris, 58, F, Md., $500
131. John N. Simmes, 42, M, Farmer, Md., $2,160
132. John L. N. Goodrick, 22, M, Constable, Md.
133. John S. Maddox, 46, M, Farmer, Md.
134. James H. Morgan, 38, M, Farmer, Md., $4,500
135. James Dutton, 34, M, Farmer, Md., $500
136. Mandy Dyson, 45, F, M, Md.
137. Nancy Burrough, 37, F, B, Md.
138. John H. Diggs, 37, M, Farmer, Md., $12,000
139. Y. Turner, 37, M, Farmer, Md., $3,000
140. John T. Stoddard, 58, M, Farmer, Md., $20,000
141. Henry Wingate, 45, M, Agent, Md.
142. John A. Burrough, 46, M, Farmer, Md., $7,800
143. Joseph Lloyd, 43, M, Md.
144. Isaiah Posey, 53, M, Farmer, Md., $8,000
145. Edward Nott, 25, M, None, Md.
146. Toloson Shorter, 35, M, B, Md.
147. Eleanor Shorter, 26, F, B, Md.
148. Joseph Bailee, 28, M, Farmer, Md.
149. Charles Bailee, 22, M, Farmer, Md.
150. Francis Warthen, 45, M, Farmer, Md.
151. Henry Glascow, 50, M, Farmer
152. Henrietta Lancaster, 53, F, $3,000
153. Thomas Ching, 28, M, Agent
154. A. P. Simms, 43, M, Farmer, $14,000
155. William Mollyhorne, 45, M, Farmer
156. Mary Smoot, 36, F, $2,000
157. Mary A. Williams, 45, F, Md.
158. Uz V. Posey, 33, M, Farmer, Md.
159. Samuel Thomas, 25, M, M, Sailor, Md.
160. John Thomas, 35, M, B, Md., $300

161. Tom Butler, 40, M, B, Laborer, Md.
162. Charles Lancaster, 29, M, Farmer, Md.
163. John Short, 40, M, B, Laborer, Md.
164. Alexander Swann, 50, M, B, Md.
165. James S. Haden, 36, M, Farmer, Md.
166. Jack Boarman, 55, M, M, Farmer, Md. $100
167. William Boarman, 40, M, B, Md.
168. John B. McWilliams, 34, M, Merchant, Md.
169. William Elkins, 38, M, Md.
170. John Thomas, 56, M, B, Farmer, Md.
171. Benjamin A. Lancaster, 48, M, Farmer, Md., $1,800
172. Ann Barlee, 50, F, Md., $2,300
173. Joseph Herbert, 35, M, Sailor
174. Washington Lancaster, 56, M, Farmer, $4,000
175. Edward Jenkins, 39, M, Agent
176. James Hollis, 70, M, Farmer, Md., $5,200
177. James Haden, 36, M, Farmer, Md., $3,000
178. Francis Matthews, 42, M, Doctor, Md., $4,000
179. Ignatius Bailee, 24, M, Farmer, Md., $1,500
180. George Bateman, 61, M, None, Md.
181. Susan Bateman, 28, F
182. Francis Nalley, 47, M, Farmer, Md., $2,000
183. Francis Bailee, 24, M, Farmer, Md., $1,000
184. Henry Dickson, 40, M, Farmer, Md., $1,000
185. John Hemsly, 39, M, Farmer, Md., $5,000
186. Francis Goodick, 35, M, Miller, Md.
187. Columbus Lancaster, 39, M, Farmer, Md., $1,500
188. Matthew Sherbin, 23, M, Farmer, Md.
189. Samuel Herbert, 35, M, Sailor, Md.
190. Henry Bailee, 35, M, Farmer, Md., $500
191. John Bond, 29, M, Md.
192. Claracy Herbert, 65, F, Md.
193. Sara Boit, 40, F, Md.
194. Eliza Goldsmith, 48, F, Md., $2,000
195. Osborn Murphy, 60, M, Farmer, Md., $25
196. George Gordon, 46, M, M, Farmer, Md.
197. Ann Dickson, 34, F, Md.
198. John Redmon, 25, M, Miller, Md.

199. Wm. Simpson, 47, M, Farmer, Md.
200. Samuel Dyhmack, 40, M, Agent, Md.
201. Garard Hundkerford, 26, M, Farmer, Md., $4,000
202. John N. Hawkins, 27, M, Superintendent, Md., $8,000
203. Elesha Roby, 67, M, Farmer, Md., $500
205. Verlenda Davis, 64, F, Md.
206. James Osbein, 35, M. Farmer, Md., $500
207. Alfred Roby, 31, M, Farmer, Md.

Bryantown District, Aug. 2, 1850; John M. Hawkins.
208. Perry Wilmer, 24, M, Farmer, Md., $2,500
209. Herereta Roberts, 40, F, $3,000
210. Josia Roberts, 6, M, Md.
George N. Robey, 28, M, Farmer, Md.
211. Sara F. Roby, 43, F, Md., $1,000
212. Sara McDaniel, 61, F, Md.
213. Charles Woolf, 51, M, Farmer, Md., $700
214. Christianna Acton, 37, F, Md.
215. Henry Roby, 31, M, Farmer, Md., $300
216. George H. Lucas, 35, M, Farmer, Md., $600
217. Elisha Padget, 29, M, Farmer, Md.

Middletown District. Aug. 20, 1850; John M. Hawkins.
218. Mary Pickaerel, 51, M, Farmer, Md.
219. Elizabeth Williams, 84, F, Md.
220. Henry Smallwood, 85, F, B, Md.
221. John Osborn, 70, M, Farmer, Md.
222. Terresa Shorter, 30, F, B, Md.
223. Rzach Adams, 57, M, Miller, Md.
224. Samuel H. Roby, 45, M, Farmer, Md., $400
225. George F. Beven, 25, M, Teacher, Md.
226. John Cliff, 50, M, Farmer, Va.
227. Wm. Berry of Jon, 72, M, Farmer, Md.
228. Carolene Hawkins, 48, F, Md., $8,000
229. Josios Hawkins, 49, M, Farmer, Md., $10,000
230. John Max, 26, M, Miller, Md.

231. John J. Jenkins, 40, M, Farmer, Md.
232. John Hamilton, 49, M, Farmer, Md., $11,000
233. George S. Richards, 42, M, Farmer, Md., $30
234. Lurena Richards, 67, F, Md.
235. L. N. B. Hawkins, 35, M, Farmer, Md., $6,000
236. M. J. Morris, 31, M, Carpenter, Md.
237. Charles Ferrell, 62, M, Farmer, Md.
238. Henry Davis, 40, M, B, Laborer, Md.
239. Charles Markes, 30, M, Plasterer, Md.
240. Ann Markes, 75, F, Md.
241. Stuse Swann, 65, M, M, Farmer, Md.
242. William Swann, 23, M, M, Farmer, Md.
243. Robert Hatcher, 30, M, Farmer, Md.
244. Judson Wedding, 37, M, Farmer, Md., $800
245. Nathaniel Freeman, 38, M, Farmer, Md.
246. William Gardiner, 27, M, Agent, Md.
247. Ann Stonestreet, 49, F, Md., $5,600
248. William C. Baines, 38, M, Lawyer, Va.
249. John Long, 62, M, Farmer, Md., $6,000
250. John S. Long, 30, M, Farmer, Md.

Hilltop District.
Martha E. Long, 30, F, Md.
251. Catherine Brawner, 38, F, Md., $4,000
252. Elisha Jones, 61, M, Farmer, Md.
253. Walter H. Robertson, 45, M, Farmer, Md.
254. Andrew J. Frank, 35, M, Sailor, Va.
255. James L. Brawner, 36, M, Co. Surveyor, Md., $1,800
256. James H. Burch, 28, M, Agent, Md., $2,000
257. Robert Davis, 32, M, Farmer, Md.
258. Mary Handson, 110, F, B, Md.
259. Elly Ferrell, 45, M, B, Md.
260. Edward N. Stonestreet, 26, M, Farmer, Md., $2,000
261. Joseph Lacy, 47, M, Captain Vessel, Md.
262. James R. Brent, 48, M, Farmer, Md., $8,000
263. James H. Neal, 48, M, Farmer, Md., $12,000
264. Nicholas Stonestreet, 30, M, Lawyer, Md., $3,000

265. Charles A. Pye, 58, M, Farmer, Md.
266. Wm. Slaven, 35, M, Agent, Md.
267. Benjamin Notch, 34, M, Farmer, Md., $2,000
268. John F. Boswell, 47, M, Farmer, Md., $2,000
269. Wm. G. Haden, 41, M, Farmer, Md., $1,000
270. John G. St. Clair, 27, M, Farmer, Md., $3,000
271. Richard H. Bailee, 30, M, Sailor, Md.
272. Roderick G. Notson, 47, M, Farmer, Md., $8,000
273. James Savage, 54, M, Farmer, England, $1,000
274. Mary Simpson, 63, F, Md., $4,000
275. Leonard Ferrell, 42, M, Farmer, Md., $3,000
276. Wm. Long, 36, M, Farmer, Md., $3,000
277. John D. Freeman, 50, M, Farmer, Md., $12,000
278. Teresa Burger, 85, F. Md., $3,000
279. Francis B. Burger, 40, M, Farmer, Md.
280. Handson Robertson, 31, M. Farmer, Md., $6,000
281. Robert Handson, 53, M, Farmer, Md., $2,500
282. Janes Stone, 68, F, Md., $500
283. Edmon Perry, 41, M, Farmer, Md., $3,000
284. Alexands H. Robertson, 37, M, Farmer, Md., $3,500
285. Wm. B. Carpenter, 28, M, Farmer, Md., $1,000
286. Thomas Loyd, 50, M, Farmer, Md., $3,500
287. Walter M. Millar, 48, M, Farmer, Md., $6,000
288. Anice D. Alen, 58, M, Farmer, Md.
289. William Penny, 9, M, M, Md.
290. Bassle Brooks, 30, M, M, Laborer, Md.
291. Ann Robey, 47, F, Md.
292. J. B. Franklin, 45, M, Farmer, Md., $3,000
293. May A. Franklin, 68, F, Md.
294. Phlenvy Bowie, 36, M, Farmer, Md., $400
295. Humphey Davis, 48, M, Md.
296. George Simmons, 26, M, Farmer, Md, $600
297. Benjamin Simmons, 41, M, Farmer, Md., $600
298. Adeline Wedge, 49, F, M, Md., $100
299. Richard J. Garner, 32, M, Agent, Md.
300. William Royls, 28, M, B, Plasterer, Md.
301. Joseph Young, 57, M, Farmer, Md., $6,000
302. James Adams, 65, M, Farmer, Md.

303. Catherine Vencin, 73, F, Md., $2,000
304. Wm. Morris, 83, M, Farmer, Md., $1,500
305. Elizabeth Swann, 35, F, M, Md.
306. James Ferguson, 34, M, Farmer, Md., $3,000
307. Robert Ferguson, 43, M, Farmer, Md., $15,000
308. John B. Lawson, 45, M, Farmer, Md., $6,000
309. Elizabeth Lawson, 50, F, Md.
310. Edward Welch, 30, M, Laborer, Md.
311. Leon Leland, 27, M, Farmer, Md., $25
312. John E. Bowie, 49, M, Farmer, Md., $300
313. James Roberson, 65, M, Farmer, Md.
314. Osborn Cornell, 28, M, Farmer, Md., $100
315. Elizabeth Bowie, 72, F, Md.

Hill Top District. 13th day of Aug.
316. Maria Bowie, 45, F, Md.
317. Thomas Johnson, 52, M, Farmer, Md., $1,000
318. May Barker, 36, F, Md.
319. Herzekiah Franklin, 60, M, Md.
320. Richard N. Hart, 32, M, Farmer, Md., $1,500
321. Joseph A. Simmons, 23, M, Farmer, Md.
322. Handson Steward, 65, M, Farmer, Md.
323. Lydia Posey, 69, F, Md.
324. Jane Carpenter, 64, F, Md.
325. Joseph G. Gray, 30, M, Farmer, Md., $2,200
326. Peter Williams, 39, M, Farmer, Md., $3,000
327. Richard Welch, 45, M, Farmer, Md.
328. P. M. Dunnington, 40, M, Cooper, Md.
329. Wm. J. Thompson, 30, M, Farmer, Md., $1,500
330. Wm. Bowie, 33, M, Merchant, Md.
331. Peter Riczen, 76, M, Farmer, Md., $1,500
332. John Smomath, 57, M, Blacksmith, Md.
333. Richard Milstead, 50, M, Farmer, Md., $150
334. James B. Carpenter, 26, M, Farmer, Md., $380
335. Thomas Delogeer, 33, M, Md.
336. Walter Southerland, 28, M, Farmer, Md., $100
337. Catherine Coten, 60, F, Md.

338. C. Graham Brawner, 35, M, Farmer, Md., $8,000
339. John F. Prince, 47, M, Farmer, Md., $2,000
340. Ann Ferrell, 60, F, Md.
341. Wm. Simmons, 35, M, Farmer, Md., $2,000
342. Rebecca Barker, 60, F, Md.
343. George Bowie, 40, M, Farmer, Md., $3,000
344. Mary Milstead, 40, F, Md., $500
345. Wm. Coten, 40, M, Farmer, Md.
346. A. Simmons, 40, M, Farmer, Md., $2,000
347. Thonton Bell, 35, M, Farmer, Md., $2,000
348. William Cox, 45, M, Farmer, Md., $1,500
349. William Skinner, 23, M, Farmer, Md.
350. Francis A. Garriot, 26, M, Farmer, Md.
351. Oswell McDaniel, 50, M, Farmer, Md.
352. John H. D. Wingate, 39, M, Farmer, Md.
353. Walter A. Haislip, 38, M, Farmer, Md., $6,000
354. Garard Pirzin, 45, M, Farmer, Md., $2,400
355. Philbert Bowie, 40, M, Farmer, Md., $400
356. Betsy Mason, 70, F, M, Md.
357. Rubin Backster, 44, M, Farmer, Md., $1,200
358. Eleana Franklin, 32, M, Farmer, Md., $3,000
359. James Southerland, 29, M, Farmer, Md.
360. James Penny, 40, M, M, Laborer, Md.
361. James Milstead, 35, M, Farmer, Md.
362. Francis Cofer, 42, M, Farmer, Md., $2,000
363. Henry Green, 50, M, M, Md.
364. Walter Mardie, 50, M, B, Laborer, Md.
365. Mary Speck, 40, F, Md.
366. Susan Milstead, 45, F, Md.
367. James Simmons, 28, M, M, Md.
368. Betty Brooks, 18, F, M, Md.
369. Frank Simmons, 21, M, M, Laborer, Md.
370. Thomas Speak, 46, M, Farmer, Md., $1,500
371. Flora Brooks, 55, F, B, Md.
372. Peter Wheeler, 35, M, Farmer, Md.
373. George Dunnington, 37, M, Farmer, Md.
374. Richard B. Posey, 45, M, Farmer, Md., $12,000
375. Ann Cofer, 58, F, Md.

376. Ann Davis, 58, F, Va.
377. Richard C. Norman, 38, M, Farmer, Md.
378. Martha F. Mason, 45, F, Va., $15,000
379. William Rennoe, 27, M, Md., $1,500
380. Juliet Winter, 50, F, M, Md.
381. Thomas Day, 30, M, M, Laborer, Md.
382. Artamacy Budd, 69, F, Md., $5,000
383. Cyrus Wheeler, 21, M, Farmer, Md., $500
384. Ann Day, 35, F, M, Md.
385. John L. Davis, 44, M, Md.
386. Mary Scott, 60, F, Md.
387. Lewis Maddox, 43, M, Farmer, Md.
388. William F. Rennoe, 57, M, Farmer, Md., $20,000
389. George Roe, 27, M, Farmer, Md.
390. James Posey, 31, M, Farmer, Md.
391. Alexander Waters, 35, M, Farmer, Md.
392. John Murdock, 47, M, Farmer, Md., $2,000
393. Thomas Skinner, 36, M, Farmer, Md.
394. John L. Hammack, 30, M, Farmer, Md.
395. Thomas J. Milstead, 32, M, Agent, Md.
396. Sopha Caten, 54, F, Md.
397. John H. Barnes, 45, M, Farmer, Md., $2,000
398. William Southerland, 38, M, Farmer, Md.
399. Walter Luckett, 38, M, Laborer, Md.
400. Eleanor Johnson, 40, F, Md.
401. Richard Johnson, 28, M, Md.
402. William U. Johnson, 54, M. Farmer, Md.
403. William Caten, 48, M, Farmer, Md.
404. Alen B. Milstead, 33, M, Constable, Md.
405. Tom Day, 35, M, M, Laborer, Md.
406. Jerry Davis, 45, M, M, Md.
407. Francis E. Dunnington, 65, M, Farmer, Md., $5,000
408. George Luckett, 40, M, Farmer, Md.
409. Thomas Davis, 42, M, Farmer, Md., $350
410. William N. Franklin, 63, M, Farmer, Md., $2,000
411. Vena Chance, 60, F, M, Md.
412. Henry Butler, 90, M, B, Md.
413. Peter Linkins, 26, M, M, Ditcher, Md.

414. George W. Matthews, 57, M, Farmer, Md., $10,000
415. James O. Oliver, 32, M, Agent, Md., $5,000
416. Thomas Pooley, 74, M, England
417. Amelia Oliver, 22, F, Md.
418. Hugh Duffy, 35, M, Md.
419. Mary Welch, 50, F, Md.
420. Elizabeth Welch, 53, F, Md.
421. Elizabeth Queen, 56, F, M, Md., $1,000
422. Jane Gray, 31, F, Md.
423. Richard Baines, 46, M, Farmer, Md., $8,000
424. Wm. Dickson, 46, M, Farmer, Md.
425. Elizabeth Davis, 43, F, Md.
426. Henry Linkins, 45, M, M, Plasterer, Md., $1,000

Hill Top District. 19th Aug. 1850.
427. Ann Linkins, 38, F, M, Md.
428. James Robertson, 50, M, Farmer, Md.
429. Joseph Linkins, 28, M, M, Farmer, Md.
430. Warren Swann, 35, M, M, Sailor, Md.
431. Robert Gray, 57, M, Farmer, Md., $1,200
432. John Ratcliff, 32, M, Agent, Md.
433. Joseph Price, 32, M, Farmer, Md., $3,500
434. Richard Price, 32, M, Farmer, Md., $3,500
435. Thomas Posey, 56, M, Farmer, Md., $800
436. Philip Wedding, 50, M, Farmer, Md.
437. Dorothy Bowie, 80, F, Md.
438. Asa M. Posey, 67, M, Farmer, Md.
439. Catherine Alen, 61, F, Md.
440. Thomas Posey, 35, M, Farmer, Md., $400
441. John Robertson, 55, M, M, Laborer, Md.
442. Richard Posey, 33, M, Merchant, Md.
443. Francis Dunnington, 31, M, Farmer, Md., $2,000
444. John Adams, 49, M, Farmer, Md.
445. James Dent, 34, M, B, Laborer, Md.
446. Buddy Posey, 61, M, Farmer, Md., $1,000
447. Mary Jackson, 25, F, B, Md.
448. Ragan Deakans, 30, M, Farmer, Md.

449. John Kendich, 23, M, Farmer, Md.
450. Eliza Posey, 65, F, Md.
451. John Gilderwy, 50, M, Doctor, Ireland
452. John A. Golden, 31, M, Farmer
453. John Leland, 25, M, Farmer, Md.
454. Wm. Milstead, 53, M, Farmer, Md.
455. George Milstead, 17, M, Laborer, Md.
456. Jonathan Dunnington, 61, M, Farmer, Md.
457. Thomas Groves, 51, M, Farmer, Md., $2,500
458. Henry A. Milstead, 29, M, Sailor, Md.
459. Thomas Wright, 35, M, Laborer, Md.
460. Eli Pettet, 32, M, Carpenter, Md.
461. Wm. H. Brawner, 35, M, Farmer, Md., $1,700
462. Wm. J. Childs, 39, M, Farmer, Md., $3,000
463. Francis Price, 22, M, Farmer, Md., $2,000
464. T. A. Smith, 27, M, Farmer, Md., $2,000
465. Luther L. Leland, 30, M, Farmer, Md., $500
466. James W. Padgett, 30, M, Farmer, Md.
467. Catherine Rose, 35, F, Va.
468. Lorenzo Leland, 38, M, Farmer, Md., $2,000
469. Charles H. Dent, 22, M, Farmer, Md., $400
470. John Bowie, 36, M, Farmer, Md.
471. Clement Skinner, 65, M, Farmer, Md., $500
472. John Proctor, 50, M, M, Farmer, Md., $80
473. Adam Posey, 47, M, Farmer, Md., $600
474. Robert Davis, 31, M, Farmer, Md., $280
475. Handson H. Posey, 62, M, Farmer, Md., $200
476. Wm. Smith, 47, M, Farmer, Md., $1,500
477. Samuel W. Adams, 26, M, Farmer, Md., $800
478. Joseph Murdock, 31, M, Farmer, Md.
479. James D. Carpenter, 47, M, Farmer, Md., $800
480. Francis Bowie, 40, M, Farmer, Md.
481. Frederick S. Brown, 32, M, Farmer, Va.
482. John W. Newberry, 30, M, Farmer, Md., $1,500
483. James Gray, 28, M, Farmer, Md., $1,500
484. Urgizial Nally, 63, M, Farmer, Md., $6,000
485. Robert Prout, 50, M, Minister, P.E., D.C., $3,000
486. Bennett Dyson, 57, M, Doctor, Md., $2,500

Hill Top. 24 Aug. 1850.
487. Eliza Boswell, 39, M, Farmer, Md., $2,500
488. Ogleton Bradshaw, 29, M, Farmer, Md.
489. John Philips, 27, M, Agent, Va., $20,000
489. James K. Nash, 53, M, Agent, Va., $20,000
491. Edward Simmes, 52, M, Farmer, Md.
492. Thomas A. Burges, 52, M, Farmer, Md., $5,000
493. Wm. G. Nally, 49, M, Farmer, Md., $1,500
494. F. R. Speak, 37, M, Farmer, Md., $3,000
495. Samuel Handson, 34, M, Farmer, Md., $3,000
496. Elizabeth Adams, 45, F, Md.
497. Francis Quade, 45, M, Agent, Md.
498. Nathan Ratcliff, 45, M, Millar, Md.
499. J. B. Ferguson, 30, M, Farmer, Md., $10,000
500. Benjamin N. Jameson, 37, M, Agent, Md.
501. Wm. Baker, 90, M, Farmer, Md.
502. Jane Smoot, 49, F, Md.
503. Jane Johnson, 65, F, B, Md.
504. Mary F. Butler, 34, F, B, Md.
505. Robert Ratcliff, 30, M, Farmer, Md.
506. Thomas J. Speak, 32, M, Teacher, Md.
507. James Scott, 32, M, Farmer, Md.
508. George W. Carpenter, 32, M, Farmer, Md., $7,000
509. Briscoe Swann, 30, M, Farmer, Md.
510. Peter Tubman, 35, M, B, Laborer, Md.
511. Robert Kelison, 43, M, B, Md.
512. Joseph Bowie, 38, M, B, Farmer, Md.
513. Gustavus Fowler, 40, M, Farmer, Md.
514. John F.W. Basten, 40, M, Farmer, Md.
515. Robert Pye, 41, M, Farmer, Md.
516. Ann Gray, 37, F, B, Md.
517. Uzach Scott, 60, M, Farmer, Md.
518. Teresa Chiseltine, 45, F, Md.
519. Jucinda Johns, 28, F, B, Md.
520. Polly Price, 60, F, B, Md.
521. Eliza Jordan, 22, F., B, Md.
522. Nelly Tyler, 40, F, B, Md.
523. Arthillia McBain, 44, F, Md.

524. Betsy Tubman, 48, F, M, Md.
525. Emeline Groves, 33, F, Md.
526. Ignatius Posey, 32, M, Farmer, Md.
527. Wills Pye, 29, M, Farmer, Md.
528. Henry E. Groves, 33, M, Farmer, Md., $2,100
529. Ignatius Milstead, 57, M, Farmer, Md., $3,000
530. James Brawner, 68, M, Farmer, Md., $800
531. Oswell Bowie, 50, M, Farmer, Md.
532. Daniel Mudd, 24, M, Laborer, Md.
533. Alfred Cos, 51, M, B, Laborer, Md.
534. Jane Montgomery, 36, F, B, Md.
535. Sara Goodrick, 55, F, B, Md.
536. John Groves, 68, M, Farmer, Md.
537. Nancy Perry, 60, F, B, Md.
538. Rebecca Perry, 23, F, B, Md.
539. Thomas Radcliff, 88, M, Farmer, Md., $500
540. Uz Mudd, 40, M, Farmer, Md.
541. Samuel Posey, 30 M, Farmer, Md.
542. Wm. Howard, 25, M, Farmer, Md.
543. Henry S. Dent, 35, M, Farmer, Md., $2,000
544. Thomas S. Dent, 38, M, Farmer, Md., $2,000
545. James L. Dyson, 33, M, Merchant, Md.
546. R. S. Handcock, 50, M, Farmer, Md., $2,700
547. Charles H. Dent, 21, M, Farmer, Md., $500
548. Thomas Highfield, 58, M, Farmer, Md., $280
549. George C. Mason, 50, M, Md.
550. Isach Handson, 37, M, Farmer, Md.
551. Margaret Dean, 36, F, Md.

Aug. 27th.
552. Thomas P. Gray, 22, M, Farmer, Md., $2,500
553. Elizabeth Gray, 56, F, Md., $4,000
554. Catherine C. Coby, 32, F, Md.
555. Wm. G. Goley, 42, M, Farmer, Md.
556. Thomas M. Posey, 34, M, Farmer, Md., $500
557. Ann Harvy, 41, F, Md.
558. Uz Shanny, 55, M, Farmer, Md.

559. Francis Shanny, 30, M, Farmer, Md.
560. John Gray, 46, M, Farmer, Md.
561. David Shanny, 30, M, Laborer, Md.
562. James Lee, 55, M, Md.
563. John Posey, 44, M, Farmer, Md.
564. Catherine Golden, 49, F, Farmer, Md., $4,000
565. Wm. Colly, 45, M, Farmer, Md.
566. Joseph F. Owen, 40, M, Md.
567. Noble Richards, 46, M, Farmer, Md.
568. Hannibal Acton, 50, M, Farmer, Md.
569. Richard Murry, 40, M, Agent, Md., $5,000
570. Betty Lomax, 70, F, Md.
571. Henry Ferrell, 33, M, Mechanic, Md.
572. Henry A. Moor, 57, M, Farmer, Md., $9,000
573. George S. Willett, 50, M, Farmer, Md., $3,000
574. Wm. Roby, 34, M, Farmer, Md., $1,000
575. Spalding C. Moor, 41, M, Farmer, Md.
576. John Boswell, 63, M, Farmer, Md., $1,000
577. Eli Hunt, 68, M, Farmer, Md., $500
578. Wm. Molden, 45, M, Farmer, Md.,
579. Julian Montgomery, 53, M, Farmer, Md., $2,000
580. George Richards, 30, M, Laborer, Md.
581. Jonothan Turner, 44, M, Farmer, Md.
582. Betty Ferrell, 47, F, Md.
583. Sena Moor, 55, F, Md.
584. James Moor, 60, M, Farmer, Md., $2,000
585. Len Adams, 50, M, Farmer, Md., $2,700
586. Mildred J. Berry, 66, F, Md., $700
587. Judson McDaniel, 34, M, Farmer, Md.
588. Wm. F. Cooms, 29, M, Farmer, Md.
589. Walter Blanford, 52, M, Farmer, Md.
590. George Adams, 58, M, Farmer, Md., $5,000
591. Joseph Pickaerel, 65, M, Farmer, Md.
592. Aquilla Robey, 73, M, Farmer, Md.
593. Christena Padget, 42, F, Md.
594. Benedette Wilburn, 33, M, Farmer, Md.
595. Lena Lovelace, 65, F. Farmer, Md.
596. Frederick W. Roland, 45, M, Farmer, Md.

597. Mary A. Sanders, 60, F, Md.
598. Lauson Marlon, 50, M, Farmer, Md.
599. Richard Williams, 30, M, Farmer, Md.
600. Charles Willet, 75, M, Farmer, Md., $1,000
601. Alsin Hecks, 30, M, Farmer, Md.
602. John H. Bean, 64, M, Farmer, Md., $2,000
603. William N. Bean, 51, M, Farmer, Md., $4,000
604. Christina Richards, 54, F, Md., $1,000
605. Benedict Montgomery, 36, M, Farmer, Md.
606. Colesta Nally, 43, F, Md.
607. Lemuel Wilmer, 55, M, P.E. Minister, Md., $3,000

Bryantown District, Sept. 3, 1850: John M. Hawkins, Asst. Marshal.
608. Harris Hamilton, 50, M, Farmer, Md.
609. John F. Gardiner, 47, M, Farmer, Md., $800
610. Ann M. Bowling, 29, F, Md., $5,000
611. Thomas Proctor, 52, M, M, Laborer, Md.
612. Susan Howel, 50, F, Farmer, Md., $500
613. Thomas W. Bowling, 21, M, Farmer, Md., $4,000
614. Aquilla Turner, 63, M, Farmer, Md., $8,000
615. James H. A. Middleton, 61, M, Farmer, Md., $4,000
616. Alexander S. Middleton, 50, M, Farmer, Md.
617. John A Dyer, 57, M, Farmer, Md., $1,000
618. Matthew Dugan, 27, M, Ireland, $2,000
619. Robert Smith, 40, M, Farmer, Md.
620. A. W. Marlow, 28, M, Tavernkeeper, Md.
621. Charles Hardy, 28, M, Farmer, Md.
622. E. M. Berry, 46, M, Farmer, Md., $700
623. Alen McDaniel, 54, M, None, Md.
624. Underwood Soper, 56, M, Farmer, Md., $100
625. Alfred Mudd, 28, M, Farmer, Md., $1,300
626. James F. Wheatley, 39, M, Farmer, Md., $100
627. Wm. Marlow, 28, M, Md.
628. Louisa A. Willet, 37, F, Md.
629. Wm. Smallwood, 27, M, Farmer, Md., $600
630. Nancy V. Reeves, 50, F, Md.

631. James Griffin, 32, M, Farmer, Md.
632. Judson Clemens, 29, M, Farmer, Md.

Middletown District. Sept. 5th
633. Alfred Reeves, 24, M, Mechanic, Md.
634. Elias Gates, 55, M, Blacksmith, Md.
635. John B. Wilkinson, 69, M, Farmer, Md.
636. Wm. Bealle, 38, M, Farmer, Md., $8,000
637. Austin Gages, 50, M, Farmer, Md.
638. Wm. Hamilton, 35, M, Farmer, Md.
639. Solomon Willet, 66, M, Farmer, Md.
640. Josia Pickaeral, 35, M, Farmer, Md.
641. Coleb Pickarel, 25, M, Farmer, Md.
642. S. L. Berry, 35, M, Farmer, Md., $3,000
643. Thomas B. Berry, 44, M, Farmer, Md., $4,000
644. Betty Osborn, 45, F, Md.
645. R. L. Smallwood, 57, M, Farmer, Md.
646. Ubgale Reeves, 58, M, Farmer, Md.
647. Henry Etcherson, 40, M, Farmer, Md.
648. George Spalding, 26, M, Laborer, Md.
649. Wm. S. Robey, 40, M, Miller, Md.
650. Domnick Mudd, 25, M, Farmer, Md.
651. Julian Mudd, 55, M, Farmer, Md.
652. Corneleus Robey, 74, M, Farmer, Md.
653. George H. Berry, 35, M, Farmer, Md.
654. Susanna H. Gates, 70, F, Md.
655. Penelope A. Bealle, 55, F, Md.
656. Ann Willet, 55, F. Md.
657. Cecelia E. Steward, 28, F, Va.
658. Wm. H. Willet, 43, M, Farmer, Va., $800
659. Charles Kellman, 50, M, Farmer, Md., $800
660. Fryna Kellman, 60, F, Md.
661. Sysvester F. Gardiner, 60, M, Farmer, Md., $7,000
662. Alaein F. Bealle, 73, M, Farmer, Md., $4,000
663. Samuel Sherrill, 60, M, Farmer, Md., $16,000
664. George F. Harris, 26, M, Doctor, Md.
665. Wm. S. Shaw, 55, M, Farmer, Md., $600

666. Francis Montgomery, 62, M, Farmer, Md., $3,000
667. Henry B. Berry, 25, M, Farmer, Md.
668. Charles H. Wills, 26, M, Farmer, Md.
669. Wm. Dement, 21, M, Farmer, Md., $1,500
670. B. D. Spalding, 35, M, Farmer, Md., $1,500
671. Benjamin Blanford, 42, M, Farmer, Md., $2000
672. Walter A. Wilkinson, 26, M, Farmer, Md.
673. Ann E. Ferrell, 38, F, Md., $1,000
674. James Carroll, 60, M, Agent, Md., $3,000
675. Thomas S. Martin, 35, M, Farmer, Md., $1,000
676. Edward Jones, 77, M, Farmer, Md., $4,000
677. Elisha Jones, 30, M, Farmer, Md.
678. Wm. A. Wilkinson, 29, M, Agent, Md., $5,000
679. Wm. Lucas, 48, M, Laborer, Md.
680. Jane Turner, 35, F, Md.
Matthew Bowell, 24, M, Laborer
Thomas H. Edelen, 57, M, Farmer, Md.
681. Wilson Wilkinson, 30, M, Farmer, Md.
682. Mary E. Wilmer, 44, F, Md., $2,000
683. John Howard, 65, M, Farmer, Md., $300
684. Richard Holly, 40, M, Farmer, Md., $400
685. Thomas D. Clagitt, 65, M, Farmer, Md., $1,500
686. Elizabeth Collins, 65, F, B, Md.
687. Samuel Collins, 40, M, M, Md.
688. Henry Dog, 70, M, B
689. Sara Butler, 60, F, B, Md., $500
690. Henry Butler, 35, M, B, Farmer, Md., $650.
691. John M. Brown, 52, M, Farmer, Md.
692. Eliza S. Brown, 54, F, Md.
693. O. N. Bryon, 29, M, Farmer, Md., $4,000
694. Wm. H. Claggett, 35, M, Farmer, Md., $6,500
695. Lucy A. Alexander, 76, F, B, Md.
696. Richard W. Bryon, 31, M, Farmer, Md.
697. Mary E. Briscoe, 39, F, Md., $3,000
698. James Morton, 25, M, Farmer, Md.
699. Wm. H. Plowden, 32, M, Farmer, Md., $10,000
700. John Lucas, 43, M, Laborer, Md.

701. Freenduck Muncin, 34, M, Sailor, Md.
702. Robert Wade, 33, M, Farmer, Md.
703. Edward Butler, 80, M, B, Farmer, Md.
704. Edward Miles, 45, M, Farmer, Md., $10,000
705. J. Thadeus Brawner, 23 M, Farmer, Md.
706. Eliza Jameson, 64, F, Md.
707. James Camel, 55, M, Farmer, Md., $2,500
708. Maria Hardy, 48, F, Md.
709. Noble Dickson, 26, M, Farmer, Md.
710. James F. Maddox, 40, M, Md.
711. James Jackson, 38, M, M, Laborer, Md.
712. Charles Jenkins, 54, M, Farmer, Md., $2,000
713. Leonard Marbary, 58, M, Farmer, Md., $12,000
714. Uzltheniah Wade, 50, M, Agent, Md.
715. Edward R. Pye, 24, M, Farmer, Md., $4,000
716. John A. Pye, 49, M, Farmer, Md., $8,000
717. Pearcin Chapman, 46, M, Farmer, Md., $15,000
718. Hezehiah Brawner, 64, M, Farmer, Md., $20,000
719. James Whittel, 50, M, M, Farmer, Md.
720. Noel B. Hannon, 19, M, Farmer, Md., $5,000
721. George W. Backly, 21, M, Farmer, Md.
722. Samuel Backly, 61, M, Farmer, Md., $400
723. Martha Rodgerson, 35, F, Md.
724. Mary P. Dent, 44, F, Md.
725. Henry Adams, 49, M, M, Md.
726. Tubman Boswell, 37, M, Farmer, Md., $100
727. John W. Guy, 41, M, Farmer, Md., $4,000
728. Wm. W. Evert, 30, M, Farmer, Md.
729. Elizabeth A. Dement, 39, F, Md.
730. Richard Wade, 35
731. Benjamin Tubman, 28, M, Farmer, Md., $4,000
732. Richard L. Tubman, 38, M, Farmer, Md., $4,000
733. Thomas A. Jameson, 27, M, Farmer, Md., $4,500
734. Thomas Jackson, 80, M, M, Md.
735. John carrington, 42, M, Farmer, Md., $2,250
736. Walter G. Vernon, 30, M, Mechanic
737. May Downs, 50, F, Md., $2,000

Middletown District
738. George O. Monroe, 35, M, Merchant, Md.
739. Edgar Brawner, 25, M, Farmer, Md., $10,000
740. Alexander Hamilton, 25, M, Farmer, Md., $10,000
741. Samuel McPharson, 28, M, Merchant, Md.
742. Wm. B. Wilson, 54, M, None, Md.
743. Susan Cox, 56, F, Md., $200
744. Susan Monroe, 51, F, Md.
745. Hoczhiah Coby, 28, M, Laborer, Md.
746. Nathaniel Holby, 44, M, Farmer, Md., $3,000
747. Wm. G. Roby, 40, M, Farmer, Md., $5,000
748. June Yates, 82, F, Md., $3,000
749. Henry A. Hannon, 42, M, Sailor, Md.
750. John Cox, 32, M, Farmer, Md., $2,500
751. Edward Briscoe, 49, M, Farmer, Md., $5,000
752. James Harris, 62, M, Farmer, Md., $3,000
753. James Richardson, 23, M, Farmer
754. Henry Howard, 37, M, Farmer, Md.
755. Leonard Boswell, 47, M, Laborer, Md.
756. H. R. B. Cawood, 50, M, Farmer, Md.
757. Benson McPharson, 23, M, Farmer, Md., $3,000
758. Francis Roby, 55, M, Farmer, Md., $3,300
759. John B. Turner, 49, M, Farmer, Md.
760. Mary Duffy, 20, F, Md., $3,000
761. George M. Berry, 32, M, Farmer, Md., $3,000
762. Marcus Luckett, 49, M, Farmer, Md.
763. John Lomax, 60, M, Farmer, Md., $3,000
764. George H. Gardiner, 46, M, Farmer, Md., $3,000
765. Thomas F. Burch, 22, M, Farmer, Md.
766. John A. Murphy, 23, M, Farmer, Md.
767. Charles Steward, 31, M, Farmer, Md., $1,000
768. Walter Mar, 23, M, Farmer, Md.
769. Wm. B. Roby, 32, M, Miller, Md.
770. Charles Mills, 70, M, Farmer, Md.
771. Alfred Battle, 45, M, M, Farmer, Md., $600
772. Teresa Cooms, 57, F
773. Charles S. Kinnemon, 57, M, Farmer, Md.
774. James R. Clemens, 26, M, Farmer, Md.

775. Betsy Ford, 77, F, Md., $4,000
776. George M. Cooms, 26, M, Agent, Md.
777. Francis E. Green, 55, M, Farmer, Md., $10,000
778. Alexander Johnson, 21, M, Farmer, Md.
779. Josias M. Cooms, 31, M, Farmer, Md.
780. Christianne S. Ward, 49, F, Md.
781. Fallosius Cooms, 59, M, Farmer, Md.
782. John Delozier, 52, M, Farmer, Md., $300
783. Bean Howard, 42, M, Farmer, Md.
784. Wm. Richardson, 33, M, Farmer, Md.
785. Wm. I. Gardiner, 20, M, Farmer, Md., $500
786. Wm. Giddinon, 46, M, Farmer, Md., $800
787. Charles Berry, 53, M, Farmer, Md.
788. Ann Cox, 46, F, Md., $200
789. Elizabeth Hodges, 37, F, Md.
790. Frederick Maddox, 65, M, Farmer, Md., $100
791. Henry M. Roby, 43, M, Farmer, Md., $2,000
792. Thomas Y. Roby, 24, M, Farmer, Md., $2,000
793. Catherine Adam, 71, F, Md.
794. Josias Handson, 38, M, Farmer, Md., $4,000
795. Walter Mitchell, 47, M, Farmer, Md., $30,000
796. Ann Padget, 43, F, Md.
797. Wm. B. Smith, 27, M, None, Md.
798. Charles Jenkins, 50, M, Farmer, Md.
799. Wm. M. Lyon, 31, M, Farmer, Md., $1,200
800. Martha Runor, 26, F, M, Md.
801. Susan Queen, 30, F, M, Md.
802. Eleanor Hunt, 27, F, Md.
803. Caleh Hunt, 56, M, Farmer, Md., $1,200
804. Samuel H. Beall, 47, M, Farmer, Md., $2,500
805. Henry T. Mitchell, 38, M, Farmer, Md., $30,000
806. Wm. W. Cox, 54, M, Farmer, Md., $450
807. Susanna Boswell, 40, F, Md.
808. John Wise, 40, M, Farmer, Md., $1,000
809. Thomas Clemens, 58, M, Farmer, Md., $2,800
810. Joseph H. Mattingly, 29, M, Farmer, Md.
811. John M. Jenkins, 31, M, Farmer, Md., $21,000
812. Charles Sudler, 30, M, Farmer, Germany

813. Samuel H. Cox, 27, M, Farmer, $1,800
814. Wm. H. Rowe, 37, M, Farmer, Md., $1,500
815. John H. Nelson, 42, M, Farmer, Md., $1,000
816. Richard F. Nelson, 42, M, Farmer, Md.
817. Jane Smallwood, 60, F, Md.
818. Joseph Maddox, 39, M, Farmer, Md., $300
819. Wm. Thompson, 59, M, Farmer, Md., $15,000
820. Cloey Simmons, 65, F, Md.
821. Harriot Brawner, 58, F, Md.
822. John S. Skinner, 37, M, Farmer, Md., $7,000
823. Jane Knight, 23, F, M, Md.
824. Henry Dog, 45, M, M, Laborer, Md.
825. Dennis Butler, 60, M, B, Laborer, Md.
826. Wm. Thompson, 30, M, Sailor, Md.
827. Priscilla Bell, 62, F, Md.
828. Rachael Nelson, 82, F
829. John G. Mink, 38, M, Laborer, Saxony
830. Jachorah Bowie, 35, M, Laborer, Md.
831. John Butler, 50, M, B, Laborer, Md.
832. Wm. Savoy, 50, M, M, Laborer, Md.
833. James Swann, 63, M, M, Farmer, Md.
834. John S. Swann, 35, M, M, Farmer, Md.
835. Joseph Gray, 66, M, M, Md.
836. Washington Day, 39, M, M, Md.
837. Wm. Kindick, 39, M, Farmer, Md., $500

Hill Top District
838. Elizabeth Scott, 60, F, Md.
839. Samuel Carrington, 35, M, Farmer, Md.
840. Benedict Welch, 33, M, Farmer, Md.
841. Walter Stone, 33, M, Farmer, Md.
842. Pheba A. Welch, 57, F, Md.
843. John J. Mattingly, 41, M, Farmer, Md.
844. Richard Smallwood, 51, M, Mechanic, Md.

Middletown District. Sept. 19, 1850; John M. Hawkins.
845. Alexander Lyon, 35, M, Merchant, Md.
846. Joseph H. Cooksey, 35, M, Farmer, Md., $4,000

847. Charles S. Williams, 45, M, Farmer, Md., $1,700
848. Wm. B. Stone, 52, M, Farmer, Md., $18,000
849. Elizabeth Stone, 42, F
850. Joseph E. Sanders, 27, M, Farmer, Md.
851. Joseph T. Wills, 33, M, Farmer, Md.
852. Mary Sanders, 44, F
853. Henry Scroggin, 22, M, Farmer, Md., $500
854. John H. Welch, 29, M, Agent, Md.
855. Mary A. Briscoe, 21, F, $4,500
856. Wm. Acton, 36, M, Farmer
857. Green Clemens, 34, M, Farmer
858. Theodore Monroe, 57, M, Farmer
859. Leonard A. Clemens, 56, M, Farmer
860. Joseph Paget, 19, M, Md.
861. Charles Garner, 38, M, Md.
862. Betty Lyon, 69, F, Md.
863. Samuel M. Simms, 45, M, Farmer, Md., $5,000
864. Rerzin Boswell, 53, M, Farmer, Md.
865. Savy Gropes, 45, F, Md.
866. Mary Roby, 40, F, Md.
867. Sara Padget, 63, F, Md.
868. Betty H. Hughs, 58, F, Md., $10,000
869. Thomas S. Gardiner, 44, M, Farmer, Md., $8,500
870. Peter Davis, 44, M, Farmer, Md.

Bryantown District. 23rd Sept. 1850; John M. Hawkins.
871. Wm. Queen, 58, M, Farmer, Md., $8,000
872. L. Langly, 50, M, Agent, Md.
873. Ann Young, 27, F, M, Md.
874. Sally Green, 26, F, B, Md.
875. John Jackson, 60, M, Farmer, Md.
876. Alexander Queen, 30, M, Farmer, Md.
877. Walter Jameson, 40, M, Farmer, Md., $1,500
878. Eliza Jameson, 40, F, Md., $3,000
879. John C. Handcock, 35, M, Farmer, Md.
880. Nicholas V. Miles, 38, M, Farmer, Md., $6,000
881. Edward L. Gardiner, 27, M, Farmer, Md., $3,000
882. Charles Proctor, 45, M, M, Farmer, Md.

883. Charles R. Padget, 28, M, Farmer, Md.
884. Thomas F. Padget, 32, M, Farmer, Md.

Allen's Fresh District. 23rd Dept. 1850; John M. Hawkins.
885. Benjamin Dent, 48, M, Farmer, Md.
886. John B. Dent, 21, M, Farmer, Md.
887. Thomas V. Bean, 56, M, Farmer, Md., $2,000
888. Eliax Brofield, 26, M, Farmer, Md.
889. Benjamin Smoot, 39, M, Farmer, Md.
890. Mathias Cooksey, 32, M, Farmer, Md., $250
891. Terresa Cooksey, 60, F, Md., $250
892. F. Horton Edelen, 45, M, Farmer, Md., $2,204
893. Henry F. Edelen, 33, M, Farmer, Md.
894. James Hamilton, 76, M, None, Md.
895. John A. Kinermon, 26, M, M, Farmer, Md.
896. James Thompson, 50, M, M, Farmer, Md.
897. Domnick Oliver, 19, M, Farmer, Md.
898. Benedict Simpson, 63, M, Farmer, md., $1,500
899. Henry B. Shannon, 25, M, Merchant, Ireland
900. Ann K. Adams, 63, F, Md.
901. George H. Simpson, 32, M, Merchant, Md.
902. Ignatius Doosscy, 56, M, Farmer, Md.
903. John F. Budd, 20, M, Farmer, Md., $2,000
904. John F. Bailey, 25, M, None, Md.
905. Thomas Shorter, 70, M, Farmer, Md.
906. Gustavus Simpson, 61, M, Farmer, Md.
907. Benjamin H. Jameson, 45, M, Farmer, Md., $17,000
908. Joseph Saxton, 32, M, Farmer, Md., $3,500
909. John Cuitmond, 50, M, Farmer, Md., $5,000
910. Rvjan Runy, 30, M, Farmer, Ireland
911. Joseph Scott, 33, M, Agent, Md.
912. George Montin, 26, M, Sailor, Md.
913. Jeremiah Habut, 52, M, Farmer, Md.
914. Henry B. Goodwin, 48, M, Farmer, Mass., $12,000
915. John F. Lucas, 27, M, Farmer, Md.
916. Henry Mattingly, 37, M, Farmer, Md., $12,000
917. Thomas Burk, 45, M, Laborer, Md.

918. Ann M. Far, 39, F, Md.
919. John F. S. Higdon, 38, M, Farmer, Md.
920. Samuel J. Briscoe, 50, M, Farmer
921. Henry A. Short, 45, F, B, Md.
922. Wm. A. Lyon, 29, M, Farmer, Md., $1,500
923. Benjamin Good, 54, M, Farmer, Md.
924. John W. Beavin, 35, M, Farmer, Md.
925. Wm. Compton, 38, M, Farmer, Md., $5,000
926. Dyson D. Welch, 24, M, Agent, Md.
927. John F. Turner, 34, M, Farmer, Md., $3,400
928. A. Bond, 45, F, Md.
929. Zachariah Bond, 65, M, Farmer, Md., $1,200
930. George T. St. Clair, 63, M, Farmer, Md.

Allen's Fresh District, 26th day of Sept.; John M. Hawkins.
931. Jane Williams, 35, F, M, Md.
932. Wm. Swann, 66, M, M, Md.
933. Wm. Swann, 15, M, M, Md.
934. Kel W. Davis, 41, M, Farmer, Md.
935. Jucmia Hundington, 55, M, Farmer, Md.
936. Joseph Watson, 26, M, M, Laborer, Md.
937. Paisa Good, 50, M, Farmer, Md., $300
938. James Lomax, 37, M, Farmer, Md.
939. Wilson Turner, 34, M, Farmer, Md.
940. Frederick Turner, 45, M, Farmer, Md.
941. Kitty Cartright, 55, F, Md.
942. Henry Good, 47, M, Farmer, Md., $500
943. Henry G. Love, 49, M, Farmer, Md.
944. Ann Guy, 60, F, Md.
945. Ben Swann, 22, M, Farmer, Md.
946. Henry Burk, 36, M, Mechanic, Md.
947. Samuel Higgs, 50, M, Farmer, Md.
948. Elen R. St. Clair, 28, F, Md.
949. Francis Simpson, 28, M, Farmer, Md.
950. Francis Simpson, 56, M, Farmer, Md., $5,000
951. John B. Lyon, 25, M, Farmer, Md., $1,000
952. Wm. H. Gough, 30, M, Farmer, Md.

953. Edward Edelen, 60, M, Farmer, Md., $4,000
954. George Warthen, 47, M, Farmer, Md., $1,000
955. Cononies Lancaster, 58, M, Farmer, Md., $2,000
956. Alectious Lancaster, 50, M, Farmer, Md., $8,000
957. Mary H. King, 48, F, Md.
958. Lucinda Canter, 45, F, M, Md.
959. John M. S. Latimer, 44, M, Farmer, Md., $7,500
960. Michael Blackstone, M, Farmer, Md.
961. Lucretia Thompson, 24, F, M, Md.
962. Philip Ware, 33, M, Agent, Md., $5,000
963. Rergin Barnes, 48, M, Farmer, Md., $500
964. John F. Thompson, 42, M, Farmer, Md.
965. Cornelius Bailee, 51, M, Farmer, Md., $1,000
966. John B. Boarman, 26, M, Farmer, Md.
967. Philip Jenkins, 56, M, Farmer, Md.
968. Stonten W. Dent, 44, M, Farmer, Md.
969. E. Thanoh Ware, 36, M, Farmer, Md.
970. Henry A. Haden, 36, M, Farmer, Md.
971. Wm. Jenkins, 60, M, Agent, Md.
972. Joseph Edelen, 35, M, Farmer, Md., $10,000
973. Elizabeth Edelen, 56, F, Md.
974. Thomas A. Jones, 30, M, Collector, Md.
975. Wm. C. Davis, 46, M, Farmer, Md.
976. Robert Miles, 30, M, Farmer, Md.
977. John W. Boarman, 26, M, Farmer, Md.
978. Joseph Boarman, 48, M, Agent, Md.
979. Thomas McDaniel, 65, M, Farmer, Md., $7,000
980. Augustus O. Burch, 68, M, Farmer, Md., $3,000
981. Wm. Wheatly, 34, M, Mechanic, Md.
982. Rachael Whcatly, 64, F, Md.
983. Edward V. Edelen, 21, M, Farmer, Md.
984. Author D. Smoot, 38, M, Farmer, Md., $2,200
985. Wm. H. Smoot, 59, M, Farmer, Md., $6,000
986. Francis L. Boarman, 38, M, Farmer, Md., $1,500
987. Raphael Boarman, 65, M, Farmer, Md., $5,000
988. Wm. Thompson, 60, M, M, Farmer, Md.
989. James Carter, 49, M, M, Laborer, Md.
990. Jenifer Proctor, 26, M, M, Laborer, Md.

991. James Oliver, 60, M, Farmer, Md.
992. Jonas B. Harbin, 32, M, Merchant, Md.
993. James W. Oliver, 39, M, Blacksmith, Md.
994. James Numan, 35, M, M, Laborer, Md.
995. Joseph N. Oliver, 26, M, Blacksmith, Md.
996. George H. Oliver, 33, M, Wheelright, Md.
997. Benjamin F. Dent, 39, M, Farmer, Md.
998. Amelia Freeman, 38, F, Md.
999. James E. Keith, 38, M, Farmer, Md., $10,000
1000. Edward Freeman, 30, M, Agent, Md.
1001. Henry H. Freeman, 49, M, Farmer, Md., $4,500
1002. Wm. H. Freeman, 22, M, Farmer, Md.
1003. Theophilus Dent, 69, M, Farmer, Md., $10,000
1004. Nathaniel Freeman, 48, M, Farmer, Md.
1005. Ann Goodrick, 60, F, Md.
1006. Wm. Matthews, 68, M, Farmer, Md., $9,000
1007. Z. Guan, 75, M, Farmer, Md., $3,000
1008. Oswell Dyson, 58, M, Farmer, Md.
1009. Samuel T. Swann, 40, M, Laborer, Md.
1010. Sally Wood, 55, F, Md.
1011. Jane E. Johns, 32, F, Md.
1012. Ann Emory, 42, F, Md.
1013. Cecilia A. Davis, 45, F, Md., $3,000
1014. John Brafield, 30, M, Farmer, Md., $200
1015. Betsy Waters, 48, F, Md.
1016. John Brady, 54, M, Farmer
1017. Joseph N. Harrison, 27, M, Farmer, Md., $1,500
1018. Hezehiah H. Bean, 30, M, MD, Md.
1019. Samuel T. Swann, 28, M, Farmer, Md.
1020. Elizabeth Latimer, 77, F, Md.
1021. Joseph B. Gardiner, 35, M, Farmer, Md.
1022. Edward Turner, 65, M, None, Md.
1023. Wm. Albriton, 65, M, Laborer, Md.
1024. Samuel Jameson, 27, M, MD, Md.
1025. John W. McPherson, 37, M, Farmer, Md., $3,000
1026. John L. Gardiner, 32, M, Collector, Md., $4,000
1027. Louis B. Adams, 26, M, Farmer, Md.
1028. Richard Adams, 28, M, Farmer, Md., $6,000

1029. George Wright, 60, M, Farmer, Md.
1030. John F. Downing, 28, M, Merchant, Md.
1031. Benedict F. Burch, 32, M, Farmer, Md., $1,300
1032. George Maddox, 28, M, Farmer, Md.
1033. George Adams, 36, M, Farmer, Md., $3,000
1034. James Adams, 30, M, Farmer, Md.
1035. Thomas I. Canter, 50, M, Farmer, Md.
1036. Catherine Cooksey, 75, F, Md., $500
1037. Eliza Butler, 28, F, B, Md.
1038. Catherine Butler, 26, F, B, Md.
1039. Martha Ford, 24, F, B, Md.
1040. Nelson Thomas, 40, M, M, Laborer, Md.
1041. Thomas B. Smith, 38, M, M, Farmer, Md.
1042. Edward M. Waters, 42, M, Farmer, Md., $200
1043. John Bevin, 70, M, Farmer, Md., $500

Bryantown District. 5th Oct. John M. Hawkins
1044. Francis Savoy, 72, M, M, Farmer, Md.
1045. Nathan Cooksey, 53, M, Farmer, Md.
1046. Emeline Edelen, 44, F, Md.
1047. Wm. Nailor, 39, M, Farmer, Md., $800
1048. Jerry Magruder, 18, M, B, Md.
1049. Henry Proctor, 34, M, Farmer, Md.
1050. John H. Proctor, 28, M, M, Farmer, Md.
1051. Josias Proctor, 28, M, Farmer, Md.
1052. John H. Downing, 50, M, Farmer, Md., $1,000
1053. Susan Smith, 40, F, Md.
1054. May Wright, 62, F, Md., $250
1055. Ann Ford, 40, F, M, Md.
1056. Nancy Butler, 45, F, B, Md.
1057. Martha Ford, 22, F, B, Md.
1058. George F. Wilkinson, 42, M, Farmer, Md., $2,000
1059. John Wilkinson, 45, M, Farmer, Md., $2,000
1060. Thomas G. Gardiner, 35, M, Farmer, Md., $8,000
1061. Elizare Gardner, 35, M, Farmer, Md., $10,000
1062. James Ferrell, 27, M, Agent, Md.
1063. Wm. Ferrell, 31, M, Farmer, Md.

1064. Charles Allbriton, 40, M, Farmer, Md., $1,000
1065. James Goldsmith, 36, M, None, Md.

Bryantown District. 6th day of Oct.
1066. John Smith, 51, M, Farmer, Md., $800
1067. Gustaves Landgley, 45, M, Farmer, Md.
1068. Rose A. Boarman, 36, F, Md.
1069. [no entry]
1070. Horatio Reeves, 65, M, Farmer, Md., $50
1071. Walter Handcock, 70, M, Farmer, Md., $2,000
1072. John Langley, 76, M, Farmer, Md., $1,000
1073. George Edelen, 72, M, Farmer, Md.
1074. Mary J. Simpson, 32, F, Md., $2,000
1075. John B. Langley, 41, M, Farmer, Md., $600
1076. Walter Harbin, 65, M, Farmer, Md., $558
1077. Alfred Adams, 19, M, Laborer, Md.
1078. Wm. Oliver, 22, M, Farmer, Md.
1079. Joseph Jenkins, 35, M, Farmer, Md.
1080. John H. Howell, 25, M, Farmer, Md.
1081. A. G. Turner, 47, M, Farmer, Md., $1,000
1082. Wm. Cooms, 55, M, Farmer, Md.
1083. Wm. S. Keech, 43, M, Farmer, Md., $8,000
1084. Thomas Carrico, 55, M, Farmer, Md., $7,000
1085. Amelia A. Dent, 42, F, Farmer, Md., $5,000
1086. Isabel Burch, 35, F, Md.
1087. Wm. F. Bowling, 48, M, Farmer, Md., $10,000
1088. Judson Hunt, 55, M, Farmer, Md., $2,000
1089. Henry Burch, 43, M, Farmer, Md., $1,000
1090. Wm. E. Butler, 50, M, Farmer, Md.
1091. Richard Taylor, 61, M, Farmer, Md.
1092. Thomas J. Boarman, 25, M, Farmer, Md., $4,000
1093. Walter L. Dent, 27, M, Farmer, Md., $7,000
1094. Cecelia A. Lyon, 26, F, Md.
1095. Elizabeth B. Matthews, 50, F, Farmer, Md., $2,000
1096. George B. Moran, 55, M, Farmer, Md., $500
1097. Elizabeth Moran, 55, F, Md.
1098. George Carrico, 27, M, Farmer, Md., $2,000

1099. Matthew Guy, 75, M, Farmer, Md.
1100. Sarah C. Lyon, 37, F, Md.
1101. Harriet Moran, 51, F, Md.
1102. Walter B. Parker, 48, M, Farmer, Md., $250
1103. Kelita Suit, 43, M, Farmer, Md.
1104. George A. Huntt, 30, M, Farmer, Md.
1105. Levi Nutwell, 55, M, Merchant, Md.
1106. Robert Bailee, 30, M, Tailor, Md.
1107. Owen H. Dyson, 45, M, Merchant, Md.
1108. Francis E. Osborn, 38, M, Mechanic, Md.
1109. George Burch, 40, M, Farmer, Md.
1110. Mary Curtis, 20, F, M, Md.
1111. Samuel Hutchen, 35, M, M, Laborer, Md.
1112. Charles M. Moran, 36, M, Farmer, Md.
1113. Resin Davis, 56, M, None, Md.
1114. Wm. Woodburn, 60, M, Farmer, Md., $5,000
1115. Henry Reed, 35, F, B, Md.
1116. Zack Webster, 52, M, Farmer, Md., $1,400
1117. Wm. Cusick, 34, M, Farmer, Md.
1118. Elizabeth Burch, 40, F, Md.
1119. John Rolph, 32, M, Agent, Md., $12,000
1120. L. H. Canter, 24, M, Farmer, Md., $2,500
1121. David D. Lynch, 50, M, Farmer, Md.
1122. Elizabeth V. Lamar, 33, F, Md.
1123. Francis Jenkins, 35, M, Farmer, Md.
1124. George H. Langley 34, M, Farmer, Md.
1125. Richard Ferrall, 36, M, Farmer, Md.
1126. Richard Smith, 25, M, Laborer, Md.
1127. John H. Langley, 47, M, Farmer, Md.
1128. James Thomas, 47, M, Farmer, Md., $5,000
1129. John Demar, 33, M, Farmer, Md., $800
1130. Thomas Demar, 35, M, Farmer, Md.
1131. Peter Wood, 40, M, Farmer, Md., $6,000
1132. Rebecca Ford, 30, F, B, Md.
1133. Martha Magruder, 60, F, B, Md.
1134. Joanna Douglop, 80, F, M, Md.
1135. Rach Hawkins, 50, M, B, Md.
1136. Samuel C. Moran, 50, M, Farmer, Md.

1137. Priscilla Cembly, 30, F, M, Md.
1138. May Canter, 52, F, Md.
1139. Richard P. Wall, 25, M, Md.
1140. Cain Charles, 70, M, B, Laborer, Md.
1141. Marice P. Morton, 37, F, Md.
1142. Joseph L. Middleton, 31, M, Merchant, Md.
1143. Jason Horseman, 56, M, Fisherman, Md.
1144. Alexander Hurly, 33, M, Fisherman, Md.
1145. Evan Hurly, 35, M, Sailor, Md.
1146. Mary C. Mathany, 22, F, Md.
1147. Alexander Cawood, 25, M, Agent, Md.
1148. Richard B. Edwards, 68, M, Tavernkeeper, Md.
1149. Henry Grindle, 48, M, M, Fisherman, Md.
1150. Joseph Davy, 54, M, Merchant, Md.
1151. John T. Burch, 40, M, Miller, Md.
1152. Levin Canter, 30, M, Merchant, Md.
1153. Henry A. Canter, 21, M, Merchant, Md.
1154. Betsy Grindle, 20, F, M, Md.
1155. John Hammett, 25, M, Sailor, Md.
1156. Thomas Johnson, 56, M, Fisherman, Md.
1157. John Saxton, 30, M, Farmer, Md.
1158. Melvina Farman, 28, F, M, Md.
1159. Lelia Beven, 30, F, Md.
1160. William C. Dyer, 55, M, Md., $6,000
1161. Sary A. Montgomery, 34, F, Md., $600
1162. Francis Canter, 23, M, Md., $5,000
1163. Samuel Smoot, 23, M, Farmer, Md., $500
1164. John L. Moran, 29, M, Laborer, Md.
1165. Eleana Moran, 65, M, Farmer, Md.
1166. Mary Burk, 45, F, Md.
1167. Sophia Boarman, 34, F, Md.
1168. George F. Adams, 19, M, Farmer, Md., $3,000
1169. Thomas Buckler, 45, M, Farmer, Md.
1170. Mary A. Greer, 60, F, Md.
1171. Joseph Montgomery, 49, M, Farmer, Md., $1,000
1172. Harriett Butler, 45, F, B, Md.
1173. Rebecca Grop, 39, F, B, Md.
1174. Ivan Bowen, 41, M, Laborer, Md.

1175. Thomas I. Cagre, 25, M, Farmer, Md.
1176. Mary Yucky, 50, F, Md.
1177. Elizabeth Curtis, 28, F, B, Md.
1178. Uz Swann, 39, M, Farmer, Md.
1179. Henry M. Lyon, 48, M, Laborer, Md.
1180. Thomas F. Burch, 40, M, Agent, Md., $5,000
1181. Catherine Montgomery, 65, F, Md., $1,000
1182. George Smith, 27, M, Farmer
1183. James Aud, 53, M, Farmer, Md., $800
1184. Henny Bowling, 30, F, B
1185. Dorothy Gardiner, 65, F, $5,000
1186. Allonies Gardiner, 40, M, Md.
1187. Ann E. Deakens, 48, F, Md., $1,000
1188. Hezekiah Williams, 32, M, Farmer, Md., $500
1189. Benjamin Smith, 49, M, Farmer, Md.
1190. George Waters, 55, M, Farmer, Md., $500
1191. William Goldsmith, 55, M, Farmer, Md.
1192. John Proctor, 45, M, M, Farmer, Md.
1193. John D. Thomas, 64, M, Farmer, Md., $3,000
1194. Leonard Edelen, 23, M, Md.
1195. Edward C. Gardiner, 27, M, Merchant, Md.
1196. Elly Proctor, 26, M, M, Laborer, Md.
1197. Henry Gardiner, 23, M, Farmer, Md., $3,000
1198. Clara Gardiner, 49, F, Md.
1199. Olevia A. Ferrell, 28, F, Md.
1200. Mary C. Ferrell, 20, F, Md.
1201. Alfred W. Gardiner, 32, M, Farmer, Md., $5,500
1202. William T. Canter, 36, M, Miller, Md.
1203. Robert Dyson, 36, M, Farmer, Md.
1204. John N. Pickerel, 36, M, Farmer, Md.
1205. Ruth A. Deaken, 46, F, Md., $1,000
1206. Sally McPherson, 60, F, Md., $500
1207. Thomas M. Queen, 38, M, Farmer, Md.
1208. Robert L. Burch, 39, M, Merchant, Md.
1209. Henry M. Robey, 44, M, Farmer, Md.
1210. Mary Robey, 42, F, Md.
1211. Ignatius Butler, 60, M, B, Md.
1212. Mary Adams, 100, F, B, Md.

Allen's Fresh.
1213. George Dent, 40, M, Farmer, Md., $10,000
1214. John Holt, 35, M, B, Laborer, Md.
1215. James P. Smith, 37, M, Agent, Md.
1216. William B. Marshall, 35, M, Ferryman, Md.
1217. Thomas D. Nettle, 47, M, Agent, Md., $10,000
1218. John Higgs, 30, M, Agent, Md.
1219. Maria Nettle, 50, F, Md.
1220. Philip Marshall, 48, M, Farmer, Md., $3,000
1221. Elizabeth Clagett, 28, F, Md.
1222. Thomas Johnson, 50, M, Farmer, Md., $2,000
1223. Elizabeth Dent, 33, F, Md.
1224. Charles H. Sherburn, 29, M, Merchant, Md., $4,000
1225. Robert B. Burroughs, 54, M, Farmer, Md.
1226. Charles Shaw, 42, M, Farmer, Md., $8,000
1227. Kitty Ford, 60, F, B, Md.
1228. James N. Semmes, 41, M, Farmer, Md., $2,000
1229. Yates Barber, 20, M, Farmer, Md., $4,000
1230. John M. Todd, 34, M, P.-E. Minister, Md., $2,000
1231. William Marx, 30, M, Farmer, Md.
1232. Absalom Tennison, 44, M, Farmer, Md., $4,000
1233. John H. Jenkins, 24, M, Mechanic, Md.
1234. Walter Franklin, 32, M, Agent, Md.
1235. Adeline Curtis, 45, F, B, Md.
1236. Francis D. Murphy, 35, M, Agent, Md.
1237. George W. Clemens, 36, M, Tailor, Md.
1238. John L. Colton, 24, M, Merchant, Md.
1239. James Murphy, 21, M, Blacksmith, Md.
1240. John H. Burroughs, 38, M, Farmer, Md., $3,500
1241. Joseph Stone, 23, M, Farmer, Md.
1242. Francis, H. Digges, 40, M, Md., $12,000
1243. Michael Martin, 54, M, Wheelwright, Md.
1244. Thomas O. Daily, 52, M, Mason, Ireland
1245. A. Pickerell, 49, F, Md.

Middletown District.
1246. John Matthews, 67, M, Farmer, Md., $50,000
1247. Catherine Posey, 37, F, Md.

1248. Mary Noris, 55, F, B, Md.
1249. Letivius Butler, 50, M, B, Farmer, Md.
1250. Mary A. Mason, 30, F, M, Md.
1251. Robert S. Reeder, 25, M, Lawyer, Md.
1252. James M. Burch, 40, M, Farmer, Md., $900
1253. Richard T. Meredith, 24, M, Tailor, Md.
1254. Ann T. Cox, 64, F, Md., $10,000
1255. Marrion Maddox, 45, F, Md.
1256. Stacha A. Warthen, 32, F, Md.

Bryantown District.
1257. Barton Robey, 52, M, Carpenter, Md.
1258. John Morris, 25, M, Farmer, Md.
1259. Joseph Proctor, 50, M, M, Farmer, Md.
1260. Josias Handcock, 45, M, Farmer, Md.
1261. John W. Owen, 38, M, Merchant, Md.
1262. Mary B. Owen, 71, F, Md.
1263. John P. Roberson, 39, M, Sheriff, Md.
1264. Mary Hindle, 50, F, England
1265. Harrison Thompson, 45, M, Farmer, Md.
1266. William Murphy, 45, M, Farmer, Md.
1267. Ann Mury, 44, F, Md.
1268. William Boswell, 38, M, Farmer, Md.
1269. William Matthews, 38, M, Lawyer, Md., $5,000
1270. Francis Thompson, 58, M, Farmer, Md., $10,000
1271. Sally Bean, 60, F, Md.
1272. Edward D. Boone, 39, M, Farmer, Md., $4,000

Middletown District.
1273. Alfred Pickerel, 24, M, Farmer, Md.
1274. Emily Bowling, 28, F
1275. Caleb Wedding, 48, M, Farmer
1276. Joseph R. Hunt, 43, M, Farmer, Md.
1277. Henry Ward, 27, M, Mechanic, Md.
1278. Rose E. Tippett, 35, F, Md.
1279. Thomas Mudd, 37, M, Farmer, Md., $600

1280. Richard Cook, 60, M, Farmer, Md., $500
1281. Theodore Roby, 60, M, Laborer, Md.
1282. Benjamin Gardiner, 27, M, Farmer, Md.
1283. Thomas D. Boarman, 26, M, Farmer, Md.
1284. Mary Gray, 50, F, Farmer, Md.
1285. Lemuel McDaniel, 29, M, Farmer, Md.

Bryantown.
1286. Theodore Roby, 25, M, Farmer, Md.
1287. Jerry Dyer, 27, M, Farmer, Md., $5,000
1288. James Montgomery, 38, M, Farmer, Md.
1289. Joseph Thompson, 45, M, Farmer, Md.
1290. John B. Norris, 37, M, Farmer, Md.
1291. John F. Swann, 33, M, M, Laborer, Md.
1292. Theophilus Smoot, 31, M, Farmer, $7,000
1293. Catherine Dent, 80, F, Md., $300
1294. Ann H. Parker, 45, F, Md.
1295. Richard Dyer, 31, M, Farmer, Md., $1,200
1296. Richard Harbin, 36, M, Farmer, Md.
1297. Henry Langly, 45, M, Farmer, Md., $100
1298. Reuzen Harbin, 65, M, Farmer, Md., $2,000
1299. Philip Courtny, 65, M, Minister, Ireland
1300. John L. Johnson, 30, M, Farmer, Md.
1301. William L. Berry, 27, M, Merchant, Md.
1302. Walter F. Boarman, 52, M, Farmer, Md., $12,000
1303. John F. Hardy, 25, M, Farmer, Md., $750
1304. John P. Edelen, 27, M, Farmer, Md., $1,000
1305. Joseph E. Simms, 42, M, Farmer, Md., $3,000
1306. Henry L. Mudd, 51, M, Farmer, Md., $7,000
1307. Smith Butler, 47, M, M, Laborer, Md.
1308. George Gardiner, 62, M, Farmer, Md., $6,000
1309. George W. Proctor, 50, M, M, Laborer, Md.
1310. George H. Gardiner, 34, M Farmer, Md., $3,500
1311. William A. Mudd, 39, M, Farmer, Md., $5,000
1312. Ignatius Gardiner, 60, M, Farmer, Md., $6,000
1313. Ann E. Bean, 41, F, Md., $1,000
1314. Sara A. Cooksey, 45, F, Md., $500

1315. George A. Dyer, 28, M, Farmer, Md., $2,000
1316. Theodore Mudd, 65, M, Farmer, Md., $5,000
1317. John S. Gibbons, 20, M, Md.
1318. Benjamin H. Goldsmith, 49, M, Farmer, Md., $500
1319. Oswell Gibbons, 58, M, Farmer, Md., $6,000
1320. William Gibbons, 26, M, Farmer, Md., $6,000
1321. Henry Cantor, 53, M, Farmer, Md., $2,000
1322. Sarah Floyd, 53, F, Md., $12,000
1323. G. G. Davis, 61, F
1324. Sara J. Davis, 40, F, Md., $10,000
1325. Hezekiah Luckett, 34, M, Agent, Md.
1326. William Ferguson, 41, M, Farmer, Md., $6,000
1327. George Jenkins, 40, M, Farmer, Md., $10,000
1328. William Hamilton, 27, M, Farmer, Md., 10,000
1329. George Brent, 33, M, Lawyer, Md.
1330. John P. Ferguson, 42, M, Farmer, Md., 30,000
1331. William Little, 42, M, Agent, Md.
1332. John S. Howard, 50, M, Agent, Md.
1333. William Brown, 30, M, Agent, Md.
1334. George Tailor, 51, M, farmer, Md., $4,000
1335. Wat Swann, 32, M, M, Laborer, Md.

4. Lists of Married and Professional Persons in Charles County

Charles County Marriages. (Taken from Maryland records in the Maryland Historical Society.)
BY REV. JOHN BOLTON
Osburn, Henry to Ann Tompson, June 23, 1779.
Tompson, Baptist to Mary Lancaster, Nov. 7, 1779.
Edelin, Francis to Sarah Tompson, Nov. 8, 1779.
Montgomery, Thomas to Rebecca Southwell, Dec. 16, 1781.
Langley, Joseph to Sarah Hill, Jan. 5, 1782.
Wheatly, Bennet to Polly Morris, Jan. 17, 1782.
Edelin, Edward to Eleanor Boarman, Feb. 12, 1782.

Cash, John to Chloe Callicoe, Feb. 8, 1782.
Goodrick, Joseph to Eliza Nash, Aug. 5, 1782.
Simpson, Joseph to Mary Ann Montgomery, Aug. 19, 1782.
Hill, Fran. Xarerius to Lidia True, Sept. 12, 1782.
Osburn, Walter to Mary Miles, Oct. 8, 1782.
Hagan, Raphael to Rebecca Deviel, Oct. 9, 1782.

By Rev. John C. Brockenborough, Rector of William and Mary Parish

Shaw, Samuel to Mary Parish, June 4, 1799.
Lipscombe, Spotswood to Eliza. Smith Pendleton, July 7, 1799.
Smoot, Horatio to Heathy Smoot, July 7, 1799.
Aderton, Joseph to Ann Latimer, Aug. 1, 1799.
Reeves, Thos. C. to Rebecca Ratcliffe, Aug. 8, 1799.
Gardiner, John Chunn to Esther Cawood, Oct. 1, 1799 (in St. Mary's Co.)
Simpson, George to Margaret Bateman, Dec. 24, 1799.
Smith, Samuel to Mary Dutton, Jan. 1, 1800.
Wiseman, Robert to Eliza. Philips, Jan. 14, 1800.
Shaw, Edward to Cloe Posey, Apr. 15, 1800.
Easley, Kemble to Ann Ratcliffe, July 25, 1800.
Bateman, Richard to Margt. Wakefield, Dec. 23, 1800.
Tompkins, Wm. to Mary Farr, Dec. 26, 1800.
Govrick, Elijah to Eliza. Bateman, Jan. 6, 1801.
Chunn, Charles to Jane T. Bowen, Apr. 28, 1801.
Farr, John B. to Jane Cawood, Aug. 9, 1801.
Hemrican, Matthew to Eliza. Penn, Oct. 15, 1801.

By Rev. Henry Fendall [Prot. Episcopal]

King, John to Susa. Lynch (of St. Paul's Parish P. G's Co.), Nov. 1777.
Rowe, John to Mary Ward (King George's Parish), Dec. 23, 1777.
Adams, Samuel to Sarah Nelson (Durham Parish), Dec. 28, 1777.

Penny, Thos. to Amelia Adams (Durham Parish), Jan. 4, 1778.
Davis, Zachariah to Sarah Wright (Durham Parish), Jan. 5, 1778.
Nally, Nathan Barton to Sarah Taylor (Durham Parish), Jan. 6, 1778.
Gray, Benja. to Mary Stewart (Durham Parish), Feb. 15, 1778.
Stewart, James to Cath. Milstead (Durham Parish), Mch. 15, 1778.
Grant, John to Eliza. greenfield Tyler (King George's Parish, Prince George's Co.), Mch. 16, 1778.
Lomax Zeth to Eleanor Gray (Durham Parish), Mch. 19, 1778.
Ryson, Lancelot to Clare Cash (both of Stafford Co., Va.), Mch. 26, 1778.
Woodward, Samuel to Ann Posey (Durham Parish), Apr. 3, 1778.
Beal, Francis to Penelope Ford (Port Tobacco Parish), Apr. 12, 1778.
Jacobs, — to Ann Grahame, Apr. 30, 1778.
Wells, Samuel to Martha Oliver (P.G. Co.), Aug. 13, 1778.
Ward, Wm. to Verlinda Harrison (Durham Parish), July 27, 1777.
Fields, Wm. to Clare Poor (Durham Parish), Aug. 11, 1777.
Waters, John to Eliza Carter (Durham Parish), Sept. 20, 1777.
McConchie, Wm. to Eliza Muncaster (Durham Parish), Sept. 25, 1777.
Walker, Richard to Mary Gilpen (P. G. Co.), Aug. 25, 1778.
Moore, John Smith to Margt. Musgrove (P. G. Co.), Sept. 20, 1778.
Cox, John to Margt. Howard (P. G. Co.), Sept. 2, 1778.
Lanyhill, Leonard to Ann Anly (Calvert Co.), Oct. 30, 1778.
Naylor, Batson to Eleanor Austin (P. G. Co.), Nov. 8, 1778.
Gabard, John to Margt. Lucas, Mch., 1778.

By Rev. Walter H. Harrison

Wheeler, Benedict to Cath. Travers, Dec. 23, 1779.

Watkins, Thomas to Lucy Belt, Dec. 26, 1779.
Rye, Warren to Sarah Smith, Jan. 23, 1780.
Posey, Uriah to Catherine Skinner, Jan. —, 1780.
Deacons, Ambrose to Ann Chatham, Jan. 26, 1780.
Haislip, John to Easter Nelson, Jan. 27, 1780.
Grows, John to Christiana Jenkins, Jan. 30, 1780.
Murdock, James to Phebe Delosien, —, 1780.
Manning, Joseph to Eliza. Dunnington, Mch. 15, 1780.
Nelson, John to Eliza. Burgess, Apr. 9, 1780.
Turner, Walter to Eliza. Blancet, Apr. 23, 1780.
Simmons, Joseph to Mary Deacons, May 15, 1780.
Braund, Joseph to Emily Maddox, May 23, 1780.
Chapman, John to Sarah Jonke, June 1, 1780.
Elgin, William to Ann Anderson, June 18, 1780.
Maddox, Samuel to Anne Warde, July 9, 1780.
Cookssy, Hezekiah to Eliza Grey, July 13, 1780.
Thatcher, Ignatius to — Saporly, July 16, 1780.
Fitzgerald, John to Ann Green, Aug. 24, 1780.
Lawler, Wm. to Mary Sacke, Aug. 31, 1780.
Milstead, Thomas to Eliza. Ratcliffe, Sept. 16, 1780.
Griffin, Rosse to Sarah Ratcliffe, Sept. 21, 1780.
Dunnington, Hezekiah to Aa. Magriger, Oct. 9, 1780.
Smith, John to Rebecca Jewel, Nov. 13, 1780.
Bartly, William to Ann Smoot, Nov. 19, 1780.

BY REV. IGNATIUS MATTHEWS [ROMAN CATHOLIC]

Reeder, John to Chloe Green, Oct. 22, 1779.
Dixon, Jacob to Mary Lancaster, 1781-2.
Higdon, Ignatius to Eliza. Taylor, 1781-2.
Cooms, Richard to Clare Green, 1781-2.
Ally, Shadrack to Eliza. Gates, 1781-2.

BY REV. JOHN MCPHERSON OF PICCAWAXON, OR WILLIAM AND MARY PARISH

King, Robert to Judith Wood, June 13, 1777.
Syme, Nicholas to Eliza. Johnson, July 25, 1777.
Reeves, Thomas to Mary Scroggan Oakley, Sept. 28, 1777.

Scroggan, John to Ann Mastin, Oct. 29, 1777.
Smith, James to Winnie Rogers, Dec. 23, 1777.
Mastin, Francis to Charity Cooksey, Jan. 10, 1778.
Duley, Thomas to Eliza. Bateman, Feb. 6, 1778.
Rock, William to Charity Adams, Feb. 23, 1778.
Collins, John to Eliza. Scroggan, May 10, 1778.
Pollock, Thomas to Susanna Curd, May 19, 1778.
Ashton, Henry Elexr. to Mary Dent, May 25, 1778.
Edwards, John to Mary Turner, June 4, 1778.
Oakly, John Scroggan to Mary Ann Mahoney, June 5, 1778.
Cleyburn, Wm. Dandridge to Ann Dandridge, June 21, 1778.
Griffy, Benja. to Susanna Modisit, Aug. 26, 1778.
Hungerford, Thos. to Violetta Gwinn, Nov. 17, 1778.
Farr, John to Mary Watts, Nov. 25, 1778.
Tyler, William to Mariamore Trueman Stoddrt, Jan. 10, 1779.
Robinson, Willm. to Mary Sims, Apr. 8, 1779.
Smoot, John to Anny Ford, Apr. 8, 1779.
Nelson, Willm. to Sally Smallwood, Apr. 13, 1779.
Carrol, John to Eliza. Hamilton, May 9, 1779.
Wilder, John Brown to Mary Ann Smoot, May 27, 1779.
Jenkins, Philip to Eliza. Hungerford, June 8, 1779.
Maddox, John to Sarah Fernandis, June 20, 1779.
Higgs, Jonathan to Eliza. Ford, June 20, 1779.
Penn, John to Eleanor Dutton, July 20, 1779.
Nettle, Thomas Dutton to Muriel Dutton, July 20, 1779.
Shaw, Dr. Louis Dene to Jenny Clements, Sept. 16, 1779.
Baillie, Andrew to Mary Leftrich, Oct. 1, 1779.
Boswel, Walter to Eleanor Smallwood, Oct. 14, 1779.
Smoot, Isaac to Mary Lock, Oct. 28, 1779.
Halkerstone, John to Eliza. Hanson, Nov. 4, 1779.
Lamond, John Christerson to Eliza. Hall, Nov. 18, 1779.
Franklin, John to Virlinda Cox, Dec. 8, 1779.
Gwinn, John to Jean Ludwell Bruce, Dec. 22, 1779.
Washington, Thornton to Milly Berry (of Va.), Dec. 26, 1779.
Hodgson, George to Nancy Jenkins, Dec. 30, 1779.
Mason, Lot to Sally Haselip, Jan. 12, 1780.

May, Richard to Mary Pitman, Jan. 24, 1780.
Mahony, Clement to Sarah Ann Oakley, July 17, 1780.
Clark, Ignatius to Ann Hilton (from St. Mary's), July 6, 1780.
Pasco, William to Ann Flaxion, Oct. 14, 1780.
Linkins, Henry to Chlaeh Alin, Oct. 28, 1780.
Roberts, John to Susannah Mason, Nov. 11, 1780.
Guy, Joseph to Sarah Smith, Dec. 13, 1780.
Robertson, Mitchel to Rose Mastin, Dec. 24, 1780.
Albritton, Charles to Cath. Burridge, Jan. 4, 1781.
Truson, Robert to Esther Ray, Jan. 6, 1781.
Marshall, William to Eliza. Hanson, Jan. 22, 1781.
Howard, Benja. to Mary Ann Buckley, Jan. 30, 1781.
Linkin, Abraham to Eleanor Borden, Jan. 30, 1781.
Ware, Francis, Jnr. to Ann Pickerell, Jan. 31, 1781.
Gambia, Richard to Sarah Gardner, Apr. 4, 1781.
Sims, James to Sarah Key, June 9, 1781.
Dent, —— to Mary Ann Hancock, Dec. 18, 1781.
Smoot, Josiah to Ann Douglass, Dec. 22, 1781.
Smoot, Henry to Eliza. Warren, Dec. 23, 1781.
Hanson, Walter to Sarah Hatch Maddox, Dec. 25, 1781.
Rigg, Charles to Eliza. Andrews, Dec. 28, 1781.
Burridge, Thos. to Joanna Chapman, Jan. 18, 1782.
Price, James to Eliza. St. George, Jan. 31, 1782.
Ghant, George to Eliza —— (Calvert Co.), Jan. 31, 1782.
Scott, John to Agnis Hadden, Feb. 5, 1782.
Minitree, Paul to Eleanor Smoot, Apr. 6, 1782.
Howard, Baker to Ann Philips, Apr. 6, 1782.
Forbes, John to Eliza. Marshall, Apr. 21, 1782.
Gray, Wilson to Eliza. Limms [Simms?], Apr. 26, 1782.
Brady, Thomas Gerard to Susanna Brown, May 11, 1782.
Scott, Thomas to Alice Philpot, July 9, 1782.
Stark, Richard to Eliza. Gatewood, Aug. 23, 1782.
Compton, Alex. to Mary Joy, Oct. 4, 1782.
Bateman, Izreel to Sarah Simkson, Nov. 18, 1782.
King, Townley to Rebeckah King, Dec. 16, 1782.
Allen, Bartholomew to Frances Ramsey, Jan. 20, 1783.
Wakefield, Abel to Margt. Jenkins, Dec. 30, 1782.

Massey, Robert to Sarah Warren, May 3, 1783.
Poslyn, William to Sarah Hammel, Aug. 27, 1783.
Billingsley, John to Charity Ford, Oct. 28, 1783.
Douglas, Benjn. to Sarah Marshall, Oct. 27, 1783.
Hawkins, Smith to Eleanor Laidles, Nov. 5, 1783.
Marshall, Thomas to Sarah Maddox, Dec. 6, 1783.
Bateman, Richd. to Mary Ann Hatton, Dec. 22, 1783.
Bunbery, John to Mary Baltrop, Apr. 30, 1784.
Smith, James to Constania Ford, May 1, 1784.
Lawless, Benja. to Eliza. Samuel, June 28, 1784.
Winter, Charles Bruce to Eliza. Mason, June 26, 1784.
Brook, Mathew to Ann Fearson, Dec. 28, 1784.

BY REV. BENJA. ROLLS.

Boone, Alesus to Mary Smith, Jan. 8, 1779.
Semmes, Thomas to Mary An Brawney, Feb. 1779.
Scott, Aquila to Henrietta Semmes, Apr. 14, 1779.
Mudd, Ezekiel to Eliza. Edelen, May 12, 1779.
Lancaster, John Jnr. to Aloysia Jerningham, July 31, 1779.

BY REV. HENRY PILE [ROMAN CATHOLIC].

"Oliuer", William to Nancy Blackstock (License granted Feb. 16, 1785).
Edelin, George to Sarah Edelin (License granted May 14, 1785).
Riney, James to Anne Semes, Dec. 27, 1785.
Haydon, Clement to Fawney Wakefield, Jan. 13, 1786.
Fenwick, James to Henrietta Mary Lancaster, Feb. 14, 1786.
Brent, Wm. Chandler to Eleanor Neale, May 24, 1786.
Hamersley, Henry to Olivia Jerningham, Oct. 1, 1786.
Simpson, Charles to Sarah Bentels, Nov. 19, 1786.
Hamilton, Edward to Mary Anne Boarman, Nov. 20, 1786.
Reeder, Benjn. to Eleanor Slaughton, Dec. 23, 1786.
Wathen, Martin to Eliza. Anderson, May 23, 1787.
Edelen, Oswald to Mary Thompson Bond, Oct. 25, 1787.
Queen, Joseph to Eddie "Jermingham," Dec. 2, 1787.
Mattingley, Raphael to Winefred Higdon, Dec. 29, 1788.

Middleton, James to Nancy Corry, Apr. 23, 1789.
Burtles, Willm. to Sarah Wathen, June 28, 1789.
Simpson, Thos. to Judith Wathen, Nov. 12, 1789.
Luckett, Benj. to Eliza. Semmes, Jan. 10, 1790.
Berien, Walter to Charity Simpson, Jan. 12, 1790.
Wathen, Martin to Eliza. Anderson, May 23, 1787.
Duggin, Robert to Teresa Brady, July 10, 1791.
Semmes, Mark to Catherine Simpson, Aug. 9, 1791.
Hayden, James to Anne Robertson, Sept. 4, 1791.
Dixon, Samuel to Eleanor Scott, Jan. 10, 1792.
Shettleworth, Allen to Anne Witherington, Feb. 9, 1792.
Witherington, James to Mary Miles, Feb. 20, 1792.
Long, Josias to Ann Friend, Jan. 13, 1793.

BY REV. THOMAS THORNTON.

McDaniel, Thomas to Ann Chattann, June 14, 1777.
Smithson, Wm. Eaton to Rhoda Robey, Sept. 1, 1777.
Gill, Thomas to Sarah Jones, Sept. 3, 1777.
Smith, John to Eliza. Rawlings, Sept. 3, 1777.
Shively, Bernard to Eleanor Longford, Sept. 22, 1777.
Vermilion, Benja. to Tabatha Burch, Oct. 14, 1777.
Talburt, John to Ann Davis, Oct. 19, 1777.
Carney, Daniel to Alice Lovelace, Nov. 1, 1777.
Hatton, Joseph to Martha Jones, Nov. 5, 1777.

BY REV. FRANCIS WALKER, OF WM. & MARY PARISH.

Philpot, Benja. to Eliza. Smoot, Aug. 3, 1786.
Minitree, Paul to Nancy Dorset, Aug. 1, 1786.
Bateman, John to Ann Oakley, Sept. 13, 1786.
Warren, John to Eliza. Shaw, Sept. 20, 1786.
Billingsley, Clement to Eleanor Warren, Nov. 21, 1786.
Duncan, James to Sarah Leach, Apr. 4, 1787.
Martin, John to Lydia Hickman, May 24, 1787.
Marshall, Robert to Joanna Douglass, May 26, 1787.
Nicholas, John to Sally Raines, June 4, 1787.
Tomkins, John to Nancy Norwood, Sept. 27, 1787.
Fisher, John to Eleanor Robertson, Nov. 24, 1787.

Jenkins, William to Eliza. Simpson, Dec. 23, 1787.
Smith, John to Ann King, Dec. 23, 1787.
Shaw, John to Sarah Vincent, Jan. 3, 1788.
Vincent, Thomas to Eliza. Wilder, Jan. 6, 1788.
Saider, John to Cath. Ann Penn, Jan. 8, 1788.
King, Rt. Rev. Reuben to Mary Ann Vincent, Feb. 3, 1788.
Posey, Thomas to Mary Dutton, Mch. 25, 1788.
Contee, Benja. to Sarah Rt. Lee, Mch. 30, 1788.
Weems, John to Alice Lee, Apr. 8, 1788.
Maddox, John to Martha Harris, Apr. 22, 1788.
Jordon, Saml. to Eliza. Thompson, July 31, 1788.
Bateman, Levin to Ann Simpson, Oct. 28, 1788.

BY REV. GEORGE H. WORSLEY, RECTOR OF PORT TOBACCO PARISH.

Bennett, Patrick and Mary Squire, Nov. 3, 1780.
Cromwell, Joseph and Kezia Stansbury, Dec. 11, 1780.
Cochran, George and Eleanor Shaw, Dec. 21, 1780.
Hicks, Abraham and Sarah Gorsuch, May 13, 1781.
Gallaway, Thomas and Cath. Dallis, Feb. 25, 1780.
McComas, Edward D. and Sarah Selby of Harford Co., Nov. 14, 1780.
Dick, David and Mary Wilson, Nov. 14, 1780.
James, Thomas and Mary Eager, Nov. 15, 1780.
Nelson, David and Rachel Baker, Nov. 16, 1780.
Jury, Richard and Nancy Stallion, Nov. 23, 1780.
Baker, Isaac and Ann Stewart, Nov. 23, 1780.
Brown, James and Hannah Hitchcock, Dec. 5, 1780.
Osborne, William and Nancy Lytle, Dec. 19, 1780.
Welch, Edward and Dorothy Clements, June 11, 1782.
McPherson, John and Elizabeth Readen, June 25, 1782.
Fleury, William and Esther Maddox, July 2, 1782.
Richardson, Wm. and Jane Bramhall, July 16, 1782.
McPherson, Wm. and Mary Smoot, July 16, 1782.
Worry, Samuel and Elizabeth Underwood, Aug. 25, 1782.
Clements, Walter and Nancy Garrett, Aug. 28, 1782.
Chandler, John and Cath. Posey, Sept. 5, 1782.
Long, Jonathan and Eleoner Going, Nov. 10, 1782.

Russell, Henry and Chole Smallwood, Nov. 10, 1782.
Smallwood, Bayne and Chole McCatee, Dec. 3, 1782.
McDonald, Jonathan and Violetta Wedding, Dec. 15, 1782.
Maddox, Benjamin and Bennedicta Fernandis, Dec. 21, 1782.
Carter, George and Gizzel Brawner, Dec. 23, 1782.
Gates, James and Lydia Padgett, Jan. 1, 1783.
Lurly, John and Hephsehe Harris, Jan. 2, 1783.
Roby, Zachariah and Elizabeth Pickrell, Jan. 16, 1783.
Simmons, Aaron and Sarah Thompson, Feb. 2, 1783.
Glasgow, William to Eleanor Morland, Feb. 10, 1783.
Lock, Thomas to Catherine Estep, Feb. 16, 1783.
Roland, Geo. to Marta Slater, Feb. 25, 1783.
Berry, John to Elizabeth Willett, Mch. 2, 1783.
Vermillion, Uriah to Susannah Barker, Mch. 16, 1783.
Menace, Robert to Eleanor Young, April 11, 1783.
Henson, Walter to Elizabeth Henson, April 20, 1783.
Fisher, Martin to Mary Daily, April 20, 1783.
Gody, Matthew to Mary Mahony, April 29, 1783.
Magruder, Nathaniel to Mary Billingsley, May 4, 1783.
McPherson, John to Elizabeth Thompson, May 12, 1783.
Berry, Ryon to Ann Owen, June 12, 1783.
Wood, John to Ann Welch, June 20, 1783.
White, John to Eleoner Long, June 27, 1783.
Von, John to Agatha Edington, July 17, 1783.
Miller, Christopher to Wismey McIntosh, July 26, 1783.
Wheeler, Ignatius to Ann Morris, Aug. 19, 1783.
Gardner, Hezekiah to Mary H. McPherson, Sept. 18, 1783.
Dyson, Bennet to Verlinda Chunn (St. Mary's Co.), Oct. 8, 1783.
Southean, Richd. to Catherine Southean, Oct. 15, 1783.
Gray, Zachariah to Susannah Parker, July 22, 1777 (of Charles Co.—m. in Montgomery Co.)
Downs, Wilson to Mary Roland, Dec. 27, 1779 (both of Charles Co.,—m. in P. G's Co.)
Thomas, Hezekiah to Jane White, June 27, 1780 (Charles Co. —m. in P. G's Co.)
Carpenter, John to Frances Perry, Jan. 28, 1779 (Chas. Co. —m. in P. G's Co.)

Risen, Chandley to Mary Hamilton, May 14, 1779 (Chas. Co.
—m. in P. G's Co.)
Garner, Wm. to Mary Ann Fimses, Nov. 14, 1779 (Chas. Co.
—m. in P. G's Co.)
Suit, Walter to Susanna Davis, Aug. 26, 1777 (Chas. Co.—m.
in St. Mary's Co.)
Boone, Alexius to Mary Smith, Jan. 8, 1777.
Summers, Thomas to Mary Ann Brawney, Feb. 8, 1779.
Scott, Aquilla to Henrietta Semmes, Apr. 17, 1779.
Mudd, Ezekiel to Elizabeth Edelen, May 12, 1779.
Lancaster, John, Jr. to Aloysia Jerningham, July 31, 1779.

Medical Doctors (from *The Maryland Directory*, 1878)

ALLEN'S FRESH; population 35
S. W. Dent
John H. Reeder

BEANTOWN; population 30
None

BRYANTOWN; population 120
W. I. Boarman
P. W. Hawkins
G. D. Mudd
S. A. Mudd

COX'S STATION; population 25
B. A. Jamison

DONCASTER; population 50
John W. Miller
Wm. H. Price

GLYMONT; population 75
N. Chapman

HARRIS LOT; population 85
F. M. Lancaster
A. J. Smoot

HUGHESVILLE; population 50
Thos. A. Carrico

LA PLATA; population 35
E. V. Edelen
Wm. N. Sanders

MATTAWOMAN; population 10
None

NEWBURG; population 75
Francis Price
John Reender

NEWPORT; population 60
A. M. Brooke
S. W. Dent

PISGAH; population 100
R. K. Compton
J. W. Miller

POMONKEY; population 50
N. Chapman
R. K. Compton
Chas. H. Pye
J. W. Thomas

PORT TOBACCO; population 200
None
(Dentist) A. D. Cobey

RIVERSIDE; population 20
M. N. Millar

TOMPKINSVILLE; population 40
None

WHITE PLAINS; population 32
Peter W. Hawkins

Attorneys (listed in John Livingston's Law Register for 1852, from Brown and Klapthor, p. 113).
ALLEN'S FRESH: William D. Merrick (Retired)
BRYANTOWN: John J. Hughes
HARRIS LOT: Peter W. Crain (on the Bench)
PORT TOBACCO: Richard Barnes (on the Bench)
William C. Barnes
George Brent
John G. Chapman (Retired)
Gerard W. Crain
James Ferguson
George P. Jenkins (Retired)
George W. Matthews
John W. Mitchell
Walter Mitchell (Retired)
Robert S. Reeder
Frederick Stone
William B. Stone (Retired)
Nicholas Stonestreet

5. Writing Your Personal History

Suggestions, Questions You Might Ask (from The Everton Publishers, Inc., Logan, Utah).

1. Your birth: when, where, parents, surrounding circumstances and conditions.

2. Your childhood: health, diseases, accidents, playmates, trips, associations with your brothers and sisters, unusual happenings, visitors in your home, visits to grandparents, relatives you remember, religion in your home, financial condition of parents.

3. Your brothers and sisters: names, date of birth, place of birth, accomplishments, names of spouses, date and place of marriage, their children.

4. Your school days: schools attended, teachers, courses studied, special activities, associates, achievements, socials, report cards, humorous situations, who or what influenced you to take certain courses or do things you might not otherwise have done.

5. Your activities before, after, and between school sessions: vacations, jobs, attendance at church, other church functions, scouting, sports, tasks at home, fun, and funny situations.

6. Your courtship and marriage: Meeting your spouse, special dates, how the question was popped, marriage plans, the wedding, parties and receptions, gifts, honeymoon, meeting your in-laws, what influenced you most in your choice of spouse.

7. Settling down to married life: your new home, starting housekeeping, bride's biscuits, spats and adjustments, a growing love, making ends meet, joys and sorrows, your mother-in-law, other in-laws.

8. Your vocation: training for your job, promotions, companies you worked for, salaries, associates, achievements, your own business.

9. Your children: names, dates and places of birth, health of mother before and after, how father fared, characteristics, habits, smart sayings and doings, growing up, accomplishments, schooling, marriage, vocations, sicknesses, accidents, operations.

10. Your civic and political activities: positions held, services rendered, clubs, fraternities and lodges you have joined.

11. Your church activities: as a young person, through adolescence, churches attended, church positions, church associates, church certificates, answers to prayers, necessity and power of love.

12. Your avocations: sports, home hobbies, dramatic and musical activities, reading habits, gencalogy, travels, favorite songs, movies, books, writers, poems, etc.

13. Special celebrations or holidays you remember: Easter, Christmas, national and local holidays, vacations.

14. Your plans and hopes for the future.

15. Your ancestors: your impressions of those you knew personally; a general sketch of those you did not know; father, mother, grandparents, great grandparents, other relatives.

16. Your encouragement and counsel to your descendants: carrying on family traditions and activities; their obligations to their country, church and family; your suggestions to your progeny and others on honesty, humility, health, diligence, perseverance, thrift, loyalty, kindness, reverence, the Bible and other religious and edifying books; service to fellow men; your religious beliefs; etc.

Sources to Consider in Writing Your Personal History (from Capt. Arthur C. Bushey, USN (ret.), Genealogist)

Newspaper accounts of a wedding anniversary, engraved announcements of weddings, family reunions, notifications of change of business, notification to all concerned that a man will not be responsible for his wife's debts, etc.

Delayed birth certificate for those born prior to 1900.

Passport or visa.

Voter registration card or identification.

Military or Veteran's Administrative records.

Scottish Rite and Shriner's records.

Personal copies of titles and related financial documents of all properties held.

Old listings in the Blue Book or other such directory.

Old leases.

Family scrapbook.

Other Sources.
Professional people may be of help. You may obtain a list of researchers from the:

> Historical Society of Charles Co.
> Genealogical Committee
> Port Tobacco, Md. 20677

A list of professional genealogists may be obtained from the:

> Maryland Historical Society
> 201 W. Monument Street
> Baltimore, Maryland 21201

Enclose a stamped self-addressed envelope.

The new "Family Tree Starter Kit" may be helpful. Cost is $6.95, from:

> Tarharka Publishing Co.
> P. O. 3063
> Annapolis, Md., 21403

Bibliography

Editor's Note: This Bibliography lists the sources used in compiling the Bicentennial Edition of *Charles County, Maryland, A History.* Standard bibliographic form for history works is used: author, title, place and date of publication. The name of the publisher is given only to avoid confusion, or where other publication information is not provided. In some cases incomplete data are available, and the interested reader is referred to the Archives and/or Libraries at Annapolis and/or Baltimore, or the Charles County Public Library at La Plata, as well as materials housed by the Charles County Board of Education or at the Charles County Courthouse, both at La Plata.

The reader is also referred to the two other bibliographies in this text: Sources for Religion, beginning on page 193 and Sources for Genealogical Research, beginning page 330. Most of the titles are not repeated; where the work is a good source for information besides religion or genealogy, it appears here as well.

Books and Articles

Andrews, Matthew Page, *History of Maryland, Province and State.* New York, 1929.

_____.*Tercentenary History of Maryland.* S.J. Clarke Co., 1925.

Beitzell, Edwin, *Life on the Potomac River.* Published by author, 1968.

Boatner, Mark Mayo, III, *Encyclopedia of the American Revolution.* New York, 1966.

Bozman, John L., *History of Maryland.* Baltimore, 1837.

Brown, Paul Dennis, and Margaret Brown Klapthor, *History of Charles County, Maryland.* Tercentenary ed. La Plata, Md. 1958.

Burgess, R.H., and H.G. Wood, *Steamboats Out of Baltimore.* Tidewater Publishers, 1968.

Burns, Vincent Godfrey, *Memories and Melodies of Maryland.* Washington, D.C., 1964.

Calvert, Benedict Leonard, *Report to Charles Lord Baltimore.* N.p., n.d.

Calvert, Cecil, *A Relation of Maryland.* Reprint, Ann Arbor, Mich., 1966.

Chapelle, Howard I., various books. Washington, D.C., 1932 through 1970.

Charles County Board of Education, *General Information or History.* La Plata, Md., 1948.

Corrigan, the Rt. Rev. Owen B., *A Model County Parish and Its Records.* Reprinted from the Records of the American Catholic Hist. Soc., Philadelphia, 1924.

Crowl, Philip A., *Maryland During and After the Revolution.* Baltimore, 1943.

Davis, George Lyn-Lachlan, *The Day Star of American Freedom.* New York, 1955.

Department of Education of Maryland, "Approved Non-public and Non-academic Schools," 1951.

DePuy, W.H., *The People's Atlas of the World.* Phillips and Hunt, 1886.

Earle, Swepson, *The Chesapeake Bay Country.* N.p., 1923.

Evans, Cerinda W., *Notes on Shipbuilding and Shipping in Colonial Virginia.* Newport News, Va., 1957.

Ferguson, Alice L. and Henry G., *The Piscataway Indians of Southern Maryland.* Published by author, 1960.

Flexner, Abraham, and Frank P. Bachman, *Public Education in Maryland (A Report to the Maryland Educational Survey Commission).* N.p., 1916.

Foster, Vera A., *Your Maryland.* N.p., 1965.

Harrison, Fairfax, *Landmarks of Old Prince William.* N.p., 1964

Harvard Guide to American History, rev. ed. Edited by Frank Freidel. Cambridge, Mass., 1975.

Hawthorne, Julian, *United States.* Vol. 1, "World's Best Histories." P.F. Collier and Son, 1898.

Hiss, Hanson, "The Knights of the Lance in the South," *Outing,* xxxi, Jan. 1898, pp. 338-44, in *Maryland Historical Magazine,* vol. 36, no. 3, Sept. 1941, pp. 264ff.

Jenkins, Gene, "Charles Countians Who Have Served in Congress," *The Record,* publication of the Historical Society of Charles County, June and December 1965.

Lantz, Emily, *The Spirit of Maryland.* Baltimore, 1929.

Leckie, Robert, *The Wars of America.* New York, 1968.

Letters of Washington and Accompanying Papers. Edited by Stanislaus Murray Hamilton. John Parke Custis to George Washington, vol. iv, p. 81. Boston, 1904.

A Library of American Literature, edited by Stedman and Hutchinson. Charles L. Webster Co., 1891.

McGrath, Francis Sims, *Pillars of Maryland.* Richmond, Va., 1950.

Manual of the Public Schools of Maryland, 1896-97. N.p., n.d.

Maryland State Board of Education Study, "Educational progress in Maryland Public Schools Since 1916," compiled by Edward G. Stapleton. N.p., 1959.

Maryland Tobacco Improvement Foundation, Inc., *Handbook on the Culture of Maryland Tobacco.* 4th edition. N.p., 1974.

Middleton, Arthur Pierce, *Tobacco Coast.* Newport News, Va., 1953.

Philips, George Morris, *Nation and State.* N.p., 1913.

Posey, Calvert R. and Judith L., *A History of the Role Charles County Played in the Civil War.* Published by author, n.d.

Queen, Sister Mary Xavier, *Grandma's Stories and Anecdotes of "Ye Olden Times."* Boston, 1899.

Radoff, Morris Leon, ed., *The Old Line State, A History of Maryland.* Baltimore, 1956.
Richardson, Hester D., *Side Lights in Maryland History.* 2 vols, reprint. Baltimore, 1967.
Ruoff, Henry W., *The Standard Dictionary of Facts.* Frontier Press, 1913.
Scharf, Thomas J., *History of Maryland.* 3 vols. John B. Piet, n.d.
Schaun, George and Virginia, *Everyday Life in Colonial Maryland.* N.p., 1960.
Semmes, Raphael, *Captains and Mariners of Early Maryland.* Baltimore, 1937.
State Board of Education of Maryland, "Course of Study of the Public Elementary Schools of Maryland, 1914." Dulany-Vernay, n.d.
State Gazette and Merchants and Farmers Directory for Maryland and the District of Columbia. Baltimore, 1871.
Steiner, Bernard C., *Maryland Under the Commonwealth.* Reprint, New York, 1971.
Stephenson, Carroll Deane, *A Journey to Philadelphia.* New York, (1976).
Steuart, Rieman, *The Maryland Line, 1775-1783.* Society of the Cincinnati of Maryland, 1969.
U.S. Bureau of Education, *Circulars of Information.* N.p., 1894.
Washington Star, *Rambler.* Washington, D.C., n.d.
Wilstach, Paul, *Potomac Landings.* New York, 1920.
_____, *Tidewater Maryland.* New York, 1931.

Periodicals*

The Maryland Gazette, 1745 to August 1837, printed at Annapolis. Available on microfilm.
Maryland Historical Magazine, since 1906.
Maryland Independent, since September 1874.
Maryland Magazine
Port Tobacco Times, 1851 to 1855, Port Tobacco, Md.

*Various articles from these periodicals

Public Documents*

Archives of Maryland.
Bylaws, Rules and Regulations of the State Board of Education, Md.
Charles County Census, 1775-1778 and 1800.
Land Records of Charles County.
Maryland, Calendar of State Papers, Red Books, no. 4, part ii.
The Maryland Code (Public Local Laws), 1860.
Minutes, Charles County Board of County Commissioners, 1941 to 1975, La Plata, Md.
Minutes, Charles County Board of Education, 1933 to 1966.
Plots, Maps, and Deeds of Charles County, 1658 to 1972.
Records, Charles County Treasurer, La Plata, Md.

*Some are available at the Library or Courthouse at La Plata; all at Annapolis.

Agricultural Pamphlets*

Cooperative Extension Service Leaflet 30.
Maryland Agricultural Statistics, Dept. of Agriculture Publication K-1.
Maryland Population, 1930-1970. Published August 1971.

Official Standards, Grades, Maryland Broadleaf Tobacco.
Sixty Years of Agricultural Census.

*These are publications of the U.S. Dept. of Agriculture, and available at or through the USDA-University of Maryland Cooperative Extension Service, at White Plains, Md., and elsewhere.

Local Schools, Anecdotal Accounts*

Artes, Dorothy, "Indian Head One-Room School" and "Glymont School."
Butler, Madeline, "Jacksontown School."
Clements, Rebecca, and Geraldine Williams, "Port Tobacco School."
Compton, Margaret Wade, "Notes on the Census for the Period from 1860-1900" and "Annual Reports of the Maryland State Superintendent of Public Education for the period 1866 to 1899."
Davis, Elsie Harris, "Hill Top Colored School."
Davis, Theodore, "Greenleek School."
Dippold, Margaret Graham, "Michael Robertson Stone."
Eisenhardt, May R., Maria Eleanor, and Anna Mercer Eisenhardt, "Thomas Mercer Carpenter."
Furey, Pearl T., "Federal Hill School of 1927."
Garner, Mary R.M., "La Plata Two-Room Elementary School, 1896-1926."
Golden, Marjorie, "Chicamuxen School."
Hill, Minnie Fields, "History of My Early Teaching Days, Wicomico School."
Kaufman, Lucille S., "Memories of a One-Room School Teacher."
Latimer, Rachel B., "William B. Billingsley—The Teacher's Friend."

Linton, Emily Marbury, "Holly Springs School."
Medley, G.E., "A Letter to 'My Dear Miss Wade'."
Middleton, Ernest A., Sr., "The Middleton One-Room School."
Norris, Dorothy Burdette, "A Few Memories of Port Tobacco School (1918-19)."
Perry, Louise Haislip, "Picture of Hill Top School, 1915-1922."
Plowden, Edna W., "Holly Springs School."
Shank, Elsie G., "Pisgah School (*ca.* 1927)."
Simmons, Edna, "The McConchie School, 1922."
Sweeney, Alfred, "Thompkinsville High School."
Wheeler, Jane G., "Cedar Point Neck School, 1926-27."
Wheeler, Wallace H., "Early Schools, " written 1935.
White, Polly, "Francis Bernard Gwynn."
Williams, P.P., "School Days of Yore," written 1935.

*These monographs can be seen in the Vertical File at the Charles County Public Library, La Plata.

Other Unpublished Materials

Conversations and correspondence with present and former residents of Charles County; papers, letters, notes, and memorabilia of residents, including: Eleanor May Carrico, Edward B. Edelen, Elizabeth Forbes Edelen, Mary Boarman Edelen, David Farr, Francis I. Ferral, Margaret Hamilton, Eleanora Bowling Kane, Spearman Lancaster, Louise Matthews, Catherine Hanson Mitchell, John T. Mudd, Mrs. George Smith, and Gladys E. Williams.

Photographs

NATIONAL REGISTER HOMES

Charles County has eight of these irreplaceable structures, which date from our nation's early years. Most have been restored to their former beauty, and all are protected by the Historical Preservation Act of 1966. Except for Mt. Carmel, they are private homes, opened to the public only on special occasions.

(Photos courtesy of Charles County Chamber of Commerce)

MAXWELL HALL, in northeastern Charles County, may date from the 1680s. Bricks in the two gigantic external free-standing chimneys differ in size, those in the east chimney slightly larger than today's standard size, those in the west chimney considerably smaller. Each of the tall, narrow, double-hung windows contains 18 panes.

MOUNT CARMEL MONASTERY, founded in 1790, was the first convent in the nation. The Carmelite nuns left it in 1831, but they have recently returned and are presently restoring the buildings. A large Crucifix and 14 Stations of the Cross are erected on the property, which is open to the public on a restricted basis.

ARABY, the girlhood home of Ann Eilbeck who married the author of Virginia's Bill of Rights, George Mason, has two stories, believed to date from about 1685 and 1720, respectively. It is a charming private home, its woodwork especially notable.

DR. SAMUEL MUDD HOME, Malcolm, has been in the Mudd family since it was built, about 1825. It was here that John Wilkes Booth had his broken leg treated, after he assassinated President Lincoln—although Dr. Mudd had no part in the conspiracy. The home was recently purchased by the State to be renovated and turned over to Charles County to be operated as an historical park.

WAVERLY was built between 1782 and 1823 by Col. Bruce, who served in Gen. Smallwood's Maryland Regiment. It was completed by Dr. Morgan Harris, who bought it in 1820, in the Federal architecture popular at the time.

◀ RICH HILL, dating from the mid-18th century, also was visited by Booth, when its owner, Southern sympathizer Samuel Cox, offered the assassin and a companion a hiding place while arranging for them to cross the Potomac into Virginia.

HABRE DE VENTURE was built in 1771 by Thomas Stone, signer of the Declaration of Independence, who is buried in the family graveyard on the property. Located at Port Tobacco, it is a Georgian-style structure, 1 1/2 stories high, with a gambrel roof.

ROSE HILL, built 1774 in the Port Tobacco Valley, was the home of Dr. Gustavus Richard Brown, physician to George Washington through his death, and later of Olivia Floyd, who spied for the Confederacy. Union General Hooker also used it as his headquarters.

(Courtesy of Charles County NAACP)

SHILOH COMMUNITY CHURCH, Newburg

(Courtesy of The Maryland Independent)

SHILOH CHURCH, La Plata, old and new

(*Courtesy of The Times Crescent*)

CHRIST CHURCH, La Plata

(Courtesy of The Maryland Independent)

ACCOKEEK BAPTIST CHURCH, old and new

TRINITY CHURCH, Newport *(Courtesy of The Maryland Independent)*

◀ST. FRANCIS DE SALES CHURCH, Benedict
  (Courtesy of The Maryland Independent)

CHRIST CHURCH, Wayside *(Courtesy of The Maryland Independent)*

(Courtesy of The Maryland Independent)
ST. JOSEPH'S CHURCH, Pomfret

ST. PAUL'S CHURCH, Waldorf, *at right*
(*Courtesy of The Maryland Independent*)

(Courtesy of The Maryland Independent)
CALVARY CHURCH, Waldorf

OLD DURHAM CHURCH, Ironsides
(Courtesy of The Times Crescent)

(Courtesy of The Maryland Independent)
ST. JOHN'S CHURCH, Pomonkey

(Courtesy of The Maryland Independent)
NANJEMOY BAPTIST CHURCH

GOOD SHEPHERD UNITED METHODIST CHURCH, Waldorf, *at right*

(Courtesy of The Maryland Independent)

TOBACCO PROCESSING in Southern Maryland is still done much as it was more than a century ago. Tobacco is harvested, *above left,* then hung in a barn to cure, *above,* then stripped, *left,* and finally hauled to market, *overleaf.* Only the hauling vehicles have changed since these pictures were taken, about 1910.

(*Courtesy of The Maryland Independent*)

SHEEP HERDING has become less prominent in Charles County.

(Courtesy of the Charles County Chamber of Commerce)

CORN SHUCKS outside barn

AN AMISH FARMER AT THE FARMER'S MARKET, near Charlotte Hall, *at right*

(Courtesy of the Charles County Chamber of Commerce)

(Courtesy of The Times Crescent)

HAY HARVESTING, aided by a coal-burning generator, used by boys at McDonogh School

DOCK AND RAILROAD WORKERS around Nanjemoy and Waldorf, about 1910, *also at bottom left*
(*Courtesy of The Maryland Independent*)

(Courtesy of The Citizen News)

GILL NETS HUNG TO DRY

(Courtesy of The Citizen News)
A CATCH OF ROCKFISH OR STRIPED BASS

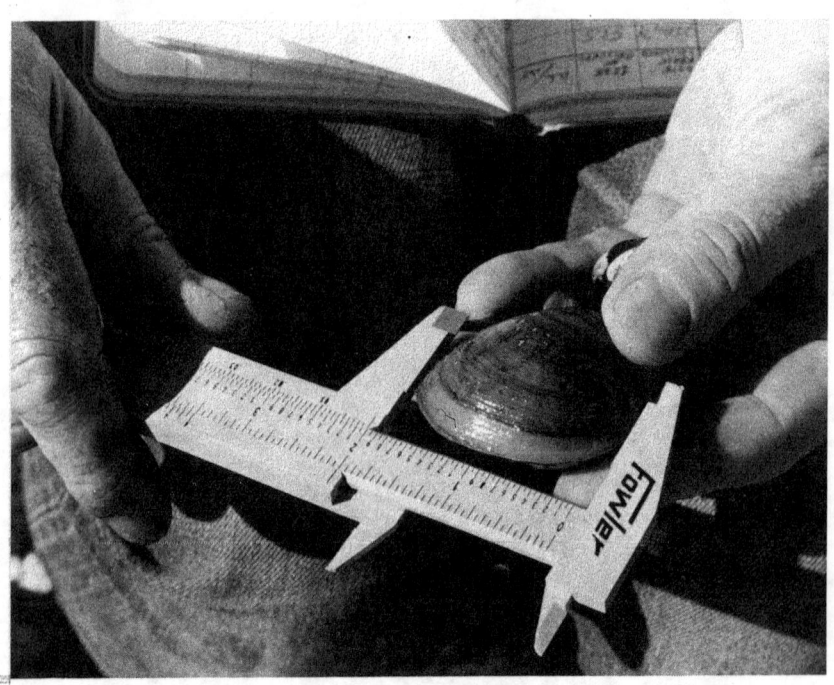

(Courtesy of The Citizen News)
A SOUTHERN MARYLAND CLAM

(Courtesy of The Citizen News)

PIER AREA

OYSTER TONGING, *at right and above*
(Courtesy of St. Mary's County Office of Tourism)

NOTABLE CHARLES COUNTIANS OF THE REVOLUTIONARY ERA

Photographs on the following pages were taken of original oil paintings, property of the Historical Society of Charles County.

JOHN HANSON

DANIEL OF ST. THOMAS JENIFER

JAMES CRAIK

GENERAL WILLIAM SMALLWOOD, *at right*

THOMAS STONE

BENJAMIN STODDERT, *at left*

(Courtesy of The Maryland Independent)
CHARLOTTE HALL ACADEMY, School Hall 1900

MEMBERS OF THE FIRST MARYLAND REGIMENT, at the restored home of Gen. William Smallwood during Charles County's annual Revolutionary War Days celebration and crafts display, *at left*
(Courtesy of Charles County Chamber of Commerce)

TYPICAL COUNTY SCHOOLHOUSES resembled this one at Waldorf, about 1920.

(Courtesy of The Maryland Independent)

LACKEY, at Indian Head, *below*, was the County's first four-year high school. Built in 1919, the structure has been razed and replaced.

(Courtesy of Charles County NAACP)
MARBURY ELEMENTARY SCHOOL

JOHN MCDONOGH (1779-1850)
founded an early Institute.
(Courtesy of The Times Crescent)

(Courtesy of The Maryland Independent)
SIDEWHEELER ON THE POTOMAC

RESTORED COUNTY COURTHOUSE,
Port Tobacco *at right*
(Courtesy of Port Tobacco Restoration Society)

BRIDGE TO COBB ISLAND was built in 1964
(Courtesy of The Maryland Independent)

(Courtesy of the Charles County Chamber of Commerce)
Attached to the dwelling of its Postmistress, the IRONSIDES POST OFFICE still operates.

The recently remodeled CHARLES COUNTY COURTHOUSE, La Plata, *at left*
(Courtesy of The Times Crescent)

(Courtesy of The Maryland Independent)
The FIRST FIREHOUSE OF THE 5TH DISTRICT FIRE DEPARTMENT, late 1940s

BRYAN'S ROAD FIRE HOUSE, built in 1963
(Courtesy of The Maryland Independent)

RYON'S STORE, Waldorf, about 1918
(*Courtesy of The Maryland Independent*)

THE BRYANTOWN HOTEL, *above*, and the

INDIAN HEAD HOTEL, *at left*, about 1900
(*Courtesy of The Maryland Independent*)

SWIMMING AT CHAPEL POINT, 1938
(*Courtesy of The Maryland Independent*)

(Courtesy of The Maryland Independent)

CROWD GREETS VISITING PRES. F. D. ROOSEVELT
at the Potomac River, 1938

THE NAVAL ORDNANCE STATION, 1942
(Courtesy of The Maryland Independent)

(Courtesy of The Maryland Independent)
MEETING OF THE CHARLES COUNTY EXTENSION SERVICE, old La Plata Firehouse, 1947

WALDORF MAIN STREET, 1918
(Courtesy of The Maryland Independent)

(Courtesy of The Times Crescent)
The PHYSICIANS' MEMORIAL HOSPITAL, La Plata

INDIAN HEAD'S MAIN STREET, 1936, *at left*
(Courtesy of John Thomas Parran Jr.)

GOVERNOR NICE BRIDGE, Rt. 301, *overleaf*
(Courtesy of the Historical Society of Charles County)

Index

Agriculture, 1-11, 42, 49, 60, 64, 74, 77, 204-07, 213-14, 218-22, 226-33, 236-37, 246, 263, 265, 278, 300, 313-14, 315, 318. *See also* Tobacco; other products by name
Airplanes, 50-52
Alexander United Methodist Church, 170
Algonquin Indians, 67, 71, 106, 307-08
Annapolis, 72, 85, 192, 199-200, 236, 310, 311, 318
Araby, 110, 120, 404 ph
Automobiles, 41, 42, 45-48, 246, 272. *See also* Roads

Baltimore, Lords. *See* Calvert
Baptist associations, 131-60 *passim*, 230-31
Baptist faith, 131-60, 165. *See also* churches by name
Benedict, 53, 54, 55, 56, 58, 59-65, 69, 97, 114, 115, 124-25, 203, 206, 248, 414 ph
Bibliography, 393-99; for Genealogy, 319, 321-22, 325-91; for Religion, 193-96
Bicycles, 44-45
Blacks, 13, 24, 62, 90-91, 117, 134, 162, 167, 179, 217-33, 236, 242, 244, 245, 247-48, 254, 256, 259-60, 266, 278, 307, 316-17. *See also* Slavery
Boarman family, 60, 67, 68, 69, 106, 114, 120, 129

Boats, 13, 18-43, 63-65, 77, 201, 219, 313-15, 316
Booth, John Wilkes, 70, 312, 40 cap, 407 cap
Bridges, 15, 16, 19, 44-45, 65, 210-11, 446 ph, 458 ph
Bryan's Road, 55, 144, 153-54, 162, 186, 212, 230
Bryantown, 53, 55, 56, 60, 66-71, 76, 97, 108, 113-20, 124, 157, 207, 303, 345, 356-57, 363-64, 368-72, 374, 375-76, 386

Calvary United Methodist Church, 170-73, 418 ph
Calvert family (Lords Baltimore), 53, 55, 65, 67, 79-81, 84, 92, 103, 107-08, 197-98, 220, 309
Camp Stanton, 62, 206
Canneries, canning, 8, 64, 265, 300
Carrico family, 69, 70, 302-03
Catholic. *See* Roman Catholic faith
Chapel Point, 58, 102-05, 114, 123, 124, 286
Charges, and circuits. *See* Methodist faith; churches by name
Charles Town. *See* Port Tobacco
Charlotte Hall Academy, 48, 157, 237, 243, 253, 258, 443 ph
Chesapeake Bay, 57, 61, 62, 64, 65, 128, 203, 273, 306
Chicamuxen United Methodist Church, 163
Christ Church (La Plata), 57, 83, 86-91, 100, 412 ph
Christ Church (Wayside), 83, 94-96, 415 ph

459

Church of Christ, 191-92
Church of Jesus Christ of Latter Day Saints (Mormons), 187-88
Church of Our Lady, Star of the Sea, 121
Churches, 15, 22, 27, 50, 278-86, 310; marriage records, 376-86. *See also* by name
Citizen News, The, viii
Civil War, 58, 62, 66, 70, 85, 86, 110, 115, 116, 122, 133, 134, 145, 163, 165, 203-06, 229, 266, 311, 313
Claggett, Rev. Thomas John, 85, 93, 94
Clubs. *See* Social life
Cobb Island, 158-59, 318
Cobb Island Baptist Church, 155, 158-59
Commerce and industry, 6-11, 23, 30, 32, 35, 44, 45, 47, 49, 54, 58, 60, 63-65, 66, 68, 69, 70-71, 72-73, 74, 76, 77, 86, 159, 198-99, 203-07, 210-15, 217-33 *passim,* 246, 265, 301-02, 313-15, 318, 428-29 ph, 451-53 ph. *See also* Economics
Communications, 17, 65, 142, 150, 160, 175, 192, 207, 235-303 *passim*
Constitution, U.S., 25, 80, 128, 202
Contee, Benjamin, 202
Cooking, 3, 35, 228. *See also* Recipes
Corn, 4, 5, 10, 25, 27, 57, 272, 426 ph. *See also* Recipes, by name
Courthouse (s), 56, 57, 58-59, 65-66, 88, 89, 197, 199, 203, 207-08, 301, 318, 447 ph, 448 ph
Craik, James, 438 ph

Daniel of St. Thomas Jenifer, 202, 308, 437 ph
Declaration of Independence, 84, 201, 279, 408 cap
DePye family, 308

Dominicans, 108
Durham Parish, 83, 91-94, 132

Economics, 1, 2, 4, 5, 6-11, 16, 18, 26, 31, 34, 35, 38, 41, 57, 58, 206-07, 209-15, 217-33 *passim,* 247-50, 263-67. *See also* Commerce and industry
Edelen family, 47-48, 52, 124, 126, 129, 277
Education, 4, 48-49, 66, 68, 70, 72, 89, 104, 115-17, 119, 123-24, 138, 139, 147, 148-49, 151, 152, 156, 157, 159, 165, 166, 167, 170, 171-72, 179, 180, 187, 190, 203, 211, 212, 217-33, 235-69, 271, 302, 318, 443-45 ph
Emergency services, 50, 213, 450 ph
England, 53, 57, 60-62, 67, 72, 79, 80, 81, 82, 84, 95, 102, 198-203, 219, 261, 273, 306-07, 315
Episcopal faith, 80-102, 143, 147. *See also* Methodist faith; churches by name

Farming. *See* Agriculture
Farr, David, 313-15
First Baptist Church of La Plata, 154-55, 159
First Baptist Church of St. Charles, 156-59
First Baptist Church of Waldorf, 145-51, 156
First Baptist Church of Welcome, 155-56
Fishing, 23, 25-37, 63-65, 125, 314-15, 430-35 ph
Floyd, Olivia, 311-12, 409 cap
Forbes, James, 202
France, 57, 65, 108, 114
Franciscans, 105

Genealogy, 319-91
Glymont, 75, 120-21, 142, 211, 243, 386

Good Hope Baptist Church (Newburg), 133
Good Shepherd United Methodist Church, 180, 421 ph
Government (of Charles County), 5, 56, 58-59, 65, 66, 71, 73, 74, 77, 82, 83, 85, 89, 220, 221, 223, 225-33 *passim,* 236-42 *passim,* 246, 252, 253, 254, 258, 262, 268, 286-87, 301-03, 306, 320; Colonial, 197-202; New nation, 202-03; Civil War, 203-06; Reconstruction, 206-08; Twentieth century, 208-15
Grace Baptist Church, 144, 153-54
Grace Lutheran Church (La Plata), 184-86
Great Britain. *See* England

Habre de Venture, 408 ph
Hamilton, Mrs. Margaret, 313
Hanson, John, 201, 202, 308, 436 ph
Holy Ghost Church (Issue), 125-27
Hughesville, 64, 70, 76, 96, 97, 98, 157-58, 246, 254, 264, 387
Hughesville Baptist Church, 157-58
Hunting. *See* Wildlife

Indenture, 4, 257. *See also* Slavery
Indian Head, 71-73, 75, 101-02, 120-21, 124, 143-45, 151-53, 164, 182, 183, 186, 192-93, 211, 212, 243, 246, 251, 266, 286, 302, 307-08, 456 ph
Indian Head Baptist Church, 143-45, 147
Indians, 1, 2, 3, 5, 6, 14, 26, 27, 28, 44, 55-56, 57, 71-73, 81, 102, 106, 218, 306-08. *See also* tribes by name
Industry. *See* Commerce and industry
Ironsides, 83, 91-94, 230
Iroquois, 306

Jesuits, 57, 103-05, 107, 108, 112, 114, 121, 122, 123, 124, 126, 130, 131, 222
Jews, 80, 98
Johnson, Thomas Jr., 199-200
Jousting, 203, 272, 309-11

King George's Parish, 83

Labor. *See* Economics
La Plata, 55, 56, 57, 58, 59, 65-66, 69, 71, 74, 83, 86-91, 107, 112, 113, 121, 122, 123-24, 142, 154-55, 156, 160, 161, 164, 174-78, 181, 182, 183, 186, 207, 244, 246, 247-48, 249, 250, 251, 263, 264, 279, 285, 286, 302, 303, 309, 312, 318, 387, 411 ph, 412 ph, 448 ph, 457 ph
La Plata United Methodist Church, 170-78
Lancaster, Spearman, 315-17
Legend and folklore, 71-72, 305-18
Lincoln, Pres. Abraham, 70, 90, 116, 206, 312, 405 cap
Loyola-on-the-Potomac Retreat House, 130-31
Lutheran faith, 180-86. *See also* churches by name

McDonough, Maurice James, 48, 113, 237 ph, 259 ph, 428 ph
Manor. *See* Proprietary system
Marbury Baptist Church, 142, 159
Marbury Church of God, 188-90
Maryland Gazette, The, 22, 226
Maryland Independent, The, viii, 59, 253-54, 256, 263
Matthews family, 127, 128, 129, 279, 281-82, 286
Maxwell Hall, 402 ph
Medical services, 50, 52, 63, 66, 68, 76, 198, 212, 232, 265, 301, 386-88, 457 ph

461

Methodist faith, 160-80, 230-31. *See also* churches by name
Metropolitan United Methodist Church, 166-70
Mitchell (John Hanson) family, 311
Mt. Carmel, 111, 127-30, 403 ph
Mt. Republic (Republican), 95, 273
Mt. Victoria, 45, 51, 95
Mudd, Dr. Samuel A., 70, 312, 405 ph (home)

Nanjemoy, 76, 83, 132-39, 142, 155, 197, 203, 207, 231, 246, 248, 263, 264, 420 ph, 428-29 ph
Nanjemoy Baptist Church, 131, 132-39, 157, 420 ph
Naval Ordnance Station, 73, 102, 151, 454 ph
Naval Powder Factory, 43, 44-45, 72-73, 121, 211-12, 246
Neale family, 104, 105, 111, 112, 125-29
Negroes. *See* Blacks; Slavery
Newspapers, 21, 23, 41, 203, 225, 252, 276-78, 279, 280-86. *See also* by name
NOS Protestant Chapel, 192-93

Old Durham Church, 83, 91-94, 100, 418 ph
Oldfields Chapel, 97
Oysters, 29, 30, 32, 33, 34, 35, 44, 64, 65, 124, 315, 434-35 ph. *See also* Fishing and Transportation (to 52), *passim*

Parishes, 115. *See also* by name
Patuxent River, 53, 60, 61, 62, 63, 64, 65, 103, 124, 148, 183, 197, 203
Piney (St. Paul's Church), 90, 100-01, 174
Piscataway Indians, 71, 306-07
Pisgah, 77, 163-65, 175, 230, 250, 262, 387

Pisgah United Methodist Church, 163-65
Pleasant Grove Baptist Church, 140-42, 230
Politics. *See* Government
Port Tobacco, 53, 54, 55, 56, 58, 66, 69, 71, 75, 76, 77, 87, 92, 93-94, 123, 130, 145, 155, 163, 197, 198-99, 202, 203, 207, 226, 230, 233, 243, 250, 256, 262, 269, 276, 279, 301, 307, 309, 321, 387, 408 ph, 409 ph, 447 ph
Port Tobacco Parish, 83, 86-91, 100
Port Tobacco River, 129
Port Tobacco Times, 16, 17, 18, 59, 108-09, 205, 276, 277, 284-85, 300
Port Tobacco Valley, cover photo
Postal Service (U.S.), 17, 18, 38, 57, 65-66, 67, 71, 73, 74, 75, 76, 77, 312, 449 ph
Potomac River, 53, 57, 63, 66, 71, 74, 92, 103, 125, 128, 131, 134, 142, 203, 204, 205, 206, 210-11, 308, 309, 312
Potomac Heights Baptist Church, 151-53
Potopaco (Potobac, Portobac) Indians, 57, 102, 306-07
Proprietary system, 3, 22, 54, 59, 197, 220. *See also* Calvert
Protestant faith, 79-102, 197-98. *See also* churches by name
Puritan Revolution, 82, 197-98

Railroads, 41, 42-43, 58, 65-66, 69, 74, 76, 77, 207
Recipes, 272-73, 287-300
 almond cookies, 298
 angel pie, 295
 baked beans, 291-92
 berry pudding, 296
 brownies, 298
 catsup, 289
 cheese fondue, 292
 chilli(e) sauce, 288-89

chocolate icing, 297
chow-chow, 289
cole slaw dressing, 291
corn bread, 272-73
crab imperial, 293
crab surprise, 293
cranberry cupcakes, 296-97
cream scones, 294-95
deviled beef patties, 290-91
elegant chicken a la king, 287
frosting (cake), 298
ginger cookies, 299
grape jelly, 290
hard sauce, 296
hot milk cake, 299
Maryland biscuit, 294
Maryland old ham, 293-94
old fashioned jumbles, 299
orange coconut cake, 297
pie crust, 295
sauce (crab), 293
scalloped crabs, 292-93
soap, 290
soft gingerbread, 299
So. Maryland stuffed ham, 294
spanish cream, 296
spider corn cake, 273
sugar cookies, 299-300
tar heel hush puppies, 272
topping (angel pie), 295-96
Recreation. *See* Social life; Jousting
Religion, 68, 70, 76, 79-196, 197-98, 202, 209, 226, 227, 228-33, 257-58, 308, 317-18, 376-86. *See also* Churches; individual churches by name; denominations by name
Restoration, 59, 66, 69, 71, 72, 301, 447 ph
Revolutionary War, 70, 84, 86, 201-02, 228, 273, 312, 313
Rich Hill, 406 ph
Ripley Community Church, 190
Rivers, 13-45 *passim*, 49, 52. *See also* by name

Roads, 13, 14, 15, 16, 17, 23, 24, 25, 43-44, 45-48, 57, 60, 66, 69, 70, 71, 73, 75, 76, 198, 204, 211-15, 272, 314-15
Roman Catholic faith, 76, 79-82, 102-31, 197-98, 230-31. *See also* churches by name
Roosevelt, Pres. Franklin D., 45, 65
Rose Hill, 409 ph

Sacred Heart Church (La Plata), 123-24
St. Catherine's Church (McConchie), 121-22
St. Charles, 73-74, 101, 150-51, 156-57, 191
St. Charles Church (Glymont), 120-21
St. Francis de Sales Church (Benedict), 124-25, 414 ph
St. Francis de Sales Church (Rock Point), 125-27
St. Ignatius Church (Chapel Pt.), cover ph, 102-05, 108
St. Ignatius Church (Hilltop), 121-22, 123
St. James Parish, 101-02
St. John's Episcopal Chapel, Parish (Pomonkey), 101-02, 182, 419 ph
St. Joseph's Church (Pomfret), 110-13, 123, 416 ph
St. Mary's Church (Bryantown), 47, 70, 113-20, 124
St. Mary's Church (Newport), 105-07, 126
St. Matthews United Methodist Church, 179, 230
St. Peter's Church (Waldorf), 107-10
St. Thomas Manor, 102-05, 108, 112, 114, 121, 122, 124, 130
Sarum, 107
School Sisters of Notre Dame, 110, 117, 119

463

Shiloh Community United Methodist Church, 165-66, 230
Shiloh United Methodist Church, 161-62, 339
Slavery, 4, 5, 8, 26, 31, 90, 166, 203-07, 208, 217-33, *passim*, 316-17. *See also* Blacks; Indenture
Smallwood, Gen. William, 92, 94, 201, 312, 407 cap, 439ph, 442 cap
Smith Chapel United Methodist Church, 179
Smith, Mrs. George, 312-13
Social life, 13-52 *passim*, 53-77 *passim*, 141, 153, 154, 165, 167-70, 173-74, 180, 188, 198, 211-12, 217-33 *passim*, 240, 249, 251-52, 262-64, 268-69, 271-303, 308, 309-11, 314-17, 318, 453-55 ph. *See also* Jousting
Stoddert, Benjamin, 440 ph
Stone, Thomas, 200-02, 223, 279, 408 ph (home), 441 ph
Surratt family, 68, 116

Taverns, 13, 20, 22, 23, 24, 25, 33, 50, 57, 67, 69, 146, 147, 148, 268, 278
Taxes, 16, 21, 83, 84, 87, 96, 114, 199, 210, 211, 213-15, 235, 236-42
Times Crescent, The, viii, 309
Tobacco, 3, 5-11, 14, 16, 22, 26, 27, 32, 44, 56, 57, 60, 64, 87, 91, 92, 96, 110, 203, 204, 218, 225, 226, 227, 236, 255, 258, 313-14, 318, 422-24 ph
Towns, 53-77. *See also* by name

Transportation, 6, 7, 8, 10, 54, 57, 58, 73, 210-15, 221, 248, 265, 268, 300, 428-29 ph, 446 ph, 458 ph. *See also* Airplanes; Boats; Bridges; Railroads; Rivers; Roads
Trinity Church, Trinity Parish, 81, 96-100

Vocational training, 159, 264

Waldorf, 69, 70, 74-75, 107-10, 114, 115, 145-51, 170-73, 187, 191-92, 230, 245, 265, 268, 417 ph, 428-29 ph, 451 ph, 455 ph
War of 1812, 58, 60-62, 85, 86, 97, 203
Washington, George, 72, 75, 93, 105, 201, 275, 276, 311, 409 cap
Watermen, 29, 34, 42, 318. *See also* Fishing
Waverly, 407 ph
We-sorts, 307
Wheat, 3, 9, 314, 315
White, Father Andrew, 26, 102, 220
White Plains Baptist Chapel, 159-60
Wicomico River, 67, 76, 107, 125
Wildlife, 1, 2, 3, 67, 198
William and Mary Parish, 83, 87, 94-96
World War I, 73, 86, 110, 208, 288
World War II, 66, 69, 86, 110, 142, 151, 164, 183, 211, 249, 288

Zachiah (Zacciah, Zecciah, Zekiah) Indians, 107
Zion Wesley United Methodist Church, 173-74, 231

www.ingramcontent.com/pod-product-compliance
Lightning Source LLC
Chambersburg PA
CBHW050424240426
43661CB00055B/2268